A Lincoln

ALFRED A. KNOPF   NEW YORK   1993

LINCOLN

An Illustrated Biography by

Philip B. Kunhardt, Jr.
Philip B. Kunhardt III
Peter W. Kunhardt

Foreword by **David Herbert Donald**
Contributing Writer **Daniel Terris**

THIS IS A BORZOI BOOK PUBLISHED BY ALFRED A. KNOPF, INC.

Copyright© 1992 by Philip B. Kunhardt, Jr., Philip B. Kunhardt III, and Peter W. Kunhardt

All rights reserved under International and Pan-American Copyright Conventions.
Published in the United States by Alfred A. Knopf, Inc., and simultaneously
in Canada by Random House of Canada Limited, Toronto.
Distributed by Random House, Inc., New York.

Library of Congress Cataloging-in-Publication Data

Kunhardt, Philip B.
   Lincoln, an illustrated biography /by Philip B. Kunhardt, Jr.,
 Philip B. Kunhardt III, Peter W. Kunhardt.—1st ed.
     p.   cm.
   Includes index.
   ISBN 0-679-40862-2
    1. Lincoln, Abraham, 1809–1865. 2. Presidents—United States—Biography.
I. Kunhardt, Philip B. II. Kunhardt, Peter W. III. Title.
E457.K94   1992
973.7′092—dc20
[B]   92-53043
                                         CIP

Manufactured in the United States of America
Published October 14, 1992
Reprinted Once
Third Printing, January 1993

CONTENTS

FOREWORD

The central figure in the American experience, Abraham Lincoln is also the most elusive. Generations of biographers have tried to recapture the man, but none has quite succeeded. Poets and novelists have attempted to describe him, only to find, as did Walt Whitman, that his face was "almost as impossible to depict as a wild perfume or fruit taste." Sculptors have produced images that range from the shambling hobbledehoy by George Grey Barnard to the deified figure by Daniel Chester French, but the essence of the man has escaped them all.

Fortunately we can form our own image of Lincoln from the remarkably full photographic record that covers most of his adult life. Even though Abraham and Mary Lincoln lived in frontier Illinois, they were, in 1846, among the first generation of Americans to have their likenesses preserved by the newly introduced daguerreotype process. As improvements in photography paralleled the increasing visibility of Lincoln's career, he sat for numerous photographs in the late 1850s. During his presidential years, his frequent visits to the photographic studio of Mathew B. Brady resulted in dozens of pictures that allow us to chart his evolution from a stiff, insecure Western politician to the master statesman, whose lined, kindly visage spoke of fatigue, of sadness, and of a profound humanity.

That this record has been preserved is due primarily to one family, which has dedicated itself to collecting the photographic history of Abraham Lincoln and his times. Back in 1897, Frederick Hill Meserve, a young New York textile commission merchant, began the process when he started searching for pictures to illustrate his father's Civil War memoirs. That quest led him to purchase thousands of Mathew B. Brady's fragile glass negatives, which otherwise might have been destroyed, and to collect tens of thousands of *cartes de visite*, those charming small photographs favored in the 1860s as calling cards. Over many years Mr. Meserve came to be the greatest collector of Civil War photographs this country has ever known, and he was recognized as the unquestioned authority on photographs of Abraham Lincoln. Freely he shared his treasures with virtually every Lincoln biographer, and it is largely through his generosity that we know what Americans of the Civil War generation looked like. Fortunately, his daughter, Mrs. Dorothy Meserve Kunhardt, shared his interests and, indeed, after his

death in 1962 she expanded the Meserve Collection to include other kinds of Lincoln memorabilia. In turn her son, Mr. Philip B. Kunhardt, Jr., was brought up to know and respect the Meserve Collection and was given much of it. Because of his careful oversight it has come appropriately to be called the Meserve-Kunhardt Collection. He has passed along the family's love of Lincoln and its mastery of photographs to his two sons, Philip III and Peter. These three are the authors of the present book.

From four generations of knowledge and experience the Kunhardts have crafted a book that on every page reflects that love and that knowledge. Their *Lincoln: An Illustrated Biography* is not simply another picture book, for their informed and accurate text places the photographs in their historical context and gives fascinating biographical information as well. Much of that text consists of Abraham Lincoln's own words, with extensive quotations from his most important letters and speeches. Excerpts from authenticated writings by Lincoln's contemporaries offer additional astute, and often amusing, commentary. Here is a portrait of Lincoln told largely in his own words and in the words of those who knew him well.

But the heart of the Kunhardts' *Lincoln* is, of course, the pictures. They present a complete photographic record of Lincoln, from his earliest, awkward daguerreotype to that final, careworn, and almost saintly portrait made by Alexander Gardner just a few weeks before his assassination. Here, too, are the faces of Mary Lincoln, as proud wife and tragic widow, and the portraits of the Lincoln children. So comprehensive is the Kunhardts' coverage that they show us Lincoln's office and his books, his house and even his outhouse, his boots and his pocketknife. Here, too, are images of Lincoln's horse, "Old Bob," who seemed delighted to pose for the camera, and of his frisky yellow dog, Fido.

Drawing on the profusion of photographs, prints, and cartoons in the Meserve-Kunhardt Collection and supplementing that vast resource with little known illustrations from other major historical libraries, the Kunhardts have re-created the Washington scene during the Civil War years. Here is virtually every important Northern political leader. Salmon P. Chase looks solemnly from their page, as if searching for the high office he never attained, while John C. Frémont hides a weak chin behind unconvincing whiskers. Chief Justice Roger B. Taney glares out balefully, while Clement L. Vallandigham's image is as slippery as that Copperhead's record. Here, too, are the generals of the armies, resplendent in their sashes and medals. Often the faces are familiar, but the poses are new. Unless you look closely, you will fail to identify Ulysses S. Grant wearing a long, flowing beard that reached his chest.

The Kunhardts' *Lincoln* reminds us how deeply involved American women were in the Civil War. In these pages, novelist Harriet Beecher Stowe stares gravely at us, perhaps recalling that Lincoln called her "the little woman who wrote the book that made this great war." Here, too, is the abolition orator Anna E. Dickinson, the prototype of Varena Tarrant in Henry James's *The Bostonians*. Julia Ward Howe looks off into the distance, as if in a rapture of inspiration after having composed "The Battle-Hymn of the Republic." A fascinating picture shows Sojourner Truth, who had led so many of her people on the underground railroad to freedom. Improving on the historical fact that Lincoln welcomed this great African-American to the White House and signed her autograph book, an ingenious photographer has superimposed the President's figure to create a plausible, if inauthentic, joint picture.

Reflecting the great strength of the Meserve-Kunhardt Collection in the history of the American theater, the Kunhardts offer portraits of many of the actors and actresses whose performance on the stage in Washington gave the weary Lincoln brief relief from the crushing burdens of his wartime presidency. Charlotte Cushman, Mrs. John C. Wood, Maggie Mitchell, James H. Hackett, and Edwin Forrest were among his favorites.

Fascinating as are all these individual portraits, many of the group photographs and scenes in *Lincoln* are even more memorable. Here, in the sharpest reproductions ever made, are Brady's pictures of dead and injured Union soldiers, so vivid that the *New York Times* said the photographer had "brought bodies and laid them in our dooryards and along the streets." These pages tell the moving story of how the Civil War affected African-Americans. No words can say more about the "peculiar institution" of slavery than the photograph of Gordon, a slave whose back was so lacerated from whip marks that it looked like a relief map. Then the Kunhardts show us slaves who ran away from their masters as Union armies advanced, many becoming laborers for the Northern armies. After 1863, the photographs depict awkward black recruits still new to their uniforms and arms, but by 1865 they reveal the handsome, disciplined faces of black soldiers who had proved themselves in combat.

What is perhaps most charming about the Kunhardts' book is not the faces of the great and historically significant personages Lincoln encountered but the pictures of the ordinary people he met. Devoting a double-page spread to every month of Lincoln's presidency, they show that even while the beleaguered President was struggling with weighty issues of war and freedom, he had time to greet Robert H. Hendershot, the valiant boy drummer of the Army of the Potomac. From his six-foot-four-inch height a bemused President welcomed to the White House the recently married "General" and Mrs. Tom Thumb. Here is Hermann the Magician, whose White House performance Lincoln inadvertently spoiled. When the prestidigitator asked to borrow the President's handkerchief for a trick, Lincoln roared, "I ain't got any!"

The final chapters of the Kunhardts' *Lincoln* deal with the most fully photographed months in Lincoln's career, the assassination and death of the President. These repeated sorrowful images of the draped catafalque, the black funeral train, the mourning crowds cumulatively suggest the immense grief that swept the nation and the intense sense of loss at the death of a leader who was only fifty-six years old when he was killed.

Recapturing the life and death of Abraham Lincoln, the Kunhardts have written the best photographic biography of Abraham Lincoln ever published, unequaled in authenticity, in comprehensiveness, and in clarity of reproduction. This is the closest we are ever likely to come to seeing Lincoln plain.

DAVID HERBERT DONALD
Harvard University

Frederick Hill Meserve and his daughter, Dorothy Meserve Kunhardt

INTRODUCTION

You will not find the name of Frederick Hill Meserve on the title page of this book, but, nevertheless, these 432 picture-laden pages would not exist today if it were not for him—grandfather of one of the authors, great-grandfather of the other two.

What authors would dare to venture out on a book project such as this, with a one-year deadline while simultaneously writing and producing a Lincoln biography for television, without having something pretty substantial to back them up? The resource we had was the Meserve Collection, along with the source material and research of its longtime caretaker, Dorothy Meserve Kunhardt.

Meserve was the country's first great collector of photography. His specialty was Lincoln, his self-imposed mission to seek out, investigate, identify, order, and preserve every picture ever taken of our sixteenth president. The late nineteenth century was a time when people were still trying to forget the Civil War. Many of the million glass negatives that recorded the great conflict were used to build greenhouses. Paper prints of the combat and the combatants were more often than not tossed aside and forgotten. Fortunately for history, the young Meserve saw something important and exciting in the magic shadows of the prints and negatives that had been made in the years surrounding his birth in 1865.

In his spare time, at the age of thirty-two, the former cowboy, engineer, surveyor, and mountaineer who was now plying a business career in New York City began searching for pictures to illustrate his father's Civil War reminiscences. One day, Meserve walked into a lower Fifth Avenue auction gallery and watched as a package of one hundred or so photographs wrapped in brown paper was placed on the block. The bidding opened at one dollar, at which point Meserve screwed up his courage and raised the ante to a dollar and ten cents. Not a hand stirred, not a mouth opened. Suddenly the gavel sounded and, sight unseen, the lot was his.

"That night," he later recalled, "I had my first experience of the sensation of intoxication—that intoxication, the only kind I have ever experienced, that comes from the possession of a rare find. I had not the knowledge necessary for full appreciation of the one hundred or more exquisite salt prints that I unwrapped, soft brown in color and unglazed, but their clarity and beauty were so evident that I was stirred. After that I attended auction after auction. My appetite had been whetted. I spent much time in old book stores and print shops, where in those days there were still floating about gems, which are now under lock and key in institutions. Then, in 1902, came the day whose events enriched the entire rest of my life."

Let Meserve's friend Carl Sandburg pick up the tale. "One unforgettable moment in the life and work of Frederick H. Meserve happened in Hoboken, New Jersey. He had talked about buying a collection of glass negatives the day before. And he went to Hoboken to see what he had and how to pack and haul it home if he bought it. On the warehouse floor lay scores of glass negatives—broken. They had sort of spilled over. There were thousands more—who cared? Meserve saw on the floor one negative not broken. He picked it up and held it to the light. His eyes ranged over it. And he could hardly believe his eyes. What he saw was a camera record, an extraordinary photographic negative, a profile of the face and right shoulder of Abraham Lincoln, a composed majestic Abraham Lincoln. What he saw was the camera record of the granitic Lincoln in February 1864, facing the awful issues of that year of smoke, agony, and ballots."

Sandburg was in the midst of putting together a book with Meserve and he was trying to describe the intensity of his co-author's collecting passion. "Up to this time Meserve had been a patient and devoted collector of the known Lincoln photographs. Now he became a tireless zealot. There are collectors who are hobbyists, fans, faddists, enthusiasts, eccentrics, cranks, bugs. Meserve is the Zealot."

Of the 15,000 Mathew Brady glass negatives Meserve unearthed that day and acquired, 7 were of Lincoln. "After a year or two I had fifty Lincoln photographs. I was six or seven years getting one hundred put together. The next eight photographs of Lincoln took me seven years to gather. And the next eight required twenty-one years."

In 1911 Meserve published a book of 100 Lincoln photographs, which, he believed at the time, comprised all the known poses. It was the first serious attempt to put together a complete look at the photographs of the prairie president. This effort was followed by the creation of the first of nine twenty-eight-volume, handmade sets of nineteenth-century photographs showing Lincoln and the people around him, as well as thousands of the President's more distant but still important contemporaries. All the time, Meserve was adding to his collection. In one year alone he acquired 75,000 theatrical photographs; in another, 10,000 cartes de visite, those extraordinarily beautiful little photographic calling cards so popular around the time of the Civil War. Still, his major interest was the Lincoln circle itself. "We can't put 'em all in," Meserve protested to Sandburg after the two men had winnowed the number down for their book. "The eighty faces are nearly a crowd." Sandburg persisted, offering this description of the faces before them. "A few saw him often, across years...in dress and undress, bowed with burdens or shaken with mirth. Others saw him briefly but saw much in those moments and wrote it vividly. Still others crossed his path definitely, to help or to hinder, and Lincoln read their faces and they were in his album of memory."

Meserve not only searched and collected and verified and studied, he also helped anyone else seriously interested in Lincoln and his times. He assisted sculptors shape the face of Lincoln on coins, on busts and statues, even on the side of a mountain; he helped artists in their attempts to capture the elusive beauty in Lincoln's face; he provided illustrations for the distinguished Lincoln biographies of the twentieth century; he was the prime source for all the Lincoln picture books. A friend to the ever growing Lincoln community, he was also one of its distinguished leaders. Kind and gentle, wise and far-sighted, he was a forebear in whom we take immense pride.

Fortunately, when Meserve died in 1962 at the age of 97, his collection passed into the hands of his daughter, who was even more of an avid picture sleuth than her father, a noted children's book author, and a diligent and imaginative Lincoln scholar in her own right. Dorothy Meserve Kunhardt was the mother of one of the authors of this book, the grandmother of the other two.

Each of us in turn was introduced by her to "the collection," which, except to her, had remained pretty much of a mystery during her father's lifetime, hidden away on the fifth floor of his midtown New York City house and in a vast, hard-to-get-to warehouse downtown. Under their new owner, the life negatives of Lincoln, Mary Todd, their children, the members of his Cabinet, and others special to the Lincoln scene, plus Lincoln letters and notes and signatures, were kept in a battery of safe-deposit boxes in the underground vaults of a New York City bank. Visiting the treasures, holding the negatives to the light, studying those long ago faces became a hushed and reverent family ritual.

The rest of the collection—tens of thousands of original prints and modern-day contact prints and copies—now occupied five windowless rooms of an uptown New York City storage company. The dry, paper smell of those rooms, their chill in winter, their dankness in the heat of summer, are memories etched into all three of us. We worked on "Lincoln" there, trying to help organize and manage and control and corner the unwieldy "animal himself."

Dorothy Kunhardt practically lived at the warehouse, pushing supermarket cartloads of materials back the many blocks to her house so she could continue her study each day far into the night. In her house was her working library, thousands upon thousands of books having to do with Lincoln in some way or other; all the original records and maps of the Civil War; official publications of the Patent Office, Congress, and every state in the Union; pamphlets and other publications on Indians, slavery, western expeditions, education, spiritualism, prisons, and a hundred other Lincoln-related subjects; bound volumes of nineteenth-century magazines and newspapers, piles of *Harper's Weekly*, stacks of *Leslie's*. Here the air was filled with dust and leather. The books were piled everywhere, walls of them coming up the stairwells, blocking the halls, on beds, stacks so high they shut out the window light. She had acquired them by haunting the rare book stores and the secondhand book shops, by corresponding with other collectors who were always on the lookout for her. She read like the wind and was in the habit of flagging pages of interest with little white slips on which were her notations. All the time she was researching different aspects of the collection, different nooks and crannies of the Lincoln story. Her files grew to overflowing. And her acquisitions did not stop with books and pictures. She collected locks of Lincoln's hair, wallpaper from the rooms in which he lived, and clippings of material from the clothes of people close to him. She owned the horsehair material that covered the couch upon which Lincoln courted Mary Todd and the sperm oil lamps that lighted the room where they were wed; she even had Mary Lincoln's traveling commode and proudly sat on it for guests. She also acquired the Lincoln scrapbooks that the keepers of the Lincoln home in Springfield had kept for generations.

We had at our disposal much of the key material that Meserve and his daughter collected, along with her comprehensive library and her research files which she had used to create a book on Lincoln and another on Mathew Brady. We did not, unfortunately, still have possession of all the key photographic material acquired over the decades. When Dorothy Kunhardt died in 1979, much of the Meserve Collection had to be sold. The National Portrait Gallery in Washington, D.C. acquired the 5,420 Mathew Brady life negatives as well as the famed, one-and-only orginal print of Alexander Gardner's haunting "cracked negative" photograph of Lincoln, long believed to be the very last picture of Lincoln ever to be taken. (Today it is thought that at least one photograph was taken later.) At auction and through private sales, many collectors and institutions acquired other Meserve original prints and Kunhardt memorabilia. The daguerreotypes, ambrotypes, tintypes, and a vast collection of *cartes de viste*, as well as a quantity of rare originals and many thousand twentieth-century prints and copies were given to the senior author of this book during his mother's lifetime. These now comprise the primary source from which this book was fashioned.

For more than three decades the senior member of our triumvirate has been working with the collection, writing and publishing from it. In the early 1980s he was assisted by his oldest son on a book about the Gettysburg Address, published in 1983. Since then, all three of us have worked with the Lincoln material and, trying to keep it up to date, have added considerably to the library.

Of course, no single collection could provide all the pictorial material to fully illustrate the extraordinary life of Lincoln, particularly his years as president. As well as tapping our own files, we have gone far afield, to the main repositories of Civil War and Lincoln material around the country. We are in debt to these many institutions, to their dedicated curators who have led us to the gems they care for, and to a number of private collectors who have been extraordinarily generous with their material. Again and again we were told that Frederick H. Meserve or Dorothy M. Kunhardt, or both, had been an important help to them at one time or another and now they were returning the courtesy. It was a most pleasant atmosphere in which to be working.

A few people who were key to this project's success must be noted here.

We are deeply indebted to the writer of our foreword, David Herbert Donald, the renowned Harvard professor who is one of the country's leading authorities on Abraham

Dorothy Kunhardt's largest cache of Lincoln relics was acquired in 1958 from Mary Lincoln's great-niece, Mary Edwards Brown, former custodian of the Lincoln home and a sentimental collector of anything that breathed of Lincoln. At top left is an inlaid box containing dozens of daguerreotypes of Lincoln's friends and neighbors. To the right is one of the Lincoln scrapbooks kept by the family from the time of the assassination on. One of the lamps that provided light for Lincoln's wedding is next, followed by books in family libraries from which Lincoln often borrowed. The framed hair is Mary Lincoln's, snipped from her head right after she died. Also in the picture are hand-wrought nails from Lincoln's home, a latch from Lincoln's kitchen door, a conductor from the house's lightning rod, and wallpaper from Lincoln's bedroom. The black horsehair material in the foreground covered the Edwardses' sofa on which Lincoln courted Mary Todd. Along with pressed flowers from Lincoln's yard and fragments of clothing worn by women and children dear to Lincoln, is the very first Springfield directory, listing "Lincoln Abraham, attorney."

Lincoln. Throughout the year Mr. Donald has patiently checked our work, corrected our errors, and suggested improvements. Others have read, critiqued, and corrected as well, and thanks to them is made on our acknowledgments page.

From the start it was obvious that if both a Lincoln book and a television show were to be created together and in a hurry, we would need additional research and writing help. It arrived in the person of Daniel Terris, a teacher of American history and literature at Harvard. In the chapters on Lincoln's presidency, Dan painstakingly constructed fifty separate essays and also wrote a great many of the captions. We salute him for his valuable and insightful role in the book.

Even though Meserve owned prints of all the pictures of Lincoln, the quality of some of them was not the highest. Sometimes they were copies of copies and had lost a bit of their original sharpness and depth. Skin tones and detail had faded or disappeared. The person who has the finest set of Lincoln prints in the world today is James Mellon. Aware of the sad condition of most Lincoln photographs, many already desecrated, stolen, or destroyed, others fading into nothingness because of "the fugitive nature" of the photographic chemicals, Mr. Mellon spent years tracking down and copying either the originals or the nearest and clearest generation of copy prints he could find. From the original glass negatives that still exist, he coaxed hitherto invisible elements. Printing enlarged positives on a special film, Mellon and his printer were able to bring out skin tones and details from the glass negatives that simply did not appear with conventional paper printing. Reproduced from the master set of prints that resulted, Mellon's book *The Face of Lincoln*, published in 1979, is the most stunning book of Lincoln photographs ever made. Now, for our book, Mr. Mellon has allowed us to work from his master set of prints and we have used the results liberally.

This book is a contemporaneous view of Lincoln, in today's perspective. To show him as he was seen and judged at the time, it relies heavily on eyewitness accounts, which have been set off in differently shaded areas throughout the book. It also contains an enormous number of Lincoln's own remarkable words. Lincoln's presidency is dealt with in a unique manner: two pages, acting as a calendar, are devoted to each of the fifty months Lincoln was in office. As we move through his days, and see what he said and wrote in context, the reader meets hundreds of the people Lincoln dealt with, as well as the issues and events he confronted. We can actually see what wore him down, what made him grow. It is his "album of memory."

We have tried not to convey a stiff, historical Lincoln. We have dealt with the different periods of his life, but in each we have tried to bring him alive and make him real. That is not always easy when describing the stuff of greatness. "He captured all the finest qualities of the great Americans who came before him, without their defects," wrote the distinguished historian Samuel Eliot Morison, "...the poise of Washington without his aloofness, the mental audacity of Hamilton without his insolence, the astuteness of Jefferson without his indirection, the conscience of John Quincy Adams without his harshness, the courage of Jackson without his irascibility, the magnetism of Clay without his vanity, the lucidity of Webster without his ponderousness."

In his costly effort to preserve democracy in America, he became the freedom-giver to the slaves, causing Frederick Douglass to remark that an ugly war was now, finally, "invested with sanctity." We see Lincoln as the giant moral figure of our history, flawed though he was, who unlike extremists to the right or left of him was able to accomplish specific, lasting achievements in human liberty. "As I would not be a slave," he once insisted, "so I would not be a master. This expresses my idea of democracy."

Remember also that he was plain, funny, kind, withdrawn. He could talk up a storm or be as quiet as the prairie on a still night. He sounded like a backwoodsman, even in high hat. Up close, it was impossible to fear him. His heart broke over fallen birds and fallen men. He could get fired up or fed up. He was absentminded. He was slow to act. Straining, he grew out of his prejudices. He wrote like a poet. He laughed like a hyena. He cried real tears. Everything about him was real.

Philip B. Kunhardt, Jr.
Philip B. Kunhardt III
Peter W. Kunhardt

A Lincoln

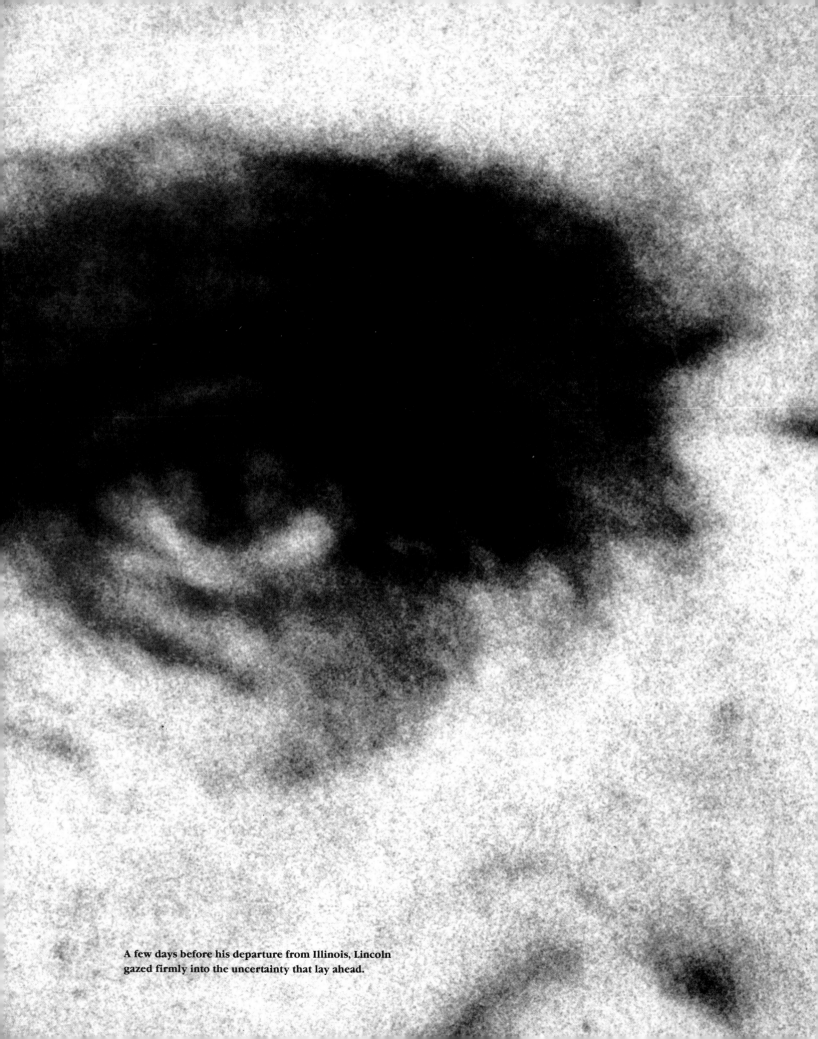

A few days before his departure from Illinois, Lincoln
gazed firmly into the uncertainty that lay ahead.

Chapter 1

TAKING THE HELM

The disintegrating Union welcomes its new leader.

HEADING EAST, WITH A NATION IN HIS HANDS

Abraham Lincoln's trip east to assume the presidency of the United States began on the morning of February 11, 1861, and ended by the early light of February 23—twelve days in all. The journey took him from his home in Springfield, Illinois, along a great curving excursion through the American North—through Indianapolis, Cincinnati, and Columbus, to Pittsburgh and then back out again into Cleveland, up to Buffalo and east to Albany, and finally south along the Hudson River to New York City and down to Washington via Philadelphia, Harrisburg, and Baltimore.

As the trip got under way, amid warnings and death threats, the state of the country was nothing less than precarious. The issue of slavery, for decades an unhealable cancer in the national tissue, was now, finally, threatening death to the Union. "Never till now has a President been chosen who was known to regard Human Bondage as...evil and...wrong," wrote radical newspaperman Horace Greeley upon Lincoln's election the previous November, and ever since, the troubles had unfurled. On December 20, South Carolina had seceded from the Union, setting off a chain reaction throughout the lower South. By early February, Mississippi, Florida, Alabama, Georgia, Louisiana, and Texas were hastening in the same direction. In Washington, President Buchanan, deeply sympathetic to the South and its rights to slavery, stood by doing nothing. When Lincoln heard a rumor that Buchanan had decided to surrender a key Union fort in Charleston, South Carolina—Fort Sumter—he exclaimed, "If that is true they ought to hang him." North and South now seemed irreconcilable.

The train itself was a Pullman sleeper, one of the first ever in use. Seventeen-year-old Robert Lincoln, the President-elect's eldest son, was particularly pleased with it, riding half the time up with the engineer and delighting at sights of men along the way shouldering rails, or else hanging out in the refreshment saloon. (He later became president of the Pullman Car Company.) The insides of the cars were lavish and comfortable, decorated with plush carpets, great overstuffed chairs, and inlaid wooden walls lined with crimson velvet beneath the windows and heavy curtains. Lincoln's car was festooned with red, white, and blue bunting and contained, to his delight, long sofas to stretch out upon during quieter moments in the day. Here he might wonder how a dirt-poor, would-be village blacksmith who had painfully mastered grammar without teachers, then forged himself into a lawyer of strict honesty, had gradually raised himself up to the presidency itself, how this odd choice of the American people would cope with a "task"—he had said it himself—"greater than that which rested upon Washington."

Accompanying Lincoln on the trip, in addition to Robert, were his wife, Mary, and their two younger sons, Willie and Tad—who joined him in Indianapolis—as well as various friends: Elmer E. Ellsworth, the popular young colonel who had been studying in Lincoln's law office; Ward Hill Lamon, the lawyer; John G. Nicolay and John Milton Hay, Lincoln's two personal secretaries; Judge David Davis, his campaign manager; and, among his political friends, Norman B. Judd, Orville Browning, and Illinois Governor Richard Yates. There was also an assortment of relatives and hangers-on. Four army men came along as protection—Colonel E. V. Sumner, Major David Hunter, and Captains John Pope and George W. Hazzard. And tucked away somewhere on board was Lincoln's hired black servant and friend, William A. Johnson.

This is how Lincoln looked as he started off for Washington. The President-elect had let his hair grow long and cultivated a brand-new beard. Below is the train schedule for the first leg of the journey, from Springfield to the Indiana border. In Illinois the train was pulled by a Hinkley locomotive named the L.M. Wiley, which was burning hickory that day. Every tie along the way, every spike, had been checked by details of trainmen who now watched each switch. Militia guarded the bridges.

Except for a second exposure of the same scene, this is the only photograph of Lincoln on his way to Washington. He has just made a speech at Independence Hall, Philadelphia, and now awaits a flag-raising ceremony to begin. Taken in the early morning, when the light was not strong enough for a good exposure, the picture shows Lincoln standing on the platform, directly above the single star at the far left of the draped flag. Leaning on the railing, Tad is just above the star at far right.

Also on board was the trip director, William S. Wood, and a special train officer ready with telegraph equipment, in case of an accident. All along the route, flagmen stood within visual distance of one another, and spare locomotives were parked in various towns, ready to be called into service if needed.

As the train left Illinois and passed the Indiana state line, a thirty-four-gun salute went off to celebrate its arrival, followed by an identical salute as the party reached Indianapolis.

In Cincinnati more than 100,000 people showed up to honor Lincoln on his birthday, and to watch him ride in a procession in a ceremonial carriage drawn by six white horses, and to hear thirty white-clad girls sing "The Star-Spangled Banner."

In town after town Lincoln was met by tremendous crowds and taxing public ceremonies. At no other time in his life would he have to make so many speeches so close together. The schedule on some days contained as many as twelve different speaking occasions, each with receptions. Henry Villard, the only journalist to accompany Lincoln on most of the trip, wrote of Lincoln's limbs becoming stiff from all the handshaking, and his voice growing hoarse from all the open-air speaking. The speeches themselves were solid and good, if not memorable, filled with awareness of the great weight of the times. "Without a name, perhaps without a reason why I should have a name, there has fallen upon me a task such as did not rest even upon the Father of his country...," he said to one state legislature. Lincoln saw himself as an "instrument," maybe not the best that could have been selected, but even he, with the help of the Almighty, was going to be able to pilot the ship of State through this voyage if he had the people's help—"for if it should suffer shipwreck now, there will be no pilot ever needed for another voyage."

In Columbus, Ohio, Lincoln was almost crushed when a crowd of 60,000 well-wishers pressed in for a closer look. Only the huge barrel chest of Lamon, thrusting itself between Lincoln and the crowd, allowed the President-elect to escape behind a pillar.

At one stop, a salutatory cannon misfired and shattered Mary Lincoln's train window, covering her with broken glass. At another point, one report had it that just outside Cincinnati, a loaded grenade was discovered hidden in a small carpetbag near Lincoln's seat.

Eldest son Robert saw more of his father on the train trip east than he would for the next four years at Harvard College.

"SHOW US THE CHILDREN!"

On the trip east, the press kept close tabs on the Lincoln family. At Poughkeepsie, The New York Times reported.

Mrs. Lincoln, who was recognized in the cars, was warmly welcomed by the crowd. "Where are the children? Show us the children!" cried a loud voice. Mrs. Lincoln immediately called her eldest son to the window, and he was greeted with a hearty cheer. "Have you any more on board?" "Yes," replied Mrs. Lincoln, "here's another"—and she attempted to bring a tough, rugged little fellow...into sight. But the young representative of the House of Lincoln proved refractory, and the more his mother endeavored to pull him up before the window the more stubbornly he persisted in throwing himself down on the floor of the car...His mother was at last constrained to give up the attempt to exhibit the "pet of the family."

In Springfield, Lincoln's tiny, vivacious, opinionated wife, Mary, posed with their young sons, Willie *(left)*, everybody's favorite, and Tad, the family pet. To tend the two on the trip east, Mary brought along a nurse.

Taken in Springfield on May 20, 1860, this picture shows
how ugly Lincoln could look on occasion.

Who was this man humming eastward to take command of a faltering nation? What could you tell from his weather-beaten face? Early in their marriage his wife, Mary, had said: "He's not pretty; he would certainly make a magnificent President."

Had that been a crazy guess or keen prophecy? His law partner and friend William Herndon said that Lincoln was a "riddle and a puzzle to his neighbors among whom he lived...an abstracted man—self-reliant... never once doubting his power to do anything any one else could do." Herndon also described how the man looked. "His structure was loose and leathery;...he had dark skin, dark hair, and looked woe-struck. The whole man, body and mind worked slowly, as if it needed oiling."

Ever since his nomination by the Republican Party nine months earlier, painters and photographers had come to Springfield to catch his likeness. What they all found was a face that was a true American original. Lincoln himself termed it "homely." He liked to pull a jackknife from his pocket and tell this story: "I was once accosted...by a stranger who said, 'Excuse me, sir, but I have an article in my possession which belongs to you.' 'How is that?' I asked, considerably astonished. The stranger took a jackknife from his pocket. 'This knife,' said he, 'was placed in my hands some years ago, with the injunction that I was to keep it until I found a man *uglier* than myself. Allow me *now* to say, sir, that I think *you* are fairly entitled to the property.'"

In the same way he employed his height for amusement, measuring against any tall man he met, Lincoln used his face as a weapon of self-deprecation. He mocked paintings and photographs that flattered him, termed "painfully truthful" those that showed up his rough edges. In a heated debate with Stephen Douglas, his opponent once called him two-faced, to which Lincoln supposedly replied, "I leave it to my audience. If I had another face, do you think I'd wear this one?"

On August 13, 1860, Preston Butler took this photograph of a self-assured, commanding Lincoln *(above)*. "They want my head, do they?" Lincoln challenged artist Charles A. Barry, "Well, if you can get it you may have it; that is, if you are able to take it off while I am on the jump." Barry did—in crayon *(below left)*. Upon seeing this Thomas Hicks portrait *(below right)*, Mary Lincoln exclaimed, "Yes, that is Mr. Lincoln. It is exactly like him, and his friends in New York will see him as he looks here at home." *Overleaf:* On these two photographs by Alexander Hesler, Lincoln commented, "That looks better and expresses me better than any I have ever seen; if it pleases the people I am satisfied."

Lincoln could appear handsome at one time, homely at another. When his hair was too long or too short, when it shot out every which way like blown wheat or stood up in spikes, Lincoln looked odd indeed. When his weak right eye wandered, or his beak of a nose was caught in sharp profile, or his thick lower lip hung down, when his hollow cheeks seemed sucked in more than usual, when his massive jaw took on a mulish set, or sadness and melancholy deadened his eyes, then his visage was construed as heavy and unpleasant. People who knew him said that his face was impossible really to describe because it was forever changing expression. Its plasticity gave it a thousand different gradations and configurations, and even when the light was unflattering or the jutting eyebrows stood out, or the cheeks went hollow, it was only for a moment. Then, in another flash, any hint of oddness or lack of expression or looseness of skin or overabundance of jaw disappeared, and as the man warmed up and his sadness fled, his features revived and his countenance turned radiant.

Artists especially did not see homeliness in Lincoln's face. In the rush to record him, Alban Conant arrived in Springfield and was pleasantly surprised: "My first sight of him was a revelation. This beaming expression of the man who stood transfigured before me I was resolved to do my best to transfer to canvas." Thomas Johnson, who came in July, considered Lincoln's face "beautiful in the extreme when compared with all the pictures that have been published over his name." What they tried to capture, which was so elusive, was inside the man. Herndon may have best summed it up: "When those little gray eyes and face were lighted up by the inward soul on fires of emotion...then it was that all those apparently ugly or homely features sprang into organs of beauty....Sometimes it did appear to me that Lincoln was just fresh from the hands of his Creator."

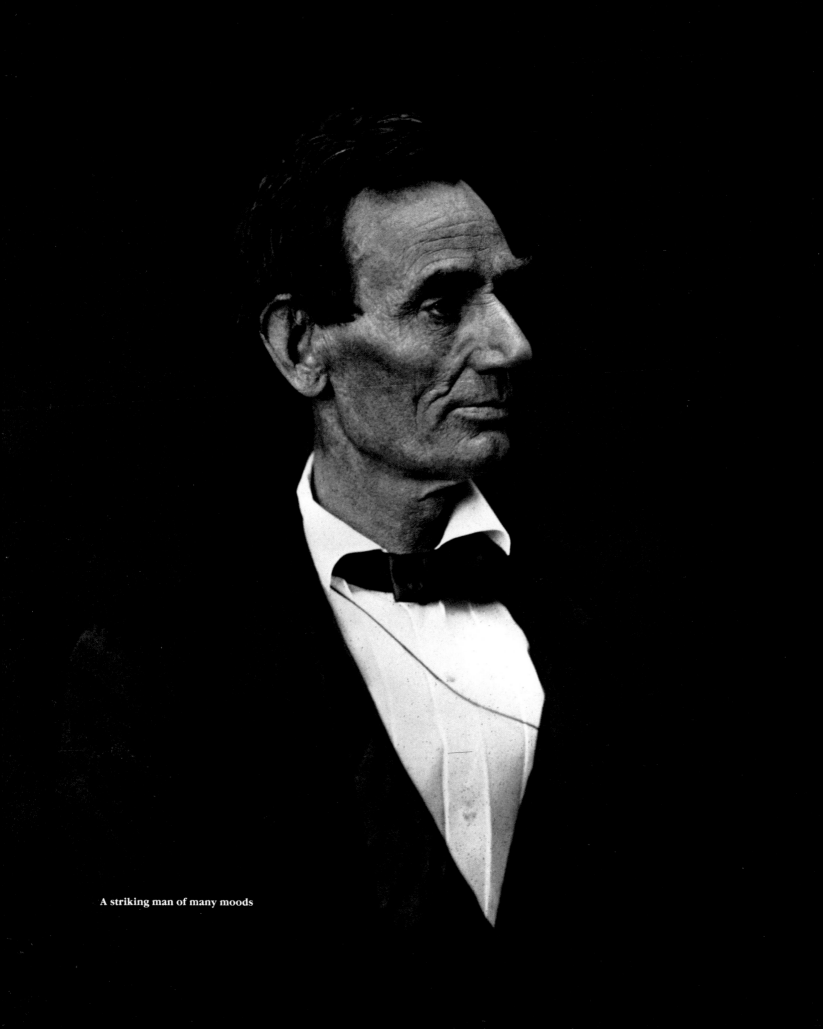

A striking man of many moods

Lincoln's Haitian barber, William de Fleurville *(right)*, lost some work when the President-elect decided to let his whiskers grow. The sudden decision surprised one old friend who described Lincoln as scrupulously clean and close shaven: "he never let his beard get the start of him."

The first photograph of the fledgling beard *(above)* was taken in Chicago on November 25, 1860, by Samuel G. Alschuler. The most famous picture of Lincoln up until then was taken in New York City during a trip to speak at the Cooper Union early in 1860. Touched up to show him smooth-cheeked, it was widely reproduced and helped Lincoln get elected. With whiskers added by an artist, the photograph looked like this *(right)*.

LINCOLN'S NEW WHISKERS MARK THE END OF HIS UNBEARDED YEARS

The man on the train heading east did not look exactly like the man for whom the nation had cast its vote. For shortly before the election a young girl named Grace Bedell from Westfield, New York, wrote Lincoln urging him to grow a beard. The idea must have crossed Lincoln's mind already, for three days earlier another letter had been posted to him, this one from ardent Republicans in New York City. "Dear Sir," it read. "Allow a number of very earnest Republicans to intimate to you, that after oft-repeated views of the daguerreotypes; which we wear as tokens of our devotedness to you; we have come to the candid determination that these medals would be much improved in appearance, provided you would cultivate whiskers and wear standing collars. . . . P.S. We really fear votes will be lost to 'the cause' unless our 'gentle hints' are attended to." Whatever advice he took, soon after, Lincoln was being attended to by "Billy the barber," who was just sharpening his razor to attack an overdue growth of beard. "Willie, let's give them a chance to grow," said Lincoln — and grow they did.

"Do you not think people would call it a piece of silly affection?" Lincoln had answered the Bedell child, meaning affectation. He was so greatly pleased by her letter that he carried it about for years and often pulled it out to show. "Affection" (affectation) or not, Lincoln was impervious to charges that he was trying to be a fashion plate or to musings that the beard was to protect his throat or to save him time in the White House. Whatever the real reason, the new whiskers were not looked upon kindly by his old Illinois friends. And they were a subject of much ridicule by the press. The December 27, 1860, *Evansville Daily Journal* commented: "They say that old Abe is raising a pair of whiskers. Some individual of the cockney persuasion remarked that he was 'a puttin' on airs!" *The Illustrated News* accused the President-elect of using a stimulating ointment known as "Bellingham's" to start his "manly adornment." And *Vanity Fair* ran a cartoon showing Lincoln at the start of the "Lincoln Whiskeropherons." Other publications, caught off guard by word of the new whiskers, solved the problem by adding their own beard to an earlier photograph.

LINCOLN'S REPLY

> Springfield, Ills Oct 19. 1860
> Miss. Grace Bedell
> My dear little Miss.
>   Your very agreeable letter of the 15th is received—
> I regret the necessity of saying I have no daughter— I have three sons— one seventeen, one nine, and one seven, years of age— They, with their mother, constitute my whole family—
> As to the whiskers, having never worn any, do you not think people would call it a piece of silly affection if I were to begin it now?
>   Your very sincere wellwisher
>   A. Lincoln

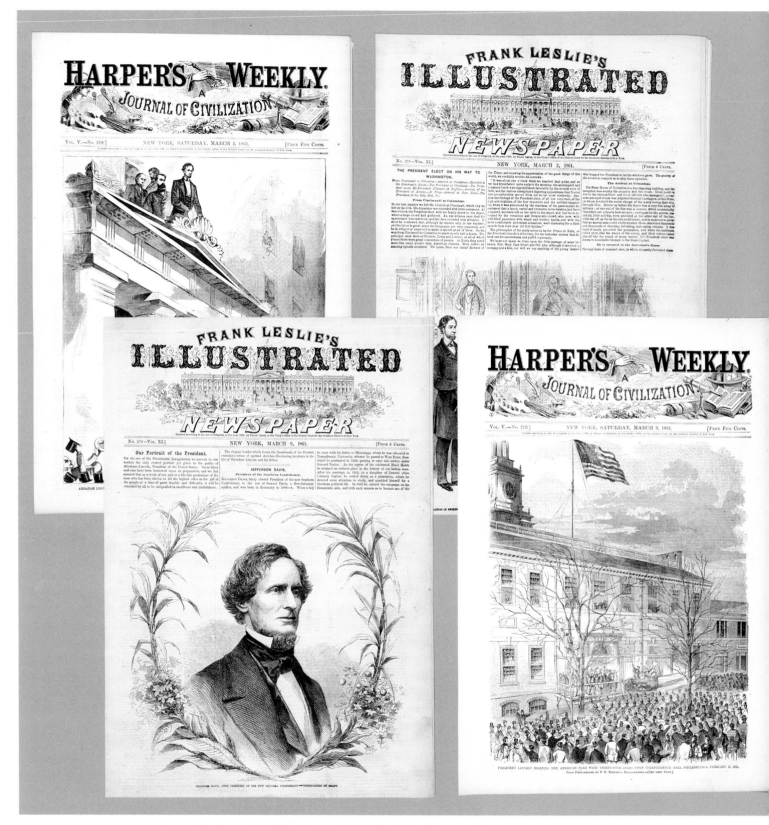

The two main pictorial weeklies of the day tracked Lincoln east. In the March 2 editions, each journal showed different events in the New York City stopover. Unlike *Leslie's, Harper's* chose the flag raising at Philadelphia over the swearing in of Jefferson Davis for its March 9 front page.

Philadelphia's Independence Hall

After his formal speech inside Independence Hall, Lincoln was led outside to a stand where, before raising the American flag with its new thirty-fourth star, representing Kansas, he spoke these farsighted words.

...excluding passion, ill-temper and precipitate action on all occasions, I think we may promise ourselves that not only the new star placed upon the flag shall be permitted to remain there to our permanent prosperity for years to come, but additional ones shall from time to time be placed there, until we shall number...five hundred millions of happy and prosperous people. [Great applause.] With these few remarks, I proceed to the very agreeable duty assigned me.

When the train reached Westfield, New York, on Lake Erie, Lincoln sought out Grace Bedell, the eleven-year-old girl who had written to him in Springfield about the beard, and showed her what he had grown.

In Buffalo, home of Millard Fillmore, Lincoln lunched with the former president, then joined Willie and Tad and a hotel-owner's son in a game of leapfrog.

Somewhere east of Albany, news reached them that the South had taken its own terrible leap. Former Secretary of War, Mississippi Senator Jefferson Davis, a moderate who for some time had opposed secession, had been sworn in as president of what was called a new nation—the Confederate States of America—with its own flag and slavery-protecting constitution. Reluctantly abandoning his hope for a military command in the Southern armies, Davis assumed the presidency with a realistic understanding of the difficulties facing the new Confederacy. At the large inaugural ceremony at Montgomery, Alabama, he soberly predicted "war, long and bloody." From this point on, the Lincoln journey took place under a gathering cloud.

But still the crowds came out to celebrate their new leader. In one stop along the Hudson River, a group of fans ice-skated over the frozen river to see him, bearing flying banners.

In New York City, where Lincoln had gained many admirers twelve months earlier at the Cooper Union address, crowds were waiting for his arrival with anticipation. By far the nation's biggest city, and the undisputed center of America's commerce, still New York was hardly Lincoln country—only 35 percent of the voters had wanted him for president. Horace Greeley, who had joined the Lincoln train for twenty miles in western New York, now released a front-page story in the *New York Independent* enthusiastically backing Mr. Lincoln in the face of a treasonous South. "The sole reason for all the hatred and malignity which now scowl upon him is this—he holds, with the founders of this Republic that human slavery is an evil to be circumscribed, not a good to be diffused and extended."

The speech Lincoln looked forward to most of all, next to his inaugural, was the address at Independence Hall, Philadelphia, scheduled for Washington's birthday. He chose as his subject the sacredness of the Declaration of Independence. "I am filled with deep emotion at finding myself standing here in the place where were collected together the wisdom, the patriotism, the devotion to principle, from which sprang the institutions under which we live....I have never had a feeling politically that did not spring from the sentiments embodied in the Declaration of Independence....I have often inquired of myself, what great principle or idea it was that kept this Confederacy so long together. It was not the mere matter of separation of the colonies from the mother land; but something in that Declaration giving liberty, not alone to the people of this country, but hope to the world for all future time. It was that which gave promise that in due time the weights should be lifted from the shoulders of all men, and that *all* should have an equal chance."

SNEAKING INTO WASHINGTON

On the night of February 22, not twelve hours after the Philadelphia speech, Abraham Lincoln ate a hasty dinner at the Jones House in Harrisburg, Pennsylvania, and then hurried to his room, where he changed his clothes and wrapped himself up in a large overcoat. In his pocket was an unfamiliar felt hat, unlike any he had ever worn, soft enough to be drawn down low over his big face as a disguise. The President-elect walked out a side door of the hotel, pulled on the hat, and approached a carriage where his friend Ward Hill Lamon was waiting, his pockets bristling with common pistols, derringers, and knives. The regular presidential train would leave on schedule with fanfare in the morning. Lincoln was to be smuggled into Washington tonight.

For some time Lincoln had been informed that the weak link in his long train trip east from Springfield would be Baltimore. With wildly secessionist sections, like parts of Washington itself, Baltimore had a chief of police named George P. Kane who hated Lincoln and could not be counted on to supply adequate protection. The slow passage through town while the train cars were pulled to a new set of tracks at the Camden Street Station was the perfect opportunity for an attack upon the incoming President.

Despite urgings to avoid travel by steamer and avoid Baltimore altogether, Lincoln had remained determined to arrive in Washington calmly by the regular route. He had declined the offer of an Ohio chemist to provide him with a special gold-plated suit of mail, silk-covered and sweat-resistant, to be worn over an ordinary undershirt.

By the time his party had reached Philadelphia on February 21, however, word of an assassination conspiracy had arrived from two sources. The first was Scottish-born railroad detective Allan Pinkerton, who spoke of murderous Baltimore ''plug-uglies'' and urged Lincoln to cancel the next day's Philadelphia address and visit to Harrisburg, and instead to get to Washington that night. The second, even more serious, came from old General Winfield Scott, who for months had been arming Washington in preparation for Lincoln's arrival and inauguration. The general warned of ''banded rowdies'' in Baltimore and ''threats of mobbing and violence.'' Scott's friend New York Senator William H. Seward added that ''about fifteen thousand men were organized to prevent [Lincoln's] passage through Baltimore,'' and were planning ''to blow up the railroad track'' and set fire to the train. Like Pinkerton, General Scott urged a secret night trip. With so many advisers pushing him, Lincoln finally agreed to turn himself over to the Pinkerton agency, insisting, however, that he first keep his appointments in Philadelphia and Harrisburg and that Mrs. Lincoln, prone to attacks of panic, be fully briefed. At Philadelphia the next morning he declared he would rather be ''assassinated on the spot'' than surrender to the threats of traitors.

Now, on the night of Washington's birthday, Lincoln was being spirited aboard a special single-car train in Harrisburg, while expert pole climbers cut the telegraph wires leading out of the city. With secrecy thus guaranteed, the train, its car lamps unlit, pulled quietly out into the night. By 10:00 p.m., it arrived in West Philadelphia, where Pinkerton was waiting to escort Lincoln to a special sleeping car on the midnight train to Baltimore. The car had been reserved under a false name, supposedly for the use of an invalid who required special access through a rear door. He was to be assisted by his sister, in

Railroad detective Allan Pinkerton

BY SPECIAL MESSENGER

General Winfield Scott sent this important message to William Seward, whose son, Frederick, relayed it to Lincoln in Philadelphia on the 22nd.

From Lt. Genl. Scott...

Feb. 21, 1861

A New York detective officer who has been on duty in Baltimore for three weeks past reports this morning [to Col. Stone] that there is serious danger of violence to and the assassination of Mr. Lincoln in his passage through that city should the time of that passage be known—He states that there are banded rowdies holding secret meetings, and that he has heard threats of mobbing and violence, and has himself heard men declare that if Mr. Lincoln was to be assassinated they would like to be the men....

All risk might be easily avoided by a change in the traveling arrangements which would bring Mr. Lincoln & a portion of his party through Baltimore by a night train without previous notice—

HIS FRIEND WASHBURNE MET THE TRAIN

I stood behind the pillar awaiting the arrival of the train. When it came to a stop I watched with fear and trembling to see the passengers descend. I saw every car emptied, and there was no Mr. Lincoln. I was well-nigh in despair, and when about to leave I saw slowly emerge from the last sleeping car three persons. I could not mistake the long, lank form of Mr. Lincoln, and my heart bounded with joy and gratitude.... Any one who knew him at that time could not have failed to recognize him at once, but, I must confess, he looked more like a well-to-do farmer from one of the back towns...coming to Washington to see the city, take out his land warrant and get the patent for his farm, than the President of the United States.

A congressman from Illinois, Elihu B. Washburne was Lincoln's informant in the capital before the journey east. He was the only person to greet Lincoln on the station platform at the secret arrival.

Huge, barrel-chested family friend Ward Hill Lamon volunteered himself as Lincoln's bodyguard for the long train journey east.

(3.) THE SPECIAL TRAIN.

reality Pinkerton agent Kate Warne. Once aboard, Lincoln was pushed up into a sleeping berth far too short for him, so that his huge legs had to be doubled up. The curtains were pulled shut on him, and everyone was ordered to be totally silent. Then, after an elaborate coded signal that Lincoln was safely on board, the train pulled out of the station. The only words spoken that night, according to Lamon, were by Lincoln, who couldn't help but crack jokes from time to time in the darkness.

At 3:15 a.m., the train arrived in Baltimore, and Lincoln's car was hitched up to a team of horses and slowly pulled through the danger area to the Washington depot, Camden Station. As they waited to begin the last leg of their journey, the clandestine group could hear a drunkard singing ''Dixie'' on the platform outside.

In Washington, Lincoln was met by his old ally Congressman Elihu B. Washburne, who for months had been worrying about his friend's safety. Then Pinkerton, Lamon, Washburne, and Lincoln sped off in horse and carriage to Willard's Hotel, where the President-elect would reside until his inauguration. There, joined by the newly designated Secretary of State Seward for coffee and fresh local fish, Washburne heard Lincoln say that he was neither mournful nor chagrined at having sneaked into Washington. ''I thought it wise to run no risk where no risk was necessary.''

It had been a safe if undignified arrival and Lincoln felt satisfied as he entered his suite. Still, he could not escape the hatred boiling in so many American hearts, for there, awaiting him on a table, was a note threatening death if he didn't resign. It called him ''nothing but a goddern Black nigger.''

At top is the hat Lincoln actually used to disguise himself. In New York City a few days before arriving in Washington, a friend presented Lincoln with a new beaver stovepipe, and the President-elect discovered the soft felt hat inside the box as well. " I had never worn one in my life," Lincoln recalled. "Having informed a very few friends of the secret of my new movements, and the cause, I put on an old overcoat that I had with me, and putting the soft hat in my pocket, I walked out of the house at a back door, bareheaded, without exciting any special curiosity. Then I put on the soft hat and joined my friends without being recognized by strangers, for I was not the same man." Since the Scotsman Pinkerton engineered the strange arrival at Washington, *Harper's Weekly* mocked it by showing a fleet Lincoln garbed in Scottish tam and military cloak *(far left)*. At left is Willard's Hotel, where Lincoln and his family lived before moving to the White House on inauguration day. And above are the final lines of the foul-mouthed letter that was awaiting Lincoln in his room at Willard's.

BUSY DAY IN THE HIGHLY CHARGED CITY

It was no secret that Lincoln's life was in danger. Three days earlier Horace Greeley's article ''Mr. Lincoln on his way'' reported that ''large rewards have been openly proffered in the Cotton States to whosoever would take his life before the 4th of March.'' Still, Lincoln's first morning in Washington was relatively calm—few even knew that he was there. After breakfast and a meeting with his Vice President-elect, Hannibal Hamlin, Lincoln called upon President James Buchanan in the White House, met all of Buchanan's Cabinet, and then went searching for General Scott. By two o'clock, the general finally turned up back at Willard's Hotel. News of Lincoln's arrival began to spread through the city. Stephen A. Douglas showed up late in the afternoon. And at some point, Lincoln went down to Brady's Studio at 352 Pennsylvania Avenue and had his picture taken. When Mary and the family arrived later in the day, they were ushered into suite #6 at the hotel. That evening, Lincoln dined privately with Senator Seward, who was beginning to like this man who had run against him for president. ''He is very cordial and kind toward me,'' Seward wrote home to New York that same day, ''simple, natural and agreeable.''

Lincoln's choice for secretary of state was William H. Seward, shown here in an 1850s daguerreotype.

The White House, as it looked when Lincoln paid his respects to outgoing President James Buchanan

Hannibal Hamlin of Maine beat out Cassius M. Clay of Kentucky to become the 1860 Republican nominee for vice president. Two months after the convention, Lincoln wrote to Hamlin: ''It appears to me you and I ought to be acquainted, and accordingly I write this as a sort of introduction of myself to you. You first entered the Senate during the single term I was a member of the House of Representatives, but I have no recollection that we were introduced. I shall be pleased to receive a line from you. The prospect of Republican success now appears very flattering, so far as I can perceive. Do you see anything to the contrary?'' It was not until after the election that the next leaders of the United States finally met in Chicago.

Lieutenant General Winfield Scott, General-in-Chief of the United States Army, in an imposing image made by the piecing together of a broken glass negative. For many weeks after Lincoln's election, Scott argued fruitlessly with President Buchanan for the reinforcement of Fort Sumter and other Federal forts in the South. Frustrated and angry at Buchanan's obstinacy, which seemed to border on treason, Scott looked forward eagerly to Lincoln's arrival. Later he would tell Lincoln, "I have dined with every President since Jefferson and...in my mind, the last should be the First."

James Buchanan, fifteenth president of the United States. The negative, from which this early print was made, was also badly damaged. Patch marks across Buchanan's middle show where the glass was refastened.

Gardner's photograph of Lincoln

Swollen and nearly paralyzed from thousands of handshakes since his departure from

Alexander Gardner ran Brady's Washington Gallery at 352 Pennsylvania Avenue. The photographs he took during Lincoln's first visit showed an exhausted subject with long hair, a newly grown beard, and a right hand swollen from shaking so many hands on the trip east. The sitting was at the request of *Harper's Weekly*, which wanted a current picture of the bearded Lincoln to lithograph for its readers *(right)*. Clad in his new long coat and his shiny, black, pointed shoes, Lincoln sat pensively as the overhead window curtains were adjusted by a long pole so that the right amount of light would illuminate him below. Gardner had asked a young artist named George H. Story to be present to help with the posing. Story later recalled that Lincoln "seemed absolutely indifferent to all that was going on about him, and he gave the

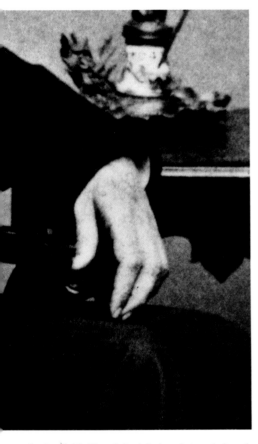

Springfield, Lincoln's right hand stayed closed and partially hidden during the sitting.

impression that he was a man who was overwhelmed with anxiety and fatigue and care.'' While five different poses were photographed, the President-elect closed his eyes for long periods, hardly moved, never parted his lips, and seemed lost in reverie. Portrait sittings were conducted in the gallery on the top floor of the building. To get there Lincoln had to climb three flights of stairs, first passing through the elaborate Brady reception room on the second floor, with its large stereoscopic viewing box, and then past the finishing and mounting rooms on the third floor before finally reaching the gallery itself with its cameras, posing chairs, and headrests, as well as its French plate-glass mirror, marble stand, clock, painted screen, curtains, table, inkstand, and a variety of other props and accessories.

Harper's Weekly used Gardner's photograph to make this engraving.

FINALLY, THE BIG DAY

Lincoln awoke in Washington to his inauguration day, and to his address. No single speech of his had ever received the painstaking attention this one had. He had written a first draft of it in Springfield, and given Carl Schurz, the ardent German-born abolitionist, a chance to look it over and criticize it. He had worked on it some more on the train from Springfield to Indianapolis, and had asked his friend Orville Browning for comments. En route to Washington he had kept it in a special gripsack, temporarily entrusted at times to Robert for safekeeping. When the teenager mislaid the satchel containing what Lincoln called his "certificate of moral character," his father had exploded. In Washington, he asked Seward to examine it word by word, and was persuaded to tone down all threats to the South. Now on the morning of the inauguration, he gathered together his family and read the speech to them.

A little past noon, a worn-out President Buchanan arrived at Willard's Hotel to escort Lincoln up Pennsylvania Avenue to the Capitol steps. The horse-drawn carriage rolled past heavily guarded streets, with riflemen on the rooftops and great guns erected near the Capitol. Never before had an inauguration taken place in such an atmosphere. The city of Washington was unabashedly opposed to Lincoln and sympathetic to the South. The President-elect was in alien territory—a city much more willing to put up with a Buchanan Democrat than with a Lincoln Republican. Washington that day was tense, quiet, barely decorated. A sizable part of the crowd that had gathered for the address had been imported from the North.

The presidential carriage entered the Capitol through a boarded tunnel and disappeared from view. When they emerged onto the Capitol's east portico, Lincoln and Buchanan walked arm in arm. Around them were the giants of government, both new and old. Chief Justice Roger B. Taney, looking shrunken and grim, stood for everything Lincoln hated. But then there were the new: Salmon P. Chase, Seward, Charles Sumner, Benjamin Wade. Even Lincoln's old adversary, Stephen A. Douglas, was here, shivering without an overcoat.

In the center of them all was Lincoln, dressed up in a new suit, hat, and boots, and carrying a gold-headed cane. Mary had thought he looked so good that morning, so dignified.

The address was to precede the swearing-in ceremonies. Senator Edward Baker of Oregon, Lincoln's old friend, introduced him. Then Lincoln stood. As he approached the little table from which he would speak, several people saw Douglas reach over and take Lincoln's hat to hold throughout the ceremony. Others saw Lincoln pull out his steel-rimmed spectacles, which he needed for reading.

Now Lincoln was in his element, speaking in the open air to a crowd. His high-pitched, passionate voice rang out like a bell across the silent crowds. It had been a dark, cold morning, but the sun broke out and beamed upon the listeners. Lincoln's speech was a strong, loving appeal to his countrymen and -women to hold together in the dark times, to resist revolution, to trust in his goodwill. As much as he hated the institution of slavery, he would not interfere with it where it was long established. He *would* hold firm on keeping it out of new territories. He *would* hold onto Union forts in the South, "...occupy and possess the property, and places belonging to the government." He called on all Americans to be friends, not enemies, for the Union

Far left: Newspaper artist Thomas Nast pictured Lincoln in the lobby of Willard's Hotel on the night before the inauguration, slumped in a chair and casually reading a paper. *Left:* Lincoln and Buchanan turn up Pennsylvania Avenue on their approach to the Capitol. *Below, far left:* Crowds gather for the inauguration beneath the Capitol's unfinished dome. *Below:* A markedly similar scene had taken place two weeks earlier as an assembled crowd heard Jefferson Davis's inauguration address in Montgomery, Alabama, capital of the newly formed Confederate States.

depended upon it, now more than ever. Thirty minutes after he had begun, he closed with this appeal. Then a brown velvet bible was held out to Lincoln, and old Justice Taney—author of the infamous Dred Scott decision and defender of slavery—administered the oath of office. That night, after the inaugural ball, Lincoln entered his room at the White House and was handed a letter warning that Fort Sumter, South Carolina, was in grave danger.

THE CONCLUSION OF LINCOLN'S FIRST INAUGURAL ADDRESS

In your *hands, my dissatisfied fellow countrymen, and not in* mine, *is the momentous issue of civil war. The government will not assail* you. *You can have no conflict, without being yourselves the aggressors.* You *have no oath registered in Heaven to destroy the government, while* I *shall have the most solemn one to "preserve, protect and defend" it.*

I am loth to close. We are not enemies, but friends. We must not be enemies. Though passion may have strained, it must not break our bonds of affection. The mystic chords of memory, stretching from every battle-field, and patriot grave, to every living heart and hearthstone, all over this broad land, will yet swell the chorus of the Union, when again touched, as surely they will be, by the better angels of our nature.

Beneath a stand on the Capitol steps, Lincoln addresses the country.

Abraham Lincoln, President of the United States, and
Jefferson Davis, President of the Confederate States:
"We must not be enemies."

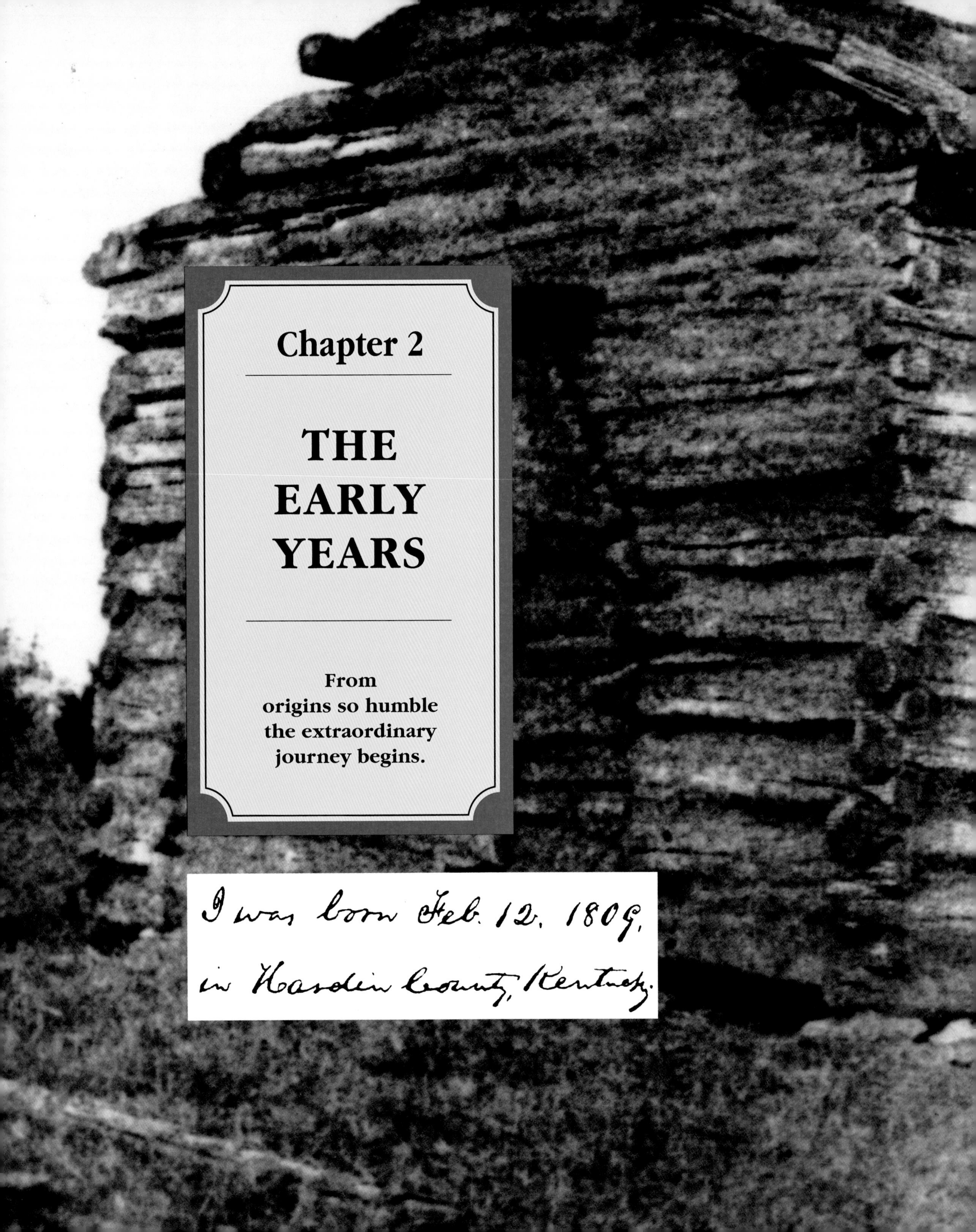

Chapter 2

THE EARLY YEARS

From
origins so humble
the extraordinary
journey begins.

I was born Feb. 12. 1809, in Hardin County, Kentucky.

The cabin where
Lincoln may
have been born.
Some claim these
are the original
logs, taken down,
refinished, then
reassembled.
Today the cabin is
enshrined in
Kentucky.

S ome spelled it "Linkhern" and others called it "Linkorn," but Abraham and his wife, Bathsheba, signed their name "Lincoln" before leaving Virginia with their five children in the early 1780s to make their way west down the Wilderness Road, following the trail the buffalo took, through mountain gaps, past Indians on the ambush, to the rich timber and bluegrass farmlands of Kentucky. There they staked claims for 2,000 acres, a modest size as far as plantations went but stretching almost as far as the eye could see, paying a total price of $800. The dream did not last long. An Indian sneaked through the woods and put a fatal shot into Abraham while he was clearing a field. Six-year-old Thomas watched in horror and would have been carried off if his older brother Mordecai had not taken aim from the nearby cabin and shot the killer dead. Forlorn and leaderless, the stricken pioneer family stuck together at first, but eventually the widow and younger children were forced to scatter about the county. Grown to almost five feet, ten inches, Thomas struck out on his own, drifted about, helped build a milldam, cut wood for hire, learned carpentry and cabinet-making, bought a horse, guarded prisoners, enlisted to fight Indians, patrolled for permitless slaves, saved his money, got himself a piece of land, and established a home for his mother. An amiable, fun-loving "piddler"—a friend called him that because he'd never try anything big—Tom was the best storyteller about. In 1806, at the age of twenty-eight, he married a girl his sisters had played with since they were little. Nancy Hanks was a tall, pretty, uneducated twenty-three-year-old with sad, gray eyes who, it was whispered, had been born "illegitimate," her mother lacking "the necessary appendage of a husband." Their wedding was the fifth Lincoln family ceremony in the community—two brothers and two sisters had been married there before him. At first Tom and Nancy lived just off the main path in the village of Elizabethtown, in a cabin close to the courthouse where a friend of theirs, Sarah Bush, was keeping house over the stone jail with her husband, Daniel Johnston, the jailer. After their first child, Sarah, was born in 1807, Tom Lincoln decided to move out of town to farm. Late in 1808 the little family was living on newly purchased property in a rough-hewn cabin eighteen feet long standing on the south fork of Nolin Creek. There, on what was called Sinking Spring Farm, just under three miles from the village of Hodgenville, in that little, rough cabin with packed dirt for a floor, with a door that swung on leather hinges, with a single window opening on the world, Nancy Hanks Lincoln went into labor one winter evening. And there, on February 12, 1809, upon a bed of poles and cornhusks and bearskins, soon after dawn on that snow-filled Kentucky Sunday, a new Abraham Lincoln was born.

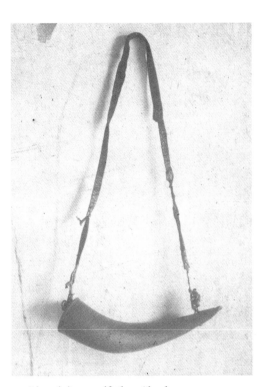

Lincoln's grandfather Abraham was wearing this powder horn *(above)* when he was killed by Indians. It was in the early 1780s, only a few years after the Declaration of Independence, that Daniel Boone *(below)*, a friend and distant kinsman, had persuaded the Lincolns to sell their farm in Virginia and move away from the Revolution to Kentucky. This portrait of Boone was painted when the great pioneer was ninety years old.

When Abraham Lincoln's father, Thomas, was a boy, he saw his father killed by an Indian. This is traditionally believed to be a picture of Thomas.

A BOY CAME RUNNING

Many decades later, cousin Dennis Hanks, who was nine at the time and lived nearby, claimed he remembered Abraham's first hours.

Babies wasn't as common as blackberries in the woods o' Kaintucky. Mother come over an' washed him an' . . . that's all the nuss'n either of 'em got. . . . Well, now, he looked just like any other baby, at fust — like red cherry pulp squeezed dry. An' he didn't improve none as he growed older. Abe never was much fur looks. I ricollect how Tom joked about Abe's long legs when he was toddlin' round the cabin. He growed out o' his clothes faster'n Nancy could make 'em.

But he was mighty good comp'ny, solemn as a papoose, but interested in everything. An' he always did have fits o' cuttin' up. I've seen him when he was a little feller, settin' on a stool, starin' at a visitor. All of a sudden he'd bu'st out laughin' fit to kill. If he told us what he was laughin' at, half the time we couldn't see no joke. . . .

Most o' the time he went bar'foot. . . . Abe was right out in the woods about a soon's he was weaned, fishin' in the creek, settin' traps fur rabbits an' muskrats, goin' on coon-hunts with Tom an' me an' the dogs, follerin' up bees to find bee-trees, an' drappin' corn fur his pappy. Mighty interestin' life fur a boy. . . .

Sometimes Abe was a little rude. When strangers would ride along and up to his father's fence, Abe always, through pride and to tease his father, would be sure to ask the stranger the first question, for which his father would sometimes knock him a rod. Abe was then a rude and forward boy. Abe, when whipped by his father, never balked, but dropped a kind of silent unwelcome tear, as evidence of his sensations or other feelings.

THE KENTUCKY YEARS

There wasn't much to this boy at first. He was little and all spindle. Learning was hard for him. His first steps were labored; he "walked slowly, but surely," a cousin remembered. There was nothing brilliant about him back then. He was a "bashful, somewhat dull, but peaceable boy." His father was stoop-shouldered, hard-working, sluggish. Little Abe was more like his mother — mild, tender, and intellectually inclined. Toddling into the village beside her, he sat on a keg of nails and sucked a lump of sugar while taking in the sights. When he was two, the Lincolns moved a few miles to another farm on the old Cumberland Trail, over which new settlers, peddlers, and itinerant preachers traveled and occasional lines of slaves were driven south to market. A year later, Nancy gave birth to another boy, but Abe's new brother, Thomas, lived only a few days. For a month here, a month there in warm weather, Abe and his sister, Sarah, made the long walk to school, and for whatever mischief he performed in the little windowless cabin, he received his share of the hazel switch, a schoolmate remembered. A "blab school" it was called because the learning was done by blabbing the lessons out loud over and over until they were known by heart. By the age of seven, Lincoln, now tall and spidery, could read well enough to take his turn at the Sunday bible readings at the cabin. Once, a playmate recalled, Abe almost drowned. "Cooning" it across Knob Creek on a log, while chasing birds, little Abe lost his balance, fell in, and had to be fished out with a sycamore branch. Sometimes his father cuffed him for being lazy or accosting strangers with questions. Even though Lincoln had no memory at all of the farm where he had been born, he remembered well the second cabin and the countryside around it. Something particular about that countryside stuck in his mind because it made a useful point about life. That's how Lincoln was: the practical things counted most.

Taken together, all of Lincoln's formal education added up to about a year. Here is his first schoolhouse, a windowless room for learning how to read and write. Zachariah Riney was his teacher here. Caleb Hazel taught Lincoln in his second school.

**ABE'S RELATIVE AND FRIEND
DENNIS HANKS**

When questioned late in life, Dennis Hanks remembered Lincoln's early stories and penmanship.

Physically he was a stout, powerful boy, fat, round, plump, and well made as well as proportioned. . . . He was a tricky man and sometimes when he went to log-house raising, corn shucking, and suchlike things he would say to himself and sometimes to others: "I don't want these fellows to work any more," and instantly he would commence his pranks, tricks, jokes, stories, and sure enough all would stop, gather around Abe, and listen, sometimes crying and sometimes bursting their sides with laughter. He sometimes would mount a stump, chair, or box and make speeches — stories and stories, anecdotes and suchlike things; he never failed here. . . .

Sometimes he would write with a piece of charcoal, or the p'int of a burnt stick, on the fence or floor. We got a little paper at the country town, and I made ink out of blackberry juice, briar root and a little copperas in it. It was black, but the copperas would eat the paper after a while. I made his first pen out of a turkey-buzzard feather. We hadn't no geese them days — to make good pens of goose quills.

Although it is falling apart in this picture, in its heyday, a quarter of a century before photography was invented, this cabin *(above)* was Lincoln's second home. He lived here for five years, until he was seven. Below is the farmland Lincoln remembered planting—and the rains unplanting.

LINCOLN REMEMBERS

Lincoln's boyhood memories.
I remember how, when a mere child, I used to get irritated when anybody talked to me in a way I could not understand....I can remember going to my little bedroom, after hearing the neighbors talk of an evening with my father, and spending no small part of the night walking up and down and trying to make out what was the exact meaning of some of their, to me, dark sayings. I could not sleep, although I tried to, when I got on such a hunt after an idea, until I had caught it; and when I thought I had got it, I was not satisfied until I had repeated it over and over; until I had put it in language plain enough, as I thought, for any boy I knew to comprehend. This was a kind of passion with me, and it has stuck by me; for I am never easy now, when I am handling a thought, till I have bounded it north and bounded it south, and bounded it east and bounded it west....

My earliest recollection...is of the Knob Creek place....I remember that old home very well. Our farm was composed of three fields. It lay in the valley surrounded by high hills and deep gorges. Sometimes when there came a big rain in the hills the water would come down through the gorges and spread all over the farm. The last thing I remember of doing there was one Saturday afternoon; the other boys planted the corn in what we called the big field; it contained seven acres—and I dropped the pumpkin seed. I dropped two seeds every other hill and every other row. The next Sunday morning there came a big rain in the hills; it did not rain a drop in the valley, but the water coming through the gorges washed ground, corn, pumpkin seeds and all clear off the field.

ON TO INDIANA

Lincoln was seven when his restless father decided to pull up stakes and push west to Indiana, soon to become the nineteenth state. With two horses carrying their belongings, it took them two weeks to make the hundred-mile journey. After crossing the Ohio River on a flatboat at Thompson's Ferry, Lincoln's father had to "cut his way to his farm, felling the forest as he went." Once arrived at the uncleared land near Little Pigeon Creek, Lincoln had an axe thrust into his hands, and from then on he was seldom without "that most useful instrument."

As a boy, Abe was already fiercely honest and self-reliant, sometimes lonely and withdrawn, more often exuberant and outgoing. The more he wondered about why people existed in the first place and what, anyway, human nature was all about, the more inscrutable life seemed. His confusion was compounded when first his old "aunt" and "uncle," Tom and Betsy Sparrow, perished in 1818 from a deadly scourge his father called the "milk-sick." And, even worse, after nursing them in their last hours, Lincoln's own mother followed. Life looked bleak indeed for the nine-year-old as he helped fashion her coffin, pull her on a sled to a hillside, and put her in the ground. A decade later his sister would die too, leaving Lincoln, head in hands, sobbing, when he got the news, and feeling completely alone in the world, except for his stepmother—somehow his father didn't count. In 1819, after a decent interval following Nancy's death, Thomas traveled back to his old Kentucky home and approached the widow of the former county jailer, Sarah Bush Johnston, the friend of Nancy's whom he, too, had known as a young girl and had even courted. "Miss Johnston," said he, "I have no wife and you no husband. I came a-purpose to marry you." Shortly after, the new union was sealed, and Tom arrived back in Indiana with not only his kind, loving "Sally" in tow but her three children as well. Now, with the orphaned "cousin" Dennis Hanks moved in, there were eight jammed into the cabin: three boys in the loft, three girls below in one corner, the parents in another.

In school, when he managed to get there, Lincoln stood out. He composed poems. He wrote essays on the subjects he felt strongly about: cruelty to animals, temperance, the sacredness of the American form of government. Later, he scratched out satires with his feather quill; one he called the "Chronicles of Reuben" became notorious in the way it made fun of the institution of marriage through a lightly disguised tale of the bedroom escapades of some of the neighbors. No one quite knew how to size Lincoln up. On the one hand, he was plowboy, rail-splitter, coon skinner, hog butcher. At ten he got kicked in the head by a horse and for a while was thought to be dead. He felled trees, pulled the cross saw, husked the corn, helped with house-raising. He was a swill-cleaning farm lad, with all the rough barnyard language and coarse humor of the backwoods, and with a frisky interest in his teenage stepsister Matilda. On the other hand, he was lost in the clouds—an insatiable reader who knew all the long words and a lot of the big ideas, as he sought out every book within fifty miles and ferreted out the pertinent information. "My best friend," he claimed, "is the man who'll get me a book I ain't read." He didn't read for pleasure, this odd, moody, muscular yet fleshy young man who could mimic the preachers' sermons without missing an inflection, who could mount a stump and give a speech on a variety of interesting subjects to his speechless

The Lincolns' Indiana cabin

"SHE KNEW SHE WAS GOING TO DIE"

Dennis Hanks describes the death of Lincoln's mother, Nancy Hanks, and the arrival a year later of Lincoln's stepmother, Sarah Bush Johnston.

She knew she was going to die and called the children to her dying side and told them to be good and kind to their father, to one another, and to the world, expressing a hope that they might live as they had been taught by her to love men, love, reverence, and worship God. Here in this rude house, of the milk sickness, died one of the very best women in the whole race, known for kindness, tenderness, charity, and love to the world. Mrs. Lincoln always taught Abe goodness, kindness, read the good Bible to him, taught him to read and to spell, taught him sweetness and benevolence as well....

[The second] Mrs. Lincoln proved an excellent stepmother. When she came into Indiana, Abe and his sister were wild, ragged, and dirty. Mrs. Lincoln had been raised in Elizabethtown in somewhat a high life; she soaped, rubbed, and washed the children clean, so that they looked pretty, neat, well, and clean. She sewed and mended their clothes, and the children once more looked human as their own good mother left them.

Lincoln's mother's grave (It was not until after her famous son's death that a stone or any other marker told where Nancy Hanks was buried.)

At fifteen Lincoln's stepsister Sarah Elizabeth Johnston married Dennis Hanks.

"A CONSTANT AND VORACIOUS READER"

John Hanks, another of Lincoln's cousins, moved in with the Lincoln family around 1823 and here recalls Abe's teenage years.

When...Abe...and I returned to the house from work, he would go to the cupboard, snatch a piece of corn bread, take down a book, sit down in a chair, cock his legs up as high as his head, and read. He and I worked bare-footed, grubbed it, plowed, mowed, and cradled together, plowed corn, gathered it, and shucked corn....

Lincoln devoured all the books he could get or lay hands on; he was a constant and voracious reader....He would go out in the woods and gather hickory bark, bring it home, and keep a light by it and read by it, when no lamp was to be had—grease lamp—handle to it which stuck in the crack of the wall. Tallow was scarce. Abraham was a good hearty eater, loved good eating....In the summer he wore tan linen pants and flax shirt and in the winter he wore linsey-woolsey....

Cousin John Hanks went down the Mississippi with Lincoln in 1831.

peers, who could keep an audience in stitches for hours with his drolleries. He read instead for information and explanation. It had started with Dilworth's speller and the bible back in Kentucky. Now, in Indiana, thrilling new worlds were being revealed as Aesop's *Fables* and *Pilgrim's Progress* and *Robinson Crusoe* were joined by Weems's *Life of Washington*, the *Life of Benjamin Franklin*, Shakespeare, Burns, ancient history, the law. In Franklin he found the model poor boy who had raised himself to greatness. In George Washington he met the embodiment of the American dream, the fatherly hero who had forged the country out of the democratic ideal. In the *Arabian Nights*, adventure and romance filled him with wonderful dread and yearning. "Abe'd lay on his stumick by the fire," Dennis Hanks remembered, "and read out loud to me'n Sairy, an' we'd laugh when he did....I reakon Abe read the book a dozen times, and knowed those yarns by heart." Dennis considered the *Arabian Nights* "a pack of lies." "Mighty fine lies," was Lincoln's answer.

At fifteen Lincoln was almost six feet tall, and people were astonished at his wiry strength, this gawky long-legs with too much shin showing below the pants, who once picked up a 600-pound chicken coop and carried it single-handed to its new foundation. When it came to wrestling, side holds were his specialty and no one could put him down. No one could match his mind either. It wasn't simply a God-given genius Lincoln possessed. His mind didn't automatically leap to solutions. Instead it was a slow but sure mind. It had to ponder and struggle. It had to repeat and memorize. It had to analyze and dissect. It had to listen and contemplate and figure out and decipher. It had to put two and two together. This mind had to confer with itself. Lincoln himself described it as "very hard to scratch anything on it and almost impossible after you get it there to rub it out."

He had decided early that the tedious life of endless, hard physical labor was not for him. It was one thing to work along the Ohio River, cutting wood and piling it on the bank for the captains of steamboats to buy. Even his steady job at Taylor's Mill ferrying passengers across the Anderson River at its junction with the Ohio would do—at least he was on his own. But when his father rented him and his axe out for twenty-five cents a day, that was too much. He always took a book along in his back pocket.

Lincoln's eyes were opening to the world through the written word, but it was a world that existed in his head—he had not personally experienced anything much beyond the confines of a patch of backwoods—twenty or thirty scattered, isolated families living meager farm-and-cabin lives. When an opportunity to break out came his way, he grabbed at it—a flatboat to build, a 1,200-mile journey down the Ohio River and the mighty Mississippi, to carry farm produce to New Orleans. The experience led to a permanent separation from home. After helping his restless father move farther west once more, this time to Illinois, then raising a new cabin and fencing a new field, Lincoln was off downriver to New Orleans again, this time with a promise of a job in a brand-new town at journey's end. And so the tiny Illinois settlement of New Salem was to come into Lincoln's life, a place where he could be his own man. It was not much on the map, just about twelve families, and close to the size of Chicago that year of 1831. Hardened by privation and loss, guided by horse sense, driven by ambition and dreams, off he set.

Multiplication Continued

Examples

of Land Measure

The Single Rule of Three

Late in life, Lincoln's stepmother *(left)* looked as gentle and kindly as she did when, at thirty-one, she became the second Mrs. Lincoln. Upon her arrival in the Lincoln household, "Sally"—the name she was known by—won little Lincoln's heart by replacing his cornhusk bed with a feather mattress she had brought. Although she couldn't read or write, she encouraged Lincoln with his lessons. Above are pages from Lincoln's boyhood workbooks.

A maze of rails like the thousands Lincoln split

"HE NEVER TOLD...A LIE"

Recalling her stepson Abe, Sarah Bush Johnston Lincoln had some of the most vivid memories of all.

Abe was about nine years of age when I landed in Indiana. The country was wild, and desolate. Abe was a good boy; he didn't like physical labor, was diligent for knowledge, wished to know, and if pains and labor would get it, he was sure to get it. He was the best boy I ever saw.... Abe read the Bible some, though not as much as said; he sought more congenial books suitable for his age. I think newspapers were had in Indiana as early as 1824 and up to 1830 when we moved to Illinois. Abe was a constant reader of them.... Abe had no particular religion, didn't think of that question at that time, if he ever did. He never talked about it. He read diligently, studied in the daytime, didn't after night much, went to bed early, got up early, and then read, eat his breakfast, got to work in the field with the men. Abe read all the books he could lay his hands on, and when he came across a passage that struck him, he would write it down on boards if he had no paper and keep it there till he did get paper, then he would rewrite it, look at it, repeat it. He had a copybook, a kind of scrapbook, in which he put down all things and then preserved them. He ciphered on boards when he had no paper or no slate, and when the board would get too black, he would shave it off with a drawing knife and go on again. When he had paper, he put his lines down on it.... Abe, when old folks were at our house, was a silent and attentive observer, never speaking or asking questions till they were gone, and then he must understand everything, even to the smallest thing, minutely and exactly; he would then repeat it over to himself again and again, sometimes in one form and then in another, and when it was fixed in his mind to suit him, he became easy and he never lost that fact or his understanding of it. Sometimes he seemed perturbed to give expression to his ideas and got mad, almost, at one who couldn't explain plainly what he wanted to convey. He would hear sermons [by the] preacher, come home, take the children out, get on a stump or log, and almost repeat it word for word.... He rose early, went to bed early, not reading much after night. Abe was a moderate eater... he sat down and ate what was set before him, making no complaint; he seemed careless about this. I cooked his meals for nearly fifteen years. He always had good health, never was sick, was very careful of his person, was tolerable neat and clean only, cared nothing for clothes, so that they were clean and neat, further cut no figure with him, nor color, new stuff, nor material; was careless about these things. He was more fleshy in Indiana than ever in Illinois.... He never told me a lie in his life, never evaded, never quarreled, never dodged nor turned a corner to avoid any chastisement or other responsibility. He never swore or used profane language in my presence nor in others' that I now remember of.... He loved animals generally and treated them kindly; he loved children well, very well.... Abe didn't care much for crowds of people; he chose his own company, which was always good. He was not very fond of girls, as he seemed to me....

For the rest of his life, Lincoln remembered the day he earned his first dollar. It opened up for him the possibilities of heading out on his own, not just to survive but to succeed.

[Y]ou never heard, did you, how I earned my first dollar? . . . I was about eighteen years of age. . . . I was contemplating my new flatboat . . . when two men came down to the shore in carriages with trunks. . . . "Will you," said one of them, "take us and our trunks out to the steamer?" . . . I was very glad to have the chance of earning something. I supposed that each of them would give me two or three bits. . . . I sculled them out to the steamboat. . . .

Each of them took from his pocket a silver half-dollar, and threw it on the floor of my boat. I could scarely believe my eyes as I picked up the money. . . . [Y]ou may think it was a very little thing . . . but it was a most important incident in my life. I could scarely believe . . . that I, a poor boy, had earned a dollar in less than a day, — that by honest work I had earned a dollar. The world seemed wider and fairer before me. I was a more hopeful and confident being from that time.

THE YEARS AT NEW SALEM

New Salem came and went fast. It seemed almost as if the little community sprouted on a bluff above the Sangamon River just so Lincoln could make use of it. And then, when he was ready to leave, the hamlet slid slowly and silently into the night.

New Salem was only two years old when Lincoln came down the Sangamon River in April 1831. He returned in July and settled in, and on August 1—election day—he made acquaintance with the inhabitants by hanging around the polling place. The town grew up around a saw-and-grist mill and the dam that powered it. Anticipating that steamboats would come up the river and the spot could turn into a boomtown, people started settling there. Pretty soon a general store or two opened, then a tavern, a couple of saloons, and a school for the children of the several dozen families that made up New Salem at its peak. Newly liberated from his own family, Lincoln had been hired to run Denton Offutt's store and work at the mill, and it was not long before the likable young giant who could whack down tall trees and tell tall tales all in the same breath was a Salem fixture, someone worth knowing. Even Jack Armstrong, the local strong man and the leader of the Clary's Grove boys, thought so after wrestling Lincoln practically even in a public match. Fair and square, this Lincoln—always looking to do a kindness, watching out for the underdog, honest almost to a fault—once walked miles to return pennies to an overcharged customer. But what was this two-fisted storekeeper doing joining the New Salem Debating Society and persuading the local schoolmaster to lend him books and teach him elocution and grammar? When they heard Lincoln speak, his new friends had the answer: here was somebody special, here was a thinker, here was someone who ought to take up politics. When the opportunity arose in early March of 1832, he tossed in his hat for the state legislature.

The grocery clerk in the failing store got a big boost when he was chosen to pilot the steamer *Talisman* on the last leg of an exploratory trip from Cincinnati to Springfield. Lincoln met the steamer at the mouth of the flooded Sangamon and helped guide her upstream to Springfield, where a dance was given to celebrate the event. For the trip downstream a week later, with the river's water dropping rapidly, Lincoln saw the *Talisman* safely past New Salem, having to knock down some of the milldam to do it. Soon after, Lincoln's campaign for the legislature was interrupted again, this time by the Black Hawk War and two months of service in the Illinois militia. He was delighted when his volunteer company elected him captain, even though there were more mosquitoes to fight than Indians. Mustered out without seeing action, Lincoln found his horse had been stolen, so he had to walk practically the whole way from Wisconsin back to New Salem. It left him only a bit over two weeks to campaign and thus probably cost him the election, even though he carried his hometown and came in eighth in a field of eighteen—"the only time I have been beaten by the people," he liked to point out. But even in defeat, Lincoln had begun to make his special mark, wandering from house to house, helping with the chores while swapping stories, hearing problems, getting votes. Two years later that kind of intimacy with a wider portion of the electorate would win him a seat in the state legislature. In the meantime, Offutt's store had gone broke, and a similar venture Lincoln owned along with partner William

The man above made Lincoln an instant celebrity in New Salem. Jack Armstrong was the most powerful wrestler in the county, and even though the new arrival didn't much like to "tussle and scuffle," he took on the leader of the Clary's Grove boys in a public go. Some said it was a draw, others that Lincoln was the winner. Whatever the truth, the match ended in handshakes, the two became best friends, and the town had a new hero. *Below:* Black Hawk was a leader of the Sauk and Fox tribes, whose seemingly hostile crossing to the east bank of the Mississippi in 1832 caused panic and led to Lincoln's two months as a captain in the militia. In this portrait Black Hawk is wearing a wampum necklace and a medal showing an unnamed government agent.

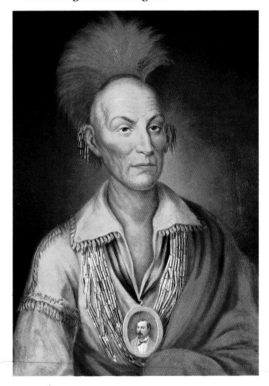

Long after the town of New Salem disappeared, the ruins above were the only evidence left of the mill that drew people to the little river town in the first place. In 1834, as deputy surveyor, Lincoln mapped the approach to the town from Musick's Ferry *(below)*. At the top of his drawing is the Sangamon River, where the mill stood.

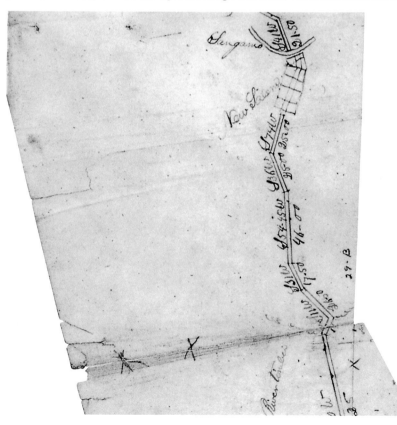

To the People of Sangamon County
FELLOW CITIZENS: Having become a candidate for the honorable office of one of your representatives in the next General Assembly of this state, in accordance with an established custom, and the principles of true republicanism, it becomes my duty to make known to you—the people whom I propose to represent—my sentiments with regard to local affairs....

So began Lincoln's very first communication to "the people," a document printed in the Sangamo Journal *at Springfield. After advocating the improvement of the Sangamon River for navigation, stating his case against usury and in favor of education and the existing laws, Lincoln closed with an endearing statement about himself and his need to be liked.*

Every man is said to have his peculiar ambition. Whether it be true or not, I can say for one that I have no other so great as that of being truly esteemed of my fellow men, by rendering myself worthy of their esteem. How far I shall succeed in gratifying this ambition, is yet to be developed. I am young and unknown to many of you. I was born and have ever remained in the most humble walks of life. I have no wealthy or popular relations to recommend me. My case is thrown exclusively upon the independent voters of this county, and if elected they will have conferred a favor upon me, for which I shall be unremitting in my labors to compensate. But if the good people in their wisdom shall see fit to keep me in the background, I have been too familiar with disappointments to be very much chagrined. Your friend and fellow-citizen,

A. Lincoln.
New Salem, March 9, 1832.

WHAT IT WAS LIKE TO MEET HIM

Future Governor of Illinois Richard Yates describes first meeting Lincoln in 1835.
I was down at Salem with a friend, who remarked to me one day, "I'll go over and introduce you to a fine young fellow we have here—a smart, genial, active young fellow, *and we'll be certain to have a good talk*." I consented, and he took me down to a collection of four or five houses, and looking over the way, I saw a young man partly lying or resting on a cellar door, intently engaged in reading. My friend took me up and introduced me to young Lincoln, and I tell you, as he rose up, I would not have shot at him *then* for a President.... Well after some pleasant conversation...we all went up to dinner. You know we all lived in a very plain way in those times. The house was a rough log house, with a puncheon floor and clapboard roof, and might have been built, like Solomon's Temple, "without the sound of hammer or nail," for there was no iron in it.... The old lady whose house it was soon provided us with a dinner, the principal ingredient of which was a great bowl of milk, which she handed to each. Somehow in serving Lincoln there was a mistake made, and his bowl tipped up, and the bowl and milk rolled over the floor. The good old lady was in deep distress, and exclaimed, "Oh dear me! that's all my fault." Lincoln picked up the bowl in the best natured way in the world, remarking to her, "Aunt Lizzy, we'll not discuss whose fault it was; only if it don't worry you, it don't worry me."... The old lady was comforted, and gave him another bowl of milk.

John Calhoun, the official surveyor of Sangamon County, appointed Lincoln as his deputy and put him in charge of the county's north end, including New Salem.

"Aunt Hannah," as Lincoln called her, was married to Jack Armstrong, New Salem's strong man until Lincoln came along.

Isaac Onstot studied grammar and arithmetic with Lincoln by the light from the burning shavings in his father's cooper shop.

William Greene was Lincoln's assistant at the Offutt store and was probably Lincoln's closest New Salem friend. It was Greene who persuaded Yates to meet Lincoln.

Mentor Graham, shown here with his wife, was the local schoolmaster. Lincoln turned to him for help in improving his grammar and acquiring new books.

F. Berry "winked out." It left him deeply in debt (the "National Debt," he called it), morose and resigned to failure in life. Although the pay was little, he took the position of New Salem's postmaster and was able to read dozens of newspapers each week before delivering them. That fall Lincoln also became a deputy surveyor, and he used both offices from which to campaign for the legislature again in 1834. He got votes at the dances and the house-raisings, the foot races and the quilting bees, the barbecues and the wolf hunts. He got votes at the horseshoe pits, the gander pulls, the cockfights, and even at the wrestling matches, where he was usually referee because no one could beat him but everyone could trust him. And in November, at the age of twenty-five, wearing his very first suit, he set off as a state legislator for Vandalia, then the Illinois capital, where subsequently he boarded whenever the legislature was in session. He had a sense of the poetic in his ear, a sense of right in his heart, this newly elected official of the state of Illinois. Reelected in 1836 and off to practice law in Springfield twenty miles away, Lincoln bid goodbye in 1837 to the dwindling town that had given him safe harbor. The people had lost faith in the future of the river, and three years after he left, New Salem was no more.

Even though folklore has it that Lincoln's heart was broken by the tragic death of his pretty New Salem sweetheart, Ann Rutledge, there is no evidence that the two were anything but close friends. In the absence of a picture of Ann (she died four years before photography was invented), the elderly faces of her younger sister, Sallie (above), and their mother, Mary Ann (below), may indicate what the fated Ann would have looked like had she lived a long life.

The Sangamon River near where the New Salem community once stood

BLACKSMITH OR THE BAR?

When keeping store in New Salem, so goes a Lincoln legend, Lincoln bought an unopened barrel from a man moving west in a covered wagon. "I did not want it," he said later, "but to oblige him I bought it, and paid him a half dollar for it." The contents were mostly rubbish, but at the bottom of the barrel were books; and one of those books was Blackstone's *Commentaries on the Laws of England*, basic reading for any law student. Although Blackstone's never did really fall into Lincoln's lap in quite so mysterious a manner (he bought his copy in Springfield at an auction), still fate did have something to do with his interest in studying law. If he had not met Major John Todd Stuart during the Black Hawk War, Lincoln might never have had the incentive he needed to forget the blacksmith's trade, which he thought he was suited for, and follow Stuart into the legal profession. No matter how he obtained Blackstone's, he studied every word. And when he was elected to office in 1834, there was his friend Stuart again, also chosen to the legislature, still urging him to become a lawyer. Now he had the confidence. Lincoln began borrowing from Stuart's legal library and systematically studying the fundamental texts he would soon be recommending to future law students—Chitty's *Pleadings*, Greenleaf's *Evidence*, Story's *Equity* and *Equity Pleading*. Going at it "in good earnest," Lincoln "studied with nobody," he recalled, and "still mixed in the surveying to pay board and clothing bills. When the Legislature met, the law books were dropped, but were taken up again at the end of the session." Finally, Lincoln had finished all the books an actual law school would require. There was no examination yet in Illinois for admittance to the bar, which required only a testament of good moral character and enrollment by the clerk of the State Supreme Court. On March 1, 1837, Lincoln got his license to practice law, and a month and a half later, still in debt and riding a borrowed horse, he set off for Springfield. As leader of the "Long Nine" (a group of nine like-minded, farsighted Illinois legislators who all averaged six feet in height—they claimed end to end they measured fifty-five feet) he had already made a name for himself in politics. Now, with the practice of law added to his political skills, there was no telling how far Lincoln might go.

This was once the house where Lincoln "kept batch" at intervals during his seven years at New Salem. When the picture was taken, the town no longer existed and this building stood in a feed lot, its weather boarding having been removed.

Major John Todd Stuart *(right)*—a cousin of Lincoln's future wife, Mary Todd—met Captain Abraham Lincoln during the Black Hawk War. Stuart further befriended the pride of New Salem in Vandalia while both served in the State Legislature. Attempting to remain the capital of Illinois, Vandalia built a new State House in 1863 *(below)*. Stuart helped Lincoln study law and in 1837 made him junior partner in his firm at Springfield, the town destined to become Vandalia's successor, which soon rendered this building obsolete.

Abraham Lincoln

Joshua Fry Speed

A TOWN OF BLACK MUD AND STREET PIGS

When Lincoln came to Springfield in 1837, his life was exactly half over. He did not arrive unknown. The New Salem wrestler and speaker had become known in Vandalia not only as a legislator but as Springfield's talented young benefactor, for largely because of his efforts as a party leader, the capital of Illinois was being switched to Springfield, much to Vandalia's dismay. Even though launched on his new career and lodged with the friendly, twenty-two-year-old Joshua Fry Speed, Lincoln found himself lonely and out of place. "This thing of living in Springfield," he wrote, "is rather a dull business after all, at least it is so to me. I am quite as lonesome here as [I] ever was anywhere in my life. I have been spoken to by but one woman since I've been here, and should not have been by her, if she could have avoided it. I've never been to church yet, nor probably shall not be soon. I stay away because I am conscious I should not know how to behave myself."

Springfield was a town of less than 1,500 people in 1837. There were no streetlights, no sidewalks, no sewers, no paved streets. After a rain, carriages became mired in the deep, black mud, while pigs wallowed freely about town, rooting out garbage. The notorious quagmire of mud after a rain or a melt could keep Springfielders inside their houses for days at a time. The stagecoach was the principal means of travel; railroads had not yet come, even though the Long Nine had been advocating them with vigor. There were not even any roads as such leading into town—only the paths made by covered wagons streaming westward across the vast prairie. Joshua Speed remembered the high prairie grass "waving in the breeze and resembling the billows of the ocean as the shadows of the fleeting clouds passed over it."

Lincoln was a difficult man to get to know. No matter how kind and good-humored, he usually stayed distant and kept his true feelings to himself. Speed was the ideal man to break through this reserve; he had many of the same concerns Lincoln had, especially about his inadequacy for lasting love and marriage. They could talk intimately, share confidences, and trust each other, and it was not long before Lincoln had made the best friend he would ever have. Speed was not hesitant to express his friendship frankly and openly, and to tell Lincoln how deeply he felt for him. Reciprocating, Lincoln could write sentiments to Speed that were unique in their intimacy. "I will be very lonesome without you," he once wrote his friend. "You know my desire to befriend you is everlasting—that I will never cease, while I know how to do anything."

It was at Speed's store that Lincoln began to make his mark on Illinois's new capital city, which was attracting many of the finest young lawyers and politicians in the West. "Mr. Lincoln was a social man, though he did not seek company; it sought him," Speed related. "After he made his home with me, on every winter's night at my store, by a big wood fire, no matter how inclement the weather, eight or ten choice spirits assembled, without distinction of party. It was a sort of a social club without organization. They came there because they were sure to find Lincoln."

START OF A FRIENDSHIP

Joshua Speed recalls the day he met his best friend.

It was in the spring of 1837, and on the very day that he obtained his license, that our intimate acquaintance began. He had ridden into town on a borrowed horse, with no earthly property save a pair of saddle-bags containing a few clothes. I was a merchant at Springfield, and kept a large country store, embracing dry goods, groceries, hardware, books, medicines, bed-clothes, mattresses, in fact every thing that the country needed. Lincoln came into the store with his saddle-bags on his arm. He said he wanted to buy the furniture for a single bed. The mattress, blankets, sheets, coverlid, and pillow, according to the figures made by me, would cost seventeen dollars. He said that was perhaps cheap enough; but, small as the sum was, he was unable to pay it. But if I would credit him till Christmas, and his experiment as a lawyer was a success, he would pay then, saying, in the saddest tone, "If I fail in this, I do not know that I can ever pay you." As I looked up at him I thought then, and think now, that I never saw a sadder face.

I said to him, "You seem to be so much pained at contracting so small a debt, I think I can suggest a plan by which you can avoid the debt and at the same time attain your end. I have a large room with a double bed up-stairs, which you are very welcome to share with me."

"Where is your room?" said he.

"Up-stairs," said I, pointing to a pair of winding stairs which led from the store to my room.

He took his saddle-bags on his arm, went up-stairs, set them down on the floor, and came down with the most changed countenance. Beaming with pleasure he exclaimed, "Well, Speed, I am moved!"

Covered wagons bearing new settlers move through Springfield after a light snow

STRANGE LOVE FOR A SAVVY STOUT GIRL

Feeling alone in the world and upset during his first year in Springfield stemmed at least in part from an unfortunate romance. Lincoln had brought with him to his new city an ongoing involvement with a young lady that actually was more curious and uncharacteristic than romantic. Lincoln himself told the story tongue in cheek, making himself seem the butt of a rambling joke. Even so, it revealed a mean streak (which he later grew out of) as well as the aloof and inattentive side of his nature.

In the autumn of 1836, six months before his move to Springfield, Lincoln and Mrs. Bennett Abell, a close New Salem friend, struck a bargain. She had proposed to bring her single sister to New Salem from Kentucky if Lincoln would promise to marry her. At first it must have been a dare, a laughing pledge on his part that suddenly turned serious. "I, of course, accepted the proposal," Lincoln confessed to another married friend, Mrs. Orville Browning, wife of a fellow legislator in Vandalia. "[F]or you know," his letter continued, "I could not have done otherwise, had I really been averse to it; but privately between you and me, I was most confoundedly well pleased with the project. I had seen the said sister some three years before, thought her...agreeable and saw no good objection to plodding life through hand in hand with her."

In due time Mary Owens arrived on the scene and turned out to be as agreeable as Lincoln remembered; but in the three years since they'd met, she had put on weight. In fact, she had grown so corpulent that "she now appeared a fair match for Falstaff." That was not all. "[W]hen I beheld her, I could not for my life avoid thinking of my mother; and this, not from withered features, for her skin was too full of fat, to permit its contracting in to wrinkles; but from her want of teeth, weather-beaten appearance in general, and from a kind of notion that ran in my head, that *nothing* could have commenced at the size of infancy, and reached her present bulk in less than thirty-five or forty years; and, in short, I was not all pleased with her. But what could I do? I had told her sister that I would take her for better or worse; and I made a point of honor and conscience in all things, to stick to my word...." Should he squirm out of it? Should he close his eyes and plunge ahead? Or, a third alternative—could he both obey his conscience and make his escape? Lincoln took his time composing a careful letter to "Friend Mary": "...I want in all cases to do right, and most particularly so, in all cases with women. I want, at this particular time, more than any thing else, to do right with you, and if I *knew* it would be doing right, as I rather suspect it would, to let you alone, I would do it. And for the purpose of making the matter as plain as possible, I now say, that you can now drop the subject, dismiss your thoughts (if you ever had any) from me forever, and leave this letter unanswered.... What I do wish is, that our further acquaintance shall depend upon yourself. If such further acquaintance would contribute nothing to your happiness, I am sure it would not to mine. If you feel yourself in any degree bound to me, I am now willing to release you...."

When Mary Owens arrived to marry Lincoln, she'd put on so much weight that he was all for calling the whole thing off.

54

Seven months later, Lincoln found himself "completely out of the scrape," as he told Mrs. Browning, but his release had not happened as he had hoped. After delaying the matter as long as he honorably could, Lincoln finally came out and proposed to Mary. Lo and behold, she turned him down flat. "Shocking to relate, she answered, No. . . . I was mortified, it seemed to me, in a hundred different ways. My vanity was deeply wounded by the reflection, that . . . she whom I had taught myself to believe nobody else would have, had actually rejected me with all my fancied greatness; and to cap the whole, I then, for the first time, began to suspect that I was really a little in love with her. But let it all go. I'll try and out live it. Others have been made fools of by the girls; but this can never be with truth said of me. I most emphatically, in this instance, made a fool of myself. I have now come to the conclusion never again to think of marrying; and, for this reason; I can never be satisfied with any one who would be block-head enough to have me."

For all his exaggerations in the name of humor, the rejection obviously rankled Lincoln. When questioned later in life, Mary Owens explained that she had found Lincoln oversensitive on the one hand and "deficient in those little links which make up the chain of woman's happiness" on the other. One example Mary gave was his lack of assistance when they were once crossing a difficult river on horseback. "The other gentlemen were very officious in seeing that their partners got over safely. We were behind, he riding in, never looking back to see how I got along," never caring "whether my neck was broken or not."

"The last message I ever received from him," Mary recalled, "was about a year after we parted in Illinois. Mrs. Abell visited in Kentucky; and he said to her in Springfield, 'Tell your sister that I think she was a great fool, because she did not stay here, and marry me.' Characteristic of the man."

Much later, when Lincoln was president, Orville Browning wrote of the peculiar letter the young lawyer had sent his wife, curiously enough, on April Fool's Day, 1838. "We were very much amused with it, but both Mrs. Browning and myself supposed it to be a fiction; a creation of his brain; one of his funny stories, without any foundation of fact to sustain it." But when in 1862 a biographer got wind of the letter and asked to use it, Mrs. Browning asked the President how to answer. "She then first learned from him that the narrative of the letter was not fiction but a true account of an incident in actual life. He added that others of the actors than himself were still living; that it might be painful to them to see the letter in print; and that on their account he desired it should be withheld for the present; but that hereafter, when those most interested should have passed away, she might exercise her own discretion."

PLENTY OF ELIGIBLE BACHELORS MAKE SPRINGFIELD A MATCHMAKER'S PARADISE

In 1837, when Lincoln arrived in Springfield, one of the town's leading citizens was twenty-eight-year-old Ninian W. Edwards, the son of the man who had been Illinois's first territorial governor. Ninian's stunning young wife, Elizabeth Todd, had a handsome pedigree of her own as well as three younger sisters back home in Lexington, Kentucky, all of whom were coming of age. This born matchmaker invited her sisters one by one for extended visits to Springfield so that nature (with a little guidance from her) could take its course. Eligible bachelors there outnumbered marriageable young ladies by some ten to one. The young social set, led by Elizabeth Todd's "coterie," met regularly for outings, teas, games, and dances, which were often held in the parlor of the Edwards mansion. When Frances, the oldest of Elizabeth's sisters, arrived, she was introduced to the up-and-coming Lincoln, and they saw each other several times, but the match that Elizabeth favored for Frances was to a young Pennsylvanian named William Wallace. The youngest Todd sister, Ann Maria, gave her hand to Clark M. Smith, a leading Springfield merchant who dealt in groceries and dry goods. In between these two smooth and successful romances, pretty, high-strung, twenty-one-year-old Mary Todd arrived on the scene. Like her sisters, the blue-eyed Kentucky belle with the engaging personality and the quick, sarcastic tongue had been reared in luxury. Their mother had died when she was six, leaving her shaken and insecure, but private schools had given her composure and prepared her for a genteel life of stylish clothes and cultivated chatter. The vivacious visitor, who knew all the latest dance steps and could even speak French, quickly became the center of attention in the Springfield social whirl into which the young lawyer Lincoln was being drawn. Mary had plenty of suitors to choose from, including the energetic little Stephen Douglas, who was one of the most insistent. But in December 1839 at the grand cotillion in honor of the completion of the new capital building, where the assembly was meeting for the first time, Lincoln was introduced to Mary and liked what he saw.

Elizabeth Todd Edwards, matchmaker supreme

Frances Todd married William Wallace.

Ninian Edwards, son of the state's first senator

The Edwards house, center of the Springfield social scene

Mary Todd
married Abraham Lincoln.

Ann Maria Todd
married Clark M. Smith.

Stephen A. Douglas

James Shields

James C. Conkling

Edwin Webb

William Wallace

Abraham Lincoln

Joshua Speed

Clark M. Smith

Edward D. Baker

A typical Springfield bachelor card game. The dashing player at the left, James H. Matheny, was Lincoln's best man. The nine men shown at right were all part of the Springfield social scene. Here's how each made out: Douglas wooed Mary Todd but lost out; Shields challenged Lincoln to a duel; Conkling married Mary's best friend, Mercy Levering; Mary considered Webb too old to marry; Wallace married Mary's sister Frances; Lincoln finally won Mary's hand; Speed found his wife, Fanny, in Kentucky; Smith married Mary's sister Ann Maria; Lincoln named a child after Baker.

IN A TEMPESTUOUS ROMANCE, KEEPING HIS RESOLVE BECOMES THE CENTRAL ISSUE FOR LINCOLN

Mary Todd and Lincoln were attracted to each other from the start. What an unlikely pair, this couple of opposites: one short, plump, and round-faced, the other tall and thin, with long hollow cheeks; one cultured and refined, with French words peppering her lively conversation, the other sounding as if he were right off the farm with his hayseed, backwoods drawl; one witty, ebullient, radiating joy, entrancing, the other worshipful and withdrawn. The pretty chatterbox usually led the conversation, with the reticent Lincoln all ears. The way disapproving sister Elizabeth described them, "Mr. Lincoln would sit at her side and listen. He scarcely said a word, but gazed on her as if irresistibly drawn towards her by some superior and unseen power." Elizabeth thought the man was too uneducated and low-born for her sister, "a cold man...not sufficiently...intelligent in the female line." To her dismay Mary's flouncy petticoats and Lincoln's solemn black suits became fixtures on the long horsehair couch in the Edwardses' parlor. "Molly," as Lincoln called her, had her own mind and wasn't about to be told whom to fall in love with. She, alone, could see past the shabby exterior and discern a kind of king. The couple read poetry together, talked politics, traded dreams, shared their common sympathy for the human race, and thrilled to newly discovered longings. Mary was using all her wiles to get Lincoln to fall in love with her — and Lincoln wasn't resisting.

In the summer of 1840 Mary left Springfield for a visit to her uncle David Todd and his daughter Ann in Columbia, Missouri. From Columbia, Mary wrote to her best friend and closest confidante, Mercy Levering, who lived next door and was being romanced by another member of the inner circle, James Conkling. She said that she was being pursued by a grandson of Patrick Henry, "yet Merce I love him not, & my hand will never be given, where my heart is not." But even to Mercy, Mary did not admit that her heart already belonged to Lincoln.

In November, Lincoln received the first public chastisement of his career. After he gave a speech as a candidate for presidential elector, the *Illinois State Register* editorialized: "Mr. Lincoln's argument was truly ingenious. He has, however, an assumed clownishness in his manner that does not become him, and which does not truly belong to him.... We seriously advise Mr. Lincoln to correct this clownish fault before it grows upon him." Whether or not this change of style was a result of the growing tensions in his private life is impossible to say, but something strong and unsettling seemed to be affecting his usual honest, direct public self.

As the year drew to a close and with Mary still seeing other men, including his political rival, Stephen Douglas, Lincoln made the biggest decision he had ever made: to marry his Molly. Whether Lincoln formally proposed or not, he gave his promise and she accepted. Then, on New Year's Day, 1841, Lincoln's world suddenly exploded. "The fatal first" he would call it. A day that began with bedmate Joshua Speed's sudden sale of his store and decision to leave Illinois for good became the day that Lincoln broke his engagement, and therefore broke his word. Mary's niece Katherine Helm said it was jealousy — that Lincoln had caught Mary flirting with Stephen Douglas — but clearly there were other, deeper reasons as well.

As with many brooding, interior men, Lincoln had found himself intrigued

Fanny Henning inspired as turbulent a love in Lincoln's best friend, Joshua Speed, as Mary Todd did in Lincoln.

IN THE GRIPS OF "THE HYPO"

Just weeks after Lincoln's broken engagement, and then again a month later, James Conkling writes about it all to his own fiancée, Mercy Levering.
January 24, 1841.
...Poor L! how are the mighty fallen! He was confined about a week, but though he now appears again he is reduced and emaciated in appearance and seems scarcely to possess strength enough to speak above a whisper. His case at present is truly deplorable but what prospect there may be for ultimate relief I cannot pretend to say....

March 7.
...And L, poor hapless simple swain who loved most true but was not loved again — I suppose he will now endeavor to drown his cares among the intricacies and perplexities of the law. No more will the merry peal of laughter ascend *high in the air,* to greet his listening and delighted ears. He used to remind me sometimes of the pictures I formerly saw of old Father Jupiter, bending down from the clouds, to see what was going on below. And as an agreeable smile of satisfaction graced the countenance of the old heathen god, as he perceived the incense rising up — so the face of L. was occasionally distorted into a grin as he succeeded in eliciting applause from some of the fair votaries by whom he was surrounded. But alas! I fear his shrine will now be deserted and that he will withdraw himself from the society of us inferior mortals.

Back in Lexington, Kentucky, Mary's father, the powerful and socially prominent Robert Smith Todd, supposedly opposed his daughter's interest in a former backwoodsman.

by marriage and terrified of it at the same time. He feared the loss of his freedom, had not yet proved himself financially, and was certain that his capacity for loving was inadequate. He also may have suddenly doubted whether Mary was good enough or exciting enough, whether she matched up to his "dreams of Elysium." Suddenly confusion set in, and with it a deeper gloom than ever before, a depression magnified now by the realization that he had been unable to hold steady and keep his prized "resolve."

Billy Herndon, who had recently come to work in Speed's store, probably exaggerated when he later described this difficult time for the man who would become central to his life, but he did not make the story up out of whole cloth. "Did you know that Mr. Lincoln was 'as crazy as a loon' in this city in 1841? He did not sit, did not attend to the Legislature...that he was then deranged? Did you know that he was forcibly arrested by his special friends here at that time; that they had to remove all razors, knives, pistols etc., from his room and presence, that he might not commit suicide?"

To his law partner John Stuart, serving a term as congressman in Washington, Lincoln forced out his own description: "I am now the most miserable man living. If what I feel were equally distributed to the whole human family, there would not be one cheerful face on the earth. Whether I shall ever be better, I can not tell; I awfully forbode I shall not. To remain as I am is impossible; I must die or be better, it appears to me." At times Lincoln could not even get out of bed. He did not eat. He lost weight. "Hypochondria" was the going term for unstable and emotionally disturbed behavior. The "hypo," as Lincoln called it, had him in its grip. And there he remained for months, changing law partners in April, boarding now, since Speed's departure, with his friends the Butlers.

Late in the summer, through a friend, Dr. Anson G. Henry, Lincoln let Mary know that he still cared for her. Dr. Henry, unable to prescribe a medicine that would ease Lincoln's dark state of mind, suggested a change of scenery. Lincoln decided to follow the doctor's advice, and on a subsequent visit to the Speed family house in Louisville, Lincoln finally came out of his depression. During his stay he occupied a big, luxurious room in the Speeds' mansion and was assigned his own servant from among the plantation's slaves. Long walks through Kentucky fields with Joshua cleared his mind. So did his romps with Joshua's older half-sister, Mary, whom he locked in a room to keep her "from committing assault and battery on me." Kindly old Mrs. Speed gave him an Oxford Bible — "the best cure for the blues," she told him. But the one who had the blues now was her son. Twenty-six-year-old Joshua had fallen in love with sprightly, black-eyed Fanny Henning, who was living with her uncle on a farm nearby. One night, Lincoln kept the uncle busy while Joshua popped the question. But instead of rejoicing at Fanny's acceptance of his proposal, Speed, like Lincoln before him, was suddenly filled with self-doubt.

The two men returned to Springfield together. Speed wound up his business affairs before leaving for Kentucky permanently, and on another New Year's Day Lincoln was saying goodbye to Speed again. This time, however, the circumstances were reversed: Lincoln had recovered his composure and it was Speed who was nearly suicidal — did he really love Fanny, did she really love him, should he marry her? In a series of remarkably intimate and affectionate letters, Lincoln showed that he could see into Speed's life better than he could see into his own: "I do fondly hope...that you will never again need any comfort from abroad. But should I be mistaken in this—should excessive pleasure still be accompanied with a painful counterpart at times, still let me urge you...to remember in the dep[t]h and even the agony of despondency...that you love her as ardently as you are capable of loving....I incline to think it probable, that your nerves will fail you occasionally for a while; but once you get them fairly graded now, that trouble is over forever." Lincoln was reassuring himself as well as Speed that "our *forebodings*, for which you and I are rather peculiar, are all the worst sort of nonsense." He was also recapturing a belief in predestination—that what God had foreordained could not be halted—even by broken engagements or worried consciences. "Whatever he designs, he will do for *me* yet."

With renewed faith in himself, and his agony behind him, Lincoln's attention again turned to Mary, in particular to what he perceived as her unhappiness. "[I]t seems to me, I should have been entirely happy," he wrote Speed in another letter, "but for the never-absent idea, that there is *one* still unhappy whom I have contributed to make so. That still kills my soul." Speed, in turn, insisted that Lincoln should marry Mary or give her up completely. Lincoln replied: "I acknowledge the correctness of your advice too; but before I resolve to do the one thing or the other, I must regain my confidence in my own ability to keep my resolves when they are made. In that ability, you know, I once prided myself as the only, or at least the chief, gem of my character; that gem I lost—how, and when, you too well know. I have not yet regained it; and until I do, I can not trust myself in any matter of much importance."

In the summer of 1842 Mrs. Simeon Francis, the wife of the editor of the *Sangamo Journal*, stepped in. An admirer of both Lincoln and Mary Todd and a strong advocate of the match, Mrs. Francis invited each to the same party and provided a surprise meeting. "Be friends again," she told them. Secretly the two began to meet as the embers rekindled. By fall the romance had advanced to such a state that Lincoln needed only one more bit of confirmation from his friend Speed before taking action. Lincoln wrote to him, "You have now been the husband of a lovely woman nearly eight months. That you are happier now than you were the day you married her I well know; for without, you would not be living. But I have your word for it too; and the returning elasticity of spirits which is manifested in your letters. But I want to ask a closer question—'Are you now, in *feeling* as well as *judgement,* glad you are married as you are?' From any body but me, this would be an impudent question not to be tolerated; but I know you will pardon it in me. Please answer it quickly as I feel impatient to know."

Speed's answer must have further bolstered Lincoln's confidence, for as November approached, marriage was definitely on his mind again.

In the fall of 1842 Mary Todd and her close friend Julia Jayne *(above)* contributed to the lampooning of James Shields, the state auditor and a pursuer of Mary, through some anonymous contributions in the *Sangamo Journal.* Led to believe that Lincoln had been the author, Shields challenged him to a duel, and to protect Mary, Lincoln accepted, choosing large cavalry broadswords as the weapon. The two actually showed up at the appointed spot with their seconds before an exchange of formal notes cleared the air. The episode helped draw Mary and Lincoln back together—five weeks later they were married.

"THE BEST CURE FOR THE 'BLUES'"

Lincoln's visit to the Speed family farm in the summer of 1841 had been a turning point for him. One reason was the fun he had there with Speed's older half-sister, Mary. In this September letter, he shows how much he enjoyed the company of all the women, including Mrs. Speed, who gave him a bible when he left.

Miss Mary Speed
Louisville, Ky.

My Friend:

...Do you remember my going to the city, while I was in Kentucky, to have a tooth extracted, and making a failure of it? Well, that same old tooth got to paining me so much, that about a week since I had it torn out, bringing with it a bit of the jawbone; the consequence of which is that my mouth is now so sore that I can neither talk nor eat—I am litterally "subsisting on savoury remembrances"—that is, being unable to eat, I am living upon the remembrance of the delicious dishes of peaches and cream we used to have at your house.

When we left, Miss Fanny Henning was owing you a visit, as I understood. Has she paid it yet? If she has, are you not convinced that she is one of the sweetest girls in the world?...Give her an assurance of my verry highest regard, when *you* see her.

Is little Siss Eliza Davis at your house yet? If she is, kiss her "o'er and o'er again" for me.

Tell your mother that I have not got her "present" with me; but that I intend to read it regularly when I return home. I doubt not that it is really, as she says, the best cure for the "Blues" could one but take it according to the truth.

In the summer of 1841 Lincoln visited Speed at his family's house in Louisville, Kentucky.

Joshua Speed's doubts and uncertainties disappeared as soon as he married Fanny Henning. Here, the happy couple poses with Fanny's younger sister.

"I WANT TO GET HITCHED TONIGHT"

Springfield. November 4, 1842. It began as just another autumn Sunday in the prairie capital, but what happened by evening over at the Edwards house would be discussed for generations. This was the day that Abraham Lincoln and Mary Todd got married. It was a miracle, some people thought, that it ever happened at all, there had been so many obstacles. But the couple had overcome them, and now anybody who had anything to do with the wedding—from the best man and the sisters of the bride to the little girl who watched her mother tie Lincoln's tie for the ceremony—all of them remembered what they wanted to remember or what they thought they had seen and heard or what had become family tradition about the event.

It was a blur of memories. They began with James Matheny describing how he was awakened by Lincoln knocking on his door and announcing that this was to be his wedding day. With Speed unavailable in Kentucky, Lincoln asked his friend Matheny to stand up with him and be his best man. Reverend Charles Dresser, the Episcopal minister, was said to have been approached by Lincoln with a request for his services, explaining, "I want to get hitched tonight." Ninian Edwards remembered that Lincoln tracked him down on a street and informed him that he was marrying his sister-in-law that evening at the parsonage. When Ninian determined that the decision was firm and nothing would dissuade Lincoln, he ordered the place of the wedding changed. After all, "Mary was my ward and if she was going to be married, it must be from my house."

Ninian's wife, Elizabeth, remembered how her sister Mary broke the news: "She came down one morning and announced she and Mr. Lincoln would be married that night and I can tell you I was angry. I said 'Mary Todd, even a free Negro would give her family time to bake a ginger cake.'" The Edwardses felt that Lincoln had humiliated Mary when he broke off their engagement almost two years before. Now, on the porch of the Edwards house, rash words were exchanged between the sisters, words like "white trash" and "plebeian" were thrown about, and the name of their father, Robert Todd, back in Lexington was invoked. As Elizabeth remembered the broken engagement, "The world had it that Mr. Lincoln backed out, and this placed Mary in a peculiar situation, and to set herself right and to free Mr. Lincoln's mind, she wrote a letter to Mr. Lincoln stating she would release him from his engagement. Mr. Edwards and myself, after the first crush of things, told Mary and Lincoln that they had better not ever marry, that their natures, mind, education, raising, etc. were so different, they could not live happy as husband and wife, had better never think of the subject again."

After things quieted down at the Edwards house, Ninian enlisted the help of another Todd sister, Frances Wallace, for whom the Edwardses had thrown a grand wedding less than a year before. Frances remembered Elizabeth's quandary: "It was Sunday and Springfield was a very small town at that time, and she hardly knew what to do. But they would not have it any other way so she...asked me if I could help her. So I worked all day. I never worked

Mary Todd, painted later on from a daguerreotype by her niece Katherine Helm. This portrait was supposed to show how she looked at the time of her wedding.

The horsehair couch in the Edwards house upon which Lincoln and Mary sat and talked for hours on end in their courting days

The Edwardses' parlor where the Lincolns were married

These whale-oil, astral lamps decorated the Edwardses' mantel and provided light for the wedding. A granddaughter of the Ninian Edwardses recalled: "Abraham Lincoln spent many hours reading, talking, thinking, laughing and even dancing by the light they shed—and they lighted the pages of the Bible at his wedding. The wedding cake was cut and the wedding party celebrated in their glow."

harder all day in my life. And in the evening they were married, and we had a very nice little supper, but not what we would have had if they had given Mrs. Edwards time.''

Ninian Edwards's sister-in-law, Mrs. Ben S. Edwards, also lived close by and she remembered Ninian coming to get her too. He told her that ''he had left his wife greatly disturbed over the fact that she did not have time to prepare a suitable wedding feast. There were no confectioners in those days to furnish dainty refreshments.... There was only one bakery in the city of Springfield, and its choicest commodities were ginger bread and beer.... So when about noon of the wedding day Mrs. Edwards' feelings were sufficiently calmed to talk to her sister of the affair, she said 'Mary...I guess I will have to send to Old Dickey's for some of his ginger bread and beer.' Mary replied: 'Well, that will be good enough for plebeians, I suppose.'''

By evening the tense atmosphere at the Edwards house had softened. Over at the Butler house where Lincoln boarded, Mrs. Butler was making sure the groom was properly attired. Her young daughter Salome remembered: ''As my mother tied Mr. Lincoln's neck tie on him, my little brother called out 'Where are you going, Mr. Lincoln?' Mr. Lincoln jokingly replied, 'To the devil.'''

Many of the guests said that Mary's wedding dress was the same white satin brocade gown in which Mrs. Wallace had been married. ''She was not married in the white satin,'' Mrs. Wallace insisted. She had lent the dress to Mary for parties but not on this occasion. ''It was too soiled. She may have been married in a white Swiss muslin, but I think it was not a white dress at all. I think it was delaine, or something of that kind.''

Best man James Matheny said that during the ceremony Lincoln ''looked and acted as if he were going to the slaughter.'' Mrs. Wallace recalled quite a different picture of the groom: ''Lincoln was cheerful as he ever had been, for all we could see. He acted just as he always acted in company.''

Someone remembered that it was raining hard during the ceremony, with rain pelting against the windowpanes. Someone else remembered the soft light of the astral lamps on the mantel over the fireplace in front of which Lincoln and Mary stood. A good estimate of the number of guests was thirty. Both Caroline Lamb and Julia Jayne were bridesmaids. Elizabeth Todd Grimsley remembered being a bridesmaid, too, and seeing ''the ring bearing the motto 'love is eternal' placed upon her [Mary's] finger.'' The new Mrs. Lincoln may or may not have spilled a cup of coffee on her dress during the reception. The wedding cake, served on an old Sheffield cake plate, was probably, as claimed, still warm when it was cut. Nobody recorded anyone's memories of where the bride and groom spent their wedding night, but it was not long before they were living at the Globe Tavern for four dollars a week where their first child was born three days less than nine months after the big day.

The Reverend Charles Dresser married the couple.

OBSERVATIONS OF THE BEST MAN

Best man James Matheny remembered an amusing incident during the service.
[I]t was one of the funiest [sic] things imaginable.... Old Judge Brown was a rough ''old-timer'' and always said just what he thought without regard to place or surroundings. There was...a perfect hush in the room as the ceremony progressed. Old Parson Dresser in clerical robes...handed Lincoln the ring, and as he [Lincoln] put it on the bride's finger...[he said] ''With this ring I thee endow with all my goods and chattels, lands and tenements.'' Brown, who had never witnessed such a proceeding, was struck by the utter absurdity and spoke out so everybody could hear,... ''Lord Jesus Christ, God Almighty, Lincoln, the statute fixes all that.'' This was too much for the Old Parson—he broke down under it—an almost irresistible desire to laugh out checked his proceeding for a minute or so—but finally recovered and pronounced them Husband & wife.

In some of the accounts of the hurriedly put-together wedding party, Caroline Lamb *(left)* was named as a brides-maid, along with Julia Jayne, Anna Rodney and the bride's 17-year-old cousin Elizabeth Todd *(center)*. James Matheny *(right)* was best man, although no one remembered him actually standing up for Lincoln at the ceremony.

The marriage certificate *(left)* was officially signed by the best man's brother, Noah W. Matheny, the clerk of Sangamon County. The Lincolns' honeymoon was spent a few blocks away at the Globe Tavern *(below)*, where they lived for the first years of their marriage.

Of their very first photographs, made in Springfield four years after their marriage, Mary said: "They are very precious to me, taken when we were young and so desperately in love." In each instance the mirror image of the daguerreotype has been reversed in order to show how the Lincolns actually looked.

This is Lincoln's house in Springfield. Behind the picket fence are Lincoln and his son Willie, and perched on the fence is Willie's younger brother Tad. Below Tad is a friend.

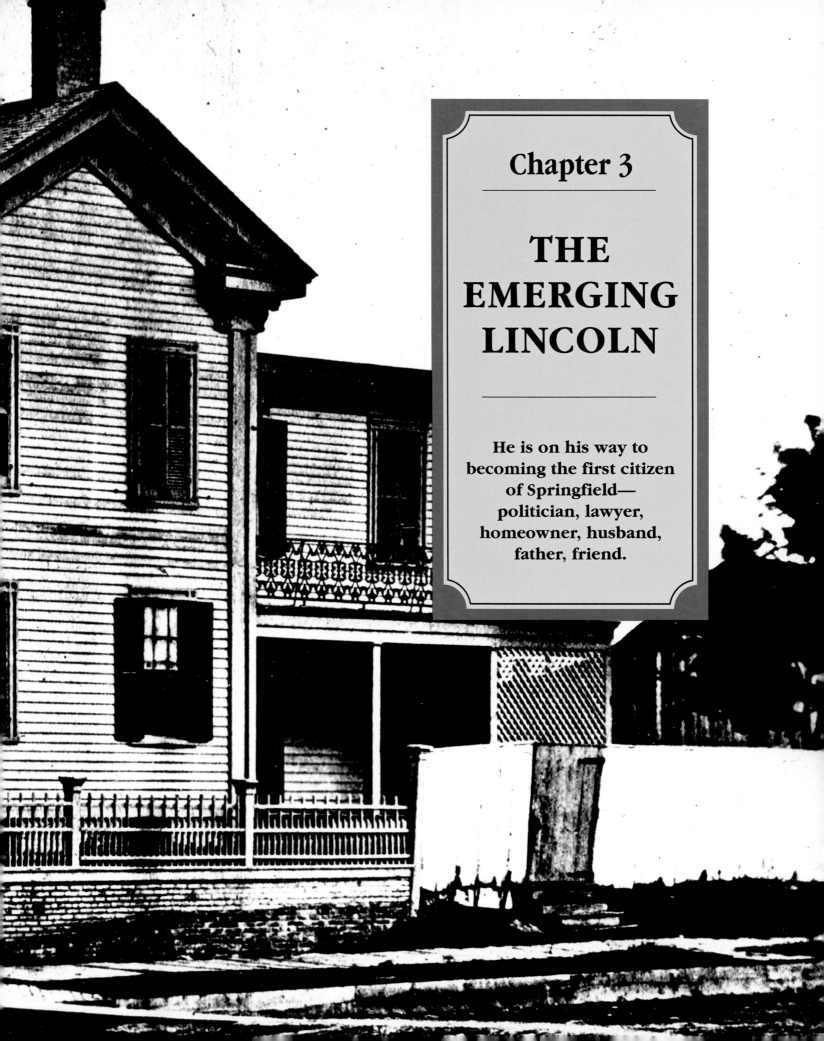

Chapter 3

THE EMERGING LINCOLN

He is on his way to becoming the first citizen of Springfield— politician, lawyer, homeowner, husband, father, friend.

FINALLY, A HOUSE OF HIS OWN

For seven years Lincoln had boarded in various places in Springfield—in the attic of a store, in people's houses, in a tavern. Now, in 1844, with his New Salem debts finally paid off and his practice giving him a comfortable income, he was able to purchase his own house. It was a one-and-a-half-story frame cottage, built with wooden pegs instead of nails. The house had a frontage of 50 feet on Eighth Street and 150 feet on Jackson. It had been built in 1839 by the Reverend Charles Dresser, who three years later married the Lincolns. Lincoln bought the property from Dresser for $1,500—$1,200 in cash, and $300 in the form of a shop Lincoln owned across the public square. In May 1844, the Lincolns and their six-month-old son, Robert, moved in. The two little rooms upstairs were too cramped to use for bedrooms, so the family slept downstairs at first. Spending $1,300 in 1856, the Lincolns raised the house to a full two stories over the front two rooms and added rooms behind as well. There was never much planting around the house; Lincoln had little interest in gardening, and the roses he once put in died soon after. Lincoln had other things on his mind.

Even when living back at the Globe Tavern, he had been contemplating running for Congress. Writing to Whig Richard S. Thomas in February 1843, he clearly stated his ambition: "Now if you should hear anyone say that Lincoln don't want to go to Congress, I wish you as a personal friend of mine, would tell him you have reason to believe he is mistaken." If Lincoln could get nominated in the pro-Whig Seventh Congressional District, his election would be a shoo-in. Unfortunately, though, two other young Whig leaders had the same idea, one being Lincoln's wife's cousin, thirty-three-year-old John J. Hardin, the other his good friend Edward Baker. After a not unfriendly interparty tug-of-war, the three came up with a solution: the seat, over the following years, would be handed down from Hardin to Baker to Lincoln. It didn't turn out quite as smoothly as planned. When the time finally came for Lincoln's turn in 1846, Baker withdrew when he was supposed to, but Hardin decided he wanted to run again. Lincoln had to pressure him not to. The thirty-seven-year-old Whig now had to take on the Democrat's choice, sixty-one-year-old Peter Cartwright, an outspoken, wily, fire-and-brimstone evangelist whose main weapon turned out to be the charge that Lincoln was a heathen. In reply, Lincoln had a handbill printed: "...That I am not a member of any Christian Church, is true; but I have never denied the truth of the Scriptures; and I have never spoken with intentional disrespect of religion in general, or of any denomination of Christians in particular....I still do not think any man has the right thus to insult the feelings, and injure the morals, of the community in which he may live. If, then, I was guilty of such conduct, I should blame no man who should condemn me for it; but I do blame those, whoever they may be, who falsely put such a charge in circulation against me." It was the only time Lincoln had ever made a public statement about his religious beliefs, but, as it turned out, it wasn't really necessary—Cartwright's campaign fizzled and Lincoln ended up with almost two-thirds of the vote.

When they bought it, the Lincolns' house had only one and a half stories. A brick wall and picket fence, shown in the picture on the preceding pages, were added to the front in 1850 and to the side in 1855.

In 1860, when an artist for *Leslie's Weekly* visited Springfield to show how the Republican nominee lived, these sketches of the front parlor and sitting room were made.

Peter Cartwright was the Democrat who opposed Lincoln for Congress in 1846.

In 1856, when the second story was added, for the first time the family had plenty of bedroom space upstairs and could devote the downstairs area to the parlors.

HEAVEN, HELL, OR CONGRESS?

The best story to come out of the Cartwright contest illustrates how quick-witted Lincoln could be. By invitation, Lincoln attended a Cartwright prayer meeting during which the old evangelist asked everybody in the room who thought they were going to heaven to stand up. Then he asked those who felt they were headed in the opposite direction to stand. When Lincoln failed to respond either time, Cartwright challenged him: "Just where are you going, Mr. Lincoln?" "I'm going to Congress," Lincoln responded.

WHIG TICKET.

For Congress.
Abraham Lincoln.

For Governor,
T. M. Killpatrick.

For Lieut. Governor.
N. G. Wilcox.

For Representative.
Stephen T. Logan,
Benjamin West,
James N. Brown,
Rezin H. Constant.

For Sheriff.
William Harvey.

For County Commissioner.
Thomas Shepherd.

For Coroner,
James W. Neal.

For a Convention.

The Whig ticket for candidates for various Illinois offices in 1846 lists Abraham Lincoln for Congress.

Above: The House of Representatives. *Below:* A view of early Washington. Lincoln boarded in one of the row houses in the left foreground.

They had reached their waning days, but at least Lincoln saw them and served with some of them, these titans of American politics in the country's second generation. For two years he was part of the Washington of these grand old war-horses. He was part of the great national democratic system that they had helped forge, an elected member of the government that made the decisions for the nation's 23 million people. Andrew Jackson had died two years earlier; John Quincy Adams would go while Lincoln was present: in the House of Representatives, he suddenly slumped over and sputtered out. For Lincoln the two years were too short for large accomplishments. But the young congressman showed promise after he began to get "the hang of the House"—as an orator first, as a Whig leader, as an elected official who would stand up and speak his conscience, even when, as in his opposition to the Mexican War, his position was the unpopular one.

Lincoln was thirty-eight when he came to Congress in 1847, Daniel Webster sixty-five. Their views coincided on the major issues. Not so with the senior senator from South Carolina. John C. Calhoun wanted to protect slavery and allow it to spread. John Quincy Adams at eighty was the most revered member of Congress; there is no record that the sixth president of the U.S. and the man who would become the sixteenth ever spoke together. Henry Clay, who was not a member of the Thirtieth Congress, was home in Lexington, Kentucky, when it got under way, but the "lone Whig from Illinois" had met him weeks earlier and listened to the great friend of the Todd family oppose the Mexican War. Lincoln's "Spot Resolutions" to Congress a few weeks later would echo Clay's stand. Clay was Lincoln's "beau ideal of a statesman" and "the man for whom I fought all my life."

Daniel Webster (1782–1852)

John C. Calhoun (1782–1850)

John Quincy Adams (1767–1848)

Henry Clay (1777–1852)

LETTERS TO AND FROM A BANISHED WIFE

Lincoln to Mary: Washington, April 16–1848–

Dear Mary:

   In this troublesome world, we are never quite satisfied. When you were here, I thought you hindered me some in attending to business; but now, having nothing but business—no variety—it has grown exceedingly tasteless to me. I hate to sit down and direct documents, and I hate to stay in this old room by myself. You know I told you in last sunday's letter, I was going to make a little speech during the week; but the week has passed away without my getting a chance to do so; and now my interest in the subject has passed away too....

   I went yesterday to hunt the little plaid stockings, as you wished; but found that...Allen had not a single pair...that I thought would fit "Eddy's dear little feet.".

   Suppose you do not prefix the "Hon" to the address on your letters to me any more. I like the letters very much, but I would rather they should not have that upon them. It is not necessary, as I suppose you have thought, to have them come free.

   And you are entirely free from head-ache? That is good—good—considering it is the first spring you have been free from it since we were acquainted. I am afraid you will get so well, and fat, and young, as to be wanting to marry again. Tell Louisa I want her to watch you a little for me. Get weighed, and write me how much you weigh.

   I did not get rid of the impression of that foolish dream about dear Bobby till I got your letter written the same day. What did he and Eddy think of the little letters father sent them? Don't let the blessed fellows forget father....

                                                          Most affectionately
                                                          A. Lincoln

Mary to Lincoln: Lexington May–48–

My Dear Husband–

   You will think indeed, that *old age,* has set *its seal,* upon my humble self, that in few or none of my letters, I can remember the day of the month, I must confess it as one of my peculiarities; I feel wearied & tired enough to know, that this is *Saturday night,* our *babies* are asleep.... Our little Eddy, has recovered from his little spell of sickness—Dear boy, I must tell you a little story about him—Boby in his wanderings to day, came across in a yard, a little kitten, *your hobby,* he says he asked a man for it, he brought it triumphantly to the house, so soon as Eddy, spied it—his *tenderness,* broke forth, he made them bring it *water,* fed it with bread himself, with his *own dear hands,* he was a delighted little creature over it, in the midst of his happiness Ma came in, she you must know dislikes the whole cat race, I thought in a very unfeeling manner, she ordered the servant near, to throw it out, which of *course,* was done, Ed—screaming & protesting loudly against the proceeding, *she* never appeared to mind his screams, which were long & loud, I assure you.... How much, I wish instead of writing, *we* were together this evening, I feel very sad away from you.... I must bid you good night—Do not fear the children, have forgotten you, I was only jesting—Even E[ddy's] eyes brighten at the mention of your name—My love to all—

                                                          Truly yours
                                                          M L–

Lincoln to Mary: Washington, June 12. 1848–

My dear Wife:

   On my return from Philadelphia, yesterday, where, in my anxiety I had been led to attend the whig convention I found your last letter. I was so tired and sleepy, having ridden all night, that I could not answer it till to-day; and now I have to do so in the H.R. The leading matter in your letter, is your wish to return to this side of the Mountains. Will you be a *good girl* in all things, if I consent? Then come along, and that as *soon* as possible. Having got the idea in my head, I shall be impatient till I see you.... Come on just as soon as you can. I want to see you, and our dear—*dear* boys very much. Every body here wants to see our dear Bobby.

                                                          Affectionately
                                                          A. Lincoln.

Above: In 1848 the Capitol's wooden dome resembled an upside-down mixing bowl. *Far left:* By the time Lincoln arrived, grand edifices such as the Patent Building had already arisen. *Left:* President James Polk and his wife pose in 1848 with the venerable Dolly Madison, still queen of Washington—the slightly blurred, turbaned lady just to the right of Polk. Only two weeks into his term, Lincoln challenged Polk to identify the exact spot where the President claimed that American blood had been shed on American soil and thus establish the legality of the Mexican War. The letters at right were written between the Lincolns after the congressman decided that his wife and two children were interfering with his work and sent them off to her family home in Lexington, Kentucky.

LINCOLN, THE LAWYER: PUTTING HIS HONESTY INTO ACTION

Lincoln found out early in his life that lawyering could be fun. When court was in session in Boonville, Indiana, the inquisitive boy happily walked the fifteen miles in order to watch and listen as visiting lawyers, with big words and seemingly vast minds, pled their clients' cases to the bellowing and gavel-pounding judges and the startled juries. It was almost as if a circus had come to town; work stopped and everybody crowded into the courthouse to enjoy the legal acrobatics and cheer their favorites on as the latest local disagreements were publicly aired, dissected, and eventually settled. Here Lincoln learned that laws were simply rules made up by people to protect their rights, such as the right to a secure and happy life, the right to own property, the right to freedom; and that, just as simply, wrongs were violations of those rights. To be part of the profession that oversaw these lofty, democratic notions was beyond hope for him, Lincoln thought, given his paltry schooling.

Much later in Springfield, having obtained his license to practice law after hard years of teaching himself, Lincoln discovered that he had little interest in a purely methodical approach to the business of justice. He needed to be out there close to the people, where he could best display his common sense and his instinct for what was right. From then on, almost half of Lincoln's law life would be spent on the move—following the Eighth Circuit judge from hamlet to hamlet, building not only a practice, but a clientele that flocked to him as his reputation grew. By the early 1850s, the Lincoln-Herndon law office had become a leading Springfield firm, handling annually between 17 percent and 34 percent of all cases in the Sangamon County circuit court. More often than not it was Herndon who performed the grueling case study research, Lincoln handling the more glamorous courtroom activities. It was often hard, boring work, and fees were split down the middle. Big-city cases involving railroads, waterways, land ownership, or fledgling industry were desirable because they brought in more money, but Lincoln worked just as hard to help settle the smaller, more personal injustices of prairie folk; accumulating wealth was only one of his life goals.

Fellow lawyers admired Lincoln for his ability to wage legal warfare without personally wounding a colleague. Juries looked up to him for his careful honesty. Galleries loved his slow, logical, but passionate deliberations. Leonard Swett, one of his colleagues (who, along with Eighth Circuit Judge David Davis, would be responsible for getting Lincoln nominated by the 1860 Republican Convention), told how formidable Lincoln could be in action:

> As he entered the trial, where most lawyers would object he would say he "reckoned" it would be fair to let this in, or that; and sometimes, when his adversary could not quite prove what Lincoln knew to be the truth, he "reckoned" it would be fair to admit the truth to be so-and-so. When he did object to the court, and when he heard his objections answered, he would often say, "Well, I reckon I must be wrong." Now, about the time he had practiced this three-fourths through the case, if his adversary didn't understand him, he would wake up in a few minutes

Lincoln's first law partner was John T. Stuart, an urbane, well-educated Kentuckian who pushed Lincoln into studying law and then took him on as his junior partner in the spring of 1837.

Nine years older than Lincoln, Stephen T. Logan was the leading lawyer in the county. Lincoln's second partner was a little gnome with a repellant voice who loved precision and severity.

After twice being a junior partner and not caring for it, Lincoln took on William H. Herndon as a full partner in late 1844 and stuck with him through seventeen years of windy orations, drinking bouts, and hero worship.

A *Leslie's Weekly* rendition of the Lincoln-Herndon law office exaggerated its size and orderliness. The "office was the dingiest and most untidy law-office in the United States, without exception," wrote fellow lawyer Henry C. Whitney. From the street the rented room was got to by a flight of narrow stairs and overlooked a flat ware-house roof, coated with tar and pebbles. In summer the tar softened and gave off a pungent, resinous odor which wafted through the office on hot, breezy days.

learning that he had feared the Greeks too late and find himself beaten. He was wise as a serpent in the trial of a cause, but I have had too many scars from his blows to certify that he was harmless as a dove. When the whole thing was unraveled, the adversary would begin to see that what he was so blandly giving away was simply what he couldn't get and keep. By giving away six points and carrying the seventh, he carried his case, and the whole case hanging on the seventh, he traded away everything which could give him the least aid in carrying that. Any man who took Lincoln for a simple-minded man would very soon wake up with his back in a ditch.

David Davis, a powerful, 300-pound man who shared more beds with Lincoln and tried more cases in which he was involved than any other judge, believed that his friend had few equals: "He seized the strong points of a cause and presented them with clearness and great compactness. His mind was logical and direct, and he did not indulge in extraneous discussion. Generalities and platitudes had no charm for him.... The framework of his mental and moral being was honesty, and a wrong case was poorly defended by him.... In order to bring into full activity his great powers it was necessary that he should be convinced of the right and justice of the matter which he advocated."

Two specimens of the Lincoln face: in Danville, Illinois, in 1858 or 1859 while attending court in Vermilion County; and in an unknown place, probably somewhere in Illinois, about 1858.

HALF THE TIME HE IS RIDING THE CIRCUIT

Lincoln's law practice was anchored in Springfield, where most of the time people with grievances in central Illinois had to bring their disputes for settlement. But twice a year a judge took justice out to the people. At fixed sessions of two days to a week, this special magistrate sat at the various little county seats sprinkled far and wide over the prairies and tried to mete out fair rulings on the crimes and contentions of each locality. Joining this movable tribunal across what was known in Illinois as the Eighth Circuit was a merry band of lawyers who sought out clients at each stop and defended them with verve and skill. "Our methods of travel were...primitive," wrote Henry Whitney of Lincoln's "nomadic life." "Railroads had just made their advent...and five of eight county seats were reached by modes other than rail." In the 1850's, the Eighth averaged some 140 miles north and south, 100 east and west, and, by the shortest route, it took a 500-mile trip to visit all fourteen county seats. Lincoln, Stuart, Logan, Davis, and Baker were the "big five" of the early horseback days, which were overseen by no-nonsense Judge Samuel H. Treat. When Lincoln returned from Congress, his corpulent, high-spirited friend David Davis had been elected to preside, and for years the two of them were the only ones to navigate the entire course twice a year—three months starting in February, another three beginning in September—Davis out of duty, Lincoln by choice. Roads were almost nonexistent, flimsy bridges were easily washed away, mud made the going slow. Lincoln was usually at the head of the legal caravan, his long legs depth finders for flooded streams that had to be forded. Once, after a big rain, the troupe of lawyers, along with Judge Davis, carrying their clothes safely over their shoulders, rode naked across a stream, with Lincoln in the lead. They slept on floors of farmhouses or doubled up in tavern beds. The courts themselves were primitive, clients had to be interviewed in semi-privacy, defense strategy often calculated on the spot. During trials, Lincoln was all business, listening attentively when he was not involved in a case, assisting his fellow lawyers with advice, pleading his own cases in the slow drawl he had become famous for, always with dignity and common sense. When the official day ended and the lawyers gathered around a fire or at a tavern to swap stories, sing, or play cards, Lincoln was more often than not the center of attention, whether mimicking someone from the day's proceedings, "heaving in" a coarse joke and bringing down the house, or participating in a mock trial to try a colleague for too much hilarity or whatever other "high crimes and misdemeanors" Judge Davis could dream up to charge him with. Out on the circuit, Lincoln could give in to his occasional fits of melancholy and work them out in his own good time. He could mingle with "the people" he put such faith in; he could visit their homes, talk crops, assess their livestock, their children, their politics. And, best of all, he could forget fancy manners, city dress, civilized refinements. Here, while making his living at what he did so well, he could live a carefree, nomadic life, far from the responsibilities of his office and home.

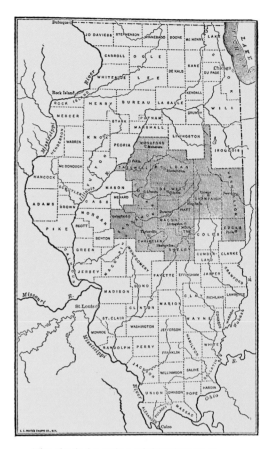

The shaded portion of this Illinois map indicates the Eighth Circuit as organized in 1847. In both 1853 and 1857 the circuit was reduced in size, but even when Sangamon County was transferred to another circuit, Lincoln kept on traveling the Eighth.

For several years Henry C. Whitney traveled the circuit with Lincoln and later set down his recollections in writing.
When I first knew him his attire and physical habits were on a plane with those of an ordinary farmer: — his hat was innocent of a nap: — his boots had no acquaintance with blacking: — his clothes had not been introduced to the whisk broom: — his carpet-bag was well worn and dilapidated: — his

umbrella was substantial, but of a faded green, well worn, the knob gone, and the name "A. Lincoln" cut out of white muslin, and sewed on the inside.... He probably had as little taste about dress and attire as anybody that ever was born: he simply wore clothes because it was needful and customary: whether they fitted or looked well was entirely above, or beneath, his comprehension.... He had no clerk, no stenographer, no library, no method or system or business, but carried his papers in his hat or coat pocket. The consideration and trial of each case began and ended with itself; he was continually roused to devise a new policy—new tactics—fresh expedients, with each new retainer.... This life on the circuit was in the nature of a "school of events" to him, and taught him to deal, offhand, and on the spur of the moment, with emergencies.... One evening, Lincoln was missing immediately after supper: he had no place to go, that we could think of—no friend to visit—no business to do—no client to attend to: and certainly no entertainment to go to: hence "Where is Lincoln?" was the question. I visited all the law offices and stores, but got no trace whatever: and at nine o'clock—an early hour for us—Davis and I went, grumbling and hungry for mental food, to bed, leaving the problem unsolved. Now, Lincoln had a furtive way of stealing in on one, unheard, unperceived and unawares: and on this occasion, after we had lain for a short time our door latch was noiselessly raised—the door opened, and the tall form of Abraham Lincoln glided in noiselessly. "Why Lincoln, where *have* you been?" exclaimed the Judge. "I was in hopes you fellers would be asleep," replied he: "Well, I have been to a little show up at the Academy:" and he sat before the fire and narrated all the sights of that most primitive of country shows, given chiefly to school children. Next night, he was missing again; the *show* was still in town, and he stole in as before, and entertained us with a description of new sights—a magic lantern, electrical machine, etc. I told him I had seen all these sights at school. "Yes," said he, sadly, "I now have an advantage over you in, for the first time in my life, seeing these things which are of course common to those, who had, what I did not, a chance at an education, when they were young."

"Old Bob," Lincoln's horse, pulled his master and his buggy over the Illinois prairie.

Court's in session; everybody's gathering. The scene is Paris, Illinois, the seat of Edgar County.

This is the east side of Springfield's Public Square, across the street from the building where Lincoln and Herndon had their law office. The three-story Logan Building is the last edifice at the far left. On its second floor was the United States courtroom where Lincoln tried more than seventy cases.

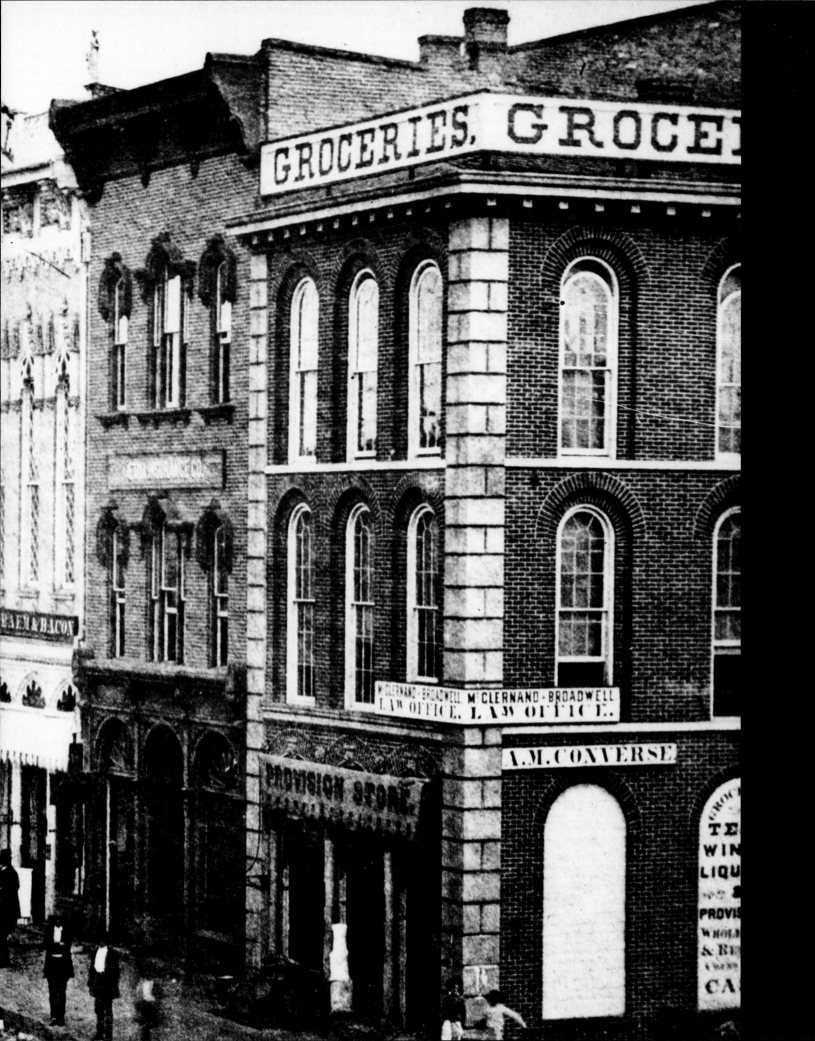

LINCOLN'S CLOSEST ASSOCIATE DISCUSSES HIS PARTNER

Billy Herndon was nine years younger than Lincoln and probably knew him better than did any other man. He first met his future law partner as a boy of thirteen, later bunked down with Lincoln and Speed in a room over Speed's store where they both worked. Lincoln was like a big brother to him, and in return Herndon did his every wish, particularly when it came to politics. Lincoln proposed the partnership in late 1844, even before Herndon had got his license to practice. "I can trust you, Billy," Lincoln said, "if you can trust me," and the pact was made. Perhaps Lincoln hoped that the scholarly Herndon would bring order to his cluttered practice, but he soon found his partner could be just as disorganized as he. One note to a client confessed that key paperwork had been "lost or destroyed and cannot be found among papers of Lincoln and Herndon." Here are some observations Herndon set down on Lincoln the lawyer, considered among the most reliable of all his reminiscences.

In the office, as in the court room, Lincoln, when discussing any point, was never arbitrary or insinuating. He was deferential, cool, patient, and respectful. When he reached the office, about nine o'clock in the morning, the first thing he did was to pick up a newspaper, spread himself out on an old sofa, one leg on a chair, and read aloud, much to my discomfort. Singularly enough Lincoln never read any other way but aloud. This habit used to annoy me almost beyond the point of endurance. I once asked him why he did so. This was his explanation: "When I read aloud two senses catch the idea; first I see what I read; second, I hear it, and therefore I can remember it better." He never studied law books unless a case was on hand for consideration—never followed up the decisions of the supreme courts, as other lawyers did. It seemed as if he depended for his effectiveness in managing a law suit entirely on the stimulus and inspiration of the final hour. He paid but little attention to the fees and money matters of the firm—usually leaving all such to me. He never entered an item in the account book. If anyone paid money to him which belonged to the firm, on arriving at the office he divided it with me. If I was not there, he would wrap up my share in a piece of paper and place it in my drawer—marking it with a pencil, "Case of Roe vs. Doe—Herndon's half."

Lincoln in Urbana, Illinois, in April 1858

On many topics he was not a good conversationalist, because he felt he was not learned enough. Neither was he a good listener. Putting it a little strongly, he was often not even polite. If present with others, or participating in a conversation, he was rather abrupt, and in his anxiety to say something apt or to illustrate the subject under discussion, would burst in with a story. In our office I have known him to consume the whole forenoon relating stories. If a man came to see him with the purpose of finding out something, which he did not care to let him know and at the same time did not want to refuse him, he was very adroit. In such cases Lincoln would do most of the talking, swinging around what he suspected was the vital point, but never nearing it, interlarding his answers with a seemingly endless supply of stories and jokes. The interview being both interesting and pleasant, the man would depart in good humor,

believing he had accomplished his mission. After he had walked away a few squares and had cooled off, the question would come up, "Well, what did I find out?" Blowing away the froth of Lincoln's humorous narratives he would find nothing substantial left.... Lincoln's restless ambition found its gratification only in the field of politics. He used the law merely as a stepping stone to what he considered a more attractive condition in the political world.... I feel warranted in saying that he was at the same time a very great and a very insignificant lawyer.... I was not only associated with Mr. Lincoln in Springfield, but was frequently on the circuit with him.... I easily realized that Lincoln was strikingly deficient in the technical rules of the law. Although he was constantly reminding young legal aspirants to study and "work, work" yet I doubt if he ever read a single elementary law book through in his life. In fact, I may truthfully say, I never knew him to read through a law book of any kind. Practically, he knew nothing of the rules of evidence, of pleading, or practice, as laid down in the text-books, and seemed to care nothing about them. He had a keen sense of justice, and struggled for it, throwing aside forms, methods, and rules, until it appeared as pure as a ray of light flashing through a fog-bank. He was not a general reader in any field of knowledge, but when he had occasion to learn or investigate any subject he was thorough and indefatigable in his search. He not only went to the root of the question, but dug up the root, and separated and analyzed every fiber of it. He was in every respect a case lawyer, never cramming himself on any question till he had a case in which the question was involved. He thought slowly and acted slowly; he must needs have time to analyze all the facts in a case and wind them into a connected story. I have seen him lose cases of the plainest justice, which the most inexperienced member of the bar would have gained without effort. Two things were essential to his success in managing a case. One was time; the other a feeling of confidence in the justice of the cause he represented. He used to say, "If I can free this case from technicalities and get it properly swung to the jury, I'll win it." But if either of these essentials were lacking, he was the weakest man at the bar. He was greatest in my opinion as a lawyer in the Supreme Court of Illinois. There the cases were never hurried.

The attorneys generally prepared their cases in the form of briefs, and the movements of the court and counsel were so slow that no one need be caught by surprise....

I used to grow restless at Lincoln's slow movements and speeches in court. "Speak with more vim," I would frequently say, "and arouse the jury—talk faster and keep them awake." In answer to such a suggestion he one day made use of this illustration: "Give me your little pen-knife, with its short blade, and hand me that old jack-knife, lying on the table." Opening the blade of the pen-knife he said: "You see, this blade at the point travels rapidly, but only through a small portion of space till it stops; while the long blade of the jack-knife moves no faster but through a much greater space than the small one. Just so with the long, labored movements of my mind. I may not emit ideas as rapidly as others, because I am compelled by nature to speak slowly, but when I do throw off a thought it seems to me, though it comes with some effort, it has force enough to cut its own way and travel a greater distance." This was said to me when we were alone in our office simply for illustration. It was not said boastingly....

The Wright case...was a suit brought by Lincoln and myself to compel a pension agent to refund a portion of a fee which he had withheld from the widow of a revolutionary soldier. The entire pension was $400, of which sum the agent had retained one-half. The pensioner, an old woman crippled and bent with age, came hobbling into the office and told her story. It stirred Lincoln up, and he walked over to the agent's office and made a demand for a return of the money, but without success. Then suit was brought. The day before the trial I hunted up for Lincoln, at his request, a history of the Revolutionary War, of which he read a good portion. He told me to remain during the trial until I had heard his address to the jury. "For," said he, "I am going to skin Wright, and get that money back." The only witness we introduced was the old lady, who through her tears told her story. In his speech to the jury, Lincoln recounted the causes leading to the outbreak of the Revolutionary struggle, and then drew a vivid picture of the hardships of Valley Forge, describing with minuteness the men, barefooted and with bleeding feet, creeping over the ice. As he reached that point in his speech wherein he narrated the hardened action of the

Billy Herndon, as he looked in old age

defendant in fleecing the old woman of her pension his eyes flashed, and throwing aside his handkerchief, which he held in his right hand, he fairly launched into him. His speech for the next five or ten minutes justified the declaration of Davis that he was "hurtful in denunciation and merciless in castigation." There was no rule of court to restrain him in his argument, and I never, either on the stump or on other occasions in court, saw him so wrought up. Before he closed, he drew an ideal picture of the plaintiff's husband, the deceased soldier, parting with his wife at the threshold of their home, and kissing their little babe in the cradle, as he started for the war. "Time rolls by," he said in conclusion; "the heroes of '76 have passed away and are encamped on the other shore. The soldier has gone to rest, and now, crippled, blind, and broken, his widow comes to you and to me, gentlemen of the jury, to right her wrongs. She was not always thus. She was once a beautiful young woman. Her step was elastic, her

face fair, and her voice as sweet as any that rang in the mountains of old Virginia. But now she is poor and defenseless. Out here on the prairies of Illinois, many hundreds of miles away from the scenes of her childhood, she appeals to us, who enjoy the privileges achieved for us by the patriots of the Revolution, for our sympathetic aid and manly protection. All I ask is, shall we befriend her?" The speech made the desired impression on the jury. Half of them were in tears, while the defendant sat in the court room, drawn up and writhing under the fire of Lincoln's fierce invective. The jury returned a verdict in our favor for every cent we demanded. Lincoln was so much interested in the old lady that he became her surety for costs, paid her way home, and her hotel bill while she was in Springfield. When the judgment was paid we remitted the proceeds to her and made no charge for our services. Lincoln's notes for the argument were unique: "No contract. —Not professional services. —Unreasonable charge. —Money retained by Def't not given by Pl'ff. —Revolutionary War. —Describe Valley Forge privations. —Ice—Soldier's bleeding feet. —Pl'ffs husband. —Soldier leaving home for army. —*Skin Def't.* —Close."...

His habits were very simple. He was not fastidious as to food or dress. His hat was brown, faded, and the nap usually worn or rubbed off. He wore a short cloak and sometimes a shawl. His coat and vest hung loosely on his gaunt frame, and his trousers were invariably too short. On the circuit he carried in one hand a faded green umbrella, with "A. Lincoln" in large white cotton or muslin letters sewed on the inside. The knob was gone from the handle, and when closed a piece of cord was usually tied around it in the middle to keep it from flying open. In the other hand he carried a literal carpet-bag, in which were stored the few papers to be used in court, and underclothing enough to last till his return to Springfield. He slept in a long, coarse, yellow flannel shirt, which reached halfway between his knees and ankles. It probably was not made to fit his bony figure as completely as Beau Brummel's shirt, and hence we can somewhat appreciate the sensation of a young lawyer who, on seeing him thus arrayed for the first time, observed afterwards that, "He was the ungodliest figure I ever saw."

THE PRAIRIE LAWYER

Far Left: In Pittsfield, Illinois. *Left:* In Beardstown, Illinois, still in the white suit he wore while winning acquittal in the Duff Armstrong murder case a few hours earlier

Raised by a free Baptist family with anti-slavery convictions, Lincoln knew that his father's decision to leave Kentucky for Indiana in 1816 was at least in part a desire to get the family away from the ugly presence of slavery and to start off fresh in free territory.

In slaveless, white Indiana and Illinois Lincoln had little experience of black people. The terrifying problems of slave unrest and mounting white violence lay far away in older states like South Carolina and Virginia, where slaves had been bought and sold for generations. Illinois's problems were simple ignorance and prejudice, and self-educated Lincoln was not immune to either. He believed, in common with virtually all his neighbors, that Negroes were probably by nature inferior to whites, were unfit to vote or to serve on juries or, of course, to marry outside their race. As the perfect subjects for crude, frontier humor, Lincoln had no compunction referring to grown black men as "boys," and for years enjoyed telling stories involving "pickaninnies," "Sambos," "darkies," and "niggers." With such limited, pioneer origins, it is amazing how far Lincoln journeyed on the subject of race over the years ahead. But the journey was slow to begin.

In 1828, at the age of nineteen, when Lincoln brought a cargo of produce down the Mississippi to New Orleans with a farmer's son, he witnessed black slave markets for the first time. His most prominent memory of the trip, however, was of an attack "by seven negroes" who tried "to kill and rob" them. He liked to remember how he and Allen Gentry had fought them off like swashbucklers and escaped down the river on their flatboat, proud of their superior cunning. Taking the thousand-mile river trip to New Orleans a second time in 1831, Lincoln was supposed to have been aghast at the slave markets, promising one day he would "hit it hard"—one of the myths that project abolitionist views into his boyhood. Some of these views were taking hold, though, a few years later.

When Lincoln was twenty-eight, he and his friend Dan Stone became the only state legislators in Illinois to take a stand against slavery, calling it "an injustice" and condemning lynch mobs that terrorized blacks and abolitionists. But they had gone on to condemn "abolition doctrines" as well, claiming that these tended to "increase rather than abate" slavery's evils. On an 1841 riverboat trip on the Ohio River with his best friend, Joshua Speed, alongside a cargo of shackled slaves, Lincoln still betrayed a lack of sensitivity. Describing the slaves in a letter to Speed's sister, Lincoln told of "twelve negroes...chained six and six together...strung together precisely like so many fish upon a trot-line...being separated forever from the scenes of their childhood, their friends, their fathers and mothers." Nevertheless, "they were the most cheerful and apparantly [sic] happy creatures on board." They "fiddled," they "cracked jokes," they "played various games with cards." It was a blessing of God that these poor creatures were not more aware of their lot. But from here, it was a short leap to the common stereotype—that slaves actually enjoyed their fate. Most Southerners, like future president of the Confederacy Jefferson Davis, believed that slaves had it good on the plantations, and that the life there was ideal for them, because, as Davis put it, Africans were "a child race." Lincoln's letter to Mary Speed about his encounter on the river was the letter of a backwoodsman, still not fully serious, trying his hardest to

This cartoon embodied one of the most deep-rooted of American stereotypes—the happy-go-lucky black slave who was not overly concerned about his freedom.

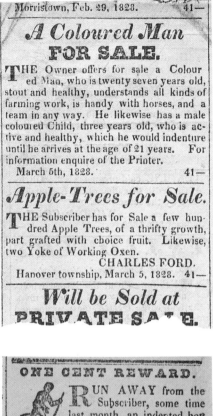
Newspaper ads of the early and middle nineteenth century show how black men and women were treated precisely like commodities.

impress a pretty Kentucky girl whose family owned slaves.

In reality the incident on shipboard had bothered Lincoln. It was apparently not enough to affect his new law practice: Lincoln had no problem in 1847 with earning a fee for returning a Kentucky slave to her owner in accordance with the fugitive slave laws. But over the years, that early encounter with slavery worked away at him. And by midlife, Lincoln remembered the same trip with Speed in markedly different terms: "In 1841 you and I had a tedious low-water trip, on a Steam Boat from Louisville to St. Louis. You may remember, as I well do, that...there were, on board, ten or a dozen slaves, shackled together with irons. That sight was a continual torment to me...which has, and continually exercises, the power of making me miserable."

It was this empathy for other people's suffering that was slowly transforming Lincoln's outlook. His two years in the U.S. Congress in the late 1840s expanded his horizons, too, and exposed him to slave auctions in the capital itself. Disgusted by the sight of black men and women being treated "precisely like droves of horses," Lincoln introduced a bill in Congress that would have forever outlawed slavery in the District of Columbia. It failed. And so did Lincoln's attempt to secure a second term in office. When he returned to Springfield from Washington, it was with a new realization of how deeply rooted slavery was in the country and how difficult it would be to eliminate it from places where it had been long established. He now hated the institution, not only because it was immoral and un-Christian, but because it undermined the American Dream, whereby each person had the right to "dig out his destiny" and to enjoy the fruit of his own labor. "This is a world of compensation," he declared, "and he who would be no slave must consent to have no slave." But for the next half-dozen years, as his law practice grew and thrived, Lincoln resigned himself to the compromise that at least the ugly practice could be kept out of the nation's expanding West.

THE FOUR LINCOLN BOYS

ROBERT TODD LINCOLN

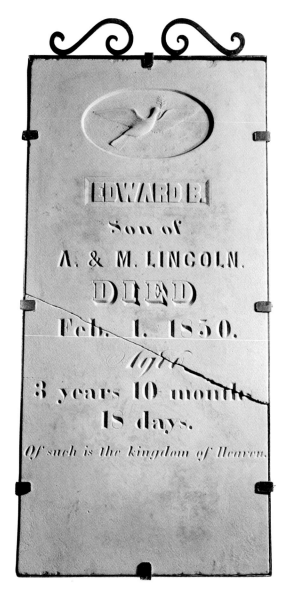

EDWARD BAKER LINCOLN

Lincoln had excitedly wanted to name his firstborn "Joshua" after his friend Speed, but in the end he and Mary chose the name of Mary's father. Robert was born on August 1, 1843, in a simple room in the Globe Tavern, a stopover for two stagecoach lines, where the couple boarded. On the square afterward, Lincoln ran into his dentist, Dr. French, and told him he had feared the baby would have one long leg like his "and one short one, like Mary's," but in fact, little Bobby was fine. Even so, he was no one's favorite. He cried a lot, his eyes were crossed, and, when the Lincolns bought a house of their own, he constantly ran away. Lincoln described him as "the rare-ripe type," brighter at five than he would ever be again. The only thing he inherited from his father was his dimple. Completely undisciplined, Robert was sent to a private school in Springfield at a tuition of $25 a year. But still, years later, he failed fifteen out of sixteen of his Harvard entrance examinations and was told to bone up for a year at Phillips Exeter Academy in New Hampshire, where he excelled in athletics as a jumper.

Named after Lincoln's friend Ned Baker, their second child was born on March 10, 1846, in the house the Lincolns had purchased from the Episcopal minister who had married them. "We have another boy," Lincoln wrote to his friend Joshua Speed at the time of Eddy's birth. "He is very much such a child as Bob was at his age—rather of a longer order. Bob is 'short and low,' and, I expect, always will be." During his congressional term in Washington, Lincoln wrote Mary, who was visiting her family in Kentucky with the two boys. "Don't let the blessed fellows forget father," Lincoln implored. "Kiss and love the dear rascals." Never photographed, Eddy died when he was not quite four, on February 1, 1850. The cause of death was either consumption, as the U.S. Census of 1850 stated, or pulmonary tuberculosis, as researchers today believe. He was buried beneath this headstone, which was later cracked in the middle from being used as a stepping stone at the entrance of the Edwards plot.

WILLIAM WALLACE LINCOLN

The Lincolns' third boy arrived December 21, 1850, ten months after the second's demise. Both mother and father hoped Willie would help them forget. But nothing could; a decade later, Mary still broke down when Eddy was mentioned. Named after Mary's brother-in-law William Wallace, the Lincolns' close friend and family doctor, the fair-skinned, blue-eyed, studious Willie had a memory like his father's and liked to learn railroad schedules by heart. Lincoln's law partner Billy Herndon, who had as close a look at the Lincoln children as anyone outside the family, had this to say about their indulgent parent: "He exercised no government of any kind over his household.... His children did much as they pleased...he restrained them in nothing (approving of much of their antics)." Explaining his philosophy of child rearing, Lincoln said: "It is my pleasure that my children are free and happy, and unrestrained by parental tyranny. Love is the chain, whereby to bind a child to its parents."

THOMAS LINCOLN

Born April 4, 1853, the Lincolns' fourth boy had a big head, a cleft palate, and was the wrong sex — the parents were hoping for a girl. Six days after Tad's birth, Lincoln left to try cases on the Eighth Circuit, and when he returned months later, he found his "Tadpole" becoming the most spoiled brat of the family — "my little troublesome sunshine," his mother called him. When he was home, Lincoln took Tad everywhere, looking at him with particularly gentle eyes when he talked in that queer, breathy, nasal way. "Why are you carrying that big boy all the way to your office, Mr. Lincoln?" asked his sister-in-law Frances Wallace. "Oh, don't you think his little feet get tired?" Lincoln answered. Lincoln found Tad's sayings unusually bright, and he never failed to understand the misshapen baby words. "Now wasn't it bright," he asked the neighbors, "when Willie was begging for a toy and I said, 'Give it to him, Tad, to keep him quiet,' he said, 'No, sir, I need it to quiet myself.'"

CLOSE TIES TO THE NEIGHBORHOOD CHILDREN, WHO WOULDN'T LEAVE LINCOLN ALONE

Lincoln had a special fondness for Josie Remann, a little girl who grew up in a house on his block, only a short walk from the center of town. He carried Josie about on his shoulder, took her to the circus, and treated her like the daughter he never had.

An early biographer suggested that Lincoln adored his own children but didn't care much for other people's. The evidence says otherwise. When neighborhood boys strung string across his path to knock off his stove-pipe hat as he strode home, all he did was retrieve the hat, place it back on his head, and take all the little pirates around the corner to the store for cookies. He gave the little ones "hossy rides" by letting them straddle his foot and bouncing them up and down. He played handball with the older boys, and chess, and beat them at marbles, kneeling down in the dust among them. He guarded them from their own firecrackers, taught them how to salute the flag, and contributed bits of money toward their little businesses. He sought out boys and girls whose parents were unable to buy tickets to the circus and took them himself, often holding them high so they could see everything. Once he noticed a small boy parading up and down the alley behind his house with a paper hat on his head, beating time on a pan; he made sure that, at Christmas, Santa Claus left the boy a real drum. Always deep in thought, still he seemed to be aware when children jumped around him pulling on his coattails, and he listened to their questions and sometimes even answered. To Lincoln's delight, his favorite little neighbor girl later married one of his wife's nephews.

Growing up in Springfield at the same time, about ten blocks away, were Lincoln's wife's nephews, the Ninian Edwards boys. Their mother, Elizabeth Todd Edwards, wore this miniature photograph of her sons in a small brooch. Albert, the older boy, was three at the time of the Lincoln wedding and was allowed to stay up late to watch. When he and Josie Remann grew up, they were married.

When four-year-old Eddy Lincoln died, his mother would not open her child's bureau until, one evening, watching her friend Mary Remann sewing for her son Henry, she gave her all of Eddy's clothes. In the photograph *(at left)* little Henry is wearing Eddy's tartans. Henry *(above)*, grew up to be Willie Lincoln's closest friend and wrote letters to him in the White House up until Willie's death.

LONG PHOTOGRAPHIC EXPOSURE TIMES WOULDN'T LET HIM SMILE

Believed to have been taken in Springfield,
Illinois, during the summer of 1858

Place unknown, probably taken in 1858

Taken in Chicago, Illinois, October 4, 1859

Taken in Springfield, May 20, 1860

Probably taken by Roderick M. Cole, in Peoria, Illinois, about 1858

Place unknown, probably taken in 1859

Probably taken in Springfield or Chicago, spring or summer 1860

Probably taken in Springfield, spring or summer 1860

A WIFE LEFT LONELY HALF THE TIME

For better or worse they had taken each other; like any couple, each had to put up with the other's failings and frailties as well as take comfort in their strengths. Lincoln was devoted but often aloof. His moods could change quickly and inexplicably, from laughter to sadness, from friendly and outgoing to silent and withdrawn. Mary was sensitive yet blunt, understanding yet driven by ambition for her husband. Lincoln was strong-minded yet he had a timid streak. Mary was a good provider and a thoughtful mother, but she was tense, insistent, in a hurry. Lincoln never seemed to be in a hurry. "Howdy! Howdy!" he greeted people on the streets, with time on his hands for a chat. Mary was prim and neat and formal. Lincoln had no pretensions; formality was foreign to him, and tidiness did not come naturally. Mary's mind was quick, her instincts impulsive, her sarcasm sharp; she often expressed her wishes as orders. "The long and the short of it," Lincoln liked to sum the two of them up—he towering, she a mere five feet four. Nine years older, Lincoln often treated Mary more like a child than a wife, guiding her, praising her, reprimanding, making concessions, trying to protect her from critics and from herself. Like a little girl, she basked in his attention. Even her violent headaches were blessings in disguise, for they provoked Lincoln's kindest and most sympathetic side. When she lost her temper, he laughed at her kindly, skirted the issue, gave in to her. But Mary was not only the little girl seeking approval and affection, she was often still that vivacious woman with a fine mind whom he married, who was well informed and could talk wisely about politics and social issues. Lincoln listened and respected her judgment about people and their motives, of which she was a better judge than he. Most of the time they got along well, adjusting to each other's needs and moods, living a normal Springfield social life. They occasionally entertained people at home, and the Lincoln table was known for its succulent Kentucky dishes.

Little things meant a lot to Mary. She had been brought up in a world of manners and decorum. Husbands didn't lie around on the floor of their parlor reading, or answer the door in their slippers and shirtsleeves; they didn't tell an arriving guest that the wife "will be down soon as she gets her trotting harness on." The kind of husband Mary would have preferred would not demand silence in the house when he was thinking, would not absentmindedly pick at the food she had so carefully prepared, would not so often forget to do the chores she asked of him.

As Lincoln's law practice grew and his income increased, his trips out on the circuit sometimes lengthened to six or more weeks at a time. It was the work he loved best, sometimes three months in the spring and another three months in the fall, broken whenever he was close enough to get home for a weekend. With these prolonged absences, Mary's irrational fears began to mount. She was sure that her children would meet some terrible fate or the house would be robbed or disaster in some form or other would strike. Sometimes she could not sleep at night and called for neighbors to be with her; James Gourley claimed she once invited him to join her in bed. Sometimes she paid a young boy to sleep in the house. A perfectionist in everything, she needed something more than motherhood and housekeeping to be perfect about. Life in Springfield was not rewarding enough. Where were the beautiful dresses, the lavish parties, the power and glory she had dreamed of? As her pent-up anger increased,

James Gourley, the Lincolns' next-door neighbor, talks on Lincoln

I lived next-door neighbor to Lincoln nineteen years; knew him and his family relations well; he used to come to our house with slippers on, one suspender and old pair of pants, came for milk; our room was low and he said: "Jim, you have to lift your loft a little higher, I can't stand in it well." He used to say to my wife that little people had some advantages; it did not take quite so much wood and wool to make their house and clothes.

Lincoln never planted any trees; he did plant some rose bushes once in front of his house; he planted no apple trees, cherry trees, pear trees, grapevines, shade trees, and suchlike things; he did not, it seems, care for such things.

He once, for a year or so, had a garden and worked in it; he kept his own horse, fed and curried it, fed and milked his own cow; he sawed his own wood generally when at home. He loved his horse well....

Mrs. and Mr. Lincoln were good neighbors. Lincoln was the best man I ever knew....

Lincoln, by an unknown photographer, sometime during May or June of 1860

Mrs. Lincoln was a very nervous, hysterical woman who was incessantly alarming the neighborhood with her outcries. It was a common thing to see her standing out on their terrace in front of the house, waving her arms and screaming, "Bobbie's lost! Bobbie's lost!" when perhaps he was just over in our house. This was almost an every day occurrence....

Once when Robert could just barely walk Mrs. Lincoln came out in front as usual, screaming, "Bobbie will die! Bobbie will die!" My father ran over to see what had happened. Bobbie was found sitting out near the back door by a lime box and had a little lime in his mouth. Father took him, washed his mouth out and that's all there was to it. The trouble was ended.

Another time Mrs. Lincoln cried, "Fire, Fire!" When the neighbors ran in they found just a little fat burning in a frying pan on the cook stove. Again she screamed, "Murder!" Mr. Eastman who lived near on their side of the street, ran in this time and found an old umbrella fixer sitting on the back porch, waiting for the "Mrs." to come back. As the man went down the steps, he muttered something not very complimentary to Mrs. Lincoln. "I wouldn't have such a fool for my wife!" The cause of her fright was the man's heavy beard, which was a rare sight in those days, it was a smooth age as is the present....

Mr. Lincoln seemed to accept his wife's eccentricities and nervous displays with philosophic calm. To one friend who remarked on a humiliating public exhibit of her temper he said: "It does her lots of good and it doesn't hurt me a bit." Another time he had occasion to hear the complaints of a farmer who had sold Mrs. Lincoln some produce. The produce was unsatisfactory, so when the man returned the following week she talked so plainly to him that he took his hurt pride to Mr. Lincoln. After listening attentively until the man had finished, Mr. Lincoln said: "My friend, you don't know how much I regret this, but in all candor, can't you take for fifteen minutes what I have taken for fifteen years?" The man had nothing more to say.

Ever since she was a young woman, Mary was convinced she would marry a man who would one day be president.

her fuse grew shorter; more and more often she needed something to explode over. Once she interrupted a discussion her husband was having with another lawyer to find out if Lincoln had done a certain errand. When she learned he hadn't, she unleashed a tirade of insults and then left, slamming the door behind her. To his surprised guest, Lincoln explained: "If you knew how much good that little eruption did, what a relief it was to her, and if you knew her as well as I do, you would be glad she had had an opportunity to explode." There were times when Lincoln was banished from his house without breakfast. Once Mary pelted him with a hail of potatoes; another time she chased him with a butcher knife; on still another occasion she hit him hard in the nose with a piece of firewood. During one of these embarrassing outbursts, a neighbor watched him retaliate by picking her up by the back of her dress and thrusting her inside the house, admonishing her not to make such a scene in public.

Lincoln kept his buggy in this barn at the rear of his house, along with his horse, Old Bob (to distinguish him from young Bob), and a cow that he milked twice a day when he was home. To the right is the privy the family used. The photograph below was taken from the barn area at the back of the property and shows the yard with its planked walkways and the back of the Lincoln house after the extension was added in 1856. The house was painted a pale chocolate color, the window shutters a deep green.

As Lincoln slowly but surely pulled his way upward economically, impoverished relatives began to look to him for hand-outs. "He . . . did not think money . . . a fit object for any man's ambition," wrote friend Ward Hill Lamon. "But he knew its value, its power, and liked to keep it when he had it." Nowhere was Lincoln's demanding work ethic better revealed than in his strict but kind-hearted refusal, in 1848, to make an eighty-dollar loan to his ne'er-do-well stepbrother John D. Johnston.

You are not *lazy*, and still you *are* an *idler*. I doubt whether since I saw you, you have done a good whole day's work, in any one day. . . . This habit of uselessly wasting time, is the whole difficulty; and it is vastly important to you, and still more so to your children that you should break this habit. . . . [W]hat I propose is, that you shall go to work, "tooth and nails" for some body who will give you money [for] it . . . I now promise you that for every dollar you will, between this and the first of next May, get for your own labor . . . I will then give you one other dollar. . . .

Now if you will do this, you will soon be out of debt, and what is better, you will have a habit that will keep you from getting in debt again. . . . [I]f you will but follow my advice, you will find it worth more than eight times eighty dollars to you.

Newsboys sold this picture, saying—as Lincoln told it—"Here's your likeness of Old Abe. Will look a good deal better when he gets his hair combed." Actually Lincoln mussed it up himself, just before the picture was taken, telling the photographers that his friends wouldn't recognize him without his hair in a "bad tousle." He might have been right, for in another picture *(opposite)* his grooming helps give him an unfamiliar look.

Chapter 4

THE
MAKING
OF A
PRESIDENT

The 1850s is the decade
that proves his leadership
and thrusts him into the
forefront of the nation.

An early look at the Republican nominee

The second
earliest known
photograph of
Lincoln was taken
in 1854 in Chicago.

In 1856 John Frémont was a candidate for the presidency. Lincoln had been nominated at the convention for vice president, but another candidate defeated him.

One of the reasons for Lincoln's return to politics was to fight against the election of James Buchanan as president.

For five long years following his term in Congress, and his refusal of the administration's offer of the Oregon governorship, Lincoln lay low, campaigning for fellow Whigs such as Winfield Scott, but pursuing no political office for himself. They were good years—years of quiet growth and continuing self-education—and they saw a steady deepening of Lincoln's mind and character. As railroads etched their way across the country and the West continued to grow, Lincoln contented himself that at least the Missouri Compromise had outlawed slavery from the huge open terrains of Kansas and Nebraska—and thus from America's long-term future. But the Missouri Compromise was like a lid on a boiling pot, and in 1854 a heated new congressional act, stoked by the chairman of the Senate's Committee on Territories, Stephen A. Douglas of Illinois, finally blew off the lid.

The effect on Lincoln of the Kansas-Nebraska Act was electrifying, rousing him "like nothing…before," he said, and reigniting all his dormant political ambitions and passions. "It is wrong," he insisted; "wrong in its…effect, letting slavery into Kansas and Nebraska—and wrong in…principle, allowing it to spread to every other part of the wide world, where men can be found inclined to take it." "When we were the political slaves of King George, and wanted to be free, we called the maxim that 'all men are created equal' a self-evident truth; but now when we have grown fat, and have lost the dread of being slaves ourselves, we have become so greedy to be *masters* that we call the same a 'self-evident lie.'"

When Douglas claimed that all he was advocating was "popular sovereignty"—the right of local territories to make their own decisions on slavery—Lincoln scoffed. Slave owners were like hungry cows, he said; remove the property fences from the free soil meadows and they would rush in and despoil. There was no prettifying the matter: slavery was an evil that must be sealed off, asphyxiated, and set on a path to certain extinction.

In the summer of 1854, to get a toehold back into politics, Lincoln decided to campaign for a position in the Illinois State Assembly. In November he easily won, but then suddenly changed his mind and resigned. What he wanted instead was a seat in the United States Senate, where he felt he could make a real difference.

In February 1855 he sought and failed to gain the coveted Senate seat, which went instead to Lyman Trumbull, husband of Mary's old friend Julia Jayne. Though Mary was furious, all Lincoln would say was, "I regret my defeat moderately, but…am not nervous about it." To his friend Joshua Speed, Lincoln attempted to define himself politically, contrasting his views to those of the newly formed anti-Catholic, anti-foreigner "Know-Nothing" party. "I think I am a Whig; but others say there are no Whigs, and that I am an abolitionist…. I am not a Know-Nothing that is certain….How can anyone who abhors the oppression of negroes, be in favor of degrading classes of white people?"

It was now clear to Lincoln that a new coalition of "anti-Nebraska" forces was needed, to be composed not just of Whigs, but of liberal Democrats, Free-Soilers, and perhaps even certain of the anti-slavery "Know-Nothings." "I have no objection to 'fuse' with any body provided I can fuse on ground which I think is right," Lincoln decided.

By early 1856, Lincoln was helping to create a new political party in Illinois

(continued on page 108)

Dred Scott, as he looked in the early 1850s

The most famous and controversial Supreme Court case of Lincoln's day, shocking Lincoln into action and becoming the chief subject of his political oratory, concerned not only slavery but the status of every black person in the United States. In 1846, with the help of abolitionist lawyers, the slave Dred Scott had sued for his freedom, on the basis that his master had taken him out of Missouri and into free areas in the West, thereby rendering him free. Scott's case had risen steadily through the legal system and finally landed in the Supreme Court itself, dominated by a former slave owner from Maryland, Chief Justice Roger B. Taney. Taney's decision, reached finally in March 1857 (delayed long enough so as not to interfere with Buchanan's inauguration), reaffirmed early American legal opinions that Negroes were "beings of an inferior order. . .and altogether unfit to associate with the white race." Furthermore, they possessed "no rights which the white man was bound to respect." Therefore, wrote the Court, blacks were not, and never had been, citizens of this country and thus had no right to sue. In addition, the Missouri Compromise, which had outlawed slavery from certain parts of the West, was deemed unconstitutional and therefore null and void.

Lincoln's reaction to the decision was one of disgust and disagreement. Taney had deliberately skewed the record, Lincoln argued, when he claimed that blacks had never possessed any rights in America. In fact, as two dissenting justices in the case had written, free blacks in five of the original states had been full voting citizens at the time of the writing of the Declaration of Independence and the Constitution. The Taney Court was baldly setting back the clock on human rights. "In those days, our Declaration of Independence was held sacred by all, and thought to include all," Lincoln wrote, "but now, to aid in making the bondage of the negro universal and eternal, it is assailed, and sneered at, and construed, and hawked at, and torn, till, if its framers could rise from their graves, they could not at all recognize it."

William "Duff" Armstrong was saved by Lincoln and an almanac.

To afford the expenses of his political activities and campaigns, Lincoln needed as much money as possible from his ongoing law practice. In August 1857, after a protracted battle in court, he received $5,000, the highest fee he had ever been paid, for services rendered to the Illinois Central Railroad. That fee alone would underwrite his Senate contest against Douglas the following year.

Money was important to Lincoln, but never all-important; at times he was willing to serve clients who could not pay. And the passion he could mount on the stand in the name of justice had little or nothing to do with his pocketbook. The most eye-catching and theatrical of Lincoln's courtroom feats occurred in the spring of 1858, when he defended the son of old New Salem friends in a murder case. Things looked bad for William "Duff" Armstrong, who had been charged with a killing at a camp-meeting brawl the previous summer. An eyewitness had just testified that by the light of the full moon he had watched the 11:00 p.m. assault, and, even though he had been 150 feet away, the moonlight was so bright that the witness was positive Duff had done it. During his cross-examination of the witness, Lincoln called for an 1857 almanac, turned to August 29, the date of the murder, and showed the court that the moon that night had been a mere sliver, barely past its first quarter, and that in any case it had gone down before 11:00 p.m., rendering the night pitch black. Then, in moving oratory, Lincoln recounted how the Armstrongs had taken him in, a pitiful, penniless stranger when he first arrived in New Salem as a young man, and that he himself had rocked baby Duff in his cradle and was absolutely certain that no son of Hannah Armstrong could ever commit the base act of murder. Now, with Hannah's husband in his grave, if the jury were to take her son's life, only desolation lay ahead. Tears ran down Lincoln's cheeks as he put the finishing touches on the most heart-wrenching and eloquent plea to a jury he would ever make. "They'll clear him before dark, Hannah," Lincoln said to the agonized widow as he helped her from the courtroom. And the jury did.

called the Republicans. Arising simultaneously in states across the North, the new party's first and primary goal was to prevent Democrat James Buchanan from winning the presidency. It failed. Then, just two days after Buchanan's inauguration, as if to celebrate the new regime, the Supreme Court issued its long-awaited Dred Scott decision. The ruling declared the Missouri Compromise ''unconstitutional'' and denied that Negroes could ever be considered American citizens.

During the chaotic days that followed, Stephen Douglas made a sudden, politically orchestrated turnabout, and appeared to join the anti-Nebraska forces. Eastern Republicans were elated by Douglas's ''conversion'' and rushed to his support. Perhaps, after all, he was the very man who could win for them in 1860. Illinois Republicans, who had known ''Doug'' all his life, were unconvinced. ''We want no such ominous wooden horse run into our camp,'' proclaimed one Republican newspaper; ''All eyes are turned toward Mr. Lincoln...as the unanimous choice of the people.''

On June 16, 1858, in what has been called the single most important day in his career, the Illinois State Republican Convention nominated Lincoln to run against Stephen Douglas for the United States Senate. Hearing of it, Douglas told a friend, ''I shall have my hands full. He is...the strong man of his party...full of wit, facts, dates—and the best stump speaker...in the West. He is as honest as he is shrewd, and if I beat him my victory will be hard won.'' That night, in a speech before the excited Republican assembly, Lincoln likened the country to a ''House Divided.'' ''I believe this government cannot endure, permanently half *slave* and half *free*,'' he told his entranced listeners. ''It will become *all* one thing, or *all* the other.''

The remarkable speech had been months in the planning, and years in evolution. To critics who found it too radical and warned that it had jeopardized his candidacy, Lincoln answered, ''You will see the day when you will consider it the wisest thing I ever said.'' Its chief aim was not only to stake out high ethical ground, but also to prove to his party and to the nation that Douglas was not the leader to follow. ''How can he oppose the advances of slavery? He don't *care* anything about it,'' Lincoln argued, comparing Douglas to a toothless lion. ''Let the Republican party...dally with Judge Douglas,'' he later elaborated, ''and they do not absorb him; he absorbs them.''

On July 24, Lincoln proposed to his opponent an exhaustive series of joint speeches, before huge, common audiences. Douglas agreed, as long as the encounters were limited to seven. Of the almost two hundred speeches given in the summer and fall of 1858 by these two men, those seven debates were the ones that counted the most. Covering thousands of miles, the candidates crisscrossed the state and spoke to crowds of ten thousand and more. It was oratory, politics, and outdoor entertainment all rolled up into one. Exclaimed one New York reporter, ''The prairies are on fire.''

''No more striking contrast could have been imagined than between these two men as they appeared on the platform,'' wrote Carl Schurz, who attended the sixth debate, at Quincy. ''By the side of Lincoln's tall, lank, ungainly form, Douglas stood almost like a dwarf....As I looked at him, I detested him deeply.''

Hard-driving, Vermont-born Stephen Douglas was the most prominent and widely respected public figure in America, looming far above the little-known

The seven Lincoln–Douglas debates during the late summer and fall of 1858 were the highlight of the campaign, in towns all over the state. Ten thousand people attended the opening three-hour debate in Ottawa, Illinois, and there were fifteen thousand at the second in Freeport. What audiences heard was the greatest public oratory in the nation's history. Although Douglas eventually won the Senate race, the debates launched Lincoln on his own path to the presidency. *Below*: A Democratic newspaper covering the final debate at Alton refers to Lincoln as the "Artful Dodger."

THE CAMPAIGN IN ILLINOIS.

THE LAST JOINT DEBATE.

DOUGLAS AND LINCOLN AT ALTON.

5,000 TO 10,000 PERSONS PRESENT!

LINCOLN AGAIN REFUSES TO ANSWER WHETHER HE WILL VOTE TO ADMIT KANSAS IF HER PEOPLE APPLY WITH A CONSTITUTION RECOGNIZING SLAVERY.

APPEARS IN HIS OLD CHARACTER OF THE "ARTFUL DODGER."

TRIES TO PALM HIMSELF OFF TO THE WHIGS OF MADISON COUNTY AS A FRIEND OF HENRY CLAY AND NO ABOLITIONIST, AND IS EXPOSED!!

GREAT SPEECHES OF SENATOR DOUGLAS.

Lincoln. The owner, through marriage, of a Mississippi plantation with 140 slaves, Douglas claimed over and over again in the debates that slavery was a neutral institution and that the decision to permit it or not should be left in the hands of each locality. How could slavery be considered an evil, he asked, when the founding fathers themselves had possessed slaves, and when the Constitution assured its existence? Why *couldn't* the nation exist "forever divided" on this issue? Furthermore, wasn't this after all a white man's country? "I hold that the signers of the Declaration of Independence had no reference to negroes at all when they declared all men to be created equal," he insisted. "They did not mean negro, nor the savage Indians, nor the Fejee Islanders, nor any other barbarous race. They were speaking of white men...men of European birth and...descent....This government was established...by white men for the benefit of white men...and should be administered by white men, and none others."

Lincoln, wrote Schurz, labored under severe disadvantages in these debates. "His voice was not musical, rather high-keyed, and apt to turn into a shrill treble in moments of excitement....His gesture was awkward. He swung his long arms sometimes in a very ungraceful manner. Now and then he would, to give particular emphasis to a point, bend his knees and body with a sudden downward jerk, and then shoot up again with a vehemence that raised him to his tip-toes...." But whereas there was a cynical, defiant quality in Douglas's effort, there was in Lincoln "a tone of earnest truthfulness, of elevated, noble sentiment, and of kindly sympathy, which added greatly to the strength of his argument..."

"One class looks upon the institution of slavery *as a wrong*, and...another class...*does not*," summed up Lincoln in the final debate at Alton. "That is the issue that will continue in this country when these poor tongues of Judge Douglas and myself shall be silent. It is the eternal struggle between...right and wrong—throughout the world."

"The...race," Lincoln wrote after losing to Douglas in November, "...gave me a hearing on the great and durable question of the age...and though I now sink out of view, and shall be forgotten, I believe I have made some marks which will tell for civil liberty long after I am gone." Ironically, Lincoln's loss carried with it the key to his own future. Having shown he could obtain a popular majority against America's premier politician, despite losing the districts, Lincoln had proven his enormous potential as a national figure. Almost immediately his name began being discussed as a possible candidate for president in 1860.

By the summer of 1859, though "absolutely without money...for even household purposes," Lincoln was back in the political arena, speaking to far-flung crowds in Iowa, Indiana, Wisconsin, Kansas, and Ohio. Traveling often alone in an open buggy across the windy plains, again and again he told audiences, "Never forget that we have before us this whole matter of right or wrong."

In the middle of October, Lincoln received an invitation to bring his message to New York, home of the single most prominent Republican in the country, William H. Seward. This event, scheduled for the upcoming February, seemed like his greatest opportunity yet.

Lincoln displays his unusual height in an 1860 portrait by an unknown photographer, possibly made for sculptor Leonard Volk, who visited Springfield in May to make the casts of Lincoln's hands the day after his nomination. Volk said Lincoln loved to measure himself against other tall men. After telling them to "stand fair," he could stretch himself out "like India rubber."

LINCOLN DISTANCES HIMSELF FROM JOHN BROWN'S ANARCHY

The most fiery abolitionist of them all was a half-crazed, white freedom fighter named John Brown (shown at left wearing the patriarchal beard that was his hallmark after 1857). Sensing a divine mission to liberate the slaves, Brown turned his attention to strife-torn Kansas, where in May 1856 he and several of his sons descended upon three pro-slavery settlers and hacked them to pieces with broadswords. On October 16, 1859, to further his plan of an independent black state in the Appalachian Mountains with himself as president, Brown attacked a Federal armory in Harpers Ferry, Virginia. After a bloody struggle, in which two of Brown's sons were killed, the revolutionaries were cornered in an engine house and captured by U.S. Marines under the command of Colonel Robert E. Lee. On December 2, John Brown was hanged by the neck before a jeering crowd.

Lincoln's reaction to the affair was true to character: he despised the anarchy and lawlessness that Brown represented, and attempted to distance himself from the raid. "John Brown was no Republican," he insisted. His effort was nothing but "an attempt by white men to get up a revolt among slaves, in which the slaves refused to participate."

Nevertheless, for many Northerners Brown's passionate struggle for black freedom was a burning torch lighting the way toward the future. Before his execution, the old warrior himself had said, "You may dispose of me easily but the negro question—the end of that is not yet." And, as a newly popular song in the North put it, John Brown's body might now lie a-moldering in the grave, but "his truth is marching on."

The little engine house in Harpers Ferry, Virginia *(at left in photograph)*, where John Brown's career was cut short in 1859

Douglas and Lincoln: the determined
players in the seven great debates

NOW THE LITTLE-KNOWN WESTERNER GETS HIS CHANCE TO DAZZLE THE EAST

On February 25, Lincoln arrived in New York City to give a lecture, originally scheduled for the Reverend Henry Ward Beecher's church in Brooklyn. Lincoln had been pleased when the site of his speech was switched to the larger and more prestigious hall of the Cooper Union. This was his chance to demonstrate the quality of his mind and his style to the Eastern leaders who were needed to support any real run for the top office.

Success, though, was hardly guaranteed. In fact, when Lincoln had set off for New York four days earlier, the *Illinois State Register* predicted failure. "Subject, not known. Consideration, $200 and expenses. Object, presidential capital. Effect, disappointment." Equally gloomy was Lincoln's host, Henry C. Bowen, who first laid eyes on the candidate in Bowen's Ann Street office. "I faced a very tall man wearing a high hat and carrying an old-fashioned, comical-looking carpet-bag," Bowen recalled. "My heart went into my boots as I greeted the tall stranger. His clothes were travel-stained and he looked tired and woe-begone...[I]n this first view of him, there came to me the disheartening and appalling thought of the great throng which I had been so instrumental in inducing to come and hear Lincoln...." Two nights later, after braving a snowstorm, that throng sat transfixed as the long-limbed, shaggy, and ungainly guest speaker displayed passionate intensity combined with precise logic. The founding fathers, Lincoln insisted, in contrast to what men like Stephen Douglas and Roger Taney were saying, had had anti-slavery intentions. He could prove this by a study of the political voting records of the thirty-nine men who signed the Constitution. Again and again, these men had outlawed slavery from the Federal territories, proving they intended its ultimate extinction. "As those fathers marked it," said Lincoln of his heroes, "so let...[slavery] be again marked, as an evil not to be extended."

Some of the speech was conciliatory, and Lincoln took care to advocate no interference with slavery where it was long established, and no abolitionism of the John Brown variety. But with those who said they "could not abide the election of a Republican President" because it would destroy the Union, Lincoln had lost his patience. "That is cool. A highwayman holds a pistol to my ear, and mutters through his teeth, 'Stand and deliver, or I shall kill you, and then you will be a murderer!'"

His final word to Republicans everywhere was not to compromise on the great issue, but to stay true to the founding ideals of the country. "Let us have faith that right makes might, and in that faith, let us, to the end, dare to do our duty as we understand it." During the prolonged standing ovation hats and handkerchiefs waved all over the vast auditorium. No one in the city had expected such straight talk on the subject, so tough and so intelligent. "Since the days of Clay and Webster," the New York *Tribune* reported, "no man has spoken to a large assemblage of the intellect and mental culture of our city. Mr. Lincoln is one of nature's orators, using his rare powers solely and effectively to convince, though the inevitable effect is to delight and electrify....No man ever before made such an impression on his first appeal to a New York audience."

Mathew Brady had become the country's foremost portrait photographer, and when the Civil War broke out, he sponsored the first team of "photo-journalists" to cover it.

Brady's New York gallery was more elaborate than the branch in Washington and featured a stunning array of photographic portraits of great statesmen.

Having already spent two nights in New York, on Monday, the day of his address, Lincoln was taken to Brady's New York gallery and into a world of cameras and chemicals, and walls hung with photographs of the great. The original negative that Brady made of Lincoln was printed, then the hard facial lines touched up, and this version copied and widely circulated *(right)*. The softened image was also engraved for a variety of influential publications. Later Lincoln said that the speech and the photograph were the forces that propelled him into the White House. But at the time he was not so impressed. A few weeks after the sitting, Lincoln wrote a picture seeker that he could "easily get one at New York. When I was there I was taken to one of the places where they get up such things, and I suppose they got my shaddow [sic], and can multiply copies indefinitely."

Brady's first famous photograph of Lincoln, known as the "Cooper Union" portrait

A portrait camera that Brady used in his gallery

THE GREATEST MAN SINCE ST. PAUL

In his 1888 biography of Lincoln, Noah Brooks quoted an eyewitness of Lincoln's Cooper Union address.

When Lincoln rose to speak, I was greatly disappointed. He was tall, tall—oh, how tall! and so angular and awkward that I had, for an instant, a feeling of pity for so ungainly a man. His clothes were black and ill-fitting, badly wrinkled—as if they had been jammed carelessly into a small trunk. His bushy head, with the stiff black hair thrown back, was balanced on a long and lean head-stalk, and when he raised his hands in an opening gesture, I noticed that they were very large. He began in a low tone of voice—as if he were used to speaking out-doors and was afraid of speaking too loud. He said "Mr. *Cheerman*," instead of "Mr. Chairman," and employed many other words with an old-fashioned pronunciation. I said to myself: "Old fellow, you won't do; it's all very well for the wild West, but this will never go down in New York." But pretty soon he began to get into his subject; he straightened up, made regular and graceful gestures; his face lighted as with an inward fire; the whole man was transfigured. I forgot his clothes, his personal appearance, and his individual peculiarities. Presently, forgetting myself, I was on my feet with the rest, yelling like a wild Indian, cheering this wonderful man. In the close parts of his argument, you could hear the gentle sizzling of the gas-burners. When he reached a climax, the thunders of applause were terrific. It was a great speech. When I came out of the hall, my face glowing with excitement and my frame all a-quiver, a friend, with his eyes aglow, asked me what I thought of Abe Lincoln, the rail-splitter. I said: "He's the greatest man since St. Paul." And I think so yet.

Broadway near Brady's New York gallery in the 1860s

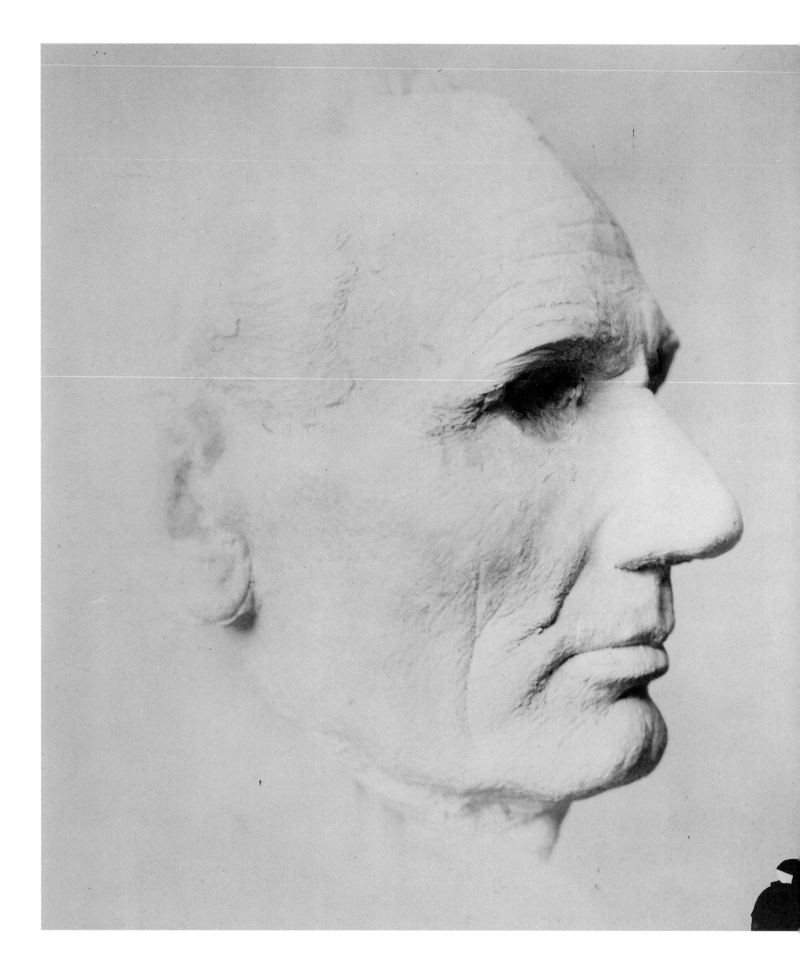

"THE ANIMAL HIMSELF," THIS TIME IN PLASTER

Returning to Illinois after a round of successful New England appearances following his Cooper Union speech, Lincoln was acting as counsel in a Chicago case over disputed land when in late March he was asked to pose for the noted sculptor Leonard W. Volk. To save him several sittings, Volk took a cast of Lincoln's face. The usual process entailed rubbing the skin very lightly with oil, matting down the hair about the temples and forehead with clay, and then applying over the entire face plaster of Paris the consistency of thick cream. While it hardened, this plaster grew hotter and hotter, which was sometimes disagreeable to "the patient," as Volk called his subjects. With quills in his nostrils for breathing and holes left for the eyes, Lincoln sat upright in a chair, watching himself in a mirror. After about an hour the plaster had hardened enough to be removed. The mask "clung pretty hard," Volk recalled. "He bent his head low and took hold of the mold and worked it off himself," pulling out some hairs in the process and making his eyes water. Lincoln found the experience "anything but agreeable." To see the results, he returned the following Sunday morning, preferring to visit the sculptor's fifth-floor studio rather than go to church. "I don't like to hear cut and dried sermons," he told Volk. "No, when I hear a man preach, I like to see him act as if he were fighting bees!" The mask was done. To make the positive image from the negative cast, Volk had poured liquid plaster into the mold he had made from Lincoln's face—the "waste" mold—which was discarded after the mask had hardened. The resulting plaster image was an exact replica of Lincoln's features, the only immediate, tangible connection we have today with the face of the unbearded Lincoln. Upon seeing it, Lincoln exclaimed, "There is the animal himself!"

Volk's life mask of Lincoln's face *(left)* and hands *(below)*

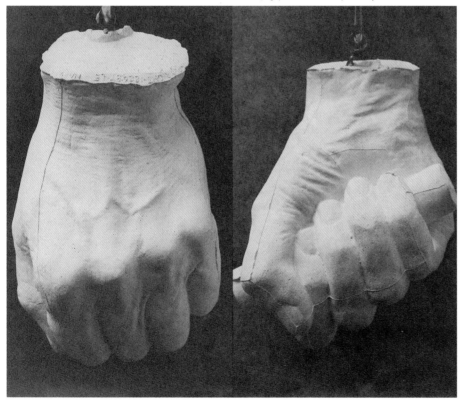

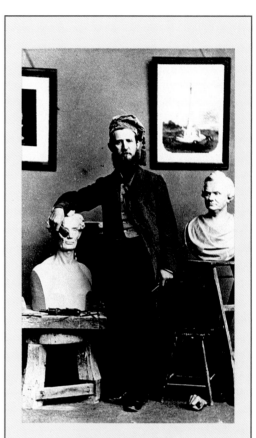

CASTING THE HANDS

Later, Volk (shown above working on a bust of Lincoln) met his "patient" again, this time in Springfield.

I found him ready, but he looked more grave and serious than he had appeared on the previous days. I wished him to hold something in his right hand, and he looked for a piece of pasteboard, but could find none. I told him a round stick would do as well as anything. Thereupon he went to the woodshed, and I heard the saw go, and he soon returned to the dining room whittling off the end of a piece of broom handle. I remarked to him that he need not whittle off the edges.

"Oh, well," said he, "I thought I would like to have it nice."

When I had successfully cast the mould of the right hand I began the left, pausing a few moments to hear Mr. Lincoln tell me about a scar on his thumb.

"You have heard that they call me a rail-splitter....Well, it is true that I did split rails, and one day while I was sharpening a wedge on a log, the axe glanced and nearly took my thumb off, and there is the scar, you see."

"THE TASTE IS IN MY MOUTH A LITTLE"

With just two months remaining before the Republican National Convention, Lincoln and his advisers at last began to see his candidacy as viable. The Cooper Union trip had changed the way fellow Illinoisans looked at Lincoln—he seemed bigger now, more "national" in scope. And Norman Judd's success at luring the Republican National Convention to Chicago, rather than to Edward Bates's home town of St. Louis, had given a tremendous boost to Lincoln's prospects. Lincoln himself began now to feel "that the presidential nomination was in his reach," remembered Billy Herndon. "My name is new in the field," wrote Lincoln in March, "and I suppose I am not the *first* choice of a very great many." But that didn't mean he might not be a strong second choice and thus an attractive compromise figure for many of the delegates. As late as mid-April, Lincoln insisted he was ready and willing to support Seward or Chase or Bates or whichever candidate should be selected to carry forward the Republican cause; but as the convention loomed on the horizon, Lincoln admitted to a friend, "The taste *is* in my mouth a little."

The populist "rail-splitter" image suddenly emerged with gusto, striking a responsive chord with the public and lighting the candidacy with unexpected, dramatic fire. Lincoln's boyhood friend and cousin John Hanks appeared at the state convention in Springfield in early May shouldering rails that Abe had split as a boy. If not those, he had "mauled many and many better ones since he had grown to manhood," said Lincoln, to wild cheering. Illinois Republicans, once divided, decided now to send their man to Chicago with unanimous backing.

No public hall in Chicago was big enough to house the Republican Convention of 1860, so the city built one—the "Wigwam." The two-story frame structure at the corner of Lake and Market streets was 200 feet long, 100 feet wide, could hold 10,000 people and cost the citizens of the city $35,000. The delegates were seated on the main floor, with the audience standing— men only. Women could rest on board seats in the gallery. The thousands who couldn't get inside congregated in Market Street Square during the balloting for candidates, the results of which were passed up to messengers on the roof who then called out how each state had gone to the boisterous crowd below.

Judge David Davis, Lincoln's old Eighth Circuit companion, headed a small group, most of them lawyers, who twisted arms and pulled strings for Lincoln at the Republican Convention. With two rooms at Chicago's Tremont Hotel as Lincoln headquarters, Davis worked around the clock, engineering the fight for his friend's nomination.

Leonard Swett worked closely with Davis and persuaded supporters of Seward and Cameron to make Lincoln their second choice. "Make no contracts that will bind me," Lincoln communicated to his managers. Swett and Davis knew to ignore this and in return for votes gave Cameron, at the very least, the right to apply for a Cabinet post through them.

In May 1861, just before the Republican Convention, *Harper's Weekly* published this centerfold spread of "the prominent candidates." Seward, appearing in the middle, dominated the group, while Lincoln, depicted by a poor adaptation of Brady's "Cooper Union" portrait, was lost in the crowd of ten other hopefuls. In the biographical sketches that followed, Lincoln's was the last. In part, it said "he became intimately acquainted with the industrial classes, and they now claim him as one of their number— 'The Flatboatsman!' "

Norman Buel Judd was responsible for bringing the convention to Chicago, used his power on the Republican National Committee to arrange the delegate seating in his absent candidate's favor, and, when the time came, placed Lincoln's name in nomination.

Jesse Kilgore Dubois, one of the chief managers on the Lincoln team, was smooth but provincial. As far back as 1854 he had told Lincoln, "I am for you against the world." Other attorney friends who worked behind the scenes included Orville H. Browning, Judge Stephen T. Logan, and Ward Hill Lamon. Springfield delegate Nathan M. Knapp also played an important role.

THE REPUBLICANS MAKE A SURPRISING CHOICE

Republican delegates from all over the country poured into Chicago by the thousands for the three-day convention. On Wednesday morning, May 16, ready for action, they packed themselves into the "Wigwam," the hastily constructed convention hall touted as the most gigantic indoor meeting place in the nation, able to hold some ten thousand delegates and visitors. The convention itself was a brawling, whiskey-filled mélange in which the nation's future would be thrashed out and decided by bartering and deal-making. Wednesday and Thursday were spent haggling over a platform. All told, it would be less strident than the platform of 1856, but still a radical statement, denouncing popular sovereignty, denying territories the right to institute slavery, and condemning all talk of secession as "contemplated treason."

These first two chaotic days allowed Lincoln's managers to do their work. New York's William Seward was clearly the front-runner, and widely expected to win. Of the other four major candidates, two—Cameron and Chase—were believed unelectable, with little support outside their home states of Pennsylvania and Ohio. This left only two real competitors for Seward, both Westerners— Edward Bates of Missouri and Abraham Lincoln of Illinois.

Cannily, Lincoln's managers realized that it was Bates's delegates, not Seward's, they needed to go after. They believed that if they could win over the Pennsylvania and Indiana delegates committed to Bates, then Lincoln would have a fighting chance against Seward on the second ballot. "Prospects fair.... Friends at work night & day," wired Jesse Dubois to Lincoln on Wednesday. "Am very hopeful.... Don't be excited.... Telegraph or write here very little," wired an exhausted Judge Davis late on Thursday.

On Thursday evening, two of Lincoln's key supporters showed up at an Indiana–Pennsylvania caucus. They were Gustave Koerner, the former lieutenant governor of Illinois, who was working hard to gain German-American votes, and Orville H. Browning, Lincoln's Illinois law colleague. According to Koerner, Browning's passionate endorsement of Lincoln to these delegates "electrified the meeting.... The delegates then held a secret session," Koerner went on, "and we soon learned that Indiana would go for Lincoln at the start, and that a large majority of the Pennsylvanians had agreed to vote for him for their second choice."

On Friday morning the nominations began, amid screaming crowds containing professional "shriekers" for each candidate. "Imagine all the hogs ever slaughtered in Cincinnati giving their death squeals together," described journalist Murat Halstead, assigned to the Wigwam, "[and] a score of big steam whistles going...and you conceive something of the same nature."

The shrieking for Lincoln, even louder than when Seward's name was placed in nomination, gave the first inkling that this was going to be a closer contest than anyone had thought. Back home in Springfield, knowing something was up, Lincoln attempted to steady his nerves by playing handball. Charles Zane remembered that "Lincoln played ball pretty much all day before his nomination, played at what is called 'fives,' knocking a ball up against a wall that served as an ally.... Lincoln said 'This game makes my shoulders feel well.'"

When the first ballot came in, Seward, as expected, was far in the lead. But with 233 votes needed for a majority, he was still 60 votes shy of victory. The astonishing fact of this first count was that Lincoln had gained so many

Horace Greeley appeared at the Chicago convention oblivious to a "Seward" likeness pinned to his coattails by a prankster. In point of fact, Greeley was an ardent Bates man, determined to aid in fellow New Yorker Seward's downfall. In the end, Greeley's politicking helped elect Lincoln.

"GIVE US LINCOLN"

Addison G. Proctor, the youngest delegate to the convention of 1860, later reminisced on what took place behind the scenes. There had come to that Convention, largely from the East, a well organized body of delegates demanding the nomination for the Presidency of Senator William H. Seward of New York...by all odds the most prominent man of his party at that time....

Vermont was there asking for the nomination of her able and popular Senator Jacob Collimer....

New Jersey was there asking for the nomination of her Judge and Senator, William L. Dayton....

Pennsylvania was there asking for the nomination of her able, aggressive Senator Simon Cameron....

Ohio was there urging the nomination of her splendid specimen of Senator and Statesman, Salmon P. Chase....

Missouri...was there asking for the naming of her eminent Jurist, Judge Edward Bates.

of the other votes—102 of them—that no one else was even close.

On the second ballot, Lincoln picked up even more—largely from Pennsylvania—whereas Bates was slipping badly and Seward seemed to have topped out. Without help from the populous states of Pennsylvania, Illinois, and Indiana, Seward was doomed.

By the third ballot, a final change of four Ohio votes triggered a landslide of switchers wanting to get on the bandwagon. Lincoln had won—his final tally, 132 votes more than was needed.

"There was a noise in the Wigwam like the rush of a great wind," wrote reporter Halstead, describing the moment of victory, "and in another breath the storm was there. There were thousands cheering with the energy of insanity." As the applause continued, a huge photograph of Lincoln was hauled up in front of the crowd and the Wigwam went wild.

"God bless you We are happy & may you ever be," wired a breathless Ward Hill Lamon to his friend Lincoln. "City wild with excitement," added Jesse W. Fell. From the roof of the Wigwam great cannons were fired off, and when the good news reached Springfield, it was immediately greeted by a one-hundred-gun salute. A day of giddy excitement followed for the people of Illinois. Their own Lincoln had won.

In the evening of May 16, a huge crowd gathered outside the candidate's home. They had known him for so long, had seen him come up the hard way, and now they were beaming with pride. Lincoln spoke to them from his front step and then invited as many as could fit to come inside and continue the celebration. A voice in the crowd called out to him, "We will get you a larger house on the fourth of next March."

Summer 1860:
the confident nominee

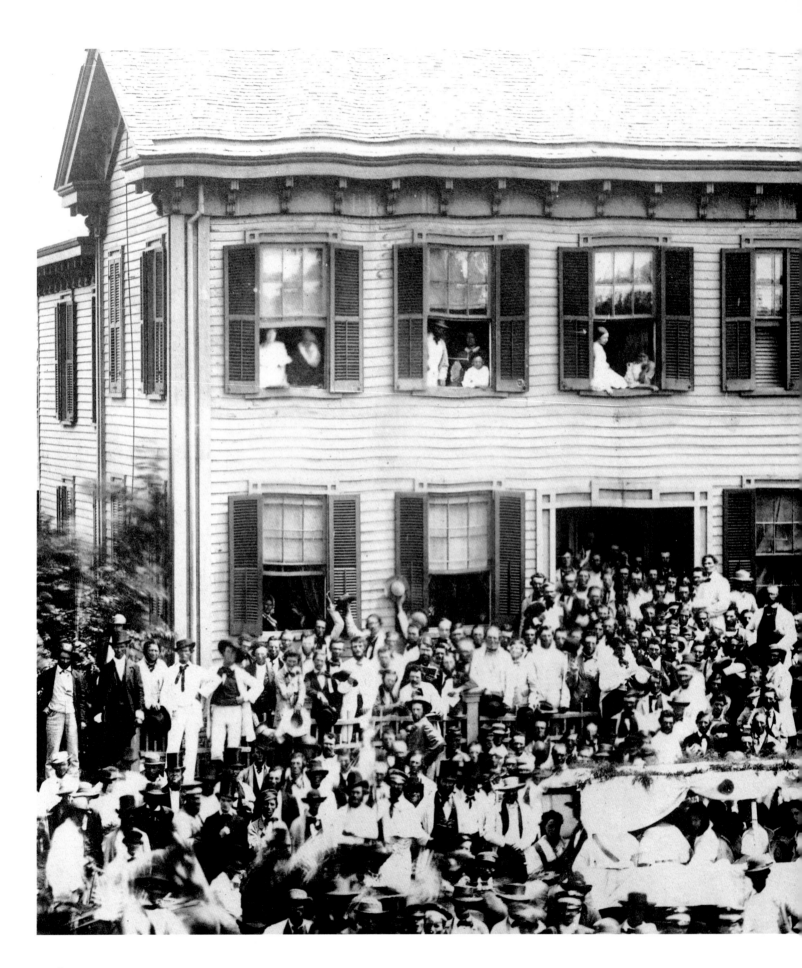

1860 WAS A YEAR SPRINGFIELD WOULD NEVER FORGET

It was the year the city's most prominent citizen was not only nominated for president but elected as well. In between these two extraordinary events was a circus-like summer of small-town pomp and circumstance, of pride and ceremony. Everybody wanted to get close to the local hero, to shake his hand, to catch his smile. One of the glamour events was the August Republican rally that passed the Lincoln home on its way to the fairgrounds, where tubfuls of lemonade and whole steers cooked in pits awaited. The parade was so long it took eight hours to pass the Lincoln home. A photographer who set up his camera across the street caught the spirit of the day, the summer, the Springfield year.

At the right of the doorway in the photograph is the nominee in his white suit. Out of the far-left downstairs window peeks Mary Lincoln in dress bonnet while Willie Lincoln, still shaky from a long bout with scarlet fever, watches from the second floor, second window from the left. The focal point of the parade is a covered wagon with its top rolled up and seating thirty-three maidens dressed in white, representing the states. In a buggy, Kansas follows, hoping to become number thirty-four and holding a sign that asks "Wont you let me in."

These are the very first out-of-door photographs of Lincoln we know of. (Cameras caught him out in the open on only four other occasions in which he is positively identified.) At left is a blowup of a small portion of the parade picture shown on the preceding pages, taken by an unknown photographer on August 8, 1860. The clean-shaven, gaunt nominee in his white suit towers over his friends and neighbors, his tousled hair falling over his forehead and giving him the look of a big man at high noon on a hot August day. *Right:* Taken the same summer, this picture is also an enlargement of a small section of its original negative. Again in front of his house, it shows Lincoln holding on to his picket fence with ten-year-old Willie just below his shoulder and seven-year-old Tad astride the fence and leaning on the corner post.

CAMPAIGN STRATEGY OF KEEPING LINCOLN UNDER WRAPS PAYS OFF

Suddenly, unexpectedly, a local Illinois moderate had become his party's candidate and the nation's probable next president. Not everyone in the North was delighted. Seward, who saw in Lincoln little more than a "country lawyer," and who had warned that he would leave the Republican Party if he were not nominated for president, insisted Lincoln's selection had been based on treachery. The abolitionist Wendell Phillips called Lincoln a mere "huckster in politics," and one Democratic editor, bemoaning Lincoln's lack of credentials, wrote, "His nomination is an outrage on an intelligent people." In fact, despite the huge hullabaloo over Lincoln's nomination, nobody quite knew who this man was: a congressional also-ran without real national stature; "half-horse, half-alligator," mocked one critic, referring to his impoverished background in the woods and on rivers. Few suspected that a great man was on his way to the nation's helm.

By late May, the eyes of the whole nation became fixed on Springfield, and a host of visitors began to pour into the Western city to find out whom they were dealing with. One was William Seward's New York manager, political boss Thurlow Weed, who arrived expecting to detest Lincoln but then was won over by the candidate's sagacity and nerve. After long consultation concerning potential Cabinet members, Weed felt Lincoln "displayed...so much good sense, such intuitive knowledge of human nature, and such familiarity with the virtues and infirmities of politicians that I became impressed very favorably."

By summer, a campaign strategy had been hit upon. Unlike Douglas but following the custom of the day, Lincoln would stay at home in Springfield and let others speak around the country on his behalf. In one sense, he had already passed over the highest hurdle—the nomination. Better now just to remain quiet and let his opponents split their affections three ways among Douglas, John Bell, and John Breckinridge, and thus assure a Lincoln victory. In any case, it was better to risk no trouble in the public eye from those habitually wrinkled suits, that frumpy stovepipe hat, balanced on top of a skeleton-like body and head, or those sweat-stained shirts that one man said were so splotched across his back they looked like "a rough map of the two hemispheres." As "Wide-Awake Clubs" promoting "Old Abe" sprang up around the country, Lincoln himself stayed home pondering the issues.

Election day in Springfield dawned with rousing blasts of cannon fire. Everywhere there was music and excitement. At 3:00 p.m., flanked by Herndon and Ellsworth and Lamon, Lincoln walked over to the polls, passed through a huge crowd in front of the courthouse, cut his own name off the ballot so as not to vote for himself, and then checked off a straight Republican ticket.

He spent the evening with friends in the telegraph office near the Statehouse. By midnight, it was clear that Lincoln had been elected president of the United States. That called for something special—a late-night dinner at the local restaurant in honor of Lincoln and his wife, Mary. But then it was back to the office for more news, as guns fired through the night. It was 1:30 a.m. before Lincoln finally struggled home to catch a bit of sleep. Later, when the huge new fact of his presidency had begun to settle in, he is said to have told a group of friends gathered around him, "Well, boys, your troubles are over now, but mine have just begun." Though he had walloped Douglas in the electoral college by 180 to 12, Lincoln had won just 40 percent of the popular

Campaign buttons and coins *(above)* and a handsome poster for the Republican ticket *(right)*

HON. ABRAHAM LINCOLN, OF ILLINOIS.　　HON. HANNIBAL HAMLIN, OF MAINE,

FOR PRESIDENT.　　FOR VICE PRESIDENT.

THE REPUBLICAN BANNER FOR 1860.

Let the People Rejoice!

CAPITAL SHALL NOT OWN US!

LINCOLN ELECTED!

THE PEOPLE TRUE TO LIBERTY.

When Lincoln won the election, half the nation mourned, while the other half cheered, like this group of Wide-Awakes *(above)*, posing for the camera in Mohawk, New York. *Left inset*: an election headline. *Right*: President-elect Lincoln receives well - wishers and office seekers in Springfield's Statehouse.

vote, making him a minority president and without any support at all throughout the South.

On the day after the election, in Pensacola, Florida, an effigy of Lincoln was hanged by the neck. The South had been poised for this day. Stephen Douglas, the "turn-coat," was bad enough; a thousand times worse was the "nigger-loving" Abraham Lincoln. Newspapers all across Dixie reacted. "The evil days...are upon us," shouted the Dallas *Herald*. "The election of Abraham Lincoln has...put the country in peril," wrote the Richmond *Dispatch*. "The South should arm at once," declared the Augusta *Constitutionalist*.

Now, the country looked as if it were truly coming apart. In Washington, President Buchanan's own government was filled with secessionists. Assistant Secretary of State W. H. Trescott knew of and approved South Carolina's plan to secede as early as November 8. Secretary of War John B. Floyd, in the last weeks before South Carolina's secession, authorized arms purchases for Charleston. "The Cabinet may break up at any moment," wrote his agent Thomas Drayton to South Carolina's governor in late November, "and a new Secretary of War might stop the muskets going south, if not already on their way when he came into office." The week after South Carolina's secession, Attorney General Edwin Stanton accused Floyd of withdrawing a million dollars' worth of bonds from the Interior Department and replacing them with his own notes. Lincoln himself believed that "federal muskets" were being "seized to be used against the government," and that the navy had purposefully been "scattered in distant seas" to render it ineffective in event of civil war. President Buchanan seemed unwilling to do anything more than to accuse Northern abolitionists of causing the nation's troubles.

Back in Springfield, Lincoln complained that his campaign managers had made too many political deals in Chicago; told friends to hold firm on their refusal to compromise on the matter of slavery's extension; and continued to work on piecing together a Cabinet. In filling these all-important posts, he would look not just to campaign supporters such as Caleb Smith, Montgomery Blair, and Gideon Welles, but also to his powerful arch rivals in the party: Seward, Bates, Cameron, and Chase.

Lincoln's daily mail now suddenly began to include a sprinkling of hate letters. Correspondence of all sorts poured in so thick and fast in these last months in Springfield that Lincoln's personal secretary, John Nicolay, had to carry it from the post office by the basketful. If Lincoln missed going through it for even a few days, he had a pile of several hundred letters waiting for him.

Every morning until noon, Lincoln held open house in a room in the State Capitol. People crowded in day after day to gawk and hang about and touch the man and listen to his jokes, amazed that one of their own had been elected president of the United States. Finally, exhausted by the public, and needing time to read and think and write, Lincoln cut back the visiting time to just an hour and a half a day. Perceptive German-born New York *Herald* reporter Henry Villard was amazed Lincoln would keep visiting hours at all. "What his executive abilities are we still have to learn," wrote Villard, as he pondered both Lincoln and the future. "The stuff of which he is made must be as stern as the aspect of our days....I dare say, there are dormant qualities in 'Old Abe' which occasion will draw forth."

Lincoln never owned many books. On returning to Springfield, he intended to read a few of them with law partner, when . . .

GOODBYE TO ALL THE THINGS LINCOLN LOVED BEST

Lincoln, June 1860

The Lincolns'
dog, Fido

The waiting was over; it was time to say goodbye and be off to Washington. Even though Tad pleaded that he could take care of Fido on the trip east, the yellow family dog, who liked to chase his tail and receive scraps at the dining room table, was given to little neighbor Johnny Roll. Mary Lincoln had gone east to New York City in January and had stayed too long buying a new wardrobe. Once returned, she and her sisters and her newly whiskered husband greeted just about the whole town at an evening open

house on Eighth Street. Then belongings were packed away, furniture was sold, the house was rented, and Mary burned old letters in the back alley. Lincoln appeared one evening at the home of Dr. and Mrs. John Todd, elderly uncle of Mary Lincoln, and handed a satchel to his and Mary's favorite cousin, the Todds' daughter Lizzie Grimsley. It contained some of his writings and Lincoln said that if he did not come back she could do with them what she thought best. For their last few days in

Springfield the Lincolns moved to the Chenery House, where Lincoln roped the trunks himself, writing on the labels: "A. Lincoln, The White House, Washington, D.C."

On the morning of February 11, the day before Lincoln's fifty-second birthday, cold rain pelted Springfield. Mary was not in the carriage as Lincoln headed down the streets, through tunnels of well-wishers, toward the station; she and the two smaller boys would join the President-elect and Robert in Indianapolis. Some detractors

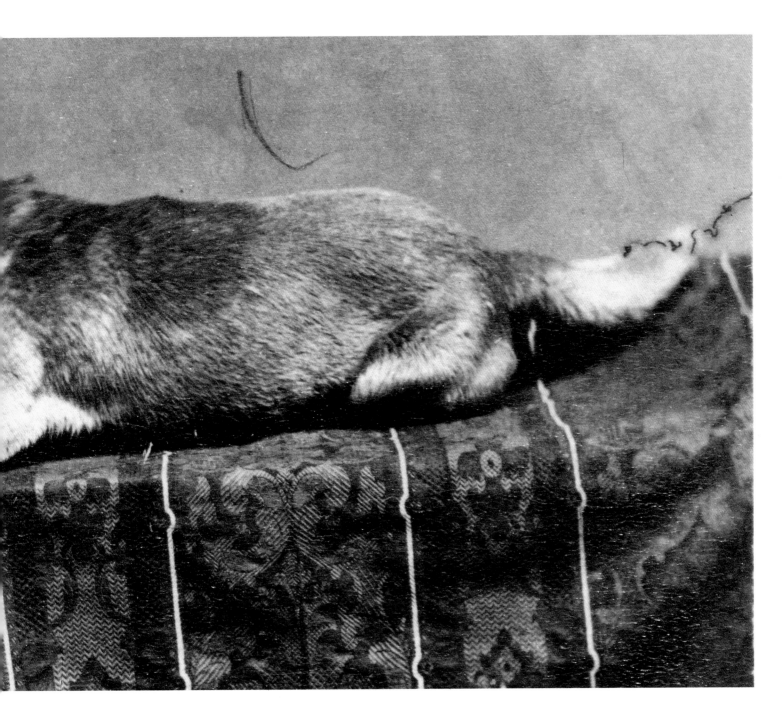

said she had gotten into an argument with her husband that morning and ended up hysterical on the hotel floor. Others heard that, for safety, General Scott in Washington had dictated how the family would travel. Still others recalled Mary at the station that morning, arriving in time to hear her husband's goodbye words.

Less than two weeks earlier, Lincoln had taken a slow train over to Charleston in Coles County, riding part of the way in the caboose of a freight, to say goodbye to his old stepmother, Sarah. She told him through her kisses that she knew she would never see him again, and he mumbled back something about meeting "up yonder." Lincoln had not said goodbye to his father a decade ago when he was dying—Thomas, who had never seen his grandchildren, never even met wife Mary, never, along with Sarah, even been invited to Springfield, though Thomas sent letters begging for a visit, saying he "craved" to see his "only child." Lincoln was too busy. "Tell him to remember to call upon ...our... Maker," he wrote his stepbrother. "Say to him that if we could meet now, it is doubtful whether it would not be more painful than pleasant."

And so there were bad memories, too, never-to-be-explained memories, unbecoming memories, as well as the good. And as Lincoln's carriage arrived at the station, awaiting him was an enormous crowd of well-wishers, each with his or her own set of memories of their prairie friend, all gathered early on this Monday morning in the rain to say goodbye.

LINCOLN'S FAREWELL

On February 11, the morning of his departure from Springfield, Lincoln took breakfast with his family in the dining room of the Chenery House. The drayman, Jameson Jenkins, a mulatto, had picked up the family luggage and brought it to the station and now he was backing his cart up to the baggage car door and unloading the trunks Lincoln had roped himself and the telescopes he had wrapped. Lincoln drove to the station in the hotel hack. It was raining. Afterward, some said it was sleeting and others, like his secretaries, Nicolay and Hay, said there were snowflakes in the air. Lincoln had requested there be no public demonstration, but still several hundred of his friends and neighbors had gathered at the Great Northern Railroad Depot. When Lincoln emerged from the station, his shawl pulled up against the rain, the Hinkley locomotive, the *L.M. Wiley*, that had been chosen to haul the two-car train the first leg of the trip to the Indiana border, was hissing steam and ready to go. Engineer Elias H. Fralick fingered his big, silver Bradley watch. It was 7:55. Lincoln climbed the steps of his special car, turned toward the crowd and removed his hat. Except for two soldiers, all the men before him followed suit. Lincoln's lawyer friend Ward Hill Lamon, who had been borrowed from the Illinois governor's staff, stood at attention on one side of Lincoln. On the other was the much smaller Elmer Ellsworth, the youthful colonel Lincoln had befriended. Together, they were charged with the President-elect's safety on the trip east. "We have known Mr. Lincoln for many years," reported a writer from the Springfield *Journal* present in the crowd. "[W]e have heard him speak upon a hundred different occasions; but we never saw him so profoundly affected....Although it was raining fast when he began to speak, every hat was lifted and every head bent forward to catch the last words of the departing chief." Lincoln had not written down any words for this final moment. He spoke slowly, his voice husky with emotion.

FAREWELL ADDRESS AT SPRINGFIELD, ILLINOIS
FEBRUARY 11, 1861

My Friends—No one, not in my situation, can appreciate my feeling of sadness at this parting. To this place, and the kindness of these people, I owe every thing. Here I have lived a quarter of a century, and have passed from a young to an old man. Here my children have been born, and one is buried. I now leave, not knowing when, or whether ever, I may return, with a task before me greater than that which rested upon Washington. Without the assistance of that Divine Being, who ever attended him, I cannot succeed. With that assistance I cannot fail. Trusting in Him, who can go with me, and remain with you and be every where for good, let us confidently hope that all will yet be well. To His care commending you, as I hope in your prayers you will commend me, I bid you an affectionate farewell.

After shaking many hands in the packed station, a remnant of which is shown above, Lincoln was led through the rain to a special train where he said goodbye to his fellow citizens from the platform of the rear car.

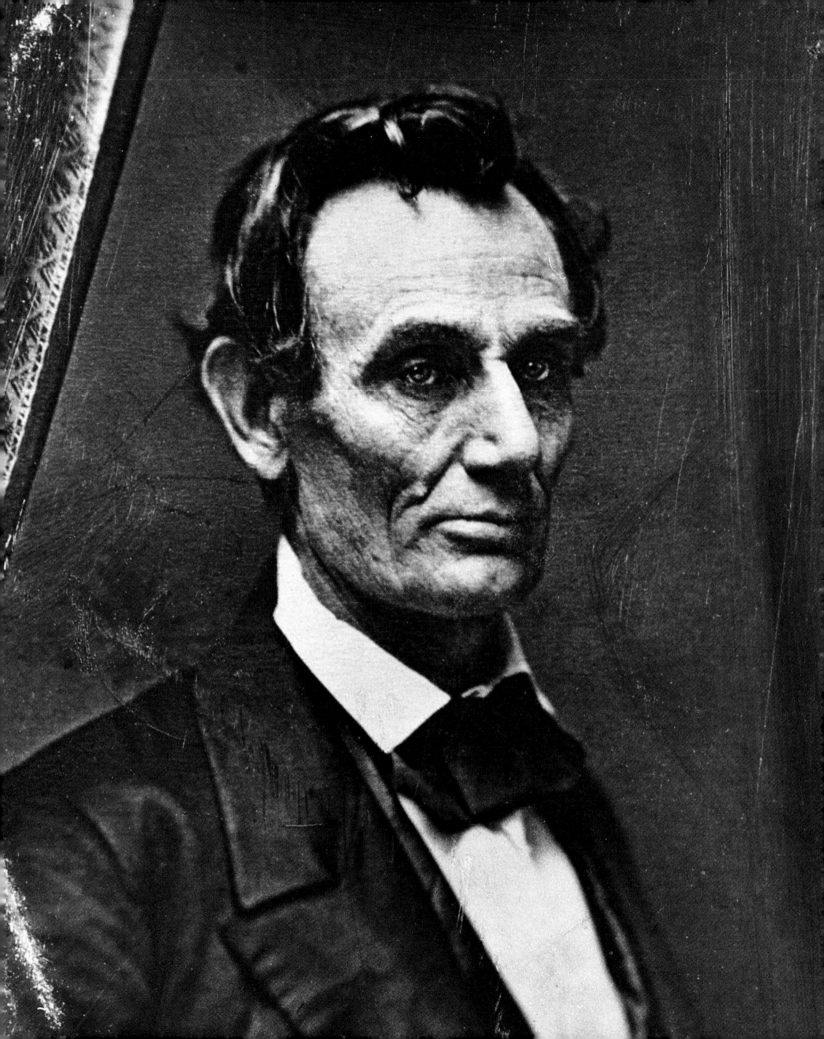

**Transition of a face: from clean-shaven
prairie lawyer to bearded president-elect
about to head east to lead the nation**

PRESIDENCY

The following five chapters provide a calendar of the crucial events of Lincoln's years in office and the people who touched his life.

Lincoln sits for his portrait a few weeks
before the start of the Civil War.

Chapter 5

1861

Lincoln's first
ten months in office
get so bad that once
he says he'd like
to hang himself.

The letter waiting for Lincoln on his first night as president was a desperate report from Major Robert Anderson, commander of the Federal troops at Fort Sumter, the little South Carolina island stronghold in the middle of Charleston's harbor. The newly formed Confederate States of America had suddenly surrounded the fortress with a flotilla of ships and a battery of cannon, and Anderson informed his commander-in-chief that he would run out of supplies by April 15.

The seven opinionated men of Lincoln's new Cabinet were outraged at the actions of the seven states that had formally seceded, but most members still wanted to preserve the peace. At their first important meeting, held at night on March 9, Lincoln asked for their opinions on provisioning the fort, and they returned a week later with their answers: Secretary of State William H. Seward, Attorney General Edward Bates, Secretary of War Simon Cameron, Secretary of the Navy Gideon Welles, and Secretary of the Interior Caleb Blood Smith all advised him not to; Secretary of the Treasury Salmon P. Chase urged restraint; and Postmaster General Montgomery Blair alone advocated the use of force to maintain the fort. Seward, Bates, and Smith even thought that Lincoln should withdraw from Sumter. General Scott sent the President a memorandum on March 28 advising him to evacuate, arguing that it would require 25,000 men and six months' time just to resupply and reinforce this fort.

Lincoln simply could not make up his mind. In part, it was because he scarcely had time to think, the flood of office seekers was so heavy. But by the end of March, Northern newspapers were clamoring that the administration do something about Fort Sumter, which had just over two weeks' provisions left. His advisers hopelessly divided—Blair arguing for the exact opposite of Seward and Welles, and Chase now trying to take both sides—Lincoln finally realized it would be his decision alone. Civil war now seemed unavoidable whatever action he took. On March 28, Lincoln struggled with the situation all night long, and the next day, a newly authoritative president ordered the navy to commence a resupply expedition after April 6. Lincoln had decided neither to evacuate nor to send troops; he would let the South fire the first shot of the war if it wanted to.

MARCH 4 During Lincoln's first month in office the Cabinet meetings are dominated by discussion of Fort Sumter, the last Union outpost in South Carolina *(inset)*. The problem: whether to withdraw the 127 men under Major Robert Anderson *(below)* or to reinforce and fight it out, or possibly just to supply them with provisions.

FORT SUMTER, CHARLESTON HARBOR, SOUTH CAROLINA.—[DRAWN BY AN OFFICER OF MAJOR ANDERSON'S COMMAND.]

MARCH 4 Lincoln's first official act is the appointment of John G. Nicolay as his private secretary.

MARCH 4 The inaugural ball is held in a temporary structure dubbed the "Palace of Aladdin" by the press. It is boycotted by those among the capital's social elite whose sympathies lie with the South.

MARCH 6 Lincoln and Scott meet with the entire Cabinet—Seward, Cameron, Welles, Chase, Smith, Bates, and Blair—but in his diary Attorney General Bates calls this first perfunctory meeting "uninteresting."

MARCH 13 Lincoln forbids Secretary of State Seward to receive officials of seceded states.

MARCH 20 Lincoln's youngest sons, Willie and Tad, come down with the measles.

MARCH 30 When a California delegation insults Lincoln's old friend Edward Baker, now senator from Oregon *(above right)*, the President loses his temper and tosses its recommendations into the fire.

MARCH 30 Worried about nepotism, Lincoln turns down "Lizzie" Grimsley, his wife's cousin, for the job of postmistress of Springfield.

On April 1, William Seward followed up his surreptitious negotiations with the rebels by suggesting to Lincoln that "someone" should relieve the President of the onerous responsibilities of executing a comprehensive foreign and domestic policy. Cutting short the secretary's ambitions to be an American "premier," Lincoln remarked curtly, "If this must be done, *I* must do it."

The fleet to resupply Fort Sumter left New York on April 9, with strict instructions not to attack rebel positions unless they were resisted or the fort itself was bombarded. Unbeknownst to Lincoln, the South had already decided to begin the war. On April 12, at 4:30 a.m., the rebels let loose a volley of shells upon the surrounded fort, and the Civil War had begun.

Three days later, after the fall of Fort Sumter, Lincoln issued a proclamation asking for 75,000 militia volunteers. Northerners flooded the recruitment offices. Searching for a leader to replace the aging Winfield Scott, Lincoln offered the command of the Union Army to Virginian Robert E. Lee. But when Virginia's secession convention voted on April 17 to join the Confederacy, the colonel decided "I cannot raise my hand against my relatives, my children, my home," and Lee went south.

It was one thing to call for volunteers. It was another to bring them to Washington. Four soldiers and nine civilians were killed on April 19 when riots broke out as the 6th Massachusetts Regiment marched through Baltimore. Lincoln was so discouraged by the slow arrival of troops that on April 24 he told the 6th Massachusetts, "I don't believe there is any North. You are the only Northern realities."

Washington itself was totally unprepared for war, with badly needed troops simply absent. For one terrible week in mid-April it appeared that the city might fall. The White House now became a barracks, mail and telegraph services were interrupted, and traitors were everywhere.

Then, on April 25, there was sudden, huge relief as the 7th New York Regiment appeared out of nowhere, marching into town amid banners and music. On the next day, with the arrival of Massachusetts and Rhode Island troops as well, Washington was finally safe. As spring came into full bloom, many predicted a Union victory within ninety days.

APRIL 2 *Correspondent William Howard Russell of the London* Times *is appalled by the state of Washington's chief fortress.* On the return of the steamer I visited Fort Washington, which is situated on the left bank of the Potomac. I found everything in a state of neglect—gun-carriages rotten, shot piles rusty, furnaces tumbling to pieces. The place might be made strong enough on the river front, but the rear is weak, though there is low marshy land at the back. A company of regulars were on duty. The sentries took no precautions against surprise. Twenty determined men, armed with revolvers, could have taken the whole work; and, for all the authorities knew, we might have had that number of Virginians...on board.

APRIL 19 Lincoln gets word that the 6th Massachusetts Infantry, on its way to defend Washington, has been attacked by a Baltimore mob and that at least thirteen are dead.

APRIL 12 At 4:30 a.m. the bombardment of Fort Sumter begins. Wealthy plantation owner and fiery secession advocate Edmund Ruffin *(inset, left)* is given the honor of firing the first shot of the shelling *(inset, right)*. The photograph below shows the fort in partial ruins the day after the shelling.

APRIL 18 Lincoln chooses canny Maryland politician Francis P. Blair *(above)* to offer Robert E. Lee command of the Union forces. Lee refuses; his first loyalty is to Virginia.

APRIL 22 *Three days before Lincoln addresses the following words to a Baltimore delegation, a group of Massachusetts soldiers, en route to relieve Washington, is killed by a Baltimore mob, becoming the war's first casualties. Governor Hicks of Maryland has wired the President not to send any more troops through this city, and a so-called peace delegation has come to Washington to demand that no Union soldiers be allowed to "pollute" any part of Maryland.*

You, gentlemen, come here to me and ask for peace on any terms, and yet have no word of condemnation for those who are making war on us. You express great horror of bloodshed, and yet would not lay a straw in the way of those who are organizing in Virginia and elsewhere to capture this city.... I have no desire to invade the South; but I must have troops to defend this Capital. Geographically it lies surrounded by the soil of Maryland; and mathematically the necessity exists that they should come over her territory. Our men are not moles, and can't dig under the earth; they are not birds, and can't fly through the air. There is no way but to march across, and that they must do.... Keep your rowdies in Baltimore, and there will be no bloodshed. Go home and tell your people that if they will not attack us, we will not attack them; but if they do attack us, we will return it, and that severely.

Three more states, Tennessee, North Carolina, and Arkansas, by now had joined the Confederacy. Their secession and the ongoing violence in Maryland convinced Lincoln that he could neither maintain the Union nor repress the rebellion without a vast show of power from the Federal government. In May, he took the unusual step of increasing the size of the regular army without congressional approval. Even more controversial, amid reports of informers, suppliers, abetters, and spies, he suspended the writ of habeas corpus in Maryland and Florida and elsewhere, allowing for military arrest without showing cause.

The suspension of habeas corpus shocked many of Lincoln's countrymen, for even in the North most Americans mistrusted the idea of massive central government. On May 28, Supreme Court Chief Justice Roger B. Taney, a Marylander, ruled that the current emergency did not justify the President's suspension. But Lincoln, not Taney, commanded the troops, and the army continued to use wartime measures to quell dissent.

Although Lincoln was still spending hours filling Federal appointments, and working hard behind the scenes to hold on to the border states of Kentucky, Missouri, and Maryland, he took advantage of the springtime weather to participate in small rituals and ceremonies around the capital. One day he crossed the Potomac into Confederate Virginia, visiting Great Falls. Twice he passed within yards of secessionist pickets.

On May 23, despite all the hopes, Virginia officially joined the Confederacy. Almost instantly Lincoln ordered the occupation of neighboring Alexandria and Arlington Heights, at the same time making clear to Virginia residents "that they are not to be despoiled." When Lincoln's instructions were carried out, among the buildings occupied was the stately mansion of Robert E. Lee.

The foray was not, however, without cost. Colonel Elmer Ellsworth, a former student in Lincoln's Illinois law office and a close friend of the entire family, commanded one of the regiments that crossed the Potomac River by night and marched into Alexandria. Ellsworth's impulsive act against a Confederate flag brought on his death, and left Lincoln crushed by the senselessness of it all.

MAY Imitating his idol, Tad Lincoln has a Zouave uniform of his own.

MAY 24 Leading his Zouaves in the occupation of Alexandria, Elmer Ellsworth *(left and top right)* climbs to the roof of the Marshall House *(above)*, cuts down a Confederate flag, and, as he comes down the stairs, is shot dead by the hotel-keeper *(right)*.

For more than a month, Lincoln had been galled at the sight of a huge Confederate flag flying over neighboring Alexandria within range of his spyglass. Suddenly Virginia's decision to join the Confederacy was finalized, and the long waiting period was over. To secure the Potomac, the President called for the immediate occupation of Virginia, and gave the job of taking Alexandria to his friend Elmer Ellsworth, commander of the famous New York Zouaves, whom Lincoln had once called "the greatest little man he had ever met."

Following a moonlit raid, and while under march to dismantle the city telegraph lines, Ellsworth caught sight of the giant flag that he knew the President hated, flying from the top of a hotel, the Marshall House. "We must have that thing down," he told his boys. Though it was not part of his orders, Ellsworth climbed to the roof, cut down the flag, and began to carry it down as a trophy of war. *New York Tribune* reporter Edward House witnessed what followed: "While on the second floor, a secessionist came out of a door with a cocked double barrelled shot gun...took aim at Ellsworth...and discharged, lodging a whole load of buckshot in Ellsworth's body, killing him instantly."

News of the incident spread across the river like lightning, reaching Lincoln just moments before he was interrupted by two visitors. "As we entered the library we [saw]...the President standing before a window, looking out across the Potomac.... He did not move till we approached very closely, when he turned round abruptly, and advanced towards us, extending his hand. 'Excuse me,' he said, 'but I cannot talk.'...[Then] the President burst into tears, and concealed his face in his handkerchief."

Later, Lincoln took time to write a letter to Ellsworth's parents:

"...In the untimely loss of your noble son, our affliction here, is scarcely less than your own....My acquaintance with him began less than two years ago; yet...it was as intimate as the disparity of our ages, and my engrossing engagements, would permit.... [He was] my young friend, and your brave and early fallen child.

May God give you that consolation which is beyond all earthly power.

Sincerely your friend in a
common affliction — A. Lincoln"

MAY 19 Aware of Lincoln's interest in the aqueduct on which he had been the chief engineer before the war, Quartermaster General Montgomery Meigs takes the President on a drive to see it. This picture at the great pipe may be of Lincoln, but there is no proof, and it is probably spurious.

MAY 30 Chief Justice Roger B. Taney contends that Lincoln has no right to suspend the writ of habeas corpus and that the military can only make arrests subject to the rules and articles of law. Lincoln and his generals pay little attention to the ruling.

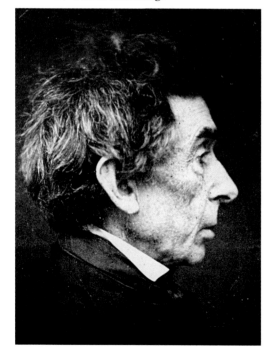

In spite of—or perhaps because of—the personal sense of loss he felt after the death of Elmer Ellsworth, Lincoln was impatient to prosecute the war. He eagerly accepted offers of new regiments from Northern governors, worked his way through books on military strategy, and personally tinkered with new weapons that inventors were trying to sell to the army. "I saw this gun myself," he wrote about one such item, "and I really think it worthy the attention of the Government."

General Scott, however, was not eager to order Union troops into battle. He proposed that Union forces surround the Confederacy on all sides and simply wait. The President had little stomach for Scott's "Anaconda" plan, believing that it could take years to "squeeze" the Confederacy into submission. He wanted action.

On June 29, Lincoln called a meeting at the White House with Scott and General Irvin McDowell, commander of the Union forces in the Potomac area. The President had been poring over maps and had determined that the army should attack a crucial rail junction at Manassas in northern Virginia, twenty miles from Washington.

The generals protested vehemently. Scott insisted that the army could not possibly be ready until fall. McDowell argued that these recently mustered soldiers were still "green." "You are green, it is true," the President replied, "but they are green too; you are green alike." Lincoln felt strongly that he could not afford to allow Northern zeal for the war to slip away through hesitancy and indecision.

JUNE Having arrived in the nick of time to save Washington, the men of the 7th New York Regiment pitch camp outside the capital and spend a quiet month of tenting and maneuvers.

JUNE 13 After reviewing military entrenchments in Virginia, Lincoln walks back over Long Bridge, the planks of which have been removed to discourage enemy cavalry.

MONTH 4

JUNE 3 Stephen A. Douglas, Lincoln's old rival for the hand of Mary Todd, a senate seat, and finally the presidency, dies unexpectedly of acute rheumatism.

JUNE 25 With Confederate General Pierre Gustave Toutant Beauregard *(above)* threatening Washington, Lincoln expresses concern.

JUNE 29 General Irvin McDowell presents Lincoln with a plan for attacking at Manassas.

At a special session of Congress on the Fourth of July, Lincoln presented one of the most carefully thought out papers of his presidency. In it he reviewed the maelstrom of events since his inauguration: the Fort Sumter fiasco, the war's first shots, the huge danger represented by secession. He defended his suspension of habeas corpus, despite Taney's objections, and asked, "[A]re all the laws, *but one*, to go unexecuted, and the government itself go to pieces, lest that one be violated?" The contest, he told Congress, was far bigger than a mere states' rights controversy. It involved a struggle for the preservation of democracy itself, "for maintaining in the world, that form, and substance of government, whose leading object is, to elevate the condition of men." The Union government, he argued, had every right to suppress this illegal rebellion.

Still, Lincoln was determined to preserve the goodwill of the crucial border states. Kentucky, Missouri, Maryland, and Delaware had all stayed within the Union, and over the next several months Lincoln assured slave owners in those states that his war aims would not include tampering with slavery within their borders.

On Sunday, July 21, Union forces under General Irvin McDowell finally followed Lincoln's plan and attacked Beauregard's forces north of the railroad junction near Manassas. The President hurried from church to the landing on the second floor of the War Department where the all-important telegraph office was located. The first news to come in was encouraging: Union forces appeared to be pushing back the Confederates. But by 7:00 p.m. the devastating word had come: the arrival of General Joseph E. Johnston's army had enabled Beauregard to vanquish McDowell, whose men had retreated across a little creek called Bull Run and were in headlong flight toward the capital.

Lincoln interpreted the defeat—and the criticism of his administration that followed —as a sign that he personally had to take more decisive action from then on.

Summoning to Washington a dashing young officer named George B. McClellan, who had won some minor engagements with rebel forces in western Virginia, Lincoln named him Commander of the Division of the Potomac, in charge of all the troops in the vicinity of Washington, D.C.

JULY 18 *Early in July, Lincoln tells Orville Browning that "all the troubles and anxieties" of his life "had not equalled those which intervened between this time and the fall of Sumter." On top of everything else is the daily pressure from office seekers. Gazing out a window toward the White House lawns, Lincoln admits to old friend Robert L. Wilson how desperate he sometimes feels.* Said he had then been President five months, and was surprised [sic] anybody would want the office.... [S]aid he was so badgered with applications for appointments that he thought sometimes that the only way that he [could] escape from them would be to take a rope and hang himself, on one of the trees on the lawn south of the President's House....

JULY 21 The first important battle of the war takes place near Manassas along a sluggish creek called Bull Run, 20 miles southwest of Washington; 847 are killed and more than 2,500 wounded. Union forces retreat over the Stone Bridge *(above)*. Throughout the night Lincoln interviews eyewitnesses and hears of his badly defeated men—"now only a rain-soaked mob."

JULY 27 Searching for a commander who will not allow another Bull Run, Lincoln replaces General McDowell with the promising but untried General George B. McClellan *(right)*. On the heels of the unexpected defeat at Bull Run, Lincoln ponders the disaster, partly due to his own impatience, which pushed ''green'' troops into battle.

George McClellan arrived in Washington, convinced that he had received a popular mandate "to save the country." Plunging into the work of instilling discipline and spirit into the Army of the Potomac, he quickly succeeded in turning the discouraged veterans of Bull Run into an impressive fighting force.

On August 2, McClellan sent Lincoln a memo outlining a plan of war calling for a major advance down the Mississippi in the West, and in the East, a threat to the Confederate seaboard with amphibious forces. Imagining vast Confederate troops arrayed before him in Virginia, McClellan balked at Lincoln's counterproposal of using the forces currently available for a second, quick thrust toward Manassas. Aggrieved, he began complaining in private letters of the "civilian" President's "meddling," and that Winfield Scott was "in his dotage."

Lincoln himself continued to expand the wartime powers of the Federal government. He issued an order forbidding commercial ties with the Confederacy. He approved a Confiscation bill that declared that captured slaves who had been forced to aid the rebel war effort would be freed and put to work by Union military commanders. He insisted on keeping Federal troops in Kentucky despite the protests of its governor. And he signed into law the first income tax in American history, a levy of 3 percent on annual incomes over $800.

The military news continued to be discouraging. Union forces had been pushed back on August 10 at Wilson's Creek, Missouri, and the Union commander, Nathaniel Lyon, had been killed. The new commander of the Department of the West, John C. Frémont, a headstrong anti-slavery advocate, and every bit as self-important as McClellan, could do little to bring order to the bitterly divided state.

On the last day of the month, however, Lincoln was awakened in the middle of the night with the news that Union forces had come from the sea to capture Forts Hatteras and Clark in North Carolina. The President was suffering with fever — even though it was summer, he needed a wood fire in his room — but the news from Carolina was the first hopeful sign that Union forces would not be permanently mired in indecision.

AUGUST 3 When Prince Jerôme Napoléon of France arrives at the White House for a state visit, he is offended to find neither butler nor doorman to show him in. Derisively known as "Plon Plon," the cousin of Emperor Napoléon III is shown here with his wife, Princess Clothilde.

AUGUST 22 Lincoln sends a request to Edward Bates of Missouri, the attorney general, to "please make out pardons in the Missouri cases...and place them in my hands."

AUGUST 6 Lincoln signs a law giving freedom to slaves who are being used by Confederates to help in the war effort. One of the results is a stream of blacks northward, like these fugitive slaves fording the Rappahannock River in Virginia.

Entered according to Act of Congress in the year 1861, by M.B. Brady, in the Clerk's office of the District Court of the U.S. for the So. District of New-York

AUGUST *Black abolitionist Frederick Douglass begins a passionate campaign to convince Lincoln to employ black soldiers in the Union Army.*

Why does the Government reject the negro? Is he not a man? Can he not wield a sword, fire a gun, march and countermarch, and obey orders like any other?...If persons so humble as we can be allowed to speak to the President of the United States we... would tell him that this is no time to fight with one hand, when both are needed; that this is no time to fight only with your white hand, and allow your black hand to remain tied....While the Government continues to refuse the aid of colored men, thus alienating them from the national cause, and giving the rebels the advantage of them, it will not deserve better fortunes [than] it has thus far experienced—Men in earnest don't fight with one hand, when they might fight with two, and a man drowning would not refuse to be saved even by a colored hand.

AUGUST 17 On General Scott's recommendation, Lincoln appoints Henry W. Halleck, known as "Old Brains," a major general.

AUGUST 28 Mary Lincoln's vacation tour with her young boys has already included a "grand hop" given in her honor by the governor of New Jersey and a trip from Albany to Auburn, New York, with Secretary of State Seward. Today she takes in Niagara Falls, which she'd visited years before with her congressman husband on a belated honeymoon.

AUGUST 31 Seward, who has given Lincoln some kittens, spots them playing in the White House hall and remarks, "Mr. L seems quite fond of them. Says they climb all over him."

Unwelcome news arrived from Missouri. General Frémont had imposed martial law on the state, and his proclamation declared that the slaves of all persons found resisting the government would be freed. His edict went well beyond the Confiscation Act, liberating blacks whether or not they were directly involved in the rebel war effort.

Lincoln, in a droll understatement, wrote Frémont that aspects of his proclamation gave him "some anxiety." Sending the general a copy of the Confiscation Act, he gently asked Frémont to modify his own order to conform with it. "This letter," Lincoln concluded, "is written in a spirit of caution and not of censure."

Although the request was polite, the urgency behind it was manifest. Lincoln was already receiving warnings from friends in Kentucky that the overtones of abolitionism in Frémont's edict were reviving the dormant secessionist spirit in the state.

Frémont, however, was intransigent. Bolstered by support from Northern radicals, he refused to change the proclamation unless Lincoln publicly ordered him to do so. Frémont's formidable wife, Jessie, arrived in Washington on the night of September 10 to plead her husband's case. Lincoln immediately summoned her to the White House for a midnight audience. She upbraided the President so strongly that he dismissed her with a thinly disguised insult: "You are quite a female politician." The next day he issued a public order rescinding Frémont's edict, even while writing to Jessie Frémont that he bore no personal ill will toward her husband. Privately, he accused the general of acting like a military dictator.

Border state Unionists were appeased by Lincoln's order, but many anti-slavery Northerners were appalled by what they saw as the President's timidity. Lincoln may be six feet four, muttered longtime abolitionist William Lloyd Garrison, but he is "only a dwarf in mind."

Lincoln's patience continued to be strained by events in the West. Reports of corruption in Frémont's department filtered back to Washington, and Lincoln expressed concern that the general's "cardinal mistake is that he isolates himself." On September 23, rebel forces captured a key Federal garrison in Lexington, Missouri. The situation was deteriorating as rapidly in the West as it had over the summer in the East.

SEPTEMBER 8 General McClellan notes: "Mr. Lincoln came this morning to ask me to pardon a man that I had ordered to be shot, suggesting that I could give as a reason in the order that it was by request of the 'Lady President' [Mrs. Lincoln]." The fortunate man is Private William Scott, sentenced to death for sleeping at his post at Chain Bridge, shown here barricaded against attack.

SEPTEMBER 18 *A letter to Lincoln from his minister to Spain, Carl Schurz*

It is my conviction, and I consider it a duty to communicate it to you, that the sympathies of the liberal masses in Europe are not as unconditionally in our favor as might be desired, and that unless the war end soon or something be done to give our cause a stronger foothold in the popular heart, they will, in the end, not be decided and powerful enough to control the actions of those governments whose good will or neutrality is to us of the greatest importance. When the struggle about the slavery question in the United States assumed the form of an armed conflict, it was generally supposed in Europe that the destruction of slavery was to be the avowed object of the policy of the

SEPTEMBER 11 Reprimanded by Lincoln for insubordination, General Frémont *(right)* sends his wife, Jessie *(left)*, daughter of Thomas Hart Benton, to defend his policies. At midnight she demands an audience and Lincoln replies, "Now, at once."

government, and that the war would, in fact, be nothing less than a grand uprising of the popular conscience in favor of a great humanitarian principle. If this opinion had been confirmed by the evidence of facts, the attitude of Europe, as determined by popular sentiment, could not have been doubtful a single moment. But it was remarked, not without a feeling of surprise and disappointment, that the Federal Government, in its public declaration, cautiously avoided the mentioning of the slavery question as the cause and origin of the conflict; that its acts... were marked by a strikingly scrupulous respect for the sanctity of slave property; and that the ultimate extinction of an institution so hateful to European minds was almost emphatically denied to be one of the objects of the war.

SEPTEMBER 24 General McClellan is determined to make his Army of the Potomac look impressive, which it does at this enormous troop review at Bailey's Crossroads, a few miles from the capital.

SEPTEMBER 27 *General McClellan, in a private letter concerning Winfield Scott*
He [the President] sent a carriage for me to meet him and the cabinet at Gen. Scott's office. Before we got through the general "raised a row with me." I kept cool. In the course of the conversation he very strongly intimated that we were no longer friends. I said nothing, merely looked at him and bowed. He tried to avoid me when we left, but I walked square up to him, looked him fully in the eye, extended my hand, and said, "Good-morning, Gen. Scott." He had to take my hand and so we parted. As he threw down the glove and I took it up, I presume war is declared. So be it. I have one strong point—that I do not care one iota for my present position.

After seven months, Lincoln's administration was in disarray. The Cabinet was meeting almost daily, bickering and frustrated at the slow pace of events. Rumors of corruption in the War Department were circulating in the capital, and the President found Secretary of War Simon Cameron "utterly ignorant and regardless of the course of things." A depressed Lincoln confessed to John Nicolay, his secretary, that "everything in the West, military & financial, is in hopeless confusion."

Rather than tackle those problems head-on, Lincoln devised another war plan on paper. His new idea was for a move on Cumberland Gap in the Appalachians, which would aid mountain Unionists and, secondarily, divert enough Confederate forces to allow McClellan in the East and Frémont in the West to make some genuine headway. But this plan, too, stalled. No memorandum could substitute for active and dynamic command.

More news from the West however, forced the President into action. He received reports from Cabinet members, and then from a congressional subcommittee, that Frémont's department was grossly mismanaging its funds, principally by rewarding inflated contracts to the general's friends. Although there was no evidence that Frémont himself was profiting by these activities, Lincoln reluctantly ordered that he be relieved of his command.

Getting the message to Frémont was not so easy. When Secretary Cameron delivered the news personally in Missouri about October 13, Frémont begged for one last chance to prove his merit on the battlefield. Although the consequent maneuvers were unsuccessful, Frémont used the confusion of war to try to prevent further orders from reaching him. Lincoln's second, and final, letter relieving the general of command had to be delivered by an army officer who crossed Union lines disguised as a farmer.

By this time, Lincoln had received another personal blow. His friend Colonel Edward Baker, whom he had known since early days in Illinois politics, was killed in a disastrous Union defeat on October 21 at Ball's Bluff, Virginia. Lincoln himself was "smote like a whirlwind." Ten-year-old Willie poured out his grief in a poem that was printed in a Washington newspaper. To the President and to many in the North, Baker's death, during a poorly planned advance, seemed to symbolize the futility of the current approach to restoring the Union.

OCTOBER 2 Secretary of War Simon Cameron will last only three more months before corruption catches up to him. Today Lincoln mentions his growing unpopularity.

OCTOBER 3 For the mother of his dear friend Joshua Speed, Lincoln inscribes this photograph of himself, taken last April at Brady's Washington gallery.

OCTOBER 21 In a dispatch about the fighting at Ball's Bluff, Lincoln learns that his great friend Colonel Edward Baker, has been killed in action. The Lincolns' second son, Eddy, who died in 1850 at the age of three, was named after Baker.

OCTOBER 19 The U.S.S. *Pensacola*, shown here at Alexandria, has just been fitted out for naval service. Today Lincoln goes aboard to inspect the changes.

George McClellan finally got his way. On November 1, Lincoln accepted the resignation of Winfield Scott, and named McClellan general-in-chief of all Union forces. When the President warned the general of the "enormous labor upon you," McClellan remained confident. "I can do it all," he insisted.

It was an effort at a clean sweep. Henry Halleck was sent to restore some order to the mess that Frémont had left in the Department of the West. Don Carlos Buell was placed in charge of the newly created Department of the Ohio, with jurisdiction over most of Kentucky and Tennessee.

Lincoln and McClellan remained at odds. The President envisioned hitting the Confederacy at several strategic points: he wanted to secure the Mississippi River, and he wanted Buell to strike at Tennessee. He was particularly anxious to liberate areas in the Appalachian region, where there was strong Unionist sentiment. McClellan, however, stubbornly held out for a concentration of forces in the eastern theater, and resented what he considered the President's civilian tinkering in military matters.

Behind Lincoln's back, McClellan complained that the Cabinet contained "some of the greatest geese I have ever seen," and referred to the President himself as "the original Gorilla." He even snubbed Lincoln openly in his Georgetown home, deliberately striding past the President and the secretary of state on his way upstairs to bed.

Another storm was brewing in November, this one on the high seas. On November 8, a Union warship, enforcing the naval blockade, stopped a British steamer, the *Trent*, in the Atlantic Ocean. The Union captain allowed the ship to continue toward England, but seized two Americans, James Mason and John Slidell, who were headed for Europe to serve as diplomatic representatives of the Confederate States of America.

Many Northerners, irritated at England's official neutrality in the war, were delighted to have the rebel emissaries detained in a Boston prison. But some of Lincoln's strongest supporters, concerned that Britain might be affronted enough to enter the war on the side of the South, pressed for their release. Since there was still no telegraph line under the Atlantic, news and commentary traveled slowly, but the first international crisis of Lincoln's administration had clearly arrived.

NOVEMBER 1 *Opening the way to new and younger military leadership, Lincoln and his Cabinet accept the resignation of Winfield Scott as general-in-chief. In Scott's letter of resignation he explains his decision and praises his President.*

For more than three years I have been unable, from a hurt, to mount a horse or to walk more than a few paces at a time, and that with much pain. Other and new infirmities—dropsy and vertigo—admonish me that repose of mind and body, with the appliances of surgery and medicine, are necessary to add a little more to a life already protracted much beyond the usual span of man... (I)t is with deep regret that I withdraw myself, in these momentous times, from the orders of a President who has treated me with distinguished kindness and courtesy, whom I know among much personal intercourse to be patriotic, without sectional partialities or prejudices, to be highly conscientious in the performance of every duty, and of unrivaled activity and perseverance.

NOVEMBER 15 A cartoon, reproduced on a *carte de visite*, tries to tell the complicated story of the *Trent* Affair, involving the capture and imprisonment of two Confederates on a British ship in neutral waters, which almost draws Lincoln into war with England. Today the President confers with Postmaster General Blair on the subject.

NOVEMBER 3 Having removed General Fremont from command of the Department of the West the day before, Lincoln wires General William K. Strong in St. Louis: "Gen. McClellan is in command of substantially the whole Army, including the Department of the West." Here, General McClellan *(second from left)* poses with his staff.

NOVEMBER 13 *Entry in John Hay's diary*

I wish here to record what I consider a portent of evil to come. The President, Governor Seward, and I, went over to McClellan's house tonight. The servant at the door said the General was at the wedding of Col. Wheaton at General Buell's, and would soon return. We went in, and after we had waited about an hour, McC. came in and without paying any particular attention to the porter, who told him the President was waiting to see him, went up stairs, passing the door of the room where the President and Secretary of State were seated. They waited about half-an-hour, and sent once more a servant to tell the General they were there, and the answer coolly came that the General had gone to bed.

I merely record this unparalleled insolence of epaulettes without comment. It is the first indication I have yet seen of the threatened supremacy of the military authorities.

Coming home I spoke to the President about the matter but he seemed not to have noticed it, specially, saying it was better at this time not to be making points of etiquette & personal dignity.

NOVEMBER 21 Lincoln watches a demonstration of how rapidly a pontoon bridge can be assembled. Achievements like this by the army engineers will be an important element in the Union's future military success.

NOVEMBER 23 Lincoln hurries back from a visit to a flotilla on the Potomac to enjoy the White House performance of Hermann, the great magician. Hermann once put the President in the spotlight by asking him for his handkerchief to use in a trick. "You've got me now," roared Lincoln. "I ain't got any!"

NOVEMBER 26 The President meets with his former rival's widow, Mrs. Stephen A. Douglas, who is worried that her family property in the South may be confiscated.

DECEMBER 8 Lincoln gives approval for a strategic telegraph line from Washington to Fortress Monroe, Virginia. *Below:* Perched on fresh-cut poles, a construction crew strings wires in the field.

Despite the paltriness of the North's military gains, Lincoln sounded optimistic when he delivered his annual message to Congress on December 3. He had raised up a huge standing army and helped prepare for a many-pronged assault upon the South. On the question of slavery, the President was still holding back from "radical and extreme measures," hoping that gradual, compensated emancipation would put a peaceful end to the heinous institution. Such restraint, it was important to consider, had kept the border states still in the Union; indeed, they were contributing troops to its cause. That cause, said Lincoln, was for a "just, and generous, and prosperous system which opens the way for all."

Congress was not overly impressed. Dismayed by the fiascoes at Bull Run and Ball's Bluff, the legislators established a Joint Committee on the Conduct of the War, and then proceeded to train their sight on the sluggishness of George McClellan, now sick with typhoid fever. Many congressmen had also lost patience with the policy of appeasing slave holders. The day after Lincoln's message, the House refused to reaffirm the Crittenden resolution it had almost unanimously passed in July, leaving open the possibility that the destruction of slavery might indeed become a more prominent war aim.

On December 18, a formal message about the *Trent* Affair finally arrived from England. The British expected the immediate release of Mason and Slidell. Lincoln spent his first Christmas Day as president in a tense Cabinet meeting, weighing the embarrassment of giving in to the demands against the threat of having to fight both the Confederacy and the British. Here, as elsewhere, Lincoln believed that posturing was counterproductive. "One war at a time," he remarked.

On the last day of the year, Lincoln met with the new Joint Committee on the Conduct of the War. Republican Senator Ben Wade of Ohio accused him of "murdering" the country with his military policy and his cautiousness on slavery. Lincoln listened respectfully and did not argue, but others privately had to agree that as 1861 came to an end, the military situation remained discouraging.

DECEMBER 18 Congressman Schuyler Colfax of Indiana, later Speaker of the House, warns Lincoln of the public's restlessness over inaction, and urges him to make the army fight.

DECEMBER 21 *Entry in the diary of Attorney General Edward Bates*
Went with the Pres[iden]t, on his invitation to see the erection of a pontoon bridge... It was quickly and beautifully done. We passed over it in the Prest's carriage... and afterwards a battery of 12 lb. field artillery—and some horsemen at the gallop. The Bridge swayed very little, even under the artillery.

Note. Col. Alexander, the commander, said this was the first time he had ever known artillery cross over a *pontoon* bridge, *in America*.

At the same time and place saw a man "walk the water" with each foot in a little water-tight canoe. He carried in his hand a slender paddle, as a help, apparently, both to preserve his erect position and incre[a]se his motion[.]

DECEMBER 11 Escorted to the Senate chamber *(left)* by Illinois Senator Lyman Trumbull *(below)*, Lincoln attends a ceremony in memory of his friend Edward Baker. One congressman estimates it has been twenty five years since the last such presidential visit.

DECEMBER 25 A letter from England's fiery John Bright *(above)* is read to the Cabinet on Christmas morning. To avert war, Bright urges Lincoln to release Confederate prisoners Mason and Slidell seized in the *Trent* Affair.

DECEMBER 29 During the evening Congressman Alfred Ely of New York tells Lincoln about his capture at Bull Run and his six months in a Richmond prison.

DECEMBER 31 *Conservative Edward Bates makes an end-of-the-year assessment.* The Genl: it seems, is very reticent. Nobody knows his plans. The Sec of war and the President himself are kept in ignorance of the actual condition of the army and the intended movements of the General — if indeed they intend to move at all — In fact the whole administration is lamentably deficient in the lack of unity and coaction[.]...

It seemed as if all military operations were to stop, just because Genl McClellan is sick! Some proposed that there should be a council of war composed of Maj. Genls, in order that somebody besides the Genl in chief, may know something about the army; and be able to take command in case Genl McC[lellan] should die or continue sick.

I differed, and told the President that *he* was commander-in-chief, and that it was not his *privilege* but his *duty* to command; and *that* implied the necessity to *know* the true condition of things....

But I fear that I spoke in vain. The Prest. is an excellent man, and, in the main wise; but he lacks *will* and *purpose*, and, I greatly fear he, has not the *power* to *command*.

While the survival of the Union was the overriding issue of the new administration, Lincoln knew that an even deeper conflict lay at the root of the war itself—the future of slavery in the states. Throughout his campaign for president, Lincoln had condemned slavery as a vast moral evil and a blight on the national landscape. His party was the party that denounced the Dred Scott decision, that reaffirmed the "all equal" clause of the Declaration of Independence, and that promised to place slavery on a course toward ultimate extinction. When it came to the question of slavery's spreading, there was "no possible compromise on it," Lincoln insisted to fellow Republicans. "On that point hold firm, as with a chain of steel."

But despite Lincoln's widespread characterization as the "high priest of abolitionism," the new President was not a thoroughgoing radical, demanding immediate freedom for America's 4,000,000 black slaves. For one thing, he owed allegiance to law. "The manner in which our Constitution is framed constrains us from making war upon [slavery] where it already exists," he told an audience in 1860. Politics was a pragmatic art, requiring slow, steady progress toward goals, and oftentimes compromise. Unjust laws, he believed, like the Dred Scott ruling, were to be reversed or altered from inside the system, not through unlawful resistance. Furthermore, there were dangers in the radical abolitionists' methods, he felt. Slavery was like "a snake in a bed where children were sleeping. Would I do right to strike...there? I might hurt the children." As for emancipation itself, from early on Lincoln favored it only if linked to financial compensation to slave owners. In his

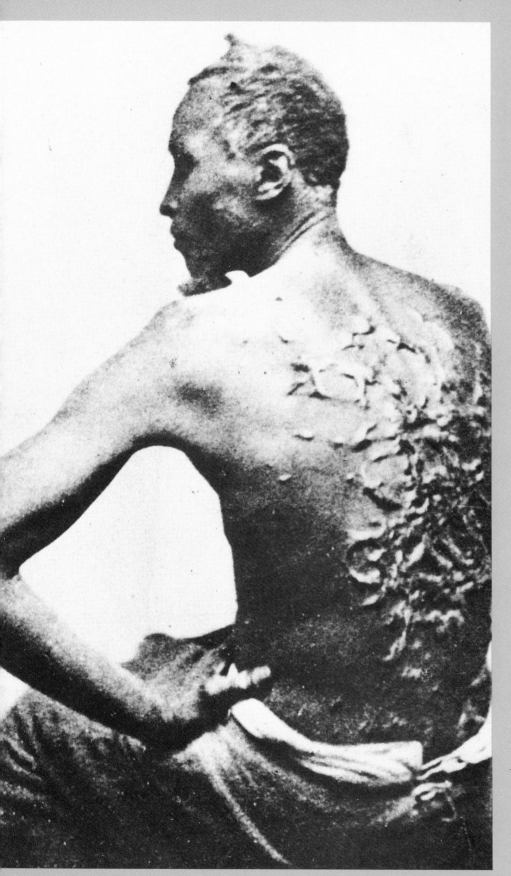

inaugural address on March 5, Lincoln reiterated an assurance to the slave states: "I have no purpose, directly or indirectly, to interfere with the institution of slavery...where it exists. I believe I have no lawful right to do so...." And that is how things would have remained, had not the outbreak of war changed all the rules.

Even so, with men fighting and dying, Lincoln's first year in office was filled with caution and contemplation. If the slaves were freed too precipitously, he believed, the key slave-holding border states of Kentucky, Maryland, Delaware, and Missouri would join the rebellion. It would be far better to offer an equitable package of Federal compensation to these loyal slave states. At the rate of $400 apiece, every slave in Delaware, Maryland, Washington, D.C., Kentucky, and Missouri could go free and the cost would be only that of running the war for just eighty-seven days ($174,000,000).

As usual, Lincoln carved out a path all his own, refusing to be swayed by extremists on either side of him. In August, he alienated conservatives by signing into law the Confiscation Act, allowing the army to seize Southern slaves for military purposes. But in September, it was the liberals who were agitated, after Lincoln rescinded General Frémont's unauthorized military proclamation of emancipation in Missouri. Giving freedom to the slaves was to be *Lincoln's* prerogative, and nobody else's. By year's end, as fugitive slaves continued to pour northward seeking refuge, even such a critic as Charles Sumner, the distinguished radical senator from Massachusetts, who had earlier called Lincoln a... "dictator," had come at the very least to appreciate the President's sincerity.

Two faces of slavery: the kindly, loyal former slave in charge of Robert E. Lee's granddaughter Tabb Bolling; and the scarred back of the slave "Gordon," whose wounds were inflicted in 1862 during a Christmas Day whipping.

167

In one of his most thoughtful and least well-known public writings, delivered to Congress on July 4, 1861, Lincoln meditates on the meaning of the newly begun war.

It might seem, at first thought, to be of little difference whether the present movement at the South be called "secession" or "rebellion." The movers, however, well understand the difference. At the beginning, they knew they could never raise their treason to any respectable magnitude, by any name which implies *violation* of law. They knew their people possessed as much of moral sense, as much of devotion to law and order, and as much pride in, and reverence for, the history, and government, of their common country, as any other civilized, and patriotic people. They knew they could make no advancement directly in the teeth of these strong and noble sentiments. Accordingly they commenced by an insidious debauching of the public mind. They invented an ingenious sophism, which, if conceded, was followed by perfectly logical steps, through all the incidents, to the complete destruction of the Union. The sophism itself is, that any state of the Union may, *consistently* with the national Constitution, and therefore *lawfully,* and *peacefully,* withdraw from the Union, without the consent of the Union, or of any other State. The little disguise that the supposed right is to be exercised only for just cause, themselves to be the sole judge of its justice, is too thin to merit any notice.

With rebellion thus sugar-coated, they have been drugging the public mind of their section for more than thirty years: and, until at length, they have brought many good men to a willingness to take up arms against the Government the day *after* some assemblage of men have enacted the farcical pretence of taking their State out of the Union, who could have been brought to no such thing the day *before....*

Our adversaries have adopted some Declarations of Independence; in which, unlike the good old one, penned by Jefferson, they omit the words "all men are created equal." Why? They have adopted a temporary national constitution, in the preamble of which, unlike our good old one, signed by Washington, they omit "We, the People," and substitute "We the deputies of the sovereign and independent

States.'' Why? Why this deliberate pressing out of view, the rights of men, and the authority of the people?

This is essentially a People's contest. On the side of the Union, it is a struggle for maintaining in the world, that form, and substance of government, whose leading object is, to elevate the condition of men — to lift artificial weights from all shoulders — to clear the paths of laudable pursuit for all — to afford all, an unfettered start, and a fair chance, in the race of life. Yielding to partial, and temporary departures, from necessity, this is the leading object of the government for whose existence we contend.

I am most happy to believe that the plain people understand, and appreciate this....

It was with the deepest regret that the Executive found the duty of employing the war-power, in defence of the government, forced upon him. He could but perform this duty, or surrender the existence of the government. No compromise, by public servants, could, in this case, be a cure; not that compromises are not often proper, but that no popular government can long survive a marked precedent, that those who carry an election, can only save the government from immediate destruction, by giving up the main point, upon which the people gave the election. The people themselves, and not their servants, can safely reverse their own deliberate decisions. As a private citizen, the Executive could not have consented that these institutions shall perish; much less could he, in betrayal of so vast, and so sacred a trust, as these free people had confided to him. He felt that he had no moral right to shrink; nor even to count the chances of his own life, in what might follow. In full view of his great responsibility, he has, so far, done what he has deemed his duty. You will now, according to your own judgment, perform yours. He sincerely hopes that your views, and your action, may so accord with his, as to assure all faithful citizens, who have been disturbed in their rights, of a certain, and speedy restoration to them, under the Constitution, and the laws.

And having thus chosen our course, without guile, and with pure purpose, let us renew our trust in God, and go forward without fear, and with manly hearts.

Union cannonballs piled by a magazine

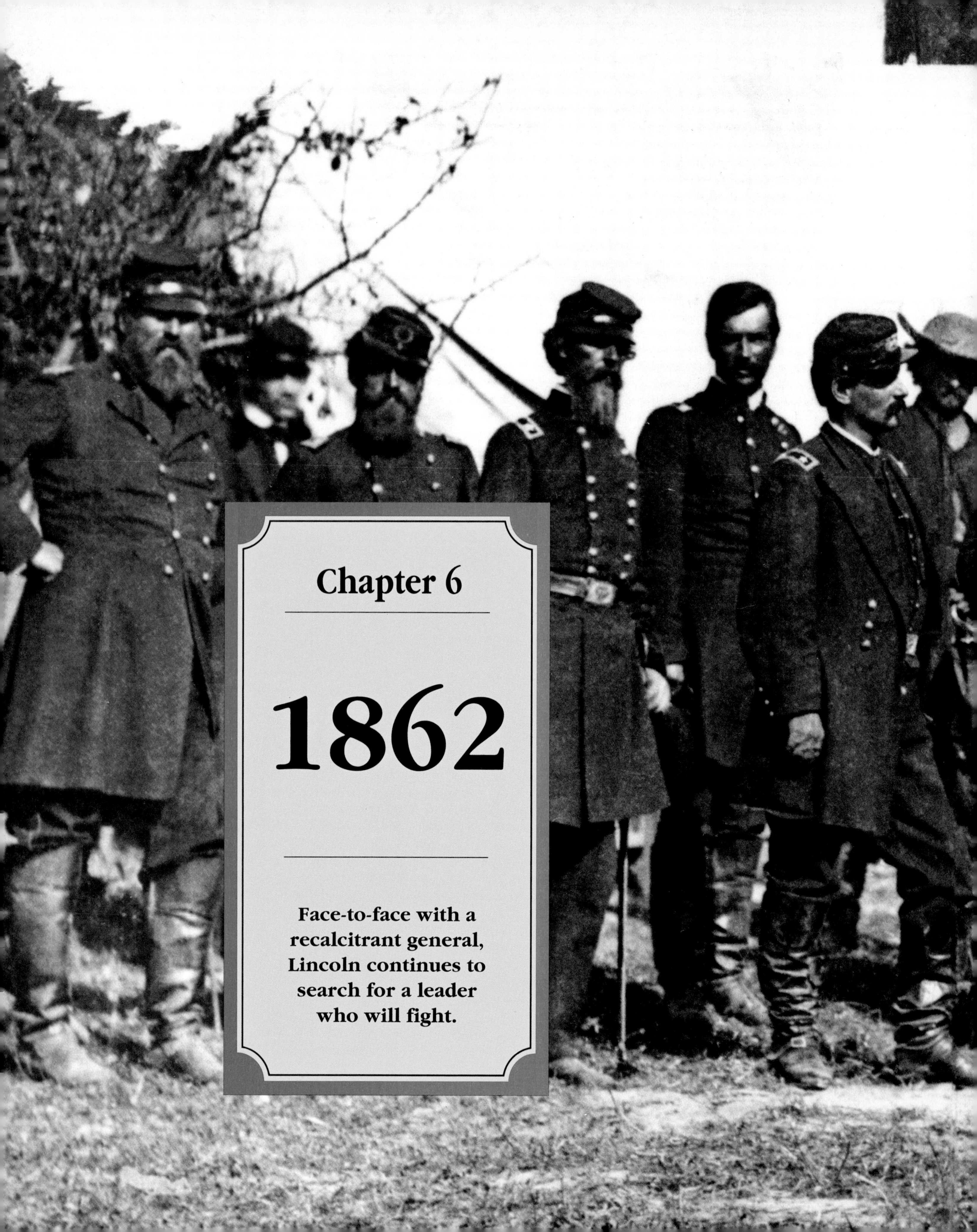

Chapter 6

1862

Face-to-face with a
recalcitrant general,
Lincoln continues to
search for a leader
who will fight.

In a showdown near Harpers Ferry after Antietam, Lincoln poses with General George B. McClellan *(facing him)* and staff.

By the beginning of 1862, the stench of corruption in the War Department had finally become intolerable. Among other travesties, so-called military expenses had included the purchase of straw hats and linen pantaloons; and the department had spent more than $100,000 on each of two warships that the navy rejected as unsafe. On January 11, Lincoln succeeded in easing Secretary of War Simon Cameron out of the Cabinet by offering him the post of minister to Russia. In his place, the President named Edwin M. Stanton, a prickly, dynamic lawyer who had been Buchanan's attorney general and who had a reputation for both harshness and indisputable integrity. "This army has got to fight," Stanton insisted. "The champagne and oysters on the Potomac must be stopped." On January 13, a major council of war was called behind McClellan's back. The Cabinet was ready to force the general to act or else relieve him of duty. Hearing of the meeting, McClellan roused himself from his sickbed and attended uninvited. When Secretary Chase demanded of him a full disclosure of his military plans, McClellan balked, refusing to answer to anyone but the President. But Lincoln himself was still hiding behind his officers, unable yet to fully assume his role as commander-in-chief. Once again, in public, he refused to force the general's hand.

But on January 31, Lincoln issued his Special War Order Number One, requiring McClellan's Army of the Potomac to march on Manassas Junction, and to begin no later than February 22. On its face, War Order Number One was impractical: it made no allowances for weather conditions, military readiness, or even the position of the enemy. Nevertheless, its specificity had to provoke McClellan into some sort of response.

"HE MUST TALK TO SOMEBODY"

JANUARY 10 *From General Irvin McDowell's minutes*
The President was greatly disturbed at the state of affairs. Spoke of the exhausted condition of the treasury; of the loss of public credit; of the Jacobinism in Congress; of the delicate condition of our foreign relations; of the bad news he had received from the West, particularly as contained in a letter from General Halleck on the state of affairs in Missouri; of the want of cooperation between Generals Halleck and [Don Carlos] Buell; but more than all, the sickness of General McClellan.

The President said he was in great distress . . . and as he must talk to somebody, he had sent for General Franklin and myself. . . .

To use his own [Lincoln's] expression, "If something was not soon done, the bottom would be out of the whole affair"; and if General McClellan did not want to use the army, he would like to borrow it, provided he could see how it could be made to do something.

JANUARY 13 The President replaces Simon Cameron as secretary of war, appointing in his place Edwin M. Stanton, who once referred to Lincoln as "that giraffe" when they were opposing counsel in the 1855 McCormick Reaper case.

JANUARY 10 After an unproductive Cabinet meeting, Attorney General Edward Bates blames the general confusion on Lincoln's weak leadership.

JANUARY 10 General Montgomery C. Meigs reports that the "President comes to me much depressed re inactivity of army and McClellan's sickness" and that Lincoln tells him, "The bottom is out of the tub."

JANUARY 12 In an evening meeting, Lincoln confides to his friend Orville Browning that he is so impatient with the war effort he is thinking of leading an army into the field himself.

SITTING MUTE

JANUARY 13 *General Montgomery Meigs records the showdown between McClellan and the Lincoln Cabinet.*

I moved my chair to the side of McClellan's and urged him, saying, "The President evidently expects you to speak; can you not promise some movement towards Manassas? You are strong." He replied, "I cannot move on them with as great a force as they have." "Why, you have near 200,000 men, how many have they?" "Not less than 175,000 according to my advices." I said, "Do you think so?" and "the President expects something from you." He replied, "If I tell him my plans they will be in the *New York Herald* tomorrow morning. He can't keep a secret, he will tell them to Tad." I said: "That is a pity, but he is the President,—the Commander-in-Chief; he has a right to know; it is not respectful to sit mute when he so clearly requires you to speak. He is superior to all."

JANUARY 26 With mortar production slowing down the Union war effort, Assistant Secretary of the Navy Gustavus V. Fox *(inset)* reports that Lincoln has decided "to take these army matters into his own hands."

McClellan parried Lincoln's War Order with a plan of his own: he would circumvent the rebel forces by moving his army by water to the Rappahannock River and take Richmond from the rear. Happy that McClellan was offering something, Lincoln agreed not to enforce his own plan.

More decisive military news, however, was coming from other parts of the country. On February 8, General Ambrose E. Burnside led a successful assault on Roanoke Island, the key to controlling the North Carolina coast. Even more significant, Federal forces took Fort Donelson in Tennessee on February 16. The little-known Union general who refused to negotiate with the rebels in that battle won a national reputation as "Unconditional Surrender" Grant. The Fort Donelson victory led to the occupation on February 25 of Nashville, a strategic center that Union forces would hold for the rest of the war.

In this month, however, the war receded to the background of the life of Abraham Lincoln. Eleven-year-old Willie Lincoln came down with a mysterious fever early in February and was confined to bed. By February 13, eight-year-old Tad Lincoln was sick too. The doctors assured their anxious parents that there was nothing to worry about, but both remembered keenly the death of their second child almost exactly twelve years earlier. Lincoln spent long hours by Willie's bedside, stroking his son's hair and trying to comfort him. "The President is nearly worn out, with grief and watching," wrote Attorney General Bates.

Willie Lincoln died on February 20 at five o'clock. "[M]y boy is gone—he is actually gone!" cried out Lincoln to John Nicolay. Mary collapsed into a frenzy of grief and remained in seclusion for days, unable even to attend the boy's funeral. Tad, fortunately, was on the mend by the time Willie was laid to rest in Oak Hill Cemetery in Georgetown. Among the letters of condolence to Lincoln was a note from General McClellan: "You have been a kind friend to me in the midst of . . . great cares and difficulties. . . . I wish now only to assure you and your family the deepest sympathy in your affliction."

FEBRUARY 2 Poet and philosopher Ralph Waldo Emerson visits the White House, and finds Lincoln to be a "frank, sincere, well-meaning man . . . not vulgar, as described; but with a sort of boyish cheerfulness."

FEBRUARY 5 Mary Lincoln hosts the first White House ball, for which she sent out 800 invitations. The elaborate bill of fare for midnight supper includes oysters, pâté de foie gras, and canvasback duck. Fancy pieces of confectionery are displayed upon a mirror in the center of

FEBRUARY 14 Lincoln anxiously awaits word from General Grant on the fighting at Fort Donelson on the Cumberland River in Tennessee. Armored ships like the *Galena (above)* helped the Union eventually to take command of the vital western rivers.

the dining room table. A large helmet, in sugar, signifies War, and a replica of Fort Pickens made of sugared cake is filled with candied quail. "Most superb affair of its kind ever seen here," comments the Washington *Star*.

FEBRUARY 16 When the Confederate general inside Fort Donelson, sensing defeat, sends a message and asks for terms, Ulysses S. Grant replies, "No terms except unconditional and immediate surrender." Grant *(left)* conducts operations at Fort Donelson from his temporary headquarters at the home of Jared Crisp *(above)*.

FEBRUARY 20 The Lincolns' eleven-year-old son, Willie, dies of what is called the "bilious fever," but which is probably either typhoid or acute malarial infection. For days Mary Lincoln is beside herself, confined to her room as Cabinet members and wives call. The body of Willie lies in state in the Green Room, the first White House funeral for a child is conducted in the East Room, and on a windy, stormy day the President places Willie's body in a borrowed vault at Georgetown's Oak Hill Cemetery. "My poor boy," Lincoln says. "God has called him home. I know that he is much better off in heaven, but then we loved him so. It is hard, hard to have him die."

No sooner had Lincoln given his grudging approval to McClellan's Urbana plan than the idea became obsolete. McClellan had hoped to sidestep Confederate forces at Manassas, and strike Richmond unexpectedly from the east. On March 9, however, the rebel forces withdrew toward their capital city.

At the same time, the Union's uncontested supremacy on the seas came under assault, in the figure of an ironclad ship called the *Virginia,* but better known by her original name, *Merrimac.* On March 8, the mammoth vessel launched its attack on Union ships in Hampton Roads, Virginia, driving right through the fifty-gun *Cumberland* and destroying the *Congress.* Panic swept through Washington as rumors flew that the rebel ship might steam up the Potomac and threaten the capital.

Early on the morning of March 9, however, the Union's own ironclad, the *Monitor,* appeared on the scene. Many experts had ridiculed the ship and its eccentric designer, John Ericsson, but Lincoln had taken a personal interest in its hasty construction during the last months of 1861. The *Monitor* was not entirely seaworthy, but its small size and revolving gun turrets gave it more maneuverability than its lumbering cousin. For more than four hours the ships bounced shot off each other's hulls. In the end, they fought to a draw, and the *Merrimac* withdrew to Norfolk. The capital and the Union blockade were out of danger.

Not so George McClellan. The evacuation of Manassas had spurred widespread criticism of the general in the North. On March 11, Lincoln relieved McClellan of the position of general-in-chief, ostensibly to allow him free rein to concentrate on leading the Army of the Potomac against Richmond.

McClellan came up with still another strategy; he proposed to Lincoln on March 13 that he would ferry the Army of the Potomac all the way down to the mouth of Chesapeake Bay, to Fortress Monroe on the James River Peninsula, and then attack Richmond from the southeast. Lincoln had his doubts, but again assented, on the condition that McClellan leave sufficient forces in place to defend Washington. On March 17, the first ships embarked from Alexandria, Virginia, beginning what would become known as the Peninsula campaign.

M - No. 64

MARCH 4 When the President appears before the Committee on the Conduct of the War at the Capitol, he cannot fail to notice the unfinished dome. Construction has been suspended for a year because "the new government has no money to spend except on self-defense." Now Lincoln is extremely anxious that Congress appropriate funds so that the hoisting of the final pillars *(below)* can start up again. "It is a sign we intend the Union to go on," says Lincoln, shown here in a picture taken this spring.

MARCH 9   The *Monitor* and the *Merrimac* engage off Hampton Roads, Virginia. The wrecks of the *Congress* and the *Cumberland,* destroyed the previous day by the *Merrimac,* can be seen in the distance. Back in Washington, Lincoln calls an emergency Cabinet meeting to discuss how to protect the capital if the *Merrimac* should succeed in its mission and head up the Potomac. Plans to block the river channel are revealed. Finally, news arrives that the *Monitor* has prevailed and that the *Merrimac* has withdrawn.

MARCH 10   Lincoln "bursts into tears" when he pays a visit to Lieutenant Commander John L. Worden *(above right),* the commander in charge of the *Monitor,* who suffered a serious eye injury in the previous day's battle. The *Monitor*'s deck *(above)* is so low to the water, Secretary of the Navy Welles says, "that it could be boarded and captured very easily." But the small size of the Union ironclad makes it an elusive target, and its revolving gun turret makes it light, quick, and lethal.

Americans had found the war enraging, frightening, and tragic over the course of its first year, but it took the staggering slaughter of the Battle of Shiloh to demonstrate its full horror. On April 6 and 7, Union forces under Ulysses S. Grant battled Confederate troops under Albert Sidney Johnston at the tiny Tennessee crossroads of Pittsburg Landing (Shiloh). Two days of fighting left a carpet of casualties: more than 3,000 men dead and over 20,000 wounded or missing out of the 80,000 soldiers from both sides who fought there. Among the dead was Mary Lincoln's half-brother, Samuel B. Todd, a Confederate officer. Critics of Grant's character and of the enormous bloodshed incurred at Shiloh pressed for the firing of the Western general. "I can't spare this man," Lincoln answered. "He fights."

On the Peninsula, McClellan was offering more excuses. Federal troops had by now learned that many of the elaborate fortifications that intimidated McClellan at Manassas had been fakes. Where the general believed that 175,000 rebel soldiers were deployed, there had probably been no more than 75,000. Now once again, as he commenced a cautious siege of Confederate-occupied Yorktown, McClellan was vastly overestimating its 15,000 rebel defenders, and pleading for more troops and supplies. On his end, Lincoln was less and less inclined to defer to his generals, other military experts, or Cabinet members. Ever since February he had thrown himself into a more aggressive leadership of the war—as if Willie's death had given him an ultimatum: become master of events, or descend into darkness. He had begun an almost daily inspection of new weapons systems, and, borrowing books from the Library of Congress, had attempted to train himself in the art of war. Now he fired back letters to his discontented General McClellan. "Your dispatches complaining that you are not properly sustained, while they do not offend me, do pain me very much," Lincoln wrote. "I have never written you, or spoken to you, in greater kindness of feeling than now....*But you must act*."

No. 194.—THE TOMB OF WASH

APRIL 2 Lincoln and his family travel by steamer to Mount Vernon, Virginia, where George Washington lived and is buried in this vault. The President remains on the boat.

APRIL 6–7 In the savage fighting near Shiloh Church in southern Tennessee, more men are killed than in all three of America's previous wars combined. One of them is Albert Sidney Johnston *(inset)*, a brilliant Confederate commander, who is hit in the leg while fighting near the Peach Orchard *(above)* and in minutes bleeds to death. Another is Mary Lincoln's half-brother, Samuel B. Todd.

APRIL 2 John Ericsson *(above)*, the ornery engineer who was the principal designer of the U.S.S. *Monitor*, is introduced to the President by Assistant Secretary of the Navy Gustavus Fox.

APRIL 4 Always seeking money, Mary Lincoln *(above left)* feels she is doing the job of a White House steward and therefore ought to get his salary. Today she instructs her husband's assistant secretary John M. Hay *(above right)* to pay her accordingly.

APRIL 24 Seventeen Federal ships, under the command of Flag Officer David Farragut *(above right)*, successfully move upstream past Forts Jackson and St. Philip on the Mississippi River, making possible the capture of New Orleans the next day. Back in Washington, a breathless Gideon Welles rushes to tell Lincoln the news.

On May 1, General Benjamin F. Butler assumed command of the occupation of New Orleans, determined to blot out secessionist sentiment there. When Butler ordered that any Southern female caught showing "contempt for any officer or soldier of the United States" should be "treated as a woman of town plying her avocation," Confederates railed against what they considered an insult to Southern womanhood, and Butler became known throughout the region as the "Beast" of New Orleans.

In the occupied coastal areas of South Carolina, General David Hunter issued his Order Number 11 on May 9 declaring all slaves in his jurisdiction to be free. This action, like Frémont's proclamation in Missouri the previous August, was at cross-purposes with Lincoln's policy, so the President nullified Hunter's order ten days later. Urging the border states to support compensated emancipation, Lincoln wrote, "The change it contemplates would come gently as the dews of heaven—not rending or wrecking anything."

At dusk on May 5, Lincoln left Washington to spend five days in the field as commander-in-chief, taking with him a mini War Cabinet. On May 8, he watched shelling from a tugboat near Fort Wool, and on May 9 he personally searched the coastline for the ideal landing site for an assault on the city of Norfolk, its harbor ominously guarded by the ironclad ship *Virginia*. On May 10, Norfolk fell. Lincoln's increasing confidence in the field was showing.

Back in Washington, while the war news continued to dominate the headlines, Lincoln quietly put his signature to one of the most far-reaching acts of American history. On May 20, he approved the Federal Homestead Law, which offered 160 acres of publicly owned land to anyone who would claim, occupy, and improve the property for a period of at least five years. Thousands of people crossed the Mississippi to stake their claim and tame the Wild West.

In the last week of May, Stonewall Jackson appeared in the Shenandoah Valley, hammering surprised Union forces at Fort Royal and Winchester, Virginia. Lincoln, thinking he saw an opportunity to cut off Jackson's army and capture it, wired McClellan a stinging command: "[Y]ou must either attack Richmond or give up the job and come to the defence of Washington. Let me hear from you instantly."

MAY 1 Taking over the occupation of New Orleans after helping to overrun the proud city, General Benjamin F. Butler is fair game for newspaper artist Thomas Nast. Swift to arrest and imprison, the military governor tries to control every aspect of the city and its citizens, and they, in turn, spit back at Butler, the flag, and anything Yankee. With a few deft lines, Nast captures the bald, sleepy-eyed, power-hungry "Beast," whom even trusting Lincoln does not trust.

MAY 5 At dusk, after a full day of interviews, appointments, and studying a new breech-loading carbine, the President, with Secretaries Stanton and Chase, leaves on a special cutter down the Potomac for a week-long stay at Fortress Monroe, Virginia *(above)*, the headquarters for the Peninsula campaign.

MAY 9 General David Hunter orders the emancipation of slaves in Union-occupied areas of Florida, Georgia, and South Carolina, but Lincoln overrules him, saying that "neither General Hunter, nor any other commander, or person, has been authorized by the Government of the United States, to make proclamations declaring the slaves of any State free."

MAY 31 General Joseph E. Johnston, commander of the Confederate Army, is badly wounded in the Battle of Fair Oaks—good news to General McClellan, for he considers Johnston a formidable foe.

The Battle of Fair Oaks, or Seven Pines, was concluded on June 1. A Confederate surprise attack had been thwarted but McClellan was shaken by the carnage. Though the Union forces gained little, the action did produce one significant development. Confederate General Joseph E. Johnston, wounded in the field, was replaced on June 1 by General Robert E. Lee. McClellan was unconcerned, even a bit exultant about the change in command; he believed his new counterpart "timid and irresolute in action."

On June 13 Abraham Lincoln and his family left the White House for the cool of their summer residence, a large cottage on the grounds of the Soldiers' Home, a few miles away. There the President turned his thoughts once again to the question of slavery. Six days later he signed into law a measure that prohibited slavery in the unorganized territories of the United States, thereby defusing the issue that had inflamed the nation throughout the 1850s. On June 20, Lincoln admitted to an anti-slavery Quaker delegation that he "sometime thought that perhaps he might be an instrument in God's hands of accomplishing a great work and he certainly was not unwilling to be."

The Peninsula campaign still refused to bear fruit. General Jeb Stuart embarrassed McClellan by leading 1,200 rebel cavalry on a four-day swing all the way around the Army of the Potomac. Then, on June 25, with McClellan's troops just miles from Richmond, Lee initiated the bloody series of engagements around the Confederate capital that was to become known as the "Seven Days."

By June 27, even though he had suffered no major setbacks, McClellan was withdrawing his troops from near the York River to a new base of operations on the James River, and pleading for more reinforcements. The general blamed Lincoln for withholding too many troops to defend Washington, and in his messages from the front he was determined to deflect the responsibility for his failures in the field. "If I save this Army now," McClellan telegraphed Stanton, "I tell you plainly that I owe no thanks to you or any other persons in Washington—you have done your best to sacrifice this Army." The War Department staff, shocked by the general's brazenness, deleted these sentences from Lincoln's copy of the message.

JUNE 1 While the President is meeting with generals and senators in the War Department to review late news from the front, the wounded Joseph E. Johnston is replaced by Robert E. Lee, who soon renames his force the Army of Northern Virginia. Even though the fifty-five-year-old Lee fails to win a victory at the Battle of Fair Oaks, this shift in command is ominous for the Union, for now it must fight against a truly great military leader.

JUNE 1 Having already sent Lincoln a telegraph message from high above Washington, inventor Thaddeus S.C. Lowe inflates a hot-air balloon similar to the one he had wired up to the White House, this one to be used as a military observation post at Gaines's Mill, Virginia.

JUNE 18 After riding horseback together to the Soldiers' Home, Lincoln and Hannibal Hamlin take dinner and then, retreating behind locked doors, Lincoln reads a draft of the preliminary Emancipation Proclamation to the Vice President.

JUNE 27 As the Seven Days' Battles are beginning at Mechanicsville and Gaines's Mill, Virginia, Lincoln, who has just placed General Frémont's forces under General John Pope, now relieves Frémont *(left)* of his command in an army shake-up.

JUNE 28 Union wounded and dying huddle at Savage Station after the previous day's battle at Gaines's Mill, where General Fitz-John Porter's Fifth Corps held off Lee's forces long enough for McClellan to continue his withdrawal to a new base on the James River. Today, in Washington, Lincoln writes, "I expect to maintain this contest until successful, or till I die, or am conquered, or my term expires, or Congress or the country forsakes me."

JULY 11 Lincoln names Henry W. Halleck, known popularly as "Old Brains," as general-in-chief of all U.S. land forces. Petulant, conservative, a distinguished author on military strategy, Halleck is a conscientious adviser to Lincoln but is roundly disliked by fellow officers.

"If you can hold your present position, we shall 'hive' the enemy yet," Lincoln assured McClellan after the bloody draw of the Seven Days and the Union Army's withdrawal to Harrison's Landing. But instead of responding to the commander-in-chief's military concerns, McClellan handed Lincoln a letter warning him not to turn the war into a war against slavery; he, for one, was not interested in fighting for such a cause. Coming on the heels of his recent military setbacks, the general's letter showed unusual arrogance.

The President decided in July to end his four-month experiment of serving as his own general-in-chief, and on July 11 he called Henry W. Halleck to Washington from the West and appointed him to oversee military operations around the country. Unlike McClellan, Halleck as general-in-chief would have no direct field responsibilities. Also in contrast to "Little Mac," Halleck had no particular relish for the post. Nevertheless, it was a step toward a modern command system.

In Congress, the struggle between radicals and conservatives came to a head in July over the second Confiscation Act. The August 1861 bill had freed only those slaves who were directly involved in the Confederate war effort; the new law extended "confiscation" to the human property of any slave owner in Union-occupied territory who had actively supported the rebellion. Uneasy about the harshness of its terms, Lincoln came close to vetoing the bill, but after some last-minute amendments he signed it into law on July 17.

Privately, Lincoln was pursuing his own "anti-slavery" agenda. On July 22, he read to his astonished Cabinet a first draft of a preliminary Emancipation Proclamation, which would free all slaves in areas still in rebellion on January 1, 1863.

Increasingly, Lincoln recognized that a Union victory would depend on a stern willingness to adopt a harder line. "Would you drop the war where it is?" he asked one correspondent who complained of Butler's strict regime in Louisiana. "Or, would you prosecute it in future, with elder-stalk squirts, charged with rose water?" To another moderate he swore "that I shall not surrender this game leaving any available card unplayed."

JULY 11 Paper currency is approved. Secretary of the Treasury Chase, assigning his own portrait to the first one-dollar bill instead of Lincoln's, will have a free campaign poster if he chooses to run for the presidency two years hence. The Currency Act follows closely on congressional approval of further refinement of the internal revenue tax, which now requires a levy of 3 percent on incomes of more than $600 per year. Because of the tax, in September Lincoln's usual monthly paycheck for $2,083.33 on his $25,000-a-year salary will be reduced by $61.

JULY 12 The President signs a bill creating the Congressional Medal of Honor, a national award for valor.

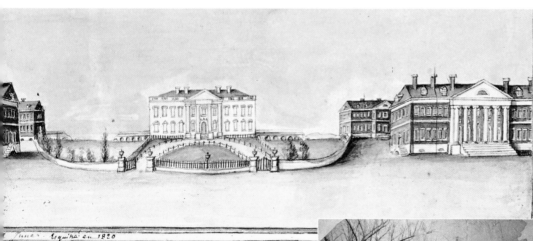

JULY 22 At the Cabinet meeting, the President reads the first draft of the preliminary Emancipation Proclamation, which he has been writing over a period of weeks in an office at the War Department. Asked by Lincoln not to "allow any one to see it," Thomas Ekert, chief of the Military Telegraph, has locked up the manuscript in a drawer of his desk each night. At Seward's suggestion, Lincoln agrees to hold off the announcement until a battlefield victory is achieved. This 1820 sketch of the White House shows what a short walk it was for Lincoln from the President's home to the War Department *(at right in drawing as well as shown in insert).*

JULY 24 Lincoln receives word of the death of Martin Van Buren, President of the United States from 1837 to 1841.

On August 3, the Peninsula campaign officially ended, and Henry Halleck ordered the Army of the Potomac back to Washington. McClellan's secretive and overcautious posture was largely responsible for the five-month fiasco, although Lincoln's withholding of troops may have contributed as well. Without an overall military commander to turn to, Lincoln had been stretched beyond his competence. McClellan, instead of working with the President, had refused to explain his repeated requests for reinforcements, or his theory that Washington was more than adequately protected.

With the military situation looking bleak, Lincoln's critics began to multiply. On August 20, *New York Tribune* editor Horace Greeley printed a passionate editorial, "The Prayer of Twenty Millions," in which he argued that "the Union cause has suffered...from mistaken deference to Rebel slavery." Calling Lincoln "timid" and "unduly influenced by ...the Border slave states," Greeley insisted that "[a]ll attempts to put down the Rebellion and at the same time uphold its inciting cause are preposterous and futile."

Lincoln refused to rise to the bait. "My paramount object in this struggle," he wrote in a public reply, "*is* to save the Union, and is *not* either to save or to destroy slavery." The President added that he intended "no modification of my oft-expressed *personal* wish that all men everywhere could be free."

Events on the battlefield did little to fulfill this wish. On July 26, General John Pope's Army of Virginia launched the offensive that Lincoln had favored seven months earlier, an advance due south toward the Rappahannock. But when Lee's brilliant strategy forced Pope to withdraw toward Manassas, the Second Battle of Bull Run (August 26–30) was no more successful than its predecessor. Pope sent news of a smashing victory, retracting it hours later with word of a rapid retreat. Henry Halleck virtually collapsed under the pressure. "He broke down," said Lincoln, "—nerve and pluck all gone." To his discouraged secretary John Hay, Lincoln said, "We must hurt this enemy before it gets away."

AUGUST 4 A delegation of Western men calls on the President and urges him to accept two regiments of black soldiers from Indiana. Lincoln agrees to use them as laborers, like these two Negro contrabands at Culpeper, Virginia *(below)*, but he is not yet ready to approve the use of blacks as regular soldiers in the armed forces.

AUGUST 21 Minnesota Mission workers and their children rest in their flight east from Sioux massacres, which have panicked thousands of settlers into abandoning their homesteads. It will take the army more than six weeks to suppress the brutal uprising of the disenfranchised Indians, and Lincoln will play a special role in the outcome.

AUGUST 7 On a sultry summer afternoon, Captain John A. Dahlgren demonstrates the "Rafael" repeater cannon to Lincoln and two Cabinet members at the navy yard in Washington.

AUGUST 8 Lincoln meets with Baron de Stoeckl, Russia's minister to the United States, and assures him that although Union enlistments are slow, a flood of volunteers would sign up in a crisis.

AUGUST 19 Twenty-three-year-old Colonel Alexander H. Todd, Mary Lincoln's favorite half-brother, dies in a skirmish following the battle of Baton Rouge. First shaken, then angry, Mary responds, "He made his choice long ago."

AUGUST 28 Today Lincoln confers with General Halleck on troop movements in Virginia as General John Pope *(above)* leads the Army of Virginia in the Second Battle of Bull Run. *Left*: Union engineers repair a bridge over the North Fork of the Rappahannock River. Their efforts make little difference; by August 30, Pope's army is routed.

After defeating the Union Army at Second Manassas, Robert E. Lee decided to press his advantage. On September 5, he crossed the Potomac River into Union Maryland, stating that the invasion of Northern soil was purely an act of self-defense. The Confederacy hoped to convince the British of the Union's military vulnerability, and to win formal recognition.

A shiver of panic ran through the lower North. The governor of Pennsylvania called up the militia and evacuated important documents from Harrisburg and Philadelphia. The Army of the Potomac under McClellan (merged, after Pope's departure, with the Federal Army of Virginia) headed warily into Maryland after Lee. "Please do not let him get off without being hurt," Lincoln begged.

On September 13, McClellan got lucky. Some of his soldiers found a few abandoned cigars wrapped up in a paper that turned out to be a copy of Lee's battle plan for the Maryland campaign. Armed with this information, McClellan struck the next day at South Mountain. When the rebels temporarily retreated, McClellan crowed, "The Enemy is in perfect panic."

South Mountain, however, was only a Confederate delaying action. The major confrontation came on September 17 along Antietam Creek, near the town of Sharpsburg. On that day, the bloodiest single day of the Civil War, nearly 5,000 men died, and more than 20,000 were wounded. Robert E. Lee lost a quarter of his army, and he was forced to call off his invasion of the North.

McClellan was ecstatic. He called his victory a "masterpiece of art," and was thrilled to see the Army of Northern Virginia heading back to rebel territory. Lincoln urged his general to pursue and destroy the rebel army, but McClellan dawdled; on September 18, Lee safely recrossed the Potomac, his invasion repulsed, his army battered but intact.

Antietam was a Pyrrhic victory, a triumph that had neither done lasting damage to the rebel army nor retaken an inch of rebel ground, but Lincoln seized on this slender reed as the moment he had been waiting for since July. On September 22, he made public his preliminary Emancipation Proclamation. A large crowd serenaded the President outside the White House, and anti-slavery advocates cheered the announcement.

SEPTEMBER 17 The Battle of Antietam is fought in the countryside near the small Maryland town of Sharpsburg and along Antietam Creek. By dusk, 26,000 men are dead, wounded, or missing. It is the single bloodiest day in American history and still is. It is also the first U.S. battlefield to be photographed before the burial of the dead. Working for Mathew Brady, photographer Alexander Gardner and his assistant James F. Gibson arrive on the scene soon after the smoke has cleared. Here, in a hand-tinted stereo view, Confederate corpses line a field near Hagerstown Pike. Dunker Church and the West Woods are in the background. A month later the sight of Gardner's pictures on display in Brady's New York gallery make a public stir. Said *The New York Times*, "If he [Brady] has not brought bodies and laid them in our dooryards and along the streets, he has done something very like it...."

"PROMISE TO...MY MAKER"

SEPTEMBER 22 *On the same day that Gardner is finishing his photographic record of the dead at Antietam, Lincoln unveils his historic proclamation, as Secretary Chase records in his diary.*
The President then took a graver tone and said: — "Gentlemen: I have, as you are aware, thought a great deal about the relation of this war to Slavery; and you all remember that, several weeks ago, I read you an Order I had prepared on this subject, which, on account of objections made by some of you, was not issued. Ever since then, my mind has been much occupied with this subject....When the rebel army was at Frederick, I determined, as soon as it should be driven out of Maryland, to issue a Proclamation of Emancipation such as I thought most likely to be useful. I said nothing to any one; but I made the promise to myself, and...to my Maker. The rebel army is now driven out, and I am going to fulfill that promise. I have got you together to hear what I have written down. I do not wish your advice about the main matter—for that I have determined for myself."

Lincoln spent most of the first week of October with the Army of the Potomac in Maryland. He surveyed the ravaged battlefield at Antietam, toured the town of Harpers Ferry, where Stonewall Jackson had taken 12,000 prisoners the month before, and slept in a tent next to McClellan's headquarters. He visited the wounded, who were lying by the thousands in makeshift hospitals throughout the state. On one occasion, overcome by wistfulness upon contemplating so many dead, he asked his friend Ward Hill Lamon "to sing one of his sad little songs." Lamon did so, and followed it up with some cheerful banjo tunes, including the irreverent "Picayune Butler." Much later, Lincoln would be accused of having blasphemed the battlefield. "Mr. Lincoln was...incapable of insulting the dead," replied Lamon. When the President returned to Washington on October 6, he sent word back to McClellan that he should move against the enemy now, while the weather was still favorable for action.

Antietam had not completely convinced the international community that the United States could be restored. On October 7, Britain's powerful chancellor of the exchequer, William E. Gladstone, proclaimed that Confederate leaders had "made a nation." While his comments came under fire in both England and the United States, they showed that the European nations might still recognize and eventually aid the Southern states.

Although the Union armies had been making slow but steady gains in the West, Lincoln once again restructured the command in that part of the country. On October 16, the Federal Department of the Tennessee was placed under the leadership of Ulysses S. Grant. Impatient with Don Carlos Buell's failure to take the key Tennessee city of Chattanooga, Lincoln named William S. Rosecrans as commander of the Department of the Cumberland on October 24.

McClellan brought out an old excuse for not chasing Lee: his cavalry's mounts were worn-out. "Will you pardon me for asking what the horses of your army have done since the battle of Antietam that fatigue anything?" Lincoln wrote angrily. Although he was popular with his own men, the criticism of McClellan among the Cabinet and throughout the North was reaching new heights of intensity, and the President's patience was nearly at an end.

OCTOBER 1 Lincoln and George McClellan meet at the headquarters of the Army of the Potomac near Harpers Ferry. Surveying the troops, Lincoln is reported to have said, "This is General McClellan's bodyguard." Later, en route to a review of cavalry and troops, Lincoln's friend Ward Hill Lamon sings a few of the sad and comic ballads that move Lincoln; the incident is later blown out of proportion, and the President and his friends are accused of making light of the sacrifices of the Battle of Antietam *(left)*.

"NO ENEMIES IN THIS PLACE"

OCTOBER 17 Lincoln directs the attorney general to make out a commission for the President's old Illinois friend Judge David Davis *(above)* as associate justice of the Supreme Court.

OCTOBER 4 *In the morning Lincoln visits wounded soldiers in the vicinity of Antietam, including General Israel "Fighting Dick" Richardson* (above), *who lies dying in a farmhouse. He also asks to visit with the Confederate wounded, as this Baltimore newspaper story relates.*

Passing through one of the hospitals devoted exclusively to Confederate sick and wounded, President Lincoln's attention was drawn to a young Georgian—a fine noble looking youth—stretched upon a humble cot. He was pale, emaciated and anxious, far from kindred and home, vibrating, as it were, between life and death. Every stranger that entered [was] caught in his restless eyes,

in hope of their being some relative or friend. President Lincoln observed this youthful soldier, approached and spoke, asking him if he suffered much pain. "I do," was the reply. "I have lost a leg, and feel I am sinking from exhaustion." "Would you," said Mr. Lincoln, "shake hands with me if I were to tell you who I am?" The response was affirmative. "There should," remarked the young Georgian, "be no enemies in this place." Then said the distinguished visitor, "I am Abraham Lincoln, President of the United States." The young sufferer raised his head, looking amazed, and freely extended his hand, which Mr. Lincoln took and pressed tenderly for some time.

OCTOBER 26 Eliza P. Gurney, a noted English Quaker, holds a prayer meeting in the White House. Lincoln tells her that we must believe that God permits the war "for some wise purpose of his own, mysterious and unknown to us."

OCTOBER 14 Lincoln grants permission for Tad to "have a little gun that he can not hurt himself with." Captain John A. Dahlgren makes him this brass cannon, a miniature of Dahlgren's own boat howitzer.

The midterm elections in the North on November 4 dealt a crushing blow to Lincoln's Republican Party. Five states that had gone for Lincoln in 1860—New York, Pennsylvania, Ohio, Indiana, and his home state of Illinois—all sent Democratic majorities to Washington in their congressional delegations. A Democrat even won the seat from Lincoln's own district in Illinois. Only strong majorities in New England kept the Republicans in control of the House.

Everyone had a different interpretation for the Republican setbacks. Democrats claimed that the Union was having second thoughts about the Republicans' radical slavery agenda and the very scope of the war effort. Carl Schurz and other Republicans complained to Lincoln that he had made too many concessions to the Democrats, that by giving them so many prominent political and military positions he had handed them the elections. The President himself refused to concede that the elections signified wavering support for the war. He argued that the Republicans had lost thousands of votes because the strongest supporters of the Union cause were on the battlefield and unable to vote at all.

In part because he did not want to alienate the Democrats further, Lincoln retained his Democratic commander of the Army of the Potomac until the day after the election, but then he finally ended General McClellan's tenure. "He is an admirable engineer," Lincoln said, "but he seems to have a special talent for a stationary engine."

The new commander of the Army of the Potomac was Ambrose E. Burnside, whose appearance was impressive but who himself felt that he was unfit for such an awesome responsibility. Under pressure to attack, Burnside put into effect a plan to move on Richmond by way of the town of Fredericksburg.

Having replaced one prominent Democrat in the field, Lincoln now removed another, withdrawing Benjamin Butler from the Department of the Gulf, thereby ending the "Beast"'s controversial rule in New Orleans.

NOVEMBER 2 For Mary Lincoln *(below right)* the social whirl on her latest trip to New York includes enjoying the company of General Robert Anderson and his wife, shown below with their son. While away, Mrs. Lincoln gives $200 from a special fund to her dressmaker, Elizabeth Keckley, for the benefit of an association to aid escaped slaves.

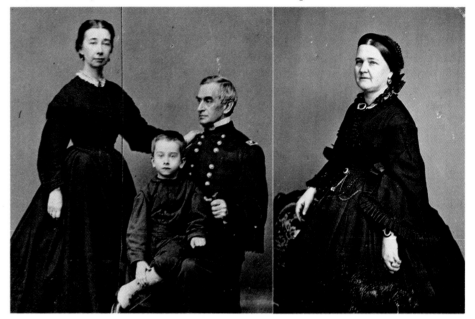

NOVEMBER 10 Julia Ward Howe, New England writer and reformer and recently the author of the popular song "The Battle Hymn of the Republic," visits the White House.

NOVEMBER 22 Lincoln is appalled by General Nathaniel P. Banks's extravagant demands for supplies after he replaces Benjamin Butler as commander of the Department of the Gulf. "I have just been overwhelmed and confounded with the sight of a requisition made by you," the President writes.

NOVEMBER 5 Lincoln finally relieves George McClellan of his command, and General Ambrose E. Burnside *(right)* becomes the new commander of the Army of the Potomac. "But I'm not fit to command an entire army," Burnside is reported to have sputtered.

A FEROCIOUS LINCOLN

NOVEMBER 24 *The President to General Carl Schurz, formerly Lincoln's minister to Spain*

I have just received, and read, your letter of the 20th. The purport of it is that we lost the late elections, and the administration is failing, because the war is unsuccessful; and that I must not flatter myself that I am not justly to blame for it. I certainly know that if the war fails, the administration fails, and that I *will* be blamed for it, whether I deserve it or not. And I ought to be blamed, if I could do better. You think I could do better; therefore you blame me already. I think I could not do better; therefore I blame you for blaming me.... Be assured, my dear sir, there are men who have "heart in it" that think you are performing your part as poorly as you think I am performing mine.

Lincoln had considered hundreds of pleas for pardons as part of his daily work, but few were as sweeping and significant as the case of the Sioux Indians that he considered this month. Starving and displaced from their hereditary lands, thousands of Sioux had taken up arms in August, killing more than 200 settlers in one day and organizing a revolt against U.S. jurisdiction. Ferocious reprisals followed the massacre, with General Pope declaring, "It is my purpose utterly to exterminate the Sioux." After two months of hasty and careless trials, resulting in a planned mass execution for 303 Indians, Lincoln demanded to see the trial proceedings. Deciding that most of the death sentences were unfair, on December 6 he limited his approval to the execution of thirty-nine Indians whom he believed to be most clearly guilty. In the end, thirty-eight Sioux were hanged at Mankato, Minnesota, on December 26 — the largest mass execution in United States history, but, thanks to Lincoln, not as large as it was intended to be.

Burnside's offensive in Virginia quickly turned into disaster at the battle of Fredericksburg on December 13. A series of futile Federal assaults on well-entrenched Confederate positions resulted in a shocking Union defeat. "It was a great slaughter pen," commented one Union officer. "They might as well have tried to take Hell."

The military and electoral setbacks of the previous months, as well as division over Lincoln's slavery policy, now provoked a major political crisis within the administration. Its chief aim was to oust William Seward, believed responsible for the general failure to prosecute the war. Behind the movement in the shadows, however, was Treasury Secretary Salmon Chase, who had hated Seward from the beginning and believed his influence over Lincoln to be malign. Between December 17 and 20, Lincoln outmaneuvered all the principals, forcing Chase to follow Seward's resignation with his own, and then convincing both men to remain in office. When the dust had settled, and Lincoln had "a pumpkin in each end" of his bag, the President proclaimed that he was "master."

DECEMBER 1 Lincoln must decide the fate of 303 Sioux Indians sentenced to death for their part in the Minnesota uprising of August and September. More than 1,700 captured Sioux are being held in a makeshift tepee village at Fort Snelling *(below)*. The compound is fenced not only to keep the Indians in but also to keep incensed mobs out.

DECEMBER 13 Ambrose Burnside's ill-conceived assault at Fredericksburg on the Rappahannock River in Virginia *(above)* is in sharp contrast to McClellan's "slows," but the results are disastrous: the Army of the Potomac suffers more than 12,000 casualties in this major defeat.

DECEMBER 6 Lincoln orders that thirty-nine of the convicted Sioux Indians—those who were charged with rape and other "barbarities"—be executed later in the month. So there will be no mistake, he phonetically writes out their names *(below)*.

"I AM SURE IT WAS RIGHT"

DECEMBER 19 *Ten months later, John Hay writes about the December Cabinet crisis.* [Lincoln] went on telling the history of the Senate raid on Seward—how he had & could have no adviser on that subject & must work it out by himself—how he thought deeply on the matter—& it occurred to him that the way to settle it was to force certain men to say to the Senators *here* what they would not say elsewhere. He confronted the Senate & the Cabinet. He gave the whole history of the affair of Seward & his conduct & the assembled Cabinet listened & confirmed all he said.

"I do not see how it could have been done better. I am sure it was right. If I had yielded to that storm & dismissed Seward the thing would all have slumped over one way & we should have been left with a scanty handful of supporters. When Chase sent in his resignation I saw that the game was in my own hands & I put it through."

DECEMBER 17 Secretary of State William Seward *(above)* and his son, Assistant Secretary Frederick W. Seward, offer their resignations in the wake of criticism from a powerful group of Republican senators. Three days later, Lincoln declines the resignations and instructs both men to resume their duties.

One day in late June, Lincoln took Vice President Hannibal Hamlin into his confidence and read to him a draft of a far-reaching executive proclamation that would, when delivered, free the nation's slaves—at least many of them. It was not a simple proclamation, and behind locked doors, in the library of the Soldiers' Home, Lincoln braced himself for criticism from the abolitionist-inclined Hamlin. What his vice president told him instead was: "There is no criticism to be made."

Two weeks later, during a carriage ride to the funeral of Edwin Stanton's infant son, Lincoln revealed his plan to Secretaries Welles and Seward. "He dwelt earnestly on the gravity, importance, and delicacy of the movement," recorded Welles in his diary. "[He] had...come to the conclusion that it was a military necessity absolutely essential for the salvation of the Union." Seward, however, at a later Cabinet meeting, urged caution, arguing that the government should wait for a military victory before proceeding, lest the proclamation be misinterpreted as a sign of defeat. Reluctantly, Lincoln agreed.

With his great plan postponed, and the war going poorly for the Union, Lincoln seemed to lose his resolve in the matter. During this long dismal summer of 1862, he turned once again to the idea of colonization. Realizing that what prejudiced Northern whites feared most was for blacks to "swarm northward" and "intermingle," competing for jobs, Lincoln had long advocated black emigration, for freed blacks to be willingly colonized to places such as Liberia, Haiti, or Central America. Like his hero Henry Clay before him, Lincoln believed blacks would be eager to return to the lands from which their ancestors had been stolen, or, at the very least, to make their escape out of white supremacist America. Insisting that such colonization be "voluntary and without expense" to the emigrés, Lincoln felt that if he could convince even a small number of them to go, it would help him immensely to accomplish the political miracle of emancipation. On August 14, he addressed a delegation of free Negroes, invited to the White House to hear his ideas.

Admitting that American blacks were "suffering...the greatest wrong inflicted on any people," and that white racism was an unalterable "fact" that would pursue blacks

On September 22, 1862, exactly one hundred days before it would go into effect, Lincoln unveiled his preliminary Emancipation Proclamation to his entire Cabinet. Artist Francis Bicknell Carpenter later painted the historic scene *(above)* with Lincoln holding his handwritten manuscript of the proclamation *(right)* in his lap, initiating what Carpenter called a "new epoch in the history of Liberty." The proclamation promised "that on the first day of January, in the year of our Lord, one thousand-eight hundred and sixty three, all persons held as slaves" within any of the rebel states "shall be then, thenceforth and forever free."

In pursuance of the sixth section of the act of congress entitled "An act to suppress insurrection and to punish treason and rebellion, to seize and confiscate property of rebels, and for other purposes" Approved July 17. 1862, and which act, and the joint Resolution explanatory thereof, are herewith published, I, Abraham Lincoln, President of the United States, do hereby proclaim to, and warn all persons within the contemplation of said sixth section to cease participating in, aiding, countenancing, or abetting the existing rebellion, or any rebellion against the government of the United States, and to return to their proper allegiance to the United States, on pain of the forfeitures and seizures, as within and by said sixth section provided—

And I hereby make known that it is my purpose, upon the next meeting of Congress, to again recommend the adoption of a practical measure for tendering pecuniary aid to the free choice or

throughout time, Lincoln proceeded to blame America's current problems on the black presence: "Our white men [are] cutting one another's throats...[and] but for your race among us there could not be war....It is better for us both, therefore, to be separated."

"The tone of frankness and benevolence which he assumes in his speech," exploded black abolitionist Frederick Douglass in New York, "is too thin a mask not to be seen through. The genuine spark of humanity is missing in it." And Isaiah Wears, the black Philadelphia leader, added, "To be asked, after so many years of oppression and wrong ...to pull up stakes...and go...is unreasonable and anti-Christian....It is not the negro race that is the cause of the war; it is the unwillingness on the part of the American people to do the race simple justice."

As the weeks unfolded, and his critics multiplied, Lincoln turned increasingly inward, in his private musings writing that he was searching out the "Will of God" on what to do about slavery.

Then, on September 17, at Antietam Creek in Maryland, the Union forces finally won a victory. It was what Lincoln had been praying for. When he was sure the news was correct, he called his Cabinet together to read them a new draft of the proclamation that had been sitting in his desk drawer all summer, declaring freedom to Confederate slaves, beginning January 1, 1863. Frederick Douglass, upon hearing the news, exclaimed that the war had suddenly, at a stroke, been "invested with sanctity." And at a Cabinet celebration at Secretary Chase's house, according to John Hay, "all seemed to feel a sort of new and exhilarated life; they breathed freer; The President's Proclamation had freed them as well as the slaves."

By early December, in his annual message to Congress, Lincoln had found the words to inspire his people down the course he—and they—were about to take. "Fellow-citizens, *we* cannot escape history....The fiery trial through which we pass, will light us down, in honor or dishonor, to the latest generation....In *giving* freedom to the *slave*, we *assure* freedom to the *free*....We shall nobly save, or meanly lose, the last best, hope of earth....The way is plain, peaceful, generous, just—a way which, if followed, the world will forever applaud, and God must forever bless."

From Lincoln's July 1862 letter to Maryland Senator-elect Reverdy Johnson, who was sent to investigate complaints against Generals Butler and John S. Phelps in Louisiana

It seems the Union feeling in Louisiana is being crushed out by...General Phelps. Please pardon me for believing that is a false pretense. The people of Louisiana—all intelligent people every where—know full well, that I never had a wish to touch the foundations of their society, or any right of theirs.... [I]t is their own fault, not mine, that they are annoyed by the presence of General Phelps. They also know the remedy—know how to be cured of General Phelps. Remove the necessity of his presence. And might it not be well for them to consider whether they have not already had *time* enough to do this? If they can conceive of anything worse than General Phelps, within my power, would they not better be looking out for it? They very well know the way to avert all this is simply to take their place in the Union upon the old terms. If they will not do this, should they not receive harder blows rather than lighter ones?

You are ready to say I apply to *friends* what is due only to *enemies*. I distrust the *wisdom* if not the *sincerity* of friends, who would hold my hands while my enemies stab me. This appeal of professed friends has paralyzed me more in this struggle than any other one thing. You remember telling me the day after the Baltimore mob in April 1861, that it would crush all Union feeling in Maryland for me to attempt bringing troops over Maryland soil to Washington. I brought the troops notwithstanding, and yet there was Union feeling enough left to elect a Legislature the next autumn which in turn elected a very excellent Union U.S. Senator!

I am a patient man—always willing to forgive on the Christian terms of repentance; and also to give ample *time* for repentance. Still I must save this government if possible. What I *cannot* do, of course I *will* not do; but it may as well be understood, once for all, that I shall not surrender this game leaving any available card unplayed.

Union artillery at Fair Oaks, Virginia, May 31, 1862

From Lincoln's annual message to Congress, December 1, 1862

A blockade of three thousand miles of seacoast could not be established, and vigorously enforced, in a season of great commercial activity like the present, without committing occasional mistakes, and inflicting unintentional injuries upon foreign nations and their subjects.... In clear cases of these kinds I have, so far as possible, heard and redressed complaints which have been presented by friendly powers....

A nation may be said to consist of its territory, its people, and its laws. The territory is the only part which is of certain durability. "One generation passeth away, and another generation cometh, but the earth abideth forever." It is of the first importance to duly consider, and estimate, this ever-enduring part. That portion of the earth's surface which is owned and inhabited by the people of the United States, is well adapted to be the home of one national family; and it is not well adapted for two, or more. Its vast extent, and its variety of climate and productions, are of advantage, in this age, for one people, whatever they might have been in former ages. Steam, telegraphs, and intelligence, have brought these, to be an advantageous combination, for one united people.

In the inaugural address I briefly pointed out the total inadequacy of disunion, as a remedy for the differences between the people.... I beg to repeat....

"...Physically speaking, we cannot separate. We cannot remove our respective sections from each other, nor build an impassable wall between them. A husband and wife may be divorced, and go out of the presence, and beyond the reach of each other; but the different parts of our country cannot do this. They cannot but remain face to face; and intercourse, either amicable or hostile, must continue between them...."

Our national strife springs not from our permanent part; not from the land we inhabit; not from our national homestead. There is no possible severing of this, but would multiply, and not mitigate, evils among us. In all its adaptations and aptitudes, it demands union, and abhors separation. In fact, it would, ere long, force re-union, however much of blood and treasure the separation might have cost....

Chapter 7

1863

This is the pivotal year for Lincoln and the Union: two great victories in July and a speech that will be remembered forever.

Lincoln *(directly above)* amid a crush of
admirers on the platform at Gettysburg

Along with Lincoln's historic Emancipation Proclamation, 1863 began with a flurry of disputes among the President's top military men. On New Year's Day, Ambrose E. Burnside met with Lincoln to promote a new assault in Virginia, via the Rappahannock, a controversial move opposed by all the general's senior subordinates. When Lincoln appealed to Henry Halleck for an opinion, the general-in-chief, chastened by events of the autumn, refused to take responsibility for any new initiative. "If in such a difficulty as this you do not help, you fail me precisely in the point for which I sought your assistance," Lincoln admonished. "Your military skill is useless to me, if you will not do this." When Halleck promptly offered his resignation, the President turned it down, agreeing at the same time to withdraw his own letter of censure. The only good military news during the first week of January was that General William Rosecrans had won a modest but significant victory in the Battle of Stone's River in Tennessee.

On January 20, Burnside did indeed lead his troops across the Rappahannock, but a series of midwinter storms ground the movement to a halt. Driving snow and rain made the Virginia roads virtually impassable, and the notorious "Mud March" ended with the army's retreat to its winter quarters.

Irritated by his subordinates' open criticisms, Burnside asked for permission to dishonorably discharge several generals under his command. Instead, on January 25, Lincoln relieved Burnside himself and named Joseph Hooker—one of Burnside's most virulent critics—as the fourth commander of the Army of the Potomac. Ambitious and hard-drinking, "Fighting Joe" Hooker's braggadocio and insubordination were his greatest drawbacks. "I much fear," wrote Lincoln on January 26, "that the spirit which you have aided to infuse into the Army ... will now turn upon you.... Beware of rashness, but with energy and sleepless vigilance, go forward, and give us victories."

As impatient as Lincoln had become with General Halleck's indecisiveness, when General John A. McClernand wrote charging the general-in-chief with "utter incompetency," the President wearily answered, "I have too many *family* controversies, (so to speak) already on my hands, to voluntarily, or so long as I can avoid it, take up another."

JANUARY 1 Today Lincoln signs the Emancipation Proclamation, which not only declares slaves free in rebel territory, but also states explicitly that blacks "will be received into the armed services of the United States." *Below:* Ex-slaves of the 1st Carolina Volunteers form up for dress parade at Beaufort, South Carolina, on the very day Lincoln's pen officially sets those in servitude free.

JANUARY 14 Lincoln writes to General John A. Dix, the commander at Fortress Monroe, Virginia *(its main sally port is shown above)*, asking whether one of the two forts under his command might, in whole or part, be "garrisoned by colored troops."

JANUARY 8 When General John A. McClernand writes Lincoln warning that the Emancipation Proclamation may have gone too far, the President replies curtly to this "interesting communication" that "to use a coarse, but an expressive figure, broken eggs can not be mended."

JANUARY 8 John P. Usher *(below)*, a Western attorney and a friend of Lincoln's, is confirmed by the U.S. Senate as the new secretary of the interior, replacing Caleb B. Smith, whose poor health forced him to resign in December.

JANUARY 16 General Samuel P. Heintzelman *(shown above with members of his staff)* meets with the President regarding the appointment of the general's son to West Point.

JANUARY 21 Lincoln endorses a letter from General Halleck to Ulysses S. Grant *(above)* explaining the President's decision to revoke Grant's December order barring Jews from his camp. "The President has no objection to your expelling traitors and Jew peddlers," Halleck writes, but he objects to the proscription of "an entire religious class."

JANUARY 25 General Joseph Hooker is named commander of the Army of the Potomac, despite Lincoln's frank admission to the handsome, always well-appointed general that "there are some things in regard to which, I am not quite satisfied with you."

The Union war effort appeared stalled. The Army of the Potomac had literally bogged down in Virginia, the fiasco at Fredericksburg was still fresh in the nation's mind, and eager volunteers were no longer overflowing the North's recruiting offices. The army was ensconced in winter huts at Falmouth, across the Rappahannock from Fredericksburg, awaiting spring.

In the West, the Mississippi River was still not fully passable, thanks to the Confederacy's control of the town of Vicksburg. The rebel batteries on the high bluffs menaced any passing boats. Since a frontal assault on the city by Sherman had failed, Grant, now the commander of the Department of the Mississippi, was busy devising alternate schemes. Lincoln, with his interest in engineering, encouraged the general to dig a canal on the western side of the river, out of reach of the Confederate batteries. Grant's men started digging, but the canal was never deep enough for boats to pass.

During February the Union experimented with running boats past the Vicksburg batteries. The ram *Queen of the West* succeeded at first but then ran aground and had to be abandoned to the Confederacy. On February 26, the Federal fleet sent an empty coal barge down the river in the middle of the night, and the looming hulk so frightened the crew on one Confederate gunboat that the rebels blew up their own ship and fled. Still, little real progress was made. For now, anyway, Vicksburg remained a stubborn thorn in the Union's side.

In Washington, Lincoln was preoccupied with political matters. He conferred with Thurlow Weed about raising money from wealthy New Yorkers for the Republican Party; he approved an act that established a system of national banks; and, in the face of a growing onslaught of job seekers, he convened the Senate to consider a long list of executive appointments and promotions.

One particularly inventive candidate made the President chuckle. Edgar Harriott of New York wrote an eloquent letter to Mary Lincoln, seeking a job as assistant paymaster in the navy and claiming that he was a descendant of the statesman John Randolph. Since it was well known that Randolph had been impotent, Lincoln sardonically endorsed the applicant's letter: "A direct descendant of one who never was a father."

FEBRUARY 5 Lincoln apologizes to General Franz Sigel for his "cross" tone in a January letter in reply to Sigel's request for additional forces. "If I do get up a little temper," the President writes, "I have no sufficient time to keep it up."

FEBRUARY 19 Lincoln nominates Commodore Charles H. Davis, the chief of the bureau of navigation, for the rank of rear admiral.

FEBRUARY 6 "I observe that the President never tells a joke now," Captain John Dahlgren, the commander of the Washington Navy Yard, notes in his diary, the day before he is named a rear admiral.

FEBRUARY 20 Lincoln meets with Hole in the Day, the chief of the Chippewas.

FEBRUARY 13 *Mary Lincoln's black mourning clothes for Willie are finally gone as the First Lady, in a low-necked, pink silk gown, hosts a reception for the celebrated midget "General Tom Thumb" (Charles S. Stratton) and his bride, Lavinia Warren, who were married to great fanfare in New York three days before (right). Grace Greenwood, the writer, is one of the guests at the honeymoon party in the East Room.*

The pigmy "General"...wore his elegant wedding suit, and his wife...her wedding dress....I well remember the "pigeon-like stateliness" with which they advanced, almost to the feet of the President, and the profound respect with which they looked up, up, to his kindly face. It was pleasant to see their tall host bend, and bend, to take their little hands in his great palm, holding Madame's with especial chariness, as though it were a robin's egg, and he were fearful of breaking it....He presented them, very courteously and soberly, to Mrs. Lincoln, and in his compliments and congratulations there was not the slightest touch of the exaggeration which a lesser man might have been tempted to make use of, for the quiet amusement of on-lookers; in fact, nothing to reveal to that shrewd little pair his keen sense of the incongruity of the scene.

FEBRUARY 21 Longtime Lincoln family friend Dr. Anson G. Henry brings news of Springfield as a dinner guest at the White House.

FEBRUARY 24 The President ventures to Grover's Theatre in Washington to see a performance by Barney Williams, an Irish comedian known for his minstrel acts in blackface.

In the flurry of activity at the end of the congressional session, Lincoln spent the first three days of March signing bills: Idaho was made a territory. Free mail delivery was approved for forty-nine cities. The President was given authorization to suspend habeas corpus whenever necessary during the war. Financier Jay Cooke was named as a government agent to help sell United States bonds. The National Academy of Sciences was established.

By far the most important piece of legislation before the President was the "Act for enrolling and calling out the National Forces." By his signature, on March 3, Lincoln created the nation's first true Federal draft — applying to men between the ages of twenty and forty-five, though containing provision for the purchase of substitutes. To head off potential trouble in the state of New York, Lincoln wrote to Governor Horatio Seymour, who opposed the draft. "I, for the time being, am at the head of a nation which is in great peril; and you are at the head of the greatest State of that nation.... [T]he co-operation of your State ... is indispensable." With lotteries to begin in the coming summer, and quotas to fill throughout the North, the act sparked a bitter debate about the government's usurpation of power.

In March, the President turned his attention to the recruiting of black soldiers. He tried, unsuccessfully, to convince General Benjamin F. Butler to return to New Orleans to lead the recruitment of blacks in Louisiana, and on March 26, he wrote to Andrew Johnson, military governor of Tennessee, saying that the presence of blacks in the army could be a powerful psychological weapon against the Confederacy. "The bare sight of fifty thousand armed, and drilled black soldiers on the banks of the Mississippi, would end the rebellion at once."

Maintaining peaceful relations with the American Indian population was a crucial aspect of the war effort west of the Mississippi, and since the army could ill-afford to detach troops there to quell any outbreaks, Lincoln spent a considerable amount of time throughout the war on Indian matters. On March 27, he met with a substantial delegation of Indian chiefs, assuring them of the United States government's goodwill.

MARCH 8 With the President's approval, Secretary of State Seward writes Lord Lyons, England's minister to the United States, requesting that the Confederacy no longer be allowed to build warships in British ports.

MARCH 13 Actor James H. Hackett, shown here in his Falstaff costume, plays his favorite role in a production of Shakespeare's *Henry IV*, with the President in the audience.

MARCH 17 In response to complaints from William Rosecrans, Lincoln tells the general: "I do not appreciate this matter of rank on paper, as you officers do. The world will not forget that you fought the battle of 'Stone River' and it will never care a fig whether you rank Gen. Grant on paper, or he so, ranks you."

MARCH 25 Continuing to supplement his steady diet of Shakespeare, Lincoln attends a production of *Hamlet* starring E. L. Davenport *(shown above as Brutus in* Julius Caesar*)*.

MARCH 27 Today Lincoln meets with a group of Indian chiefs in the East Room. After the visitors have concluded their remarks through an interpreter, the President says: "You have all spoken of the strange sights you see here, among your pale-faced brethren; the very great number of people that you see; the big wigwams; the difference between our people and your own." The President refrains from "Indian talk," as he had done in a meeting with some chiefs two years ago. "Where live now?" he had asked then. "When go back Iowa?" This time he is more judicious. "We pale-faced people think that this world is a great, round ball," Lincoln tells them, "and we have people here of the pale-faced family who have come almost from the other side of it to represent their nations here and conduct their friendly intercourse with us, as you now come from your part of the round ball.... The pale-faced people are numerous and prosperous because they cultivate the earth, produce bread, and depend upon the products of the earth rather than wild game for a subsistence. This is the chief reason of the difference; but there is another. Although we are now engaged in a great war between one another, we are not, as a race, so much disposed to fight and kill one another as our red brethren."

Right: The Washingtonians posing with Indians in the White House conservatory include Salmon Chase's stunning daughter Kate *(standing, fourth from right).*

Once again, the Army of the Potomac, 130,000 men strong, was in fighting form. But when Joseph Hooker bragged that he had assembled "the finest Army on the Planet," a worried Lincoln decided to pay him a lengthy visit.

The trip began inauspiciously on April 4 when a freakish late snowstorm forced the presidential party to stop for the night in a cove rather than proceed down the Potomac. The next day they arrived at Aquia Creek and proceeded by train to Falmouth, where Hooker's army was camped. From here Lincoln could see with a spy glass across the Rappahannock to Fredericksburg, where Lee's army waited, barely a mile away.

Hooker was completely self-assured. "My plans are perfect, and when I start to carry them out, may God have mercy on General Lee, for I will have none," he told a group of officers. Lincoln, not surprisingly, found Hooker "overconfident," but was relieved to discover that the general did at least have a plan. "Write me often. I am very anxious," he urged Hooker some days later.

Out West, on the Mississippi, Admiral David Porter managed to force twelve ships past Vicksburg on April 16. By the end of the month, Grant had crossed the river below Vicksburg and was preparing to mount a campaign from the southeast.

Back East in Washington, dreary April rains dampened spirits and hampered Hooker's plans to move against Lee. The "Mud March" had already demonstrated how much military commanders needed reliable weather information, but the science of meteorology was still in its infancy. On April 25, Francis Capen offered his services to Lincoln as a weather consultant to the War Department. But by April 27, the President had already lost his patience: "It seems to me Mr. Capen knows nothing about the weather, in advance. He told me three days ago that it would not rain again till the 30th of April or 1st of May. It is raining now & has been for ten hours. I can not spare any more time to Mr. Capen."

Despite the rains, on April 28 Hooker moved across the Rappahannock into the area known as the Wilderness, anticipating the "certain destruction" of the enemy.

APRIL 1 Lincoln writes to General David Hunter, commending him for using black troops in his attack on Jacksonville, Florida. "It is important to the enemy that such a force shall *not* take shape, and grow, and thrive, in the South; and in precisely the same proportion, it is important to us that it *shall*."

APRIL 5 En route to General Hooker's headquarters at Falmouth, Virginia, Lincoln and his party arrive in the morning at Aquia Creek on the Potomac, the site of the army's supply base *(below)*. During the trip, Lincoln jots down his idea for the design of a fast, strong naval "Steam-ram" which could guard a particular harbor, "as a Bull-dog guards his master's door."

APRIL 19 Still uneasy about General Hooker's plans, Lincoln travels "very privately" for another meeting with his general at Aquia Creek. Here Sixth Corps troops mass along the Rappahannock just before attacking Fredericksburg.

APRIL 11 Mrs. John C. Wood stars in a performance of *Pocahontas* at the Washington Theatre at which the President "laughs some."

APRIL 17 *John L. Cunningham, a twenty-two-year-old lieutenant on duty in Washington, is at Brady's with some friends when Lincoln arrives by carriage to have his picture taken. He describes the scene.*
We...hurried upstairs, to be in the operating rooms when the President came.... The operator was a Frenchman, with a decided accent. He said to the President that there was considerable call for a full-length standing photograph of him. The President jokingly inquired whether this could be done with a single negative, saying: "You see, I'm six feet four in my stockings." The operator replied that it could be done all right and left to arrange for the "standing."... The operator announced that he was ready and they went into the camera room, but the President stood where we could see and hear him. He asked whether he should stand as if addressing a jury "with my arm like this," stretching out his right arm. The operator came to him several times, placing the President's arms by his side, turning his head, adjusting his clothing, etc. "Just look natural," said the operator. "That is what I would like to avoid," Mr. Lincoln replied.

(*Left*: The photograph taken by operator Thomas Le Mere)

APRIL 15 In a letter to General Hooker, Lincoln expresses misgivings over the slow movements of General George Stoneman *(below)*, whose cavalry corps he had reviewed at Falmouth on April 6. "I do not know that any better can be done," Lincoln writes, "but I greatly fear it is another failure already."

APRIL 23 The President is reported to attend a spiritualist séance, possibly in the White House Library *(above)*. Mary Lincoln has been frequenting such gatherings over the past year, in the hope of communicating with her departed son Willie. At this session, the spirits allegedly wait until the President leaves before making their appearance known by pinching Secretary Stanton's ears and tweaking Secretary Welles's beard.

On May 2, General Hooker led his men into one of the costliest Union defeats of the entire war—the Battle of Chancellorsville. Overcoming a two-to-one disadvantage in manpower, Lee's waiting army pounced, and won big. On May 4, reeling from a head injury suffered in battle, Hooker retreated back across the Rappahannock. "Never, as long as I knew him," reported Noah Brooks of Lincoln's reaction to the news, "did he seem so broken, so dispirited, and so ghost-like. Clasping his hands behind his back, he walked up and down the room, saying 'My God! My God! What will the country say? What will the country say?'"

In the same battle, Robert E. Lee lost his most trusted subordinate. Stonewall Jackson, the hugely popular hero of the Shenandoah campaign, was fatally wounded at Chancellorsville and died in a Virginia farmhouse on May 10. "Let us pass over the river, and rest under the shade of the trees," he had whispered just before dying. When the Washington *Chronicle* praised Jackson on May 13, even Lincoln was moved to congratulate the author for his "excellent and manly article."

In May, Lincoln continued to be occupied by the problem of internal dissension. "Copperheads," Democrats who favored a negotiated settlement, were particularly strong in Illinois, Indiana, and Ohio. The most prominent Copperhead, Clement Vallandigham, in his run for governor of Ohio, was openly calling for soldiers to desert and threatening that the Western states would form their own "Peace Democracy" if war sentiment persisted in the Northeast.

On May 5, military officials in Dayton placed Vallandigham under arrest. He was tried by a military commission and convicted the next day. Vallandigham's arrest provoked a howl of outrage among Northern Democrats, but when Judge H. H. Leavitt denied the motion for a writ of habeas corpus in the Vallandigham case, Lincoln declared the decision to be worth three victories in the field. "Must I shoot a simple-minded soldier boy who deserts," Lincoln later explained, "while I must not touch a hair of a wiley agitator who induces him to desert? I think...to silence the agitator, and save the boy, is not only constitutional, but...a great mercy."

MAY 4 As the Battle of Chancellorsville comes to its catastrophic close, Lincoln is alarmed to learn that Confederate forces have reoccupied the strategic heights above the town of Fredericksburg, Virginia *(below)*.

MAY 18 Lincoln congratulates Queen Victoria of Great Britain on the marriage of her son, the Prince of Wales.

MAY 24 The President meets with an emissary sent by Horace Greeley. The New York *Tribune* editor is already actively seeking candidates to oppose Lincoln's reelection in 1864.

MAY 12 News of the death of Confederate General Stonewall Jackson reaches Washington. After a brilliant victory in the field, Jackson had been shot by his own men while riding with his staff at dusk. "I know not how to replace him," confesses Robert E. Lee.

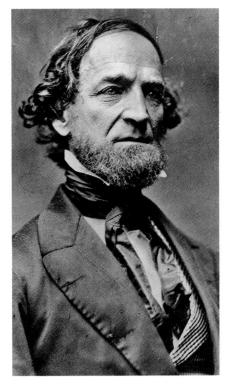

MAY 26 Lincoln acknowledges the letter of his old Illinois friend, Congressman Isaac Newton Arnold *(above)*, requesting that the President dismiss General Halleck because "the people generally believe that it is his personal hostility & prejudice that has driven from the public service, & keeps out of employment such men as Butler, Frémont, & Sigel." The President's reply suggests that he knows better. He denounces the men who prefer "political generals" over career military officers, and ends, "Without claiming to be your superior, which I do not, my position enables me to understand my duty in all these matters better than you possibly can..."

Emboldened by his crackdown on Clement Vallandigham, Ambrose Burnside, now commander of the Department of the Ohio, ordered the suppression of seditious newspapers in his jurisdiction. On June 1, he closed down the Chicago *Times,* which had recently described the Emancipation Proclamation as "monstrous" and "revolting." This time Lincoln overruled his general. On June 4, acting on behalf of freedom of the press, the President revoked the suspension of the *Times* and went on to acknowledge its distinguished nine-year history.

At Vicksburg, Grant settled into a protracted siege, generating weeks of boredom that supposedly drove the general to drink. In Virginia, Hooker devised a plan to circumvent Lee, take Richmond, and then recross the Potomac to attack the Army of Northern Virginia. The President reminded Hooker that his "true objective point" was the rebel army, which was now strung out across the state and moving north. "If the head of Lee's army is at Martinsburg and the tail of it on the Plank road between Fredericksburg and Chancellorsville, the animal must be very slim somewhere. Could you not break him?" asked Lincoln in his own characteristic manner.

With the Federal blockade creating desperate hardship for the Confederacy, and Hooker's army off balance, Lee decided to gamble all on a second invasion of the North. In response, Lincoln called out 100,000 militia in Maryland, Pennsylvania, Ohio, and what would soon be the state of West Virginia.

Simultaneously, following a quarrel about whether to relieve the garrison at Harpers Ferry, Lincoln accepted the resignation of Joseph Hooker from the Army of the Potomac. Resisting pressure from prominent Pennsylvanians and elements within the army to restore McClellan to command, on June 27 Lincoln gave the nod to George Gordon Meade, a competent if unimaginative Pennsylvanian with a background in engineering. Since it was increasingly obvious that a major confrontation with the rebels would happen soon in Meade's home state, Lincoln reasoned that the general "will fight well on his own dunghill."

As Lee's troops began to come down out of the mountains, the two huge armies of the North and the South were beginning to converge on a sleepy little Pennsylvania town called Gettysburg.

JUNE 10 The President, accompanied by Secretary of War Stanton and General Samuel Heintzelman, visits Fort Lyon, near Alexandria, Virginia, after a bad explosion there the previous day. Lincoln also wires his wife in Philadelphia, where she is on a visit with her youngest son: "Think you better put 'Tad's' pistol away. I had an ugly dream about him."

JUNE 15 Lincoln informs General Hooker at Fairfax Station, Virginia: "The facts are now known here that Winchester and Martinsburg were both besieged yesterday; the troops from Martinsburg have got into Harpers Ferry *(above)* without loss; those from Winchester, are also in, having lost, in killed, wounded and missing, about one third of their number."

JUNE 14 As Lee's army advances northward, Lincoln urges Joseph Hooker and his fun-loving subordinates (shown below horsing around) to seize the opportunity.

JUNE 24 General Darius N. Couch, at Harrisburg, Pennsylvania, where Lee's invasion is causing widespread panic, receives a telegram from the White House: "Have you any reports of the enemy moving into Pennsylvania? and if any, what?"

JUNE 27 On the eve of a major confrontation in Pennsylvania, Lincoln replaces General Joseph Hooker with General George Gordon Meade (above) as the commander-in-chief of the Army of the Potomac. Meade, known for his hot temper and high-strung nerves, is called "the old snapping turtle" behind his back.

During the first three blistering hot days of July, as Lincoln waited for news, two vast armies fought in the Pennsylvania fields outside Gettysburg. The losses each day were enormous — 17,000 the first day and 16,000 the second. Only nightfall put a halt to the carnage, though not to the screams and moans of the wounded. Day three saw a huge Confederate death march into direct Union fire, later to be known as "Pickett's charge." Five thousand men were mowed down in the space of ninety terrible minutes. By nightfall of July 3, it was all over. Lee had failed and was beginning to withdraw.

"News from the Army of the Potomac," announced Lincoln the next day, "is such as to cover that Army with the highest honor."

Equally good tidings came in from the West. Rebel forces in Vicksburg had surrendered to General Grant on July 4. Lincoln "almost hugged" his navy secretary when word reached Washington. "Now, if General Meade can complete his work, so gloriously prosecuted thus far, by the literal or substantial destruction of Lee's army, the rebellion will be over."

At first, it seemed that Lincoln's hopes might come true. The weather, so often the scourge of Union war efforts, was on their side. Heavy rains swelled the Potomac, making it impossible for Lee's retreating army to cross quickly back into Virginia.

But Meade showed no taste for pursuit and, like McClellan after Antietam, proceeded to waste day after precious day. When he finally made his move, it was too late — Lee's army had crossed back into Virginia. "We had them within our grasp," Lincoln cried out. "I am distressed immeasurably because of it."

At the same time that Lee was slipping away, huge draft riots erupted in New York City among white, mostly poor Irish immigrants, who could not afford the price of an "exemption" and who were furious at being conscripted into a war dedicated to freeing slaves. The rioters' chief victims were New York City blacks, including children.

In the South, alarmed by the Union's new Negro troops, such as the well-trained 54th Massachusetts Regiment, the Confederates declared that Northern black soldiers, if captured, would be put to death. On July 30, Lincoln warned of possible retaliation, insisting that "the government of the United States will give the same protection to all its soldiers."

SEPTEMBER 23 It doesn't take David Wills and the committee in charge of the dedication ceremony at Gettysburg long to fix upon the chief speaker for the day. Their choice is the famed silver-tongued New England orator Edward Everett *(right)*. Today Wills writes to Everett in Boston: "I am...instructed by the governors of the different states interested in the project, to invite you cordially to join with them in ceremonies, and to deliver the oration for the occasion."

As it had been for his entire presidency, Missouri remained one of Lincoln's most perplexing problems. The slave state was a hotbed of pro-rebel sentiment, and even the pro-Union forces quarreled bitterly, no matter who Washington installed as governor. On October 1, Lincoln ordered the commander of the Department of the Missouri, General John M. Schofield, "as far as practicable, to compel the excited people there to leave one another alone." When a group of Missourians arrived in Washington to criticize Schofield, Lincoln complained that the quarreling allowed a criminal element to take advantage of the confusion: "Every foul bird comes abroad, and every dirty reptile rises up."

Off-year elections were held in Ohio and Pennsylvania on October 13, and Lincoln was pleased to learn that Andrew Curtin, a staunch Unionist, was reelected governor of Pennsylvania. In Ohio, the Democratic anti-war candidate for governor was none other than Clement Laird Vallandigham, whom Lincoln had banished to the Confederacy in May, but who had resurfaced in Canada to run his campaign from afar. Now, in October, he was resoundingly defeated.

The Battle of Chickamauga spurred Lincoln to shake up the military leadership in the West. Since the defeat, Lincoln complained, General Rosecrans had acted "confused and stunned like a duck hit on the head." Now the Confederates were on the offensive: they were laying siege to Chattanooga and threatening to retake parts of Tennessee. On October 17, Rosecrans was relieved of command and replaced by General George H. Thomas, who had performed well at Chickamauga. More important, on October 16, Lincoln named Ulysses S. Grant the commander of practically the entire western theater.

Not all the matters facing the President this month were so weighty. He was asked on October 26 to pass judgment on a Captain James M. Cutts, Jr., who, among other things, had pleaded guilty to the charge that he had peeped through a Cincinnati boardinghouse keyhole, at a "lady being at the time partly undressed." Lincoln approved Cutts's court-martial, but remitted the sentence. Remembering that he had once met the Swedish minister Count Piper, Lincoln now suggested that the captain's title be changed to "Count Peeper."

OCTOBER 3 By proclamation, Lincoln declares that the last Thursday of November shall be set aside as a day of thanksgiving, promoting family gatherings and celebrations like this imaginary one in the White House, painted from photographs.

OCTOBER 17 Lincoln names General George H. Thomas, who has distinguished himself as the "Rock of Chickamauga" in September, as commander of the Army of the Cumberland, relieving William Rosecrans. "We will hold the town till we starve," Thomas swears in Chattanooga.

OCTOBER 26 Lincoln, thinking ahead, admits to Congressman Elihu B. Washburne that a second term as president would be "a great honor and a great labor, which together, perhaps I would not decline, if tendered."

OCTOBER 11 Ushered in by Secretary Seward, Charlotte Cushman, a renowned actress who often helps the war effort by working on behalf of the U.S. Sanitary Commission, pays an evening call on Lincoln.

OCTOBER 16 Ulysses S. Grant is named by Lincoln commander of the Departments of the Ohio, Cumberland, and Tennessee, placing him at the head of virtually all military operations in the West. Soon after, Grant sets up a Spartan headquarters in Chattanooga *(inset)*.

OCTOBER 30 The Lincolns see actress Maggie Mitchell at Ford's Theatre in a benefit performance of *Fanchon, the Cricket*.

When Lincoln's name was added to those who were to receive an official invitation to a cemetery dedication on the Gettysburg battlefield, it was assumed that he would not be able to attend. After all, the President received myriad invitations to every sort of event and regularly turned them down..What the ceremony planners had not reckoned on was Lincoln's desire not only to attend but to speak. Finally asked on November 2 to make "a few appropriate remarks" to go along with Edward Everett's main oration, Lincoln spent much of the first part of November composing what he would say. He also attended a production of *The Marble Heart* at Ford's Theatre, which starred a flamboyant and tempestuous young actor named John Wilkes Booth. Three days later, most of political Washington turned out for the celebrated marriage of Kate Chase, the socialite daughter of the treasury secretary. With Tad sick, it was hard for Lincoln to leave Washington for Gettysburg, Pennsylvania, on November 18, but he managed. The next day, on a crowded little platform at the newly created cemetery, he listened patiently for one hour and fifty-seven minutes to Edward Everett's eloquent bombast. Then Lincoln rose, and in little more than two minutes, delivered the ten simple sentences that constitute what has since become regarded as the single greatest speech in American history.

On the train back to Washington that night, Lincoln felt dizzy and exhausted. He was diagnosed as having varioloid, a mild form of smallpox. "Now I have something I can give everybody," the President quipped. The illness laid him low for more than three weeks.

In Tennessee, the besieged Union forces finally struck back. The Battle of Chattanooga began on November 23, as troops under U. S. Grant and George Thomas tried to break Braxton Bragg's grip on the city. Union soldiers punctuated their charges with cries of "Chickamauga," avenging their defeat of two months earlier. In the fog at Lookout Mountain on November 24 and at Missionary Ridge on November 25, the Federal troops won decisive victories. Chattanooga effectively completed the "liberation" of Tennessee, one of Lincoln's most cherished military objectives since the beginning of the war.

NOVEMBER 19 The Gettysburg Address and its author, in a photograph taken during the time Lincoln was writing his historic words

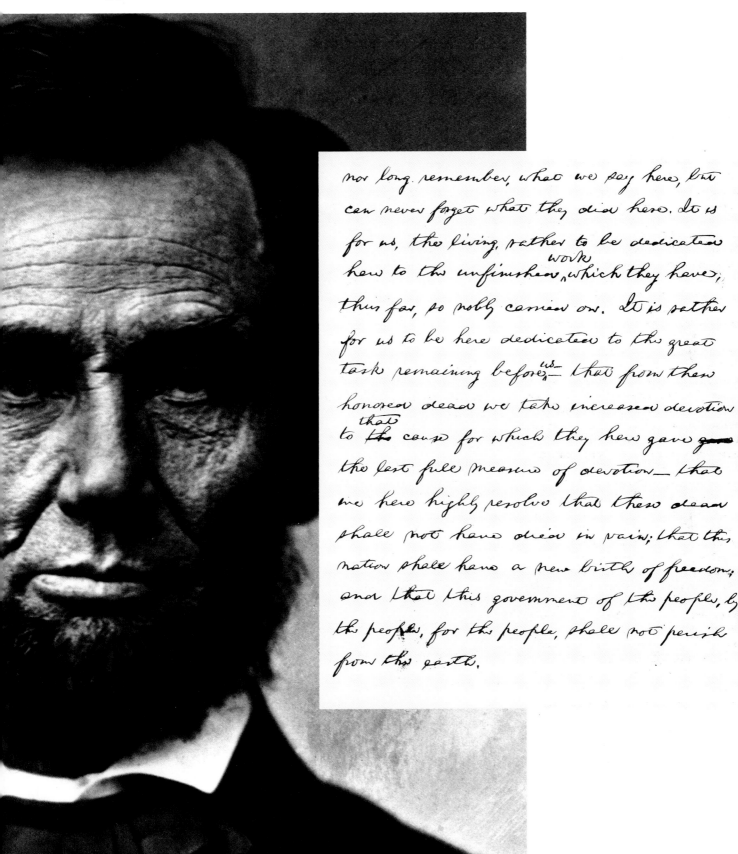

nor long remember, what we say here, but can never forget what they did here. It is for us, the living, rather to be dedicated here to the unfinished work, which they have, thus far, so nobly carried on. It is rather for us to be here dedicated to the great task remaining before us— that from these honored dead we take increased devotion to that cause for which they here gave the last full measure of devotion— that we here highly resolve that these dead shall not have died in vain; that this nation shall have a new birth of freedom; and that this government of the people, by the people, for the people, shall not perish from the earth.

Lincoln had made it clear during 1863 that no compromise with the seceded states was possible, but by year's end he was eager to welcome back into the fold those who were willing to forswear the rebellion. On December 8, the same day as his annual message to Congress, Lincoln issued a Proclamation of Amnesty and Reconstruction, offering full pardons to those who chose to "resume their allegiance to the United States" by means of a loyalty oath. Exceptions to the offer included high-ranking members of the Confederate government and military, those who had left the United States armed forces to serve with the rebels, and those who had mistreated either black or white prisoners of war. His reconstruction plan was similarly free of vindictiveness, designed to bring Southern states back into the Union as quickly as possible. Once 10 percent of those who had voted in 1860 took the loyalty oath and agreed to abide permanently by Union anti-slavery measures, a state government composed of those voters would be eligible for recognition.

"I never have seen such an effect produced by a public document," wrote John Hay following the proclamation. "Men acted as if the millennium had come....Lovejoy...said it was glorious. 'I shall live,' he said, 'to see slavery ended in America....' Kellogg of Michigan...said, 'The President...is the great man of the century....He sees more widely and clearly than anybody.'" Even such usual critics as Horace Greeley had to agree it was "devilish good!" The voices of those who wished for harsher treatment of the South were lost in the commotion, and the bilateral support that had so long evaded Lincoln was finally washing him in praise. Near the end of the year, Lincoln decided to test out for himself just how receptive the rebels might be to his offer of reconciliation. Accompanying Secretary of War Stanton to Point Lookout, Maryland, he assessed the sentiments of the ten thousand rebel prisoners of war encamped there. Perhaps it was a matter of wishful thinking, but he and Stanton "satisfied themselves that not less than a thousand, or about the tenth of the whole number, are ready to enter the service of the United States."

DECEMBER 6 Lincoln sends for Congressman Schuyler Colfax of Indiana, who has just been nominated Speaker of the House by acclamation.

DECEMBER 23 Lincoln confers with Senator James H. Lane of Kansas in one of a series of discussions about ongoing conflicts among Union factions in Missouri and Kansas.

MID-DECEMBER

Three months after the death of Confederate General Ben Hardin Helm, who fell at Chickamauga, the Lincolns are visited by his stricken widow, Mary's much younger half-sister, Emilie. Following are excerpts from Mrs. Helm's diary. Mr. Lincoln and my sister met me with the warmest affection, we were all too grief-stricken at first for speech....Sister and I dined intimately, alone. Our tears gathered silently and fell unheeded as with choking voices we tried to talk of immaterial things....Sister has always a cheerful word and a smile for Mr. Lincoln, who seems thin and care-worn and seeing her sorrowful would add to his care....Sister Mary's tenderness for me is very touching. She and Brother Lincoln pet me as if I were a child, and, without words, try to comfort me. ...General Sickles...said in a loud, dictatorial voice, slapping the table with his hand, "You should not have that rebel in your house."

DECEMBER 23 To John Hay, Lincoln relates a dream in which he is among a group of people. One of them remarks: "He is a very common-looking man." The President replies: "Common-looking people are the best in the world: that is the reason the Lord makes so many of them." Comments Hay: "Waking, he remembered it, and told it as rather a neat thing."

Mr. Lincoln instantly drew himself up and said in a quiet, dignified voice, "Excuse me, General Sickles, my wife and I are in the habit of choosing our own guests. We do not need from our friends either advice or assistance in the matter. Besides," he added, "the little 'rebel' came because I ordered her to come, it was not of her own volition."...Mr. Lincoln, in the intimate talks we had was very much affected over the misfortunes of our family; and of my husband he said, "You know, Little Sister, I tried to have Ben come with me. I hope you do not feel any bitterness or that I am in any way to blame for all this sorrow." I answered it was "the fortune of war" and that while my husband loved him and had been deeply grateful to him for his generous offer to make him an officer in the Federal Army, he had to follow his conscience and that for weal or woe he felt he must side with his own people. Mr. Lincoln put his arms around me and we both wept.

DECEMBER 19 Seamen from the Russian Atlantic Squadron are invited to an afternoon reception at the White House.

DECEMBER 21 At the War Department, Lincoln watches with interest as decoders interpret a message intercepted in the mail in New York and intended for Judah P. Benjamin, the Confederate secretary of state.

DECEMBER 31 Although Union armies recorded some impressive victories in 1863, the Army of the Potomac in the crucial eastern theater ends the year with little to show beyond the repulsion of Lee's incursion into Pennsylvania. Shown here are the army's winter quarters near Rappahannock Station, Virginia.

LINCOLN AND SLAVERY: 1863

"I have been shaking hands since nine o'clock this morning, and my right arm is almost paralyzed," said Lincoln on January 1, 1863, after being presented with a great rolled-up scroll of his proclamation by Secretary of State Seward and his son Frederick. "If my name ever goes into history it will be for this act, and my whole soul is in it." "He then turned to the table," reported John W. Forney of the Washington *Chronicle*, "took up the pen...and slowly, firmly wrote that 'Abraham Lincoln' with which the whole world is now familiar."

There were immediate outcries against the Emancipation Proclamation. If the South saw it as a "fiendish" "triumph of fanaticism," many Northern critics found it far too circumscribed. The proclamation freed only those slaves in areas inaccessible to the Union military, and was filled with exemptions, such as the entire state of Tennessee. Lincoln himself admitted "that it only aided those who came into our lines and that it was inoperative as to those who did not give themselves up." Nevertheless, the Emancipation Proclamation was the turning point in Lincoln's administration. Frederick Douglass and others would forever call the day it was signed into law "Black America's Independence Day." Not only did it transform the war, finally, into a war against slavery, but because of it, blacks became suddenly eligible and sought after to serve in the Union Army as soldiers. They are "the great *available* and yet unavailed of, force for restoring the Union," Lincoln declared. Over the next months, as recruiters took to the road to inspire black volunteers, the armies began to swell. Grant's troops in Mississippi and Tennessee received former slaves "in vast numbers — an army in themselves," flocking into the Union camps as the plantations were abandoned. In all, there

This is an 1863 poster used by Philadelphia's Supervisory Committee for Recruiting Colored Regiments. The engraving shows black soldiers at Camp "William Penn" with their white officer.

would be a grand total of 180,000 black Union soldiers.

In July 1863 the all-black 54th Massachusetts Regiment fought a heroic and historic battle at Fort Wagner, South Carolina, spearheading a desperate charge and proving itself equal to the bravest of white troops. Frederick Douglass's son Lewis, present at the attack, wrote, "How I got out of that fight alive I cannot tell.... I wish we had a hundred thousand Colored troops." Contemplating the heroism of these men, Lincoln was forever changed. He spoke less and less (and finally not at all) about colonization, and more and more about the black man's earned place in America. "You say you will not fight to free negroes," he wrote to the Springfield public in hopes of being heard by the whole country. "Some of them seem willing to fight for you.... But negroes, like other people, act upon motives. Why should they do anything for us, if we will do nothing for them? If they stake their lives for us, they must be prompted by the strongest motive—even the promise of freedom. And the promise being made, must be kept.... Peace does not appear so distant as it did.... And then, there will be some black men who can remember that, with silent tongue, and clenched teeth, and steady eye, and well-poised bayonet, they have helped mankind on to this great consummation; while, I fear, there will be some white ones, unable to forget that, with malignant heart, and deceitful speech, they have strove to hinder it."

By year's end, Lincoln had deemed his efforts a success. The Emancipation Proclamation had won him Europe's approval of the Union cause, and it had done so without any of the predicted social chaos. "It is the central act of my administration," Lincoln liked to say. It is the "one thing that will make people remember I ever lived."

In a public letter to James C. Conkling of Springfield on August 26, Lincoln praised the overall military efforts of the North, which were finally bearing fruit. With his background as a flatboat operator, a Sangamon River promoter, and inventor of a boat-lifting device, Lincoln took special interest in the progress of the war on the rivers and seas.

The signs look better. The Father of Waters again goes unvexed to the sea. Thanks to the great North-West for it. Nor yet wholly to them. Three hundred miles up, they met New-England, Empire, Key-Stone, and Jersey, hewing their way right and left. The Sunny South too, in more colors than one, also lent a hand. On the spot, their part of the history was jotted down in black and white. The job was a great national one; and let none be banned who bore an honorable part in it. And while those who have cleared the great river may well be proud, even that is not all. It is hard to say that anything has been more bravely, and well done, than at Antietam, Murfreesboro, Gettysburg, and on many fields of lesser note. Nor must Uncle Sam's Web-feet be forgotten. At all the watery margins they have been present. Not only on the deep sea, the broad bay, and the rapid river, but also up the narrow muddy bayou, and wherever the ground was a little damp, they have been, and made their tracks. Thanks to all. For the great republic — for the principle it lives by, and keeps alive — for man's vast future, — thanks to all.... Still let us not be over-sanguine of a speedy final triumph. Let us be quite sober. Let us diligently apply the means, never doubting that a just God, in his own good time, will give us the rightful result....

In his annual message to Congress, on December 8, 1863, Lincoln lets Edwin Stanton speak on the general military situation, but himself dwells extensively on the role of the navy. Without advice, early in the war, he had called for a naval blockade of Southern ports—perhaps his greatest contribution to overall military strategy in the Civil War.

The duties devolving on the naval branch of the service during the year, and throughout the whole of this unhappy contest, have been discharged with fidelity and eminent success. The extensive blockade has been constantly increasing in efficiency, as the navy has expanded; yet on so long a line it has so far been impossible to entirely suppress illicit trade. From returns received at the Navy Department, it appears that more than one thousand vessels have been captured since the blockade was instituted, and that the value of prizes already sent in for adjudication amounts to over thirteen millions of dollars.... The increase of the number of seamen in the public service, from seven thousand five hundred men, in the spring of 1861, to about thirty four thousand at the present time has been accomplished without special legislation, or extraordinary bounties to promote that increase....

In the midst of other cares...we must not lose sight of the fact that the war power is still our main reliance. To that power alone can we look, yet for a time, to give confidence to the people in the contested regions, that the insurgent power will not again overrun them. Until that confidence shall be established, little can be done anywhere for what is called reconstruction. Hence our chiefest care must still be directed to the army and navy, who have thus far borne their harder part so nobly and well....

In June 1863, Union cavalry cross the Rappahannock River near Fredericksburg.

Chapter 8

1864

Starting high, Lincoln's popularity plummets during the year; his party almost rejects him, but in November the people don't.

The President with Tad, the only member of his family with whom Lincoln was formally photographed, February 9, 1864

On a cold day in early January, following Lincoln's intense lobbying of key members of Congress, Senator John B. Henderson of Missouri introduced a joint resolution to abolish slavery throughout the United States by means of a constitutional amendment. A two-thirds majority in both houses of Congress was required to send what would be the Thirteenth Amendment to the states for ratification. The measure's chances for passage were considered better in the Senate than in the more conservative House. In fact, it failed to get the necessary two-thirds vote in the House.

The previous year had seen significant military gains for the North, but the rebel Armies of Northern Virginia and Tennessee still presented imposing obstacles. Once again, Lincoln began thinking in terms of an overall military strategy that would pressure the insurgents at several different points at the same time. Pleased by Ulysses S. Grant's continuing successes in the West, the President began to turn to the general for a comprehensive plan to crush the remnants of the rebellion. Grant, pleading that he had been so enmeshed in his own responsibilities that he had not had much time to consider these matters, submitted an unworkable plan for the Army of the Potomac to travel by water to North Carolina and take Richmond from the south. Lincoln was disappointed. Grant's idea was reminiscent of McClellan's 1862 Peninsula campaign, and it made Richmond, rather than Lee's army, its target. Nevertheless, the President was coming to believe that Grant's daring in the field might be just what was called for in the East.

As he worked to encourage the creation of new loyal governments in Louisiana and Arkansas—and, harder still, in Florida and Tennessee—Lincoln was also increasingly preoccupied with the question of the economic future of the freedmen. After giving up the idea of black colonization, the President now began to advocate a wage-labor system. He approved a policy allowing plantation owners in liberated areas to hire former slaves on a wage basis, setting aside his previous statements about the social and economic handicaps that slavery had imposed upon black Americans.

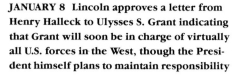

JANUARY 8 Lincoln approves a letter from Henry Halleck to Ulysses S. Grant indicating that Grant will soon be in charge of virtually all U.S. forces in the West, though the President himself plans to maintain responsibility

JANUARY 21 The Lincolns host a lavish official dinner for the members of the Cabinet, justices of the Supreme Court, and their wives, in the State Dining Room at the White House.

for the overall strategy of the war. This month, Lincoln tests Grant's willingness to adopt the vigorous, multi-front attack on the Confederacy that the President has been urging for more than two years.

JANUARY 9 Lincoln orders government buildings to be draped in black for two weeks to honor Caleb B. Smith, the former secretary of the interior, who dies in Indianapolis.

JANUARY 23 A cotton trader inquires of Lincoln whether plantation owners might recognize the freedom of slaves and then hire them back. "I should regard such cases with great favor," Lincoln answers, "and should, as the principle [sic], treat them precisely as I would treat the same number of free white people in the same relation and condition."

JANUARY 16 Outspoken young activist Anna Dickinson, who speaks vigorously on behalf of anti-slavery and women's rights causes, visits the White House, and that evening Lincoln attends her lecture at the Capitol. Dickinson had turned to oratory after losing her job at the Philadelphia Mint in 1861 for openly accusing George McClellan of treason. In the future, she will lash out at Lincoln as well.

JANUARY 24 Among Lincoln's dinner guests this night is General Rosecrans's former chief of staff, General James A. Garfield, now a congressman from Ohio, who will take up residence in the White House himself seventeen years later.

With soldiers needed for major campaigns in the spring, Lincoln began the month by ordering a draft of 500,000 more men. But as General William Tecumseh Sherman left Vicksburg to begin a campaign in Mississippi, Lincoln, in Washington, confessed to Owen Lovejoy, "This war is eating my life out."

The year 1864 was an election year, and by February political maneuvering was already well under way. Although Lincoln's popularity was still high, three years of bloody war had strengthened the hand of the Peace Democrats, who continued to press for a negotiated settlement with the Confederacy. Within his own party, Lincoln's principal problem was the radicals, who felt that the prosecution of the war was not vigorous enough and who were increasingly troubled by the generosity of the President's reconstruction policy. The most important challenger was in Lincoln's own Cabinet: Salmon Chase, secretary of the treasury, had hungered for the presidency ever since the Republican Party was born. Chase and Lincoln had frequently clashed over policy decisions and over Treasury Department appointments, which were often considered political plums. Now congressional radicals began to test the waters for a movement to support the secretary for the Republican Party nomination.

On February 22, the secretary's candidacy became a public matter when Senator Samuel C. Pomeroy of Kansas issued an open letter claiming Lincoln's reelection to be "practically impossible" and that Republicans should rally around Salmon Chase. The appearance of the "Pomeroy Circular" created a sensation, with its suggestion that a member of the President's own Cabinet should replace the head of state on the party ticket.

Although Chase hastened to apologize to Lincoln, claiming he "had no knowledge of the existence of this letter," the President judiciously waited a week before replying. Finally, deciding that the treasury secretary was less dangerous inside the administration than outside, Lincoln wrote Chase and agreed "that neither of us can be justly held responsible for what our respective friends may do without our instigation or countenance." But even while forgiving the secretary for his transgression, Lincoln slyly indicated his skepticism of Chase's claim of ignorance. After all, if the President had advance knowledge of Pomeroy's efforts, could Chase have been wholly in the dark?

FEBRUARY 9 The two photographs of Lincoln most familiar to us today are taken during a single sitting at Brady's Washington studio. At the left is the three-quarters face portrait that was adapted for the front of the five-dollar bill; above is the profile used a guide in the making of the Lincoln penny.

FEBRUARY 6 On a visit to Congressman Owen Lovejoy, Lincoln talks of the debilitating effect of the war upon him. He remarks, "I have a strong impression that I shall not live to see the end."

FEBRUARY 6 *An appraisal of Lincoln by Harriet Beecher Stowe, author of* Uncle Tom's Cabin, *is reprinted in* Littell's Living Age. *When the President met Stowe, he had said, "So you're the little woman who wrote the book that made this great war."*

Lincoln is a strong man, but his strength is of a peculiar kind: it is not aggressive so much as passive, and among passive things, it is like the strength not so much of a stone buttress as of a wire cable. It is strength swaying to every influence, yielding on this side and on that to popular needs, yet tenaciously and inflexibly bound to carry its great end; and probably by no other kind of strength could our national ship have been drawn safely thus far during the tossings and tempests which beset her way....

We do not mean to give the impression that Lincoln is a religious man in the sense in which that term is popularly applied. We believe he has never made any such profession, but we see evidence in passing through this dreadful national crisis he has been forced by the very anguish of the struggle to look upward, where any rational creature must look for support. No man in this agony has suffered more and deeper, albeit with a dry, weary, patient pain, that seemed to some like insensibility. "Whichever way it ends," he said to the writer, "I have the impression that *I* sha'n't last long after it's over."

FEBRUARY 10 *Tonight a fire destroys the President's private stables. Two of Tad's ponies are lost in the blaze. White House guard Smith Stimmel describes the incident. Left: Tad shows his riding style on the diminutive pacer Little Jeff, at City Point.*

Just then the front door of the White House flew open with a jerk, and out came the President buttoning his coat around him, and said to me, "Where is the fire, what's burning?" I said, "It seems to be around in the vicinity of the stable." With that he started off on a dog-trot down the steps and along the way leading to the stable. When he started to go to the fire, I thought to myself, "Old fellow, you are the man we are guarding, guess I'll go along." So I struck out on the double-quick and went with him, keeping close to his side; but he took such long strides that his dog-trot was almost a dead run for me.

As soon as we got around where we could see what was burning, we saw that, sure enough, the White House stable was on fire....Mr. Lincoln asked hastily if the horses had been taken out, and when told they had not, he rushed through the crowd and began to break open one of the large doors with his own hands; but the building was full of fire, and none of the horses could be saved.

On March 1, Abraham Lincoln nominated Ulysses S. Grant for the rank of lieutenant general, previously held in the field only by George Washington. The Senate confirmed the appointment on the following day. "I never met Mr. Lincoln until called to the capital," wrote Grant about his war commission. "Mr. Lincoln stated to me that he had never professed to be a military man or to know how campaigns should be conducted....All he ever wanted...was some one who would take the responsibility and act." Now Lincoln finally had such a man.

On March 9, Lincoln assigned Grant to command the armies of the United States. Although Grant preferred to make his headquarters in the West, Lincoln wanted him close to Washington to help keep the war effort from being derailed by politicians. Their compromise was that Grant himself would direct operations from a headquarters established in the field with the Army of the Potomac.

At the same time, Lincoln received the good news that Salmon Chase had withdrawn his name from consideration as a candidate for president. Lincoln's strongest potential adversary had been neutralized, but rumblings of discontent still echoed through radical circles.

One by one, the former slave states of the Union were dismantling slavery. In Maryland, where Lincoln had advocated gradual emancipation, a movement gathered steam for the immediate end to slavery. "I had thought the *gradual* would produce less confusion," wrote Lincoln in a private letter. "[But] [m]y wish is that all who are for emancipation *in any form,* shall co-operate...." The reconstruction efforts in Arkansas and Louisiana were also making progress. On March 14, loyal Arkansas voters overwhelmingly approved a new constitution that declared secession void, abolished slavery, and repudiated the Confederate debt. A moderate pro-Union governor had been elected in Louisiana, and Lincoln wrote to him to urge that at least some blacks — "as, for instance, the very intelligent, and especially those who have fought gallantly in our ranks" — be granted suffrage at the upcoming convention. Neither state actually went this far, but Lincoln continued to press for full citizenship for blacks, in particular for veterans.

MARCH 2   Lincoln sees famed actor Edwin Booth, the older brother of John Wilkes Booth, play Hamlet at Grover's Theatre. Before the show, while sitting for a painting, the President recites from memory the King's famous soliloquy confessing his guilt and his abuse of power.

MARCH 8   On the evening before the presentation of his official commission as lieutenant general, Ulysses S. Grant is a surprise guest at a White House reception. Grant, just arrived in Washington, makes his entrance to the crowded East Room at 9:30 p.m., and Lincoln and his new commander of the Union forces meet for the first time.

MARCH 15   Robert H. Hendershot *(left)*, the "gallant Drummer Boy" who won wide acclaim for his courage at the Battle of Fredericksburg, is received by the President. "[His] history is briefly written on the fine drum...which he now carries," comments Lincoln. *Above:* A drum-and-fife corps of the 93rd New York Infantry at Bealton, Virginia

MARCH 17 The war's toll is made vivid for Lincoln with the death of Ulric Dahlgren, son of Admiral John A. Dahlgren, Lincoln's ordnance chief, killed leading a cavalry raid on Richmond. Only six weeks earlier, while being shaved, Lincoln was discussing personal and military matters with him. Now the President asks General Butler to telegraph, if "you obtain the remains of Col. Dahlgren."

MARCH 25 *Francis B. Carpenter, a painter who is working on several portraits of the President, spends the evening with Lincoln.*

[L]eaning back in his chair, [he] said, "There is a poem that has been a great favorite with me for years, to which my attention was first called when a young man." ...Then, half closing his eyes, he repeated the poem, "Oh! why should the spirit of mortal be proud?"

...[H]e continued: "There are some quaint, queer verses, written, I think, by Oliver Wendell Holmes, entitled, 'The Last Leaf,' one of which is to me inexpressibly touching....

"The mossy marbles rest
  On the lips that he has pressed
    In their bloom;
  And the names he loved to hear
  Have been carved for many a year
    On the tomb."

As he finished this verse, he said, in his emphatic way, "For pure pathos, in my judgement, there is nothing finer than those six lines in the English language!"

By now, Grant had developed a plan along the lines that Lincoln himself had urged as far back as January 1862: the Army of the Potomac would continue to battle the Army of Northern Virginia.

"Wherever Lee goes, there you will go also," Grant told George Gordon Meade, who remained the commander of the Union's most powerful army. Meanwhile, Benjamin F. Butler's Army of the James would cut off the railroads south of Richmond. In the West, William Tecumseh Sherman's 100,000-strong Division of the Mississippi would invade Georgia, while Nathaniel Banks would drive on Mobile from Louisiana. Lincoln applauded the all-out nature of Grant's plan. "Those not skinning can hold a leg," he commented.

Faced with fighting against black soldiers in 1863, the Confederate government had threatened to kill captured blacks and their white officers. On April 12, one rebel apparently followed through on this threat. After General Nathan Bedford Forrest's men stormed Union-held Fort Pillow, Tennessee, and forced the Northerners to surrender, Forrest's men proceeded to massacre what may have been as many as three hundred black soldiers and their officers. As reports from Fort Pillow made their way north, pressure mounted on the President to respond in kind. Lincoln was cautious, promising full protection to black soldiers, but he was not eager to retaliate without the benefit of a full investigation. "Blood cannot restore blood, and government should not act for revenge..." he mused on one occasion. "[But if] there has been the massacre of three hundred there," he declared at another time, "the retribution shall...surely come."

Through the first part of the month, Grant came regularly to Washington to confer with Lincoln, but as spring advanced, the general elected to remain near his Eastern army to prepare for the major offensive. "You are vigilant and self-reliant," Lincoln wrote approvingly on April 30, "and, pleased with this, I wish not to obtrude any constraints or restraints upon you." Nevertheless, the President wandered nervously through the White House that same night, anxious about the upcoming campaign. He rousted his secretaries out of bed to read them selections from the English poet and humorist Thomas Hood, and he paced the hallways in his slippers, his nightshirt hanging, described John Hay, "like the tail feathers of an enormous ostrich."

APRIL 4 For the first time Lincoln meets General Philip H. Sheridan, Grant's newly appointed cavalry commander, a diminutive officer in his early thirties who will stand out as the leader of the Shenandoah Valley campaign later in the year.

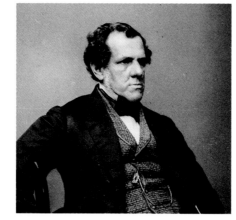

APRIL 6 The President goes to the House of Representatives to hear a speech by George Thompson, a noted English anti-slavery speaker.

APRIL 8 Lincoln attends another Shakespeare tragedy, this time seeing Edwin Forrest in *King Lear*.

APRIL 4 *In a revealing letter to Albert G. Hodges in Kentucky, Lincoln reiterates what he "verbally said the other day."* I am naturally anti-slavery....If slavery is not wrong, nothing is wrong. I can not remember when I did not so think, and feel. And yet I have never understood that the Presidency conferred upon me an unrestricted right to act officially upon this judgment and feeling. It was in the oath I took that I would, to the best of my ability, preserve, protect, and defend the Constitution of the United States. I could not take the office without taking the oath. Nor was it my view that I might take an oath to get power, and break the oath in using the power. I understood, too, that in ordinary civil administration this oath even forbade me to practically indulge my primary abstract judgment on the moral question of slavery....I did understand however, that my oath to preserve the constitution to the best of my ability, imposed upon me the duty of preserving, by every indispensable means, that government—that nation—of which that constitution was the organic law....I add a word which was not in the verbal conversation.... I claim not to have controlled events, but confess plainly that events have controlled me....If God now wills the removal of a great wrong, and wills also that we of the North as well as you of the South, shall pay fairly for our complicity in that wrong, impartial history will find therein new cause to attest and revere the justice and goodness of God.

APRIL 26 On this day alone, Lincoln reviews fifty-one court-martial cases, trying to reduce the number of military executions like the one shown above, where soldiers surround a gallows in a giant square.

APRIL 30 Women's rights activist Elizabeth Cady Stanton *(shown here at right with friend and colleague Susan B. Anthony)* is introduced to the President by painter Francis Carpenter.

"If you see the President," Grant told an associate in early May, "tell him, from me, that whatever happens, there will be no turning back." Grant had decided to launch the fiercest offensive of the entire war.

It was evident from the beginning, as Grant moved south into inland Virginia, that this was to be a brutal, relentless campaign in which losses would be heavy and continuous. No sooner had his forces crossed the Rapidan when Lee drew them into a battle in the Wilderness, an area where the terrain was so dense and ragged that the encounter was described as "a battle which no man saw or could see." "Grant has gone into the Wilderness, crawled in, drawn up the ladder, and pulled in the hole after him," Lincoln remarked.

Casualties were heavy, progress was slow, no climax had been reached, but Grant pushed ahead. It was the "supreme moment of his life," wrote General Sherman about his superior. Any other general would have fallen back by now, Lincoln said to John Hay; "it is the dogged pertinacity of Grant that wins." In one brief week in early May, Grant lost 26,000 men, killed or wounded, and still he pressed ahead. The battles at Spotsylvania Court House, North Anna, and Cold Harbor made these names infamous.

"He is a butcher," declared Mary Lincoln, who despised Grant, "and not fit to be at the head of an army." "The immense slaughter of our brave men chills and sickens us all," commented Gideon Welles. Lincoln, too, was deeply moved. White House portraitist Francis Carpenter found him unable to sleep, "pacing back and forth...great black rings under his eyes."

Simultaneously, Lincoln received word of the skeleton-like condition of Union men recently released from a Confederate prison. "Nothing has occurred in the war which causes me to suffer like this," he responded. "[T]he Confederate authorities...must... have...some...excuse!"

On May 31, a convention calling itself the "radical Democracy" met in Cleveland and nominated explorer, anti-slavery man, and failed general John C. Frémont for the presidency. His supporters, who included the zealous abolitionist Wendell Phillips, now hoped to exploit anti-Lincoln sentiment across party lines.

MAY 3 The President requests written opinions from his Cabinet members with regard to the April 12 incident at Fort Pillow, Tennessee, in which black Union soldiers were indiscriminately massacred by a victorious rebel force under General Nathan Bedford Forrest.

MAY 4 The President writes to General Sherman in Chattanooga, urging him to use military resources to aid the suffering civilian population in the area.

MAY *In his biography of Lincoln, former Illinois Congressman Isaac N. Arnold recalls the month's savage fighting and a conversation he had with the President.* During these long days of terrible slaughter the face of the President was grave and anxious, and he looked like one who had lost the dearest member of his own family. I recall one evening late in May, when I met the President in his carriage driving slowly towards the Soldiers' Home. He had just parted from one of those long lines of ambulances.... He paused as we met, and pointing his hand towards the line of wounded men, he said: "Look yonder at those poor fellows. I cannot bear it. This suffering, this loss of life is dreadful." Recalling a letter he had written years before to a suffering friend whose grief he had sought to console, I reminded him of the incident, and asked him: "Do you remember writing to your sorrowing friend these words: 'And this too shall pass away. Never fear. Victory will come.'" "Yes," replied he, "victory will come, but it comes slowly."

MAY 25 Grant's drive toward Richmond and Petersburg is sustained by an enormous

MONTH 39

MAY 14 The death the previous week of General James S. Wadsworth, from wounds received at the Battle of the Wilderness, touches the President deeply, reports John Hay.

supply effort. *Below:* The upper wharves at the supply base at City Point, Virginia

MAY 21 Late this afternoon, in front of the Massaponax Church about fifteen miles south of Fredericksburg, General Grant and his staff stop to rest during their slow progress toward Richmond through the densely wooded area called the Wilderness. The church benches have been carried outside and arranged in a circle. The photograph below shows the lieutenant general leaning over the shoulder of Major General George G. Meade (and obscuring him) as the two leaders inspect a map held flat by another officer.

The Wilderness campaign reached its climax during the first three days of June at Cold Harbor. Impatient with the inconclusiveness of the previous month's efforts, Grant mounted a massive all-out assault on Lee's entrenchments. It failed. In one furious eight-minute rage of fighting on June 3, 12,000 men were killed or wounded in Grant's costliest mistake of the war. Since early May, the Federal army had suffered 54,000 casualties, nearly the size of Lee's entire army. Critics carped that Grant was waging a war of attrition, that he would keep throwing bodies at the rebels until the sheer numerical might of the Union prevailed. Lincoln, however, stood by his general. "We accepted this war for...a worthy object," he told an audience in June, "and the war will end when that object is attained."

Despite the military problems, Lincoln had no real opposition at the Republican National Convention that convened in Baltimore on June 7. The five hundred delegates overwhelmingly nominated him for reelection, ratified a platform that called for a constitutional amendment outlawing slavery, and substituted, in the place of Vice President Hannibal Hamlin, Tennessee's military governor, Andrew Johnson. In thanking one group for its support, Lincoln recalled the saying of "an old Dutch farmer, who remarked...that 'it was not best to swap horses when crossing streams.'"

By the end of the month, Lincoln found himself once more at odds with Salmon Chase. On June 29, after a particularly sharp disagreement with Lincoln, Chase once again submitted his resignation. He was convinced that he was so valuable to the administration that the President would refuse the offer and back down on the question of appointments. To his surprise, Lincoln accepted the resignation. "This is the third time he has thrown this at me, and I do not think I am called on to continue to beg him to take it back," Lincoln explained privately to a friend. Then, in order to defuse a new attack on him by Chase's friends, Lincoln proceeded to name Chase's ally William Pitt Fessenden as the new secretary of the treasury. "When I finally struck on the name of Fessenden," Lincoln told Noah Brooks, "I felt as if the Lord hadn't forsaken me yet."

JUNE 3 Taken at the close of the Wilderness campaign, the photograph *(below)* shows skulls from earlier fighting in these woods and is a grim reminder of the terrible death toll of the past thirty days. Today, in nearby Cold Harbor, 12,000 Union soldiers are killed or wounded in just eight minutes—the deadliest fighting of the entire war.

JUNE 21 Visiting Grant's headquarters near City Point, Virginia, Lincoln has an upset stomach and turns down a glass of champagne because too many people get "seasick ashore from drinking that stuff." But he feels well enough to review the troops that afternoon astride General Grant's horse, Cincinnati *(right)*.

JUNE 8 Lincoln convincingly wins the presidential nomination at the National Union Convention in Baltimore, but his reelection is nevertheless threatened by discontent among radical Republicans on the one side and Peace Democrats on the other.

JUNE 20 The President writes but does not send a letter to the governor of Ohio encouraging him to keep an eye out for traitors. Lincoln remains concerned about the activities of Clement Vallandigham *(below)*, the noted Ohio Copperhead now pushing his peace platform from the safety of Canada.

Executive Mansion,
Washington,
June 30, 1864.

Hon. Salmon P. Chase
My dear Sir.

Your resignation of the office of Secretary of the Treasury, sent me yesterday, is accepted. Of all I have said in commendation of your ability and fidelity, I have nothing to unsay; and yet you and I have reached a point of mutual embarrassment in our official relation which it seems can not be overcome, or longer sustained, consistently with the public service.

Your Obt. Servt.
A. Lincoln

In his diary, Chase *(above)* reacts to Lincoln's letter accepting his resignation. "I had found a good deal of embarrassment from him but what he had found from me I could not imagine."

Things should have been going well for Abraham Lincoln in the summer of 1864. The main rebel armies were on the defensive in Virginia and Georgia. A competent general now commanded the Union armies. Lincoln's nomination for reelection had been rather easily secured. Yet a series of political and military crises turned this into one of the darkest seasons of Lincoln's presidency.

On July 4, in direct confrontation with Lincoln's own more forgiving plans on the subject, Congress sent to the President a reconstruction bill sponsored by Senator Ben Wade of Ohio and Congressman Henry Winter Davis of Maryland. The Wade-Davis bill would require a majority of white males in the state to swear loyalty before reorganization could take place, instead of building on a loyal 10 percent, as under the President's plan. Furthermore, citizens would have to swear an "ironclad oath" that they had never supported the rebellion. The bill also barred anyone who had served in the Confederate Army from participating in a constitutional convention.

Since the congressional session was coming to an end, Lincoln decided simply to "pocket veto" the bill; without his signature within ten days, the bill could not become law. On July 8, he publicly explained his action. What he objected to most, he said, was the plan's inflexibility. He believed that different situations required different approaches. The radicals were furious, but they bided their time crafting a response.

On the military front, it was beginning to look as though the Union would never achieve a decisive victory. Petersburg and Atlanta showed no signs of falling to Grant and Sherman. Grant's engineers succeeded in digging a 586-foot tunnel under the rebel defenses at Petersburg, but when the tunnel was detonated on July 30 and Union troops swarmed into the breach, they were unable to exploit the opening and were slaughtered by a Southern counterattack in the so-called Battle of the Crater.

To make matters worse, the Confederates under General Jubal Early mounted their most serious threat of the war to Washington, D.C. Although the military effects of the raid were inconsequential, the fact that enemy forces actually entered the District of Columbia and engaged defenders on the city's outskirts provided more fodder for the administration's critics.

JULY 1 Following Chase's resignation, Lincoln swiftly nominates William P. Fessenden of Maine as the new secretary of the treasury.

JULY 9 A tense week in Washington begins today as fourteen thousand Confederate troops under General Jubal Early *(below)* approach Silver Spring, Maryland.

JULY 11 Lincoln ventures out to Fort Stevens to survey the fighting. The President shows little regard for his own safety. "With him the only concern seems to be whether we can bag or destroy this force in our front," reports Lincoln's secretary John Hay.

JULY 10 With Early threatening, Lincoln and his family leave the Soldiers' Home, at the recommendation of Secretary of War Edwin Stanton *(below).*

JULY 10 *Noah Brooks reports on a frightening day during Jubal Early's raid on Washington.*

[T]he panic-stricken people from...Maryland...came flocking into Washington by the Seventh street road, flying in wild disorder, and bringing their household goods with them....The President and his family were at their summer residence, the Soldiers' Home, on the outskirts of Washington...but on Sunday night, the 10th, Secretary Stanton, finding that the enemy was within striking distance of that point, sent out a carriage with positive orders that the...President should return to the White House. Lincoln, very much irritated, and against his will, came back to town. He was subsequently greatly...annoyed when he found that...Captain G. V. Fox...had kept under orders a small navy vessel in the Potomac for the President's escape in case the rebel column should succeed in piercing the line of fortifications.

JULY 11, 12, 13 *Surprising those who think he lacks courage, the President takes part in the defense against Jubal Early's attack. John Hay keeps daily notes.*

July 11, 1864. The President concluded to...travel around the defenses....

At three o'clock P.M. the President came in bringing the news that the enemy's advance was at Ft[.] Stevens on the 7th Street road. He was in the Fort when it was first attacked, standing upon the parapet. A soldier roughly ordered him to get down or he would have his head knocked off....

July 12, 1864....The President again made the tour of the fortifications; was again under fire at Ft[.] Stevens; a man was shot at his side....

July 13, 1864. The news this morning would seem to indicate that the enemy is retiring from every point.

JULY 10 Lincoln wires Grant at City Point and asks him to come personally to the aid of the beleaguered capital. Grant declines, but sends the Sixth Corps, which successfully repels Early's assault. *Left:* A two-exposure view of southwest Washington, D.C., taken from the central tower of the Smithsonian Building during the Civil War

JULY 18 An unofficial emissary reports to Lincoln on a meeting with Confederate President Jefferson Davis, who continues to insist that Southern independence is a condition of peace.
Above right: Davis and his wife, Varina. *Above:* The Davises' home near Vicksburg, Mississippi

On August 3, in the wake of the attack on Fort Stevens, Lincoln encouraged Grant to reorganize the command system in Washington. Speaking from experience, the President warned Grant, "It will neither be done nor attempted unless you watch it every day, and hour, and force it."

On August 5, Senator Wade and Congressman Davis issued their reply to Lincoln's pocket veto of their reconstruction bill. Their proclamation, published in the New York *Tribune*, was an all-out assault on Lincoln's "personal ambitions" and "sinister" motives. The congressmen claimed the "right and duty to check the encroachments of the Executive on the authority of Congress." The Wade-Davis manifesto was an open declaration of war on the President by members of his own party.

Lincoln's political situation was never more precarious. The radicals were furious over Lincoln's insistence on presidential reconstruction. The Peace Democrats were gaining strength as the military campaigns failed to show quick results. Conservatives were again calling for the repeal of the Emancipation Proclamation. Republican political boss Thurlow Weed met with Lincoln on August 12 and told him bluntly that his reelection was impossible. "The people are wild for Peace," Weed wrote to Seward. On August 14, a secret council of Republican Party leaders met in New York to try to settle on an alternative candidate. "Mr. Lincoln is already beaten," despaired Horace Greeley. "[W]e must have another ticket to save us from utter overthrow." The one man the leaders could agree on, however—Ulysses S. Grant—had already made it clear that he had no intention of challenging his commander-in-chief.

The President began to reconcile himself to the possibility that he might not be in office to see the war to its end. On August 23, he prepared a memorandum: "This morning, as for some days past, it seems exceedingly probable that this Administration will not be re-elected. Then it will be my duty to so cooperate with the President elect, as to save the Union between the election and the inauguration; as he will have secured his election on such ground that he can not possibly save it afterwards."

On the final day of the month, the Democratic Party chose George McClellan as their candidate for the highest office in the land.

AUGUST 12 Poet Walt Whitman *(below)* writes in his diary that he observes the President every day going back and forth between the White House and the Soldiers' Home: "He always has a company of twenty-five or thirty cavalry, with sabres drawn and held upright over their shoulders."

AUGUST 12 Republican political boss Thurlow Weed *(below)* tells the President that his reelection is impossible.

Lincoln addresses the 166th Ohio Regiment.
August 22, 1864

I suppose you are going home to see your families and friends. For the service you have done in this great struggle in which we are engaged I present you sincere thanks for myself and the country. I almost always feel inclined, when I happen to say anything to soldiers, to impress upon them in a few brief remarks the importance of success in this contest. It is not merely for to-day, but for all time to come that we should perpetuate for our children's children this great and free government, which we have enjoyed all our lives. I beg you to remember this, not merely for my sake, but for yours. I happen temporarily to occupy this big White House. I am a living witness that any one of your children may look to come here as my father's child has.

AUGUST 14 Lincoln confers with Secretary of War Stanton on the problem of wartime destruction of private property and suggests to General Grant that he and General Lee make an agreement on the subject. *Left:* The former home of Stanton's mother, occupied by Union troops near Stevensburg, Virginia.

AUGUST 17 To Grant, still heading the siege at Petersburg, Lincoln wires, "Hold on with a bull-dog gripe [sic], and chew & choke, as much as possible."

AUGUST 31 The Democratic Party nominates George McClellan, Lincoln's former general-in-chief, for President.

AUGUST All month long, every month, burying the dead at Andersonville Prison in Georgia goes on. Dying is called "being exchanged" by the prisoners—i.e., exchanging the life of misery in the stockade for the "glorious one above."

Just as it seemed that the foundations of Lincoln's administration were about to crumble, word arrived that Sherman had finally succeeded in driving the Southern defenders out of Atlanta. The Confederate heartland's most important city was now in Union hands. Sherman rode Atlanta hard, appropriating and destroying supplies, burning buildings, evacuating residents from their homes. "If people raise a howl against my barbarity and cruelty," Sherman said, "I will answer that war is war and not popularity-seeking."

The fall of Atlanta changed the political picture in Washington almost overnight. The Republican dissidents abandoned their plans to choose an alternate candidate on September 5; John C. Frémont withdrew his independent candidacy on September 17. Republicans now banded together to prevent the election of George McClellan.

Lincoln did make one concession to the Republican radicals. On September 23, he requested the resignation of conservative Postmaster General Montgomery Blair. Originally selected to provide balance to the Cabinet, now he had become a liability at a time when Lincoln needed the support of Republican regulars. "You have generously said to me more than once," Lincoln wrote, "that whenever your resignation could be a relief to me, it was at my disposal. That time has come." Blair did indeed resign, but not without grousing that he was being "decapitated" as part of a deal to persuade Frémont to withdraw from the race for president.

In the eastern theater, a Union general was striking back at Jubal Early. Diminutive Philip Sheridan, just thirty-three years old, led the Union Army of the Shenandoah to a crucial victory at Winchester, Virginia, on September 19. Like Sherman farther south, Sheridan pursued a course of relentless destruction, ensuring that the abundance of the fertile valley would no longer be a resource for the Confederate war effort.

These developments gave a needed boost to Lincoln's reelection efforts, but they did not silence the critics. Grant, himself a frequent target, sympathized with the President's predicament in a letter to a mutual friend: "I think...for him to attempt to answer all the charges the opposition will bring against him will be like setting a maiden to work to prove her chastity."

SEPTEMBER 1 John Bell Hood's Confederate Army evacuates the city of Atlanta, destroying supplies as they leave in order to hinder the progress of the occupying Union forces under William Tecumseh Sherman.

SEPTEMBER 19 Aware that the Republican Party's chances in the upcoming elections depend on strong support from Union soldiers, Lincoln writes General Sherman in Atlanta to request that he grant leaves to as many men as possible from Indiana, where state elections are due to be held in October.

SEPTEMBER 20 When he hears the news of General Philip Sheridan's victory at Winchester, Virginia, Lincoln wires the general that he is "[s]trongly inclined to come up and see you."

SEPTEMBER 8 Feverish construction on telegraph lines around the country continues to expand the capital's contact with the hinterland. On this date Lincoln receives the first telegraphic message from the Washington Territory.

SEPTEMBER 12 Lincoln sends official congratulations to the Emperor of France, Napoleon III, on the birth of his second son.

SEPTEMBER 22 At the Cabinet meeting today, the principal topic of conversation is the withdrawal of former General John Frémont from the presidential race.

SEPTEMBER 23 Lincoln requests and accepts the resignation of Postmaster General Montgomery Blair. Although his anti-slavery credentials include serving as the lawyer for Dred Scott, the Marylander and former Democrat is not trusted by the radical Republicans, whose support Lincoln still needs to assure his reelection.

SEPTEMBER 24 Following the forced resignation of Montgomery Blair, Lincoln appoints William Dennison, the former governor of Ohio, as the new postmaster general.

On October 11, the day of the state elections, Lincoln stayed close to the telegraph office, waiting for early returns. While in Pennsylvania, Union candidates won only a narrow victory, Republicans in Ohio and Indiana tallied impressive wins. Equally gratifying, the state of Maryland approved a new constitution eliminating slavery. Lincoln had worked hard over the past few weeks to get out the soldier vote, urging generals to grant furloughs to men from those states that did not permit soldiers to vote on the field. It appeared that those efforts were paying off.

On October 18, Lincoln was pleased to receive "a deputation of Hebrews from Chicago, New York, Philadelphia and Baltimore," wrote an observer, "assuring him that their people, as a body, were in favor of his re-election." Others would be needed as well. On a War Department telegraph blank, Lincoln calculated his probable electoral support: 117 votes for the Union ticket, 114 for the "supposed Copperhead vote." It seemed almost certain he would lose New York, Pennsylvania, and New Jersey, as well as Delaware, Maryland, Kentucky, Missouri, and even his own home state of Illinois. Someone, perhaps Secretary of State Seward, added three more votes to the Union column, anticipating that Nevada would achieve statehood in time for the election. The Republicans took no chances: Nevada became the thirty-sixth state of the Union on October 31. As for himself, though he was eager to be reelected to a second term and to "hold the helm for the next voyage," Lincoln told a Baltimore delegation that wanted to give their vote to him in exchange for the pardon of a military traitor, "[I]t is not so essential that I have votes as that the rebellion be crushed."

Philip Sheridan's Shenandoah Valley campaign came to a triumphant conclusion on October 19, when he rallied his retreating troops and routed Jubal Early's forces at Cedar Creek, Virginia. At a serenade on October 21, Lincoln proposed three cheers for Sheridan, Grant, and all the soldiers and sailors who served in the armed forces. "While we are at it," he told the crowd, "we may as well consider how fortunate it was for the Secesh that Sheridan was a very little man. If he had been a large man, there is no knowing what he would have done with them."

OCTOBER 5 Lincoln spends the morning with several of his top political and military officials working out Union terms for an exchange of prisoners of war. Aiken's Landing on the James River *(below center)* is one of the sites for

OCTOBER 15 The President and several Cabinet members attend the 6:00 a.m. funeral service for Roger Taney *(left)*, chief justice of the United States. Lincoln and Taney have been divided during the past three years over the President's repeated use of wartime emergency powers to suppress individual liberties. After the service, Lincoln joins the procession to the railroad station for the special burial train to Maryland, but he does not make the trip.

such an exchange. *Below left:* The most notorious Confederate prison camp was at Andersonville, Georgia. *Below right:* Confederate prisoners of war at Camp Douglas, where 30,000 rebel soldiers were held just south of Chicago

OCTOBER 6 To Gustave Gumpert, Tad Lincoln sends a carriage bill left over from the time the older companion and the child spent together in Philadelphia *(below)*. Tad insists to his friend "Gus," "I ain't got any money to pay the man with."

OCTOBER 29 Lincoln meets with and signs the autograph album of Sojourner Truth, the former slave, now famed evangelist and orator. A likeness of Lincoln has been superimposed on a photograph of Sojourner Truth to make this composite image.

OCTOBER 31 Lincoln signs the proclamation admitting Nevada as the thirty-sixth state of the Union, just in time for its three electoral votes to help the Republicans in the upcoming presidential election. *Above:* Some of Nevada's natural beauty

On election day 1864, Washington was dark, rainy, and almost deserted, with Lincoln finding it difficult to concentrate. By nightfall, good news began to pour into the telegraph office from all over the North. With a wife even more anxious than he, "[t]he President sent over the first fruits to Mrs. Lincoln," reported John Hay, who went on to describe the rest of election night. "Despatches kept coming in all evening...showing a splendid triumph.... Towards midnight we had supper...the President...went awkwardly and hospitably to work shovelling out...fried oysters."

Given how desperate the situation had seemed just three months earlier, Lincoln's reelection was almost a landslide. Rather than the 117 electoral votes he had predicted in October, Lincoln garnered 212; he swept all the Union states except Delaware, New Jersey, and Kentucky. In the popular election he swamped McClellan by more than 500,000 votes, showing huge support all over the North, and especially among Union soldiers.

When the party finally returned to the White House and the Lincolns had retired, Ward Hill Lamon, more worried than ever about his friend's safety, lay down for the night at the Lincoln's bedroom door. John Hay noticed that, in a display of "touching and dumb fidelity," Lamon had surrounded himself with "a small arsenal of pistols and bowie knives."

On November 10, Lincoln commented on his reelection: "I am...duly grateful...to Almighty God for having directed my countrymen to a right conclusion, as I think, for their own good...."

In Atlanta, Sherman made a fateful decision. Confederate General Hood was moving his army toward Tennessee, in an effort to cut Sherman's communications and supply lines, and to draw his army out of Atlanta and back toward Union soil. Sherman decided to protect Tennessee with just half of his troops, left under the command of George H. Thomas in Nashville. With the other half, Sherman set off on November 15 on a four-pronged march eastward toward the Atlantic, abandoning supply lines altogether and allowing his army to live off the land. With no communication lines to rely on, the North heard little news of Sherman in the last two weeks of November, as his men cut a terrible swath through the Confederate heartland.

GRAND, NATIONAL UNION BANNER FOR 1864.
LIBERTY, UNION AND VICTORY.

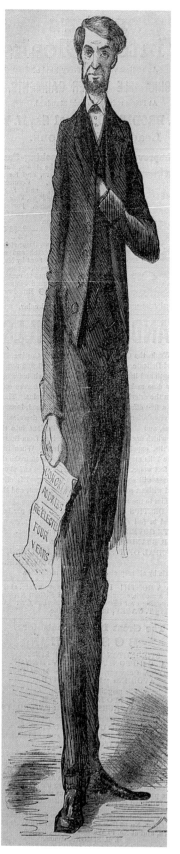

NOVEMBER 8 The election day victory for the Republicans is a triumph not only for Lincoln personally, but for the cause of continued vigorous prosecution of the war. The caricature beneath the poster for the Republican ticket at the far left shows George McClellan as Hamlet in the famous gravedigger's scene, holding Lincoln's head instead of Yorick's skull and suggesting not only Lincoln's demise but also his overfondness for Shakespeare. But the image at the right, of Lincoln standing tall, prevailed. The photograph of Lincoln at the near left was taken a few months later; it captures the satisfaction of his victory and the favorable progress of the war. Even the addition to the ticket of Andrew Johnson *(inset)*, to replace the dependable, supportive Hannibal Hamlin as vice president, could not distress the President in his hour of triumph.

RESPONSE TO A SERENADE

NOVEMBER 10 *Lincoln responds from his window to a late-night serenade.*

It has long been a grave question whether any government, not *too* strong for the liberties of its people, can be strong *enough* to maintain its own existence, in great emergencies.

On this point the present rebellion brought our republic to a severe test; and a presidential election occurring in regular course during the rebellion added not a little to the strain....

We can not have free government without elections; and if the rebellion could force us to forego [sic], or postpone a national election, it might fairly claim to have already conquered and ruined us....

But the election, along with its incidental, and undesirable strife, has done good too. It has demonstrated that a people's government can sustain a national election, in the midst of a great civil war.... It shows also how *sound,* and how *strong* we still are. It shows that, even among candidates of the same party, he who is most devoted to the Union, and most opposed to treason, can receive most of the people's votes.

In the first week of December, Lincoln filled the two most important legal posts in his administration. On December 1, he named James Speed, the brother of his old Kentucky friend Joshua, to replace the retiring attorney general, Edward Bates. And on December 6, Lincoln put forward Salmon Chase to succeed Roger Taney as the chief justice of the United States.

"I can make Georgia howl," Sherman had bragged upon being sent off on his mission to break the South's morale. Where was he now? "We all know where he went in at, but I can't tell where he will come out at," Lincoln told one group on December 6. Hated throughout the South for his harshness, this general who, it was said, preferred to fight at night when he could "envision" the activities of the enemy, and who seemed never to sleep, was finally completing his nine-month-long "march to the sea." "We are not only fighting hostile armies," Sherman wrote, "but a hostile people, and must make old and young, rich and poor, feel the hard hand of war." On December 10, he emerged on the outskirts of Savannah, Georgia, and proceeded to fight his way to the ocean to make contact with the Union fleet. "I estimate the damage done [in Georgia]," he boasted, "at $100,000,000....We have devoured the land....To realize what war is one should follow our tracks."

On December 15 and 16, George Thomas's Army of the Cumberland swept out of Nashville and all but destroyed the Confederate Army of the Tennessee. Nashville was not merely a victory; it was one of the very few battles that succeeded in what Lincoln set forth as the best way to end the war: the full destruction of an enemy army.

On December 22 Sherman telegraphed the President that Savannah was his Christmas present. Lincoln wrote back the day after Christmas, brimming over with thankfulness, and admitted to Sherman that he had had serious reservations about the wisdom of the march to the sea. "Now, the undertaking being a success, the honor is all yours....But what next? I suppose it will be safer if I leave Gen. Grant and yourself to decide."

DECEMBER 1 Lincoln names Joshua Speed's brother, James, of Kentucky as the new attorney general and wires, "Please come on at once."

DECEMBER 15 Late at night, while standing in his nightshirt and holding a candle on the second-story landing of the White House, Lincoln receives word of the defeat of Confederate General John B. Hood at Nashville.

DECEMBER 22 "I beg to present you as a Christmas gift the city of Savannah with 150 heavy guns & plenty of ammunition & also about 25000 bales of cotton," General Sherman wires the President. From Savannah, Sherman will now turn northward through the Carolinas.

DECEMBER 25 This extravagant conception of "The Union Christmas Dinner" was drawn by the nationally known cartoonist and illustrator for *Harper's Weekly* Thomas B. Nast *(right)*, after a recent visit to the White House. Throughout the war, Nast's cartoons aroused enthusiasm for the Union cause and encouraged patriotism, so much so that Lincoln was quoted as saying, "Thomas Nast has been our best recruiting sergeant."

LINCOLN AND SLAVERY: 1864

One by one, many of Lincoln's critics were turning into admirers, and that included the outspoken black orator/journalist who had ridden Lincoln hard on the slavery issue ever since his inauguration day—Frederick Douglass. Over the course of the year, Douglass became Lincoln's chief black adviser.

It is not impossible to see why the two men took to one another. Both had their beginnings in dirt-poor families; each had virtually educated himself, and then worked his way up into prominence. Lincoln could not help admiring this former slave and ship's caulker who had faced a lifetime of white hatred but who still believed passionately in America's great interracial future. The President had set him to work the previous year to inspire black recruits for the Union Army. It was partly through Douglass's influence that Lincoln had finally given up his ideas about colonization and begun to believe in Negro suffrage, in particular for soldiers.

But from the dizzying heights of the year's early months, with Lincoln at the peak of his popularity, it was a long fall to where the President stood by summer, when the war's "rivers of blood," as Greeley called them, had convinced many in the North to pursue peace at any price. By August, Lincoln's reelection looked impossible. Desperate, he briefly considered a compromise with the South on slavery, but then just as quickly stiffened his resolve, saying he would be "damned in time and eternity" for compromising.

On August 19, Lincoln summoned Douglass to the White House, prepared to offer him a novel and important role in the administration. While the governor of Connecticut was kept waiting outside the President's office, the two men discussed Lincoln's passionate regret that Southern slaves had not responded in large numbers to his Emancipation Proclamation. "Slave owners know how to keep such things

Although Frederick Douglass later described Lincoln as a "white man's president," with black Americans at best his "step-children," he himself became an important Lincoln adviser. "There is no man in the country

from their slaves,'' responded Douglass, adding that probably few had ever heard of the proclamation. Lincoln decided to place Douglass in charge of a new effort to reach the slaves, ''to warn them,'' he said, ''as to what will be their probable condition should peace be concluded while they remain within Rebel lines; And more especially to urge upon them the necessity of making their escape.''

Lincoln's idea was to make Douglass a ''general agent'' in charge of stirring up a mass exodus of slaves across Union lines. ''What he said on this day,'' wrote Douglass later, ''showed a deeper moral conviction against slavery than I had ever seen before in anything spoken or written by him.'' Those who claimed Lincoln had emancipated slaves only as a military necessity simply did not appreciate the President's huge moral concern for the slaves themselves. In a letter written on August 29, Douglass suggested a plan for how to proceed. He wanted twenty sub-agents hired under a new department and sent immediately to the front to begin spreading the message and offering assistance to runaway slaves.

The sudden Union victories that autumn rendered Douglass's new role obsolete, and he ended up playing only a limited role in Lincoln's presidential campaign, effectively muzzled by Republican leaders eager to avoid being branded as the ''Nigger Party.'' But Lincoln held a special place in Douglass's life ever after. ''In all my interviews with Mr. Lincoln,'' Douglass wrote in the 1870s, ''I was impressed by his entire freedom from popular prejudice against the colored race.'' In an era of raging white racism throughout America—in the North and the South— Lincoln was the first ''great man'' Douglass had ever met ''who in no single instance reminded me of the difference between himself and myself, of the difference of color.''

whose opinion I value more than yours,'' Lincoln said in asking for Douglass's reaction to the second inaugural address. ''Mr. Lincoln,'' the black orator responded, ''that was a sacred effort.''

From Lincoln's annual message to Congress, December 6, 1864.

The war continues. Since the last annual message all the important lines and positions then occupied by our forces have been maintained, and our arms have steadily advanced; thus liberating the regions left in rear, so that Missouri, Kentucky, Tennessee and parts of other States have again produced reasonably fair crops.

The most remarkable feature in the military operations of the year is General Sherman's attempted march of three hundred miles directly through the insurgent region. It tends to show a great increase of our relative strength that our General-in-Chief should feel able to confront and hold in check every active force of the enemy, and yet to detach a well-appointed large army to move on such an expedition. The result not yet being known, conjecture in regard to it is not here indulged.

Important movements have also occurred during the year to the effect of moulding society for durability in the Union. Although short of complete success, it is much in the right direction, that twelve thousand citizens in each of the States of Arkansas and Louisiana have organized loyal State governments with free constitutions, and are earnestly struggling to maintain and administer them. The movements in the same direction, more extensive, though less definite in Missouri, Kentucky and Tennessee, should not be overlooked. But Maryland presents the example of complete success. Maryland is secure to Liberty and Union for all the future. The genius of rebellion will no more claim Maryland. Like another foul spirit, being driven out, it may seek to tear her, but it will woo her no more....

On careful consideration of all the evidence accessible it seems to me that no attempt at negotiation with the insurgent leader could result in any good. He would accept nothing short of severance of the Union—precisely what we will not and cannot give. His declarations to this effect are explicit and oft-repeated. He does not attempt to deceive us. He affords us no excuse to deceive ourselves. He cannot voluntarily reaccept the Union; we cannot voluntarily yield it. Between him and us the issue is distinct, simple, and inflexible.

Ulysses S. Grant

Robert E. Lee

It is an issue which can only be tried by war, and decided by victory. If we yield, we are beaten; if the Southern people fail him, he is beaten. Either way, it would be the victory and defeat following war. What is true, however, of him who heads the insurgent cause, is not necessarily true of those who follow. Although he cannot reaccept the Union, they can. Some of them, we know, already desire peace and reunion. The number of such may increase. They can, at any moment, have peace simply by laying down their arms and submitting to the national authority under the Constitution. After so much, the government could not, if it would, maintain war against them. The loyal people would not sustain or allow it. If questions should remain, we would adjust them by the peaceful means of legislation, conference, courts, and votes, operating only in constitutional and lawful channels.

...A year ago general pardon and amnesty, upon specified terms, were offered to all, except certain designated classes; and, it was, at the same time, made known that the excepted classes were still within contemplation of special clemency.... Thus, practically, the door has been, for a full year, open to all, except such as were not in condition to make free choice—that is, such as were in custody or under constraint. It is still so open to all. But the time may come—probably will come—when public duty shall demand that it be closed; and that, in lieu, more rigorous measures than heretofore shall be adopted.

In presenting the abandonment of armed resistance to the national authority on the part of the insurgents, as the only indispensable condition to ending the war on the part of the government, I retract nothing heretofore said as to slavery. I repeat the declaration made a year ago, that "while I remain in my present position I shall not attempt to retract or modify the emancipation proclamation, nor shall I return to slavery any person who is free by the terms of that proclamation, or by any of the Acts of Congress." If the people should, by whatever mode or means, make it an Executive duty to re-enslave such persons, another, and not I, must be their instrument to perform it.

With his two vice presidents, outgoing Hannibal Hamlin *(left)* and Andrew Johnson, Lincoln waits to rise and make his second inaugural address.

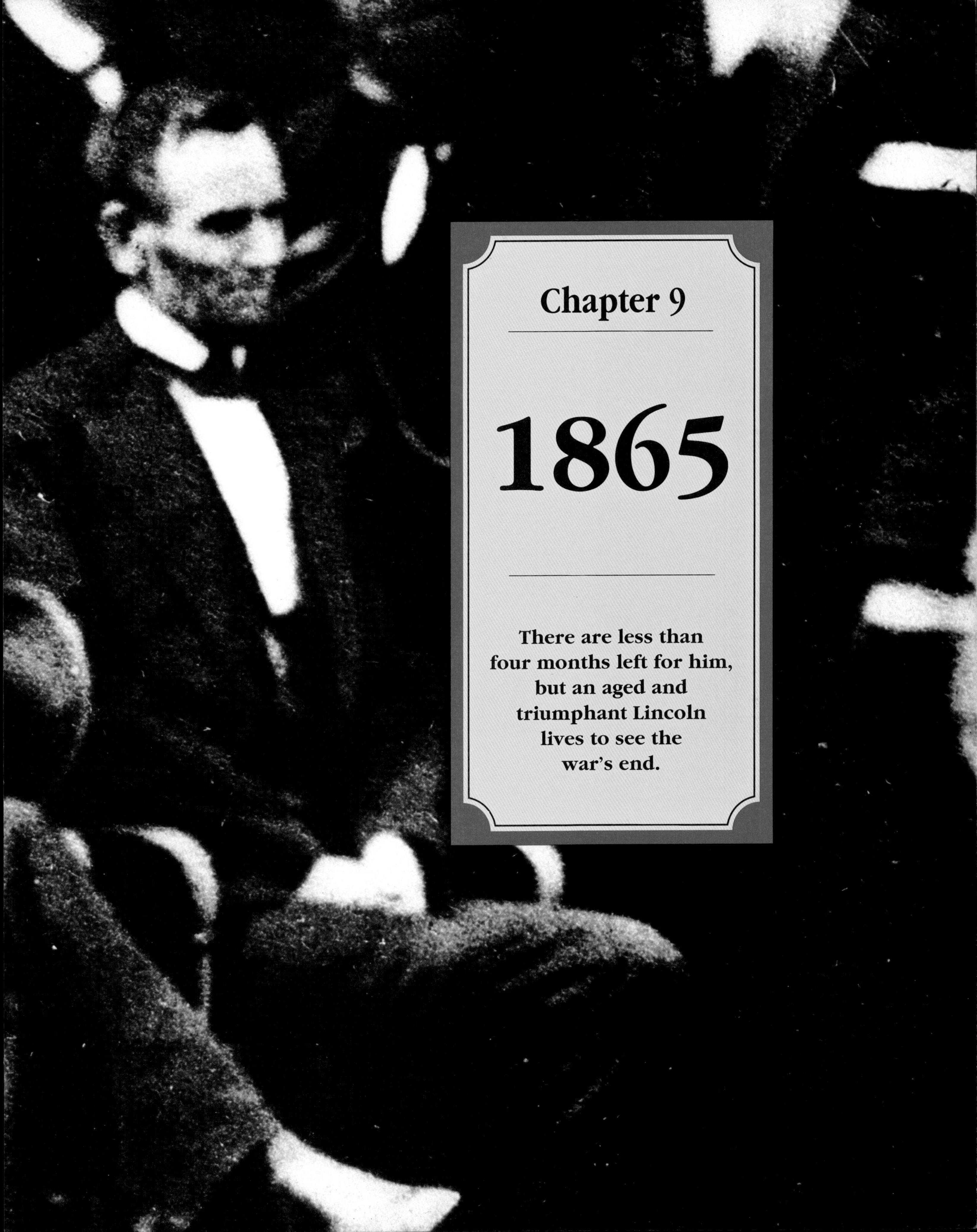

Chapter 9

1865

There are less than four months left for him, but an aged and triumphant Lincoln lives to see the war's end.

Benjamin Butler had stirred up controversy wherever he went in the war; his latest failure was irresolute leadership in the Union attempt to take Fort Fisher, in North Carolina. Grant had been trying for months to oust the intellectually brilliant but militarily erratic Butler, and on January 8, the general was finally relieved of command. One week later, Union forces under General Alfred Terry succeeded in capturing Fort Fisher.

The Confederates had only one significant fighting force left now, the Army of Northern Virginia, but Lincoln refused to be complacent. "[T]ime, now that the enemy is wavering, is more important than ever before," he wrote to Stanton on January 5.

On Sunday, January 15, the distinguished if controversial naturalist and geologist Louis Agassiz arrived at the White House for a visit with the President. Lincoln was nervous that he would be overshadowed by Agassiz's intellect but managed to hold his own, sharing insights into ancient science that even Agassiz hadn't considered, and drawing out of the Harvard professor secrets of his academic techniques. When asked afterward why he hadn't posed questions about glaciers or ice ages, Lincoln answered, "Why, what we got from him isn't printed in books; the other things are."

In Washington the towering issue of the month was the debate in the House of Representatives over the proposed Thirteenth Amendment to the Constitution. The Senate had approved the measure early in 1864, but a vote in the House had failed the previous June. When Republican James M. Ashley of Ohio once again brought up the amendment to abolish slavery, Lincoln was adamant that the measure be passed before the end of the congressional session. He began working hard to persuade a handful of Democrats who had previously opposed the amendment to switch their votes.

On January 31, Lincoln's wish was granted. The House voted 119 to 56 — two more votes than the required two-thirds majority — in favor of the new amendment. The measure could now be sent to the states for ratification. Lincoln was overjoyed that his emancipation policy, guaranteed thus far only on grounds of military necessity, and thus reversible, was now on the way to being a permanent part of the nation's basic law.

JANUARY 5 Former slave children like these will never be born to a life in the cotton fields again. But still, there are vexing problems with the industry that has driven the economy of the South for so long. Today Lincoln discusses whether his Confederate sister-in-law, Emilie Todd Helm, should be able to sell the cotton grown on her slave-holding Kentucky plantation.

JANUARY 15 Edward Everett (left), whose two-hour oration preceded Lincoln's two-minute address at Gettysburg, dies in Boston. Lincoln comments to reporter Noah Brooks: "Now, do you know, I think Edward Everett was very much overrated. He hasn't left any enduring monument."

JANUARY 6 Lincoln receives a telegram from Ulysses S. Grant requesting the prompt removal of Benjamin Butler *(left)*. The President, who has always handled the politically powerful Butler with great care, in effect tells his general-in-chief to fire Butler himself.

JANUARY 14 Lincoln puzzles over what to do about Henry S. Foote *(left)*, a former member of the Confederate Congress and an opponent of the war who fled to Union lines. Just as the Confederacy had mistrusted Clement Vallandigham, Lincoln and Seward show no great enthusiasm for Foote's thoughts on peace.

JANUARY 15 The Union puts together the largest American fleet ever assembled in order to attack Fort Fisher, North Carolina. Under heavy crossfire from the ships, eight thousand troops fight for three days and finally take the last Confederate coastal stronghold.

JANUARY 15 Noted scientist Louis Agassiz *(left)*, now teaching at Harvard College, visits the White House. Lincoln admits to him that many years ago he tried his hand at a lecture on inventions and discoveries but never finished. Agassiz urges him to do so.

JANUARY 18 James M. Ashley of Ohio *(left)* is one of the congressmen who visit the White House to confer with Lincoln about the proposed constitutional amendment prohibiting slavery throughout the United States.

JANUARY 25 Of the 106th anniversary of the birth of his favorite poet, Robert Burns *(left)*, Lincoln writes the celebration committee that "I can not frame a toast to Burns. I can say nothing worthy of his generous heart, and transcendent genius."

Lincoln was particularly pleased that Illinois was among the first states to ratify the Thirteenth Amendment. During the month of February, sixteen additional states ratified it, but when Delaware and Kentucky voted the measure down on February 8, Lincoln knew that he would need the support of at least some of the Confederate states in order to reach the required two-thirds majority.

In February, a last-ditch peace effort was under way. Earlier, Lincoln had informally permitted veteran Maryland politician Francis P. Blair to confer with Jefferson Davis in Richmond. Discouraged about Blair's prospects for success, the President remained open to any initiative, as long as it refused to compromise on either restoration of the Union or full and total emancipation.

On February 1, three representatives of the Confederacy—Vice President Alexander Stephens, Virginia Senator Robert M. T. Hunter, and Assistant Secretary of War John A. Campbell—arrived at Hampton Roads, Virginia, for talks with Union representatives. Assured by Ulysses S. Grant that their intentions were good, Lincoln came to Hampton Roads himself.

On February 3, the group met for several hours, in the salon of the steamer *River Queen*. Although the Confederates did not explicitly rule out the eventual reunion of the nation, they were unwilling to embrace it immediately. The one genuine peace talk between the warring parties ended in flat failure.

Lincoln nevertheless returned to Washington still eager to shorten the war. On February 5, he suggested to the Cabinet that the government offer a financial incentive to the seceded states to rejoin the Union. The United States could authorize payments up to $400 million to free the slaves in states that renounced secession by April 1, 1865. Even though he was pushing hard for the Thirteenth Amendment, Lincoln was still practical enough to promote a version of compensated emancipation if it could help bring the war to a swifter conclusion.

As Sherman stormed through the Carolinas, much of the city of Columbia, South Carolina, was burned to the ground on February 17 under his occupation. On February 22, Federal troops took Wilmington, North Carolina, the last major Southern port to capitulate. Grant was gradually cutting off the supply routes into Petersburg. The noose was tightening around the Confederacy.

FEBRUARY 1 Nationally known preacher Henry Ward Beecher, who has never liked Lincoln, although pretending to be a staunch admirer, confers with the President about the prospects for peace.

FEBRUARY 12 Less than a fortnight after the adoption of the Thirteenth Amendment, ending slavery forever, the Reverend Henry Highland Garnet *(left)* becomes the first black man ever to speak in the halls of Congress. The son of an enslaved African chief, Garnet escaped from bondage in 1821 and settled in New York City, becoming the pastor of the Shiloh Presbyterian Church. Now he stands addressing the "illustrious rulers of this great nation," foreseeing "a model Republic . . . in which the . . . blessings of peace are equally . . . enjoyed by all."

FEBRUARY 3 The Hampton Roads Peace Conference *(above)* is held on the steamboat *River Queen (left)*, at General Grant's headquarters. The Confederate representatives, Lincoln writes later, "seemed to desire a postponement of that question...but which course, we thought, would amount to an indefinite postponement."

FEBRUARY 17 Today Columbia, the capital of South Carolina, falls to Union forces. With the unsuccessful conclusion of the Hampton Roads conference, General Robert E. Lee (shown here flanked by Colonel Walter Taylor to his left and the general's son, General George Washington Custis Lee) continues the Army of Northern Virginia's now-hopeless attempt to defend the Confederacy.

FEBRUARY 17 *The following letter from Lincoln to Judge Advocate General Joseph Holt, one of many such attempts of Lincoln to offer clemency, was answered by Holt with a reference to Lincoln's "kind heart."*
In regard to the Baltimore and Washington Merchants—clothes dealers—convicted mostly on the testimony of one Worsley (I believe) I have not been quite satisfied. I can not say that the presumption in favor of their innocence has not been shaken; and yet it is very unsatisfactory to me that so many men of fair character should be convicted principally on the testimony of one single man & he of not quite fair character. It occurs to me that they have suffered enough, even if guilty, and...I propose giving them a jubilee...

FEBRUARY 17 Lincoln signs the army commission for his son Robert, who is finally given a position on Grant's staff after being kept out of the army for several years at the request of his mother. Six days later it is reported that the President looks and feels indisposed.

"I am very unwell," Lincoln told his long-time friend Joshua Speed in the last days of his first term in office. "My feet and hands...always cold—I suppose I ought to be in bed." Instead, he had the last acts of the congressional session to approve. The most important was the establishment of the Bureau for the Relief of Freedmen and Refugees, designed to provide temporary assistance for the freed slaves.

The morning of March 4, the day of Lincoln's second inauguration, was raw and rainy. The still unwell President rode up Pennsylvania Avenue amidst cheering throngs, and took his place on the platform in front of the recently completed Capitol dome. His speech was a masterpiece, eloquent but brief. On the verge of victory, Lincoln refused to be complacent about the Union's triumph. Instead, he urged upon the nation a relentless and searching examination of the sins that underlay the tragedy of war. In preaching "malice toward none" and "charity for all," Lincoln expressed his magnanimity toward the vanquished, a tenderness made possible by the common bond of guilt that bound the North and South. The United States had been weighed in the balance, and had been found wanting.

Lincoln expected his second inaugural address "to wear as well as—perhaps better than—anything I have produced." But he believed that "it is not immediately popular. Men are not flattered by being shown that there has been a difference of purpose between the Almighty and them. To deny it, however, in this case, is to deny that there is a God governing the world."

Eager to see the war's conclusion, on March 23 the President embarked on the *River Queen* for Grant's main headquarters at City Point, Virginia.

On March 27, William Tecumseh Sherman came up from North Carolina for talks with Grant and Lincoln. The approach of Sherman's army from the south was threatening to squeeze Lee's army, but Lincoln remained concerned that the battle for Petersburg and Richmond would still be very bloody. "I begin to feel that I ought to be at home," Lincoln wrote to Secretary of War Stanton on March 30, "and yet I dislike to leave without seeing nearer to the end of General Grant's present movement." At the end of March, Lincoln was still at the front.

At the center of this photograph, just above the little white table, Lincoln reads his second inaugural address.

MARCH 4 *The morning rain has stopped and the dignitaries make their way to the Capitol portico. Inside, having fortified himself with whiskey, Andrew Johnson has just been sworn in as the new vice president. When the crowd is still, Lincoln rises to read his second inaugural address. As Lincoln speaks, the heavy clouds open and the sun breaks through. Here is the speech in its entirety.*

[Fellow Countrymen:]

At this second appearing to take the oath of the presidential office, there is less occasion for an extended address than there was at the first. Then a statement, somewhat in detail, of a course to be pursued, seemed fitting and proper. Now, at the expiration of four years, during which public declarations have been constantly called forth on every point and phase of the great contest which still absorbs the attention, and engrosses the enerergies [sic] of the nation, little that is new could be presented. The progress of our arms, upon which all else chiefly depends, is as well known to the public as to myself; and it is, I trust, reasonably satisfactory and encouraging to all. With high hope for the future, no prediction in regard to it is ventured.

On the occasion corresponding to this four years ago, all thoughts were anxiously directed to an impending civil-war. All dreaded it — all sought to avert it. While the inaugeral [sic] address was being delivered from this place, devoted altogether to *saving* the Union without war, insurgent agents were in the city seeking to *destroy* it without war — seeking to dissol[v]e the Union, and divide effects, by negotiation. Both parties deprecated war; but one of them would *make* war rather than let the nation survive; and the other would *accept* war rather than let it perish. And the war came.

One eighth of the whole population were colored slaves, not distributed generally over the Union, but localized in the Southern part of it. These slaves constituted a peculiar and powerful interest. All knew that this interest was, somehow, the cause of the war. To strengthen, perpetuate, and extend this interest was the object for which the insurgents would rend the Union, even by war; while the government claimed no right to do more than to restrict the territorial enlargement of it. Neither party expected for the war, the magnitude, or the duration, which it has already attained. Neither anticipated that the *cause* of the conflict might cease with, or even before, the conflict itself should cease. Each looked for an easier triumph, and a result less fundamental and astounding. Both read the same Bible, and pray to the same God; and each invokes His aid against the other. It may seem strange that any men should dare to ask a just God's assistance in wringing their bread from the sweat of other men's faces; but let us judge not that we be not judged. The prayers of both could not be answered; that of neither has been answered fully. The Almighty has His own purposes. "Woe unto the world because of offences! for it must needs be that offences come; but woe to that man by whom the offence cometh!" If we shall suppose that American Slavery is one of those offences which, in the providence of God, must needs come, but which, having continued through His appointed time, He now wills to remove, and that He gives to both North and South, this terrible war, as the woe due to those by whom the offence came, shall we discern therein any departure from those divine attributes which the believers in a Living God always ascribe to Him? Fondly do we hope — fervently do we pray — that this mighty scourge of war may speedily pass away. Yet, if God wills that it continue, until all the wealth piled by the bond-man's two hundred and fifty years of unrequited toil shall be sunk, and until every drop of blood drawn with the lash, shall be paid by another drawn with the sword, as was said three thousand years ago, so still it must be said "the judgments of the Lord, are true and righteous altogether"

With malice toward none; with charity for all; with firmness in the right, as God gives us to see the right, let us strive on to finish the work we are in; to bind up the nation's wounds; to care for him who shall have borne the battle, and for his widow, and his orphan — to do all which may achieve and cherish a just, and a lasting peace, among ourselves, and with all nations.

Lincoln awoke on April 3 to news that Petersburg had finally fallen. Grant's armies had spent almost ten months besieging the crucial rail junction, key to the survival of Richmond, and its fall signaled the rapid approach of war's end. Overjoyed, Lincoln rushed to congratulate Grant. "I doubt whether Mr. Lincoln ever experienced a happier moment in his life," wrote Lieutenant Colonel Horace Porter, who was present at the scene.

On April 4, accompanied by his son Tad, Lincoln paid a visit to Richmond itself, now also in Grant's possession. "Thank God I have lived to see this," he said. "It seems to me that I have been dreaming a horrid nightmare for four years, and now the nightmare is over." As he walked through the rubble-strewn streets, jubilant blacks thronged around him. At the Confederate White House, Lincoln took a seat at Jefferson Davis's desk, to the applause of Union troops outside.

When Lincoln arrived back in the capital on April 9, Edwin Stanton was waiting at the dock with the news from Appomattox Court House: Lee had unconditionally surrendered. The President and his secretary of war threw their arms around each other, as suddenly Stanton's "iron mask" of stoicism fell away. Then Lincoln hurried over to see his friend William Seward, who was badly injured from a carriage accident and lay in bed in a bulky neck brace.

Crowds serenaded the President all day on April 10, and at one point Lincoln urged a band to strike up "Dixie," calling it "one of the best tunes I have ever heard."

On April 11, in his last public address, delivered at night from his White House window as little Tad held a lamp for him to read by, Lincoln offered a powerful defense of his vision for America. Admitting the dangers of allowing a relatively small number of voters to initiate the reconstructed state governments, he just would not accept a policy of anger and rejection, which would be "discouraging and paralyzing" for both blacks and whites. Out in the shadows, among the teeming crowds, was John Wilkes Booth. As he listened to Lincoln's speech about the future—about a united country without slavery—Booth suddenly turned to his friend David Herold and said, "Now, by God, I'll put him through."

APRIL 3 Less than a week before the war's end, a dead Confederate soldier greets the Union victors in a trench at Fort Mahone, on the outskirts of Petersburg, Virginia.

APRIL 9 The McLean house at Appomattox Court House, Virginia *(above)*, is the site for the meeting at which Robert E. Lee formally surrenders his army to Ulysses S. Grant. The agreement is signed on the table shown at right.

MONTH 50

APRIL 4 Lincoln arrives on a boat manned by twelve sailors for his triumphant tour of Richmond, Virginia, the erstwhile capital of the Confederacy, which now lies in ruins *(below)*. A painting by Dennis Malone Carter *(bottom)* shows the enthusiastic reception accorded the President.

APRIL 4 *White House guard William H. Crook accompanies Lincoln on his trip from City Point into fallen Richmond.* Admiral Porter asked the President to go to Richmond with him. At first the President did not want to go.... [H]e had no wish to see the spectacle of the Confederacy's humiliation.... I understand that when Mr. Stanton...heard that the expedition had started, he was...angry against the President. "That fool!" he exclaimed. Mr. Lincoln knew perfectly well how dangerous the trip was....

The shore for some distance before we reached Richmond was black with negroes. They had heard that President Lincoln was on his way—they had some sort of an underground telegraph, I am sure. They were wild with excitement and yelling like so many wild men.... By the time we were on shore hundreds of black hands were outstretched to the President.... In all Richmond [it was] the only welcome I saw.... It seems to me nothing short of miraculous that some attempt on his life was not made. It is to the everlasting glory of the South that he was permitted to come and go in peace.

APRIL 14 *Lincoln writes the last letter of his life, to General James H. Van Alen, who has warned him to be more careful, that such exposure as he has recently had in Richmond makes him much too vulnerable to assassination.*
My dear Sir: I intend to adopt the advice of my friends and use due precaution.... I thank you for the assurance you give me that I shall be supported by conservative men like yourself, in the efforts I may make to restore the Union, so as to make it, to use your language, a Union of hearts and hands as well as of States.
Yours truly,
A. Lincoln.

APRIL 14 Late in the afternoon, before their excursion to Ford's Theatre, the Lincolns take a leisurely drive to the Navy Yard *(above)* to see three monitors damaged in the Fort Fisher engagement. Possibly reminded of home by this white picket fence, the President speaks to his wife wistfully about a time when they can both return to Illinois and live quietly.

LINCOLN AND SLAVERY: 1865

In the long history of Lincoln's struggle against slavery, 1865 was the grand culmination—the year slavery was abolished in America by constitutional amendment. Back in 1861, with Lincoln newly installed as president, Congress had passed a Thirteenth Amendment that would have guaranteed that slavery could never be abolished; but with the outbreak of war, it had failed to find ratification by the states and quietly disappeared. In 1864, Lincoln's Republican friend Senator Lyman Trumbull of Illinois proposed a new Thirteenth Amendment, abolishing slavery forever and giving Congress the duty of enforcement. This one passed the Senate but failed in the House. Despite the setback, Lincoln had decided to stake his political future on the measure, insisting that it become the central plank of the Republican Party platform in the 1864 presidential campaign, for reconsideration in 1865 were he to win. It was clear to him now that the Emancipation Proclamation was a war powers act and could not be counted on to protect slaves in peacetime. Nor had it freed enough slaves—none at all in the Union slave states, and only a small percentage in the Confederate South. He had come to admit that it simply "did not meet the evil." The new Thirteenth Amendment, in contrast, would be a "King's cure for all the evils." "Sink or swim, live or die, survive or perish," he vowed, "I give my heart and hand to this measure."

By 1865 Lincoln was deeply involved in behind-the-scenes politicking for "his" amendment, confident that his reelection had proved that the will of the people was solidly behind him. By mid-January, still several votes short of a victory in the House, and turning to Ohio Congressman James M. Ashley and others for help, Lincoln began to target wavering Democrats, offering some of them patronage in return for ballots. "Those...votes must be procured," he was heard to say.

On January 31, following weeks of con-

The President displays the kind of firm intensity that brought about the outlawing of slavery in the United States forever. The moment finally comes in the halls of Congress when, amid pandemonium, the vote is announced, assuring the passage of the Thirteenth Amendment that Lincoln has worked so hard for.

gressional debate, the all-important vote was taken. One by one the ballots were counted. Finally, Speaker of the House Schuyler Colfax, in a trembling voice, called out that the amendment had passed by a margin of 119 to 56. "For a moment there was a pause of utter silence," wrote Noah Brooks, who was present at the scene. "Then there was an explosion, a storm of cheers, the like of which probably no Congress of the United States ever heard before. Strong men embraced each other with tears. The galleries and aisles were bristling with standing, cheering crowds... women's handkerchiefs waving and floating; hands... shaking;... arms about each other's necks, and cheer after cheer... burst after burst." Amidst the wild celebration, great guns were uncovered on Capitol Hill and fired off into the sky, announcing to the world that "slavery was no more."

Lincoln, who had been pacing the floor all the while in a flush of excitement, was suddenly "filled... with joy," seeing in the amendment's passage, said former Congressman Isaac Arnold, "the complete consummation of his... work." "The great job is ended," Lincoln exclaimed. "I... congratulate... myself, the country, and the whole world upon this great moral victory." Nibbie Slade, daughter of Lincoln's personal servant William, commented that that night the President slept like never before.

On February 4, with the amendment already ratified in Lincoln's home state of Illinois, in Rhode Island, Michigan, Maryland, New York, and West Virginia, and well on its way to being adopted by the nation, ardent Bostonian abolitionist William Lloyd Garrison publicly gave credit where credit was due. "And to whom is the country indebted... for this vital and saving amendment...? I... answer — to the humble rail-splitter of Illinois, to the Presidential chain-splitter for millions of the oppressed — to Abraham Lincoln!"

A branded slave from Louisiana,
Wilson Chinn is shown here shackled by
an instrument of torture used to punish
slaves and make escape more difficult.

On the evening of April 11, from a second-story window in the White House, Lincoln made his last public address. We meet this evening, not in sorrow, but in gladness of heart. The evacuation of Petersburg and Richmond, and the surrender of the principal insurgent army, give hope of a righteous and speedy peace whose joyous expression can not be restrained. In the midst of this, however, He from Whom all blessings flow, must not be forgotten....

The amount of constituency, so to to [sic] speak, on which the new Louisiana government rests, would be more satisfactory to all, if it contained fifty, thirty, or even twenty thousand, instead of only about twelve thousand, as it does. It is also unsatisfactory to some that the elective franchise is not given to the colored man. I would myself prefer that it were now conferred on the very intelligent, and on those who serve our cause as soldiers. Still the question is not whether the Louisiana government, as it stands, is quite all that is desirable. The question is "Will it be wiser to take it as it is, and help to improve it; or to reject, and disperse it?" "Can Louisiana be brought into proper practical relation with the Union *sooner* by *sustaining*, or by *discarding* her new State Government?"

Some twelve thousand voters in the heretofore slave-state of Louisiana have sworn allegiance to the Union, assumed to be the rightful political power of the State, held elections, organized a State government, adopted a free-state constitution, giving the benefit of public schools equally to black and white, and empowering the Legislature to confer the elective franchise upon the colored man. Their Legislature has already voted to ratify the constitutional amendment recently passed by Congress, abolishing slavery throughout the nation. These twelve thousand persons are thus fully committed to the Union, and to perpetual freedom in the state — committed to the very things, and nearly all the things the nation wants — and they ask the nation's recognition, and its assistance to make good their committal. Now, if we

reject, and spurn them, we do our utmost
to disorganize and disperse them. We in
effect say to the white men "You are
worthless, or worse—we will neither help
you, nor be helped by you." To the blacks
we say "This cup of liberty which these,
your old masters, hold to your lips, we
will dash from you, and leave you to the
chances of gathering the spilled and
scattered contents in some vague and
undefined when, where, and how." If this
course, discouraging and paralyzing both
white and black, has any tendency to bring
Louisiana into proper practical relations
with the Union, I have, so far, been unable
to perceive it. If, on the contrary, we
recognize, and sustain the new government of Louisiana the converse of all this
is made true. We encourage the hearts, and
nerve the arms of the twelve thousand to
adhere to their work, and argue for it, and
proselyte for it, and fight for it, and feed
it, and grow it, and ripen it to a complete
success. The colored man too, in seeing all
united for him, is inspired with vigilance,
and energy, and daring, to the same end.
Grant that he desires the elective franchise,
will he not attain it sooner by saving the
already advanced steps toward it, than by
running backward over them? Concede
that the new government of Louisiana is
only to what it should be as the egg is to
the fowl, we shall sooner have the fowl by
hatching the egg than by smashing it?
Again, if we reject Louisiana, we also
reject one vote in favor to the proposed
amendment to the national constitution.
To meet this proposition, it has been
argued that no more than three fourths of
those States which have not attempted
secession are necessary to validly ratify
the amendment. I do not commit myself
against this, further than to say that such a
ratification would be questionable, and
sure to be persistently questioned; while a
ratification by three fourths of all the
States would be unquestioned and
unquestionable.

I repeat the question. "Can Louisiana be
brought into proper practical relation with
the Union *sooner* by *sustaining* or by
discarding her new State Government?"

As the war nears its close, Federal supply
wagons file through Petersburg, carrying
provisions to Grant's troops.

Upon this little sharp-edged triangle of broken glass, one of the great portraits of Abraham Lincoln is etched. The photograph was taken on April 20, 1864, in Brady's Washington gallery to assist artist Francis B. Carpenter in the portrait he was doing at the White House.
Upper right: Lincoln's home for the fifty months during which his true greatness most fully emerged

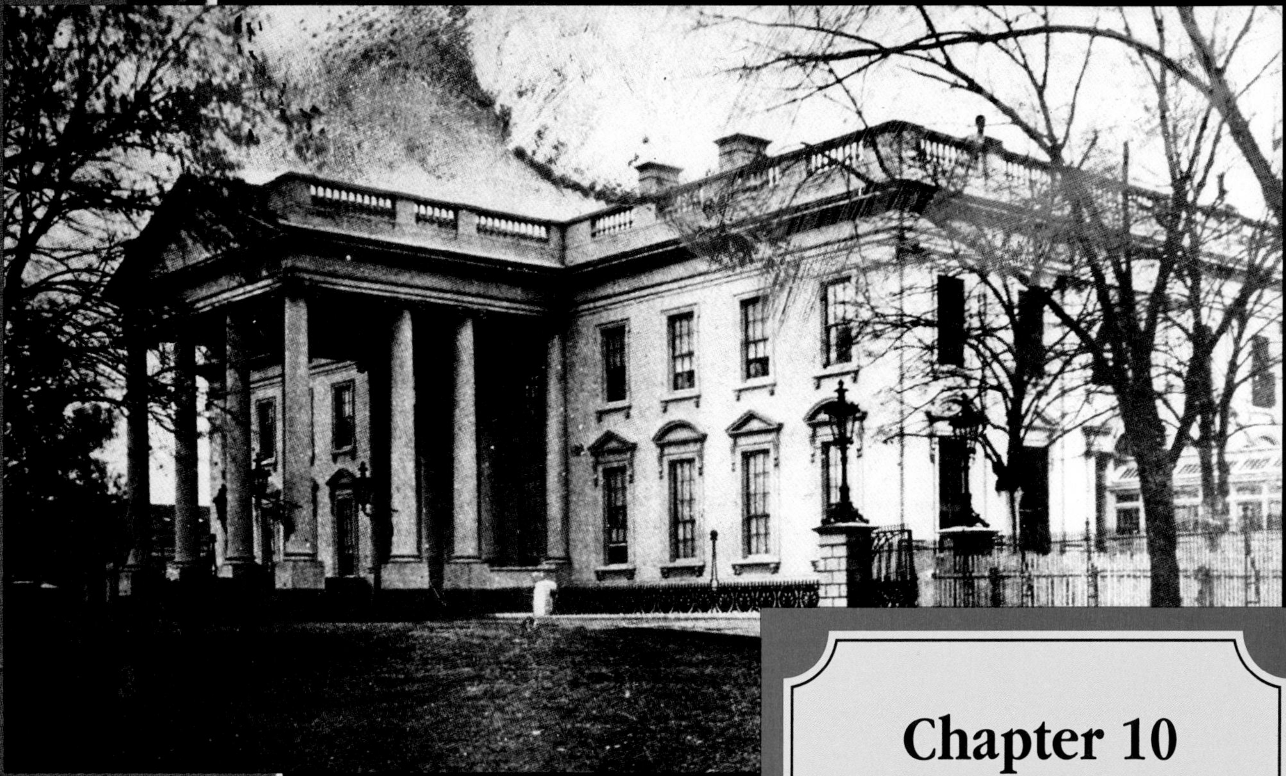

Chapter 10

THE MAN IN THE WHITE HOUSE

**He is so many things
to so many people,
it is a wonder the strain
of his everyday life
does not leave him
shattered.**

Left: Lincoln on February 9, 1864
Below: The massive East Room

Lincoln dominated his White House—some felt the life drain out of it when he was not present—but he personally did little to rearrange or modernize it. His use of the building merely followed precedent and protocol. An attic cistern for rainwater that had been the source of the flushing system from Jefferson's day had been replaced by city well water during the time of Andrew Jackson. Van Buren added a furnace. Polk's contributions included an icebox and gaslights. Pierce installed a bathroom and a more elaborate hot-air heating system. Most recently, Buchanan had added a conservatory and ordered bedroom sinks fed by Potomac River water; the pipes were installed soon after the Lincolns moved in. The First Lady went right to work refurbishing the run-down mansion, with its peeling walls, broken furniture, and thread-

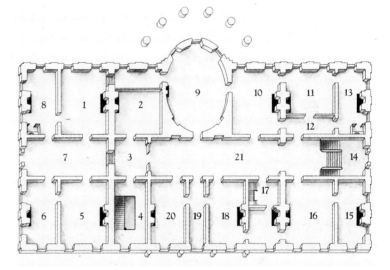

bare carpets, which made it look to one observer like some "old and unsuccessful hotel," but the only construction Lincoln himself requested was a partition in the second-floor office area, to create a private passageway between his office and the library.

The photographs at the right show a back and a front view of the Lincoln White House, separated by a numbered floor plan of the second story. On the ground floor of the mansion was the mighty East Room—forty feet wide by eighty feet long—running the entire north-south width of the building; also the Green Room, the Oval Room, the Red Room, and the State Dining Room. The President's quarters and offices were on the second floor. Directly above part of the East Room was the office of Lincoln's secretary John G. Nicolay (*8*). Located across the back of the House were Lincoln's own office

(*1*), a reception room (*2*), and a private passageway from his office to the family library (*9*). Farther along were Mrs. Lincoln's bedroom (*10*) and the President's sleeping quarters (*11*) and dressing room (*13*).

The front side of the upstairs contained John Hay's office (*6*), Nicolay and Hay's shared bedroom (*5*), and a set of office stairs (*4*). A central corridor (*19*), splitting two smaller bedrooms (*20* and *18*), opened out on a balcony used for speaking to the public on special occasions. Beyond the service stairs (*17*) was the Prince of Wales Room (*16*), where Lincoln's son Willie died. The final bedroom (*15*) was Tad's. The sketch reveals how public the private part of the White House was, with its grand staircase and landing (*14*), which led to a long central corridor (*21*), passing within a whisper of the Lincoln family rooms.

Before it was finally replaced, there was only one key to the front door of the White House, from the Jefferson era right through Lincoln's administration.

TWICE A WEEK HIS OFFICE BECOMES A "PUBLIC OPINION BATH"

Lincoln's "oval office" was rectangular. This was where he did his presidential paperwork and conducted a seemingly endless stream of interviews. It was also used as the Cabinet Room, the scene of weekly Tuesday and Friday meetings, which, when the military situation demanded it, became daily gatherings, even early-morning or late-into-the-night assemblies. Here, between these four walls, was the heart of the government of the United States. Here came the generals and admirals to report upon the progress of the war and give their recommendations; the senators and congressmen to make known their opinions, needs, desires; office seekers by the drove, waving their petitions, spouting credentials, jostling for position, and with them, wrote John Hay, "an endless stream of officers in search of promotion or desirable assignments." Here came the inventors whose schemes and tinkerings, Lincoln was aware, could alter the future. Here came fiery people pleading causes, relatives of condemned men seeking pardons, widows searching for solace. Here came old friends, and Indians, and the just plain curious. "They don't want much," said Lincoln. "They get but little, and I must see them."

Lincoln could stand at either of his two office windows and look out over the Potomac, to the Virginia hills beyond. Closer was the stunted, arrested base of the Washington Monument, whose cornerstone had been laid in 1848 and whose planned-for height of 600 feet was stopped at 153 because no more contributions could be raised. Now rubbish blew around its base, detracting even more from the seldom-visited, marshy spot just beyond the smelly old city canal that inched its way across town from beside the Capitol, cutting between the White House and the monument shaft before it emptied into the Potomac.

Lincoln's office facilities were few: a black, horsehair-covered, swivel-seated armchair; a high postmaster's desk, its alphabetized pigeonholes bringing the only sense of order to the room; wall maps with colored pushpins to designate armies and battlegrounds; a system of bell ropes which ran to a yoke in the attic and then to the different rooms of his secretaries and key White House servants. Except at night or early morning it was hard to find time alone in this office room, as so many people used it or had access. The days on which Lincoln threw open the doors to the public seemed to many like badly wasted time. Not to Lincoln. On one occasion, a visiting major, seeing how taxed the President was by the audiences, suggested they stop. "[N]o hours of my day are better employed," Lincoln replied, according to Francis B. Carpenter. "Men moving only in an official circle are apt to become merely official—not to say arbitrary—in their ideas, and are apter and apter, with each passing day, to forget that they hold power in a representative capacity. Now this is all wrong. I go into these promiscuous receptions of all who claim to have business with me twice each week, and every applicant for audience has to take his turn as if waiting to be shaved in a barber's shop.... I tell you, Major,... that I call these receptions my *public opinion baths*...and, though they may not be pleasant in all their particulars, the effect, as a whole, is renovating and invigorating."

Especially in the early days of the Lincoln administration when this sketch *(right)* was published, it was common for the corridor outside the President's room to be crowded with office seekers. To Lincoln's dismay, there weren't enough posts to fill, although he put it differently: "There are too many pigs for the tits."

Brady, A. Lincoln Washingt

This sketch of Lincoln's office, made by C. K. Stellwagen in October 1864, is the most accurate picture we have of Lincoln's workplace. The high desk at the right blocks the door to the screened-off passageway behind the reception room, the painting over the fireplace, one of Lincoln's favorites, is of Andrew Jackson. The wallpaper was dark green with gold star patterns.

On November 8, 1863, Lincoln sat with his secretaries for photographer Alexander Gardner. Although they were with him almost constantly for fifty straight months, this was the only occasion on which John Nicolay *(seated)* and John Hay posed with the President. On this Sunday, Hay wrote in his diary, "Nico & I immortalized ourselves by having ourselves done in group with the Prest."

Lincoln's secretaries handled the two to three hundred letters a day that were sent to the White House, including requests for the President's autograph. Here, on the back of a *carte de visite* with Lincoln's portrait, John Hay has verified the President's signature. Work got so heavy a third secretary, William O. Stoddard, was added to make a preliminary screening of all incoming mail.

Taken on April 26,
1864, these are the
only photographs of
Lincoln in his office.
The President's height
was disproportion-
ately in his legs;
seated (as in the
photograph at left),
his knees poked up
like prongs. The other
pair of legs belong to
John Nicolay. In the
photograph at the right,
Lincoln stands, resting
a book on the table
the Cabinet uses at
its meetings. Lincoln's
back is to his high
desk, which sits
against the door to
the passageway
behind the reception
room. The photographs
were made by Anthony
Berger, a Brady oper-
ator, to assist the
artist Francis B. Car-
penter in his massive
painting of Lincoln
reading the Emancipa-
tion Proclamation to
his Cabinet.

THE LINCOLN FAMILY

Although Lincoln was photographed on dozens of occasions, he never posed with his entire family, never even alone with his wife. The only family member who received the honor was Tad, who was brought along to sittings at both Brady's and Gardner's studios. The first time was on February 9, 1864, when Anthony Berger was the cameraman. Present was artist Francis B. Carpenter, who was then living in the White House in order to paint his Emancipation Proclamation portrait. Taken on this day were several photographs, including the faces that would later appear on the Lincoln penny and the five-dollar bill. Carpenter is credited with some of the posing, especially for the photograph of the President reading to Tad *(below)*. Carpenter's painting of how the whole family would have looked in 1861 was not even started until after the assassination, at which time he asked Mrs. Lincoln to sit for a photograph from which he could work. She wrote to him, turning him down — she was in much too nervous a state to pose — but she would help by providing him with several photographs of herself and her favorites of the boys. Using the pose from the photograph below to anchor his portrait (but reversing the image), Carpenter then added Mary and Robert and resurrected Willie as well. Mary liked the picture of Willie she had provided but wrote Carpenter that "even in *that* likeness, of Willie, justice, is not done him, he was a very beautiful boy, with a most *spiritual* expression of face."

Brady's photograph of Lincoln and Tad

Carpenter's painting *Lincoln Family in 1861*

Francis B. Carpenter, the artist, writes about parental discipline in the White House. The day after the review of Burnside's division, some photographers from Brady's Gallery came up to the White House to make some stereoscopic studies for me of the President's office. They requested a dark closet, in which to develop the pictures; and without a thought that I was infringing upon anybody's rights, I took them to an unoccupied room of which little "Tad" had taken possession a few days before, and with the aid of a couple of the servants, had fitted up as a miniature theater, with stage, curtains, orchestra, stalls, parquette, and all. Knowing that the use required would interfere with none of his arrangements, I led the way to this apartment.

Everything went on well, and one or two pictures had been taken, when suddenly there was an uproar. The operator came back to the office, and said that "Tad" had taken great offence at the occupation of his room without his consent, and had locked the door, refusing all admission. The chemicals had been taken inside, and there was no way of getting at them, he having carried off the key. In the midst of this conversation, "Tad" burst in, in a fearful passion.... Mr. Lincoln had been sitting for a photograph, and was still in the chair. He said very mildly, "Tad, go and unlock the door." Tad went off muttering into his mother's room, refusing to obey. I followed him into the passage, but no coaxing would pacify him. Upon my return to the President, I found him still sitting patiently in the chair, from which he had not risen. He said: "Has not the boy opened that door?" I replied that we could do nothing with him—he had gone off in a great pet. Mr. Lincoln's lips came together firmly, and then, suddenly rising, he strode across the passage with the air of one bent on punishment, and disappeared in the domestic apartments. Directly he returned with the key to the theater, which he unlocked himself... "Tad," said he, half apologetically, "is a peculiar child. He was violently excited when I went to him. I said, 'Tad, do you know you are making your father a great deal of trouble?' He burst into tears, instantly giving me up the key."

MISTAKES, EXTRAVAGANCE, AND WILLIE'S DEATH MAKE HAVOC OF THE FIRST LADY'S LIFE

For Mary Lincoln, her husband's presidency should have been the happy climax to her life; instead, it led her down a spiral of darkness and misery. Already shaken by criticism in the press—some of it fair, some not—Mary fell apart after Willie's death in February 1862, less than a year after the inauguration. "Mrs. Lincoln's grief was inconsolable," her seamstress and friend, Elizabeth Keckley, remembered. "The pale face of her dead boy threw her into convulsions." Try as she might, Mary never fully recovered from the shock and loss. "I feel rebellious," she exploded. "[I] almost believe that our heavenly father has forsaken us." Desperately seeking solace, answers, anything to stem her overwhelming despair, Mary turned to the spirit world. With much of America caught in the spell of the spiritualism cult, mediums were conducting séances everywhere, even, Mary now made sure, in the White House itself. Half amused, the President turned up at one or two of these sessions. But as superstitious as Lincoln was, the table rappings in the dark, the floating objects, the tweaked beards, the unworldly voices, could not persuade him to join his wife in her hysterical belief that she was really and truly communicating with her lost boys.

All too soon after Willie was taken from her, there were other deaths in the family for Mary to deal with, and although she denied it, they too were matters of wrenching grief. "I hope they are either dead or taken prisoner," she had blurted out against her Confederate half-brothers in 1862, adding that "they would kill my husband if they could, and destroy our government." But four months later, when her favorite half-brother, Alexander, perished fighting for the South, she cried out, "Oh, little Aleck, why had you to die!" A year later, news reached Mary in New York that Ben Helm, her half-sister Emilie's husband, had been killed at Chattanooga. At Mary's request, "Sister Emilie" was invited to recuperate in the White House, but instead of solace, what Emilie found unnerved her. Willie's presence was almost palpable. "After I had said good night and had gone to my room," Emilie recorded in her diary, "there was a gentle knock at the door, and [I heard] Sister Mary's voice.... She was smiling though her eyes were full of tears.... '[H]e lives, Emilie!' she said with a thrill in her voice I can never forget. 'He comes to me every night, and stands at the foot of my bed with the same sweet, adorable smile.'" The whole thing was "unnatural and abnormal."

Through eighteen years of marriage Mary had always been Lincoln's closest friend, his best adviser, his most ardent supporter. Fights aside, she had loved him warmly and devoted her life to his. She had checked his dress before he left for work each morning, mended his clothes, always had meals ready on time, gave his life stability. Now, in the White House, all that changed. The intimacy of their Springfield home was gone. Lincoln was no longer hers alone; he belonged to an endless stream of people, events, and decisions that shut her out and rendered her, in her own eyes anyway, useless. Hungering for his attention, she wrote, "I consider myself fortunate if at eleven o'clock, I...find myself in my...room and...my tired and weary Husband is there...to receive me—to chat over the occurrences of the day." Even this luxury came less and less frequently; and over time, as money problems arose, there developed a host of "forbidden subjects" between them. Plucky and determined, Mary struck back at the unfairness of it all, leaving a trail of enemies in her

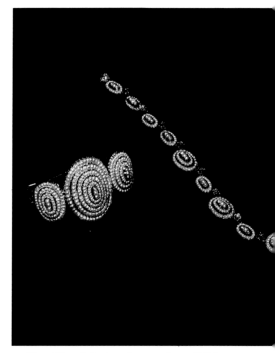

Mary Lincoln's stunning seed-pearl Tiffany necklace and earrings. The jewelry with which the First Lady decorated herself suggested that some royal coffer had

An elaborate silver service was one of Mary Lincoln's purchases for the run-

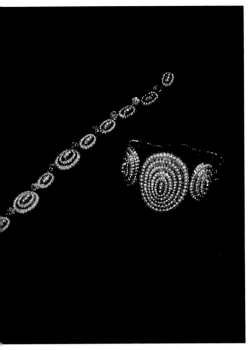

been mysteriously plundered. Instead, the jewels, along with the dozens of ballgowns she ordered, were all part of a personal debt of $27,000.

down mansion. "Flub dubs" and a "monstrous extravagance," Lincoln called them.

MRS. LINCOLN.

Entered according to Act of Congress in the year 1861, by M.B. Brady, in the Clerk's office of the District Court of the U.S. for the So. District of New-York

Mary Lincoln had to give individual picture approval before Brady could put *cartes de visite* of the First Lady on sale at his gallery. Once she wrote the New York printer, "The one at all possible is the one standing, with the large figured dress...This you might retain. On Monday I will sit for another, which we will send you, if you will destroy the others."

wake, including Secretary of State Seward and the youthful John Hay. With her husband hardly bothering to write to her anymore when she was away, and with the flattery of some attentive men blinding her to their motives, Mary formed her own coterie, some of whom turned out to be unprincipled. Her friendship with William S. Wood was so controversial that it provoked an anonymous letter to Lincoln: "If he continues as Commissioner, he will stab you in a most vital part." Her famous evening gatherings in the White House Blue Room attracted notorious womanizers such as Henry "Chevalier" Wikoff and the infamous Dan Sickles, who had once murdered his wife's lover. By late 1864 Mary was carrying on a secretive correspondence with New York politico Abram Wakeman; their letters were intimate enough that she had to urge him to burn her notes to him.

Once started, it seemed she could do nothing any longer with restraint or sensitivity. Reorganizing the White House staff, she trod on toes and stirred up bitterness in long-trusted servants. Her usually keen powers of assessing character failed her when she befriended a groundskeeper who turned out to be misusing his position, and a dapper informer who sold descriptions of life in the White House to newspapers, even a speech of Lincoln's before it was delivered. She gave private dinners and tried to get the government to pay for them. In her attempt to refurbish the shabby White House, she fell victim to power and glitter, as she overtraveled, overspent, and overindulged herself playing the grand lady. Her shopping sprees in Philadelphia, Boston, and New York became notorious, as she squandered money at the splendid emporiums and then held court afterward every evening at fancy hotels. Wallpaper from Paris, mirrors, goblets, a 560-piece set of chinaware, chandeliers, carpets, gold knives, forks, and spoons—the purchases were extravagant and endless. Soon Mary had exceeded her decoration allowance of $20,000 by $6,700. When Mary's friends attempted to convince the President to ask Congress for more money to cover the deficit, Lincoln became furious. "It can never have my approval—I'll pay it out of my own pocket first—it would stink in the nostrils of the American people to have it said that the President of the United States had approved a bill over-running an appropriation of $20,000 for *flub dubs*—for this damned old house, when the soldiers cannot have blankets!"

Mary was even less careful of her spending when it came to her personal attire, and more secretive. "There is more at stake in this election than he dreams of," she confided to Mrs. Keckley in 1864. "If he is re-elected, I can keep him in ignorance of my affairs, but if he is defeated...he will know all." The newspapers paid little attention to Mary's good work in Washington's hospitals distributing fruit and encouragement to the Union wounded, or to her compassion toward Washington's fugitive slaves. In the heated times, it made better reading to call her names, exaggerate gossip about her, focus on her excessive wardrobe and jewelry, and dwell upon her rebel family ties. She was flirtatious but also intensely jealous, and her wild outbursts on numerous occasions made her self-controlled husband cringe. What had started out so gloriously in 1860 for this spirited, dainty, dignified woman with the quicksilver temper and an unfailing dedication to her indulgent husband, who would not take her seriously, had turned by 1865 into a life out of control.

Mary Lincoln's only rival for social leadership of the new administration was the beautiful, pug-nosed, twenty-one-year-old daughter of the secretary of the treasury, Kate Chase. Determined to see her widower father become president, the beguiling, willful Kate acted as his campaign manager. To further her father's career, and hers, Kate married wealthy though scandal-ridden Senator William Sprague of Rhode Island, the richest man in New England. In November 1863 all of Washington turned out for her wedding, including the President—all, that is, except Mary Lincoln.

When the wife of General Ord rode too close to Lincoln, Mary loudly accused her of trying to impersonate her. *Above:* The general, his insulted wife, and their daughter

This is how Mary Lincoln looked at the time of the first inaugural ball. She loved to flatten down her hair and cover it with elaborate flower arrangements.

ALL ROBERT NEEDS IS A UNIFORM

Robert sports his first mustache.

Lincoln did not naturally warm to Robert, his taciturn and seemingly indifferent eldest son. Away at Phillips Exeter Academy through most of his father's triumphal year in Springfield and then at Harvard during the presidential years, Bob almost never saw him. Lincoln sent his son money and salutations but relied on his wife's trips to Boston to keep him posted. When Robert was home on vacation in Washington, his mother found him "pleasant" and "companionable" and came to dread his returns to Cambridge, but Bob never got to see his father for more than a few rushed, unsatisfactory minutes. The chip on his shoulder grew as he watched the casual banter between Lincoln and Tad, who was now seldom away from his father's side, present even at some Cabinet meetings, and a frequent visitor in Lincoln's bed. On his rare visits to Washington, Robert began straying from home, attending the theater a lot and gallivanting about town with best friend John Hay. In his senior year, he spent his free time in Washington with his sweetheart, Mary Harlan. As his graduation from Harvard approached, the telegram he most

feared arrived: "The President will not be at commencement." Bitterly disappointed, Bob returned to Washington. "One day I saw my father for a few minutes," he related. "He said: 'Son, what are you going to do now?' I said 'As long as you object to my joining the army, I'm going back to Harvard to study law.' 'If you do,' said Lincoln, 'you will learn more than I ever did, but you will never have so good a time.'" The fact that Robert was not in uniform was an embarrassment to Lincoln; but until now, the President himself had blocked Robert from signing up for the sake of Mary, who was terrified of losing still another son. In early 1865, the President wrote to General Grant: "My son, now in his twenty second year, having graduated at Harvard, wishes to see something of the war before it ends.... Could he, without embarrassment to you, or detriment to the service, go into your Military family with some nominal rank, I, and not the public, furnishing his necessary means?" Once in uniform on Grant's staff, Robert lost his reticence toward his father and Lincoln seemed, for the first time, truly proud of his eldest son.

When this photograph of Lincoln *(left)* was taken, on January 8, 1864, Robert was a senior at Harvard, in a class of ninety-nine. That month, when Robert wrote home for money, Lincoln's reply seemed curt: "I sent your draft today. How are you now? Answer by telegraph at once." Nor did the President add any niceties a week later when he warned Bob, "There is a good deal of small-pox here. Your friends must judge for themselves whether they ought to come or not." Robert seemed slightly out of step with his mother as well. In Washington at the time of the Tom Thumb reception, he declined to leave his room to meet his parents' little guests. "No, mother, I do not propose to assist in entertaining Tom Thumb," he said. "My notions of duty, perhaps, are somewhat different from yours."

As a Harvard undergraduate, Robert poses with a high hat like his father's.

WITH WILLIE'S DEATH, LINCOLN LOSES HIS FAVORITE

Dapper with cane, hat, and tie—certainly not normal wear for the younger Lincoln boys—Willie is all spiffed up for a photograph at Brady's soon after the Lincolns' arrival in Washington.

Although close friends, Willie and Tad were opposites. While Tad could be tempestuous, irreverent, demanding, loud, full of mischief, and discourteous, Willie was a model son—polite, quiet, bright, and thoughtful—very much like his father, everybody said, but with better looks. "The idolized child of the household," wrote Mary.

At eight, he had written back to his neighbor playmate when his father took him to Chicago on a business trip, modeling his letter on his favorite tale, "The Three Bears." "Me and father have a nice room to ourselves. We have two little pitchers on a washstand. The smallest one for me, the largest one for Father. We have two little towels on top of both pitchers. The smallest one for me, the largest one for Father. We have two little beds..."

Willie studied hard at his lessons, could read and write, loved to memorize railroad timetables, took pleasure in being obedient, told his parents he planned to be either a teacher or a preacher, and saved his allowance for the missionary society. When he fell sick toward the end of January 1862, it was blamed on his riding in a chilly rain, but a more likely culprit was the White House drinking water, badly polluted and capable of transmitting typhoid fever.

Even though the boy was sick, Dr. Stone advised Mary Lincoln to go ahead anyway with her lavish February 5 reception. Several times during the evening the Lincolns left their eight hundred guests and came up to check on Willie, who was feverish and breathing hard.

There had never been a state funeral in the White House for a child before, but when Willie finally died two weeks later, it seemed fitting for the powerful of Washington to gather there and say goodbye. Willie lay in the Green Room while many of the same guests who had crowded the East Room for the recent reception— senators, diplomats, officers, friends—now gathered there again to hear the Reverend Phineas D. Gurley, the Lincoln's minister from the New York Avenue Presbyterian Church, lead a deeply emotional service. Mary Lincoln was unable to leave her bed, but the devastated President bravely faced the occasion, leading the way to Oak Hill Cemetery through a city just battered by a storm, along a path of torn-off roofs and splintered steeples.

After weeks of gasping for breath and fighting fever, Willie became delirious and expired in the enormous bed in the Prince of Wales Room *(left)*. Mrs. Lincoln's dress maker and friend, Elizabeth Keckley, described the President at his dead son's side: "Great sobs choked his utterance. He buried his head in his hands, and his tall frame was convulsed with emotion. I stood at the foot of the bed, my eyes full of tears, looking at the man in silent, awe-stricken wonder. His grief unnerved him, and made him a weak, passive child." After the embalming, Willie lay in his little soldier's uniform in an imitation rosewood coffin in the Green Room *(below left)* for viewing. Following the service, he was placed at Oak Hill Cemetery in a crypt inside a tomb *(below)* offered to Lincoln by his friend William Thomas Carroll, the clerk of the Supreme Court. In the days that followed, Lincoln twice returned alone, to lift the coffin lid and gaze upon his son.

In February 1865, Lincoln and Tad strike a father-and-son pose for photographer Alexander Gardner.

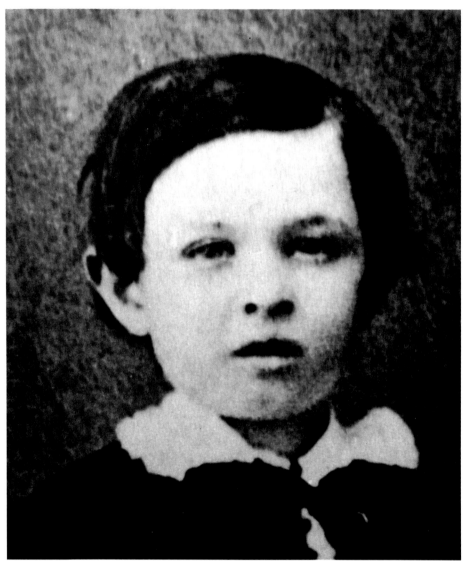

A few months after his father's death, the young man faces the world.

This photograph of Tad at eight shows a scar running from his upper lip to his nose, possibly marking a harelip which, along with a partially cleft palate, had made his speech difficult to understand.

Every time he looked at his youngest son, Lincoln felt anxious and torn. Tad was so vulnerable, so open, so weak emotionally, so undisciplined, yet so loving. Especially after Willie was gone, Lincoln wanted to protect Tad from the world, give him a special place, a hand up on life. He couldn't say "no" to him. "Let the children have a good time" was the motto of the White House when the Lincolns first moved in, remembered Julia Taft, an older playmate. It was Mary Lincoln's philosophy as well as her husband's—let them grow up naturally, without restraint or guidance, and learn to enjoy life in their own way. The lack of control and direction had been good for Willie, who had motivation and self-discipline; mercurial, elfin, eccentric

Tad couldn't handle it. Sparkling with creative mischief, he delighted in making trouble in the big, old, white mansion. He drove his goats through the executive halls, sprayed dignitaries with the fire hose, broke mirrors, locked doors, constructed sleds and wagons out of chairs, and created mock snowstorms from stacks of calling cards. He executed his Zouave doll "Jack" for sleeping at his post, got his father to pardon the Thanksgiving turkey, carved up the furniture, dipped his fingers in the inkwells, fished out the goldfish from the greenhouse tank, set up a food shop in the White House lobby, rang the call bells, pestered guests, drilled the servants, and, in general, scooted all over the place, hooting with adenoidal merriment. In the

eyes of his parents, Tad could do no wrong. "I have not the least trouble managing him," said Mary. But to outsiders, he appeared patently "spoiled." With a special nurse to provide for his basic needs, Tad still could not dress himself at the age of eight. With his education sorely neglected, in the White House he remained almost completely illiterate. The wilder Tad got, the more his father remembered his own childhood and the more he wanted to take his child into his arms. "When this is over," he told a visitor, "I tell my boy Tad that we will go back to the farm, when I was happier as a boy when I dug potatoes at 25 cents a day than I am now. I tell him I will buy him a mule and a pony and he shall have a little garden, in a field all his own."

Left: The date that Lincoln sat for this stern portrait at the Brady gallery has long been in question. On an original Brady *carte de visite* of the picture, given to Lincoln's sister-in-law in the White House, Mrs. Ninian Edwards wrote "taken April 1862." *Above:* In Alexander Gardner's August 9, 1863, portrait, Lincoln is close to a smile.

Hannibal Hamlin

Andrew Johnson

ANDREW JOHNSON, LINCOLN'S SECOND VICE PRESIDENT

Although Lincoln refrained from a public endorsement of a running mate in 1864, the Republican Convention replaced Hannibal Hamlin, the good-natured incumbent from Maine, with a candidate who most delegates felt would strengthen a shaky ticket: Andrew Johnson, military governor of Tennessee. He was that rare commodity, a man from rebel territory who not only backed the Union but also, though a recent slave owner himself, was now all for emancipation. When Johnson started out as a tailor in Greenville, Tennessee, his young wife helped to improve his mind, reading books to him as he sat cross-legged with his needle and thread. He entered politics as an alderman, then worked his way up the political ladder to state legislator, U.S. congressman, governor, and senator. He was widely known as a man of the people. But Mary Lincoln had warned her husband: "He is a demagogue and if you place him in power, Mr. Lincoln, mark my words, you will rue it some day." The day came sooner

than even Mary expected. Preceding the swearing-in of the Vice President inside the Capitol, just minutes before Lincoln was to be inaugurated outside, Johnson, recovering from a long illness, took a strong drink of whiskey in Hamlin's private office to steady his nerves. On the ceremony that followed, journalist Noah Brooks commented: "Hamlin made a brief and sensible speech, and Andrew Johnson, whose face was extra-ordinarily red, was presented to take the oath.... He was evidently intoxicated." Johnson's rambling, purposeless speech went on and on, even though Hamlin

nudged him to end. "Oh well, don't you bother about Andy Johnson's drinking," Lincoln told friends afterward. "He made a bad slip the other day but I have known Andy a great many years and he ain't no drunkard." Mary Lincoln was less charitable, saying much later, when Johnson was president and had not favored a pension for her, that her husband had "hated Andrew Johnson...Down at City Point once Andy Johnson followed us. Was drunk. Mr. Lincoln said: 'For God's sake don't ask Johnson to dine with us.' 'No, don't' said Sumner. And I did not ask him.'"

Charles Sumner

SENATOR CHARLES SUMNER, LINCOLN'S HIGH-MINDED GADFLY

The tall, erudite, impeccably dressed senator from Massachusetts looked down on Lincoln at first. An ardent abolitionist—some political enemies incorrectly said he preferred not to mingle with blacks in his personal life—Charles Sumner kept steady pressure on Lincoln to emancipate the slaves and scorned him for moving so slowly. But as time went on, and Sumner came to believe in the President's real commitment to emancipation, the two

began to appreciate each other. In a way, Lincoln was amused by the elegant Brahmin whose "profusion of dark hair," according to Noah Brooks, was "arranged with an appearance of studied negligence." Lincoln would be sitting in his office, in some casual position, his leg over the arm of a chair as he liked to do, when he would catch sight of Sumner's cane in the door. "Quick as thought he was up," wrote John Eaton, and "returned a courteous bow

with dignity." Said Lincoln to Eaton later, "When in Rome we must do as the Romans do." Acutely aware of his public, Sumner "never allowed himself, even in his own room, to fall into a position he would not take in his chair in the Senate," wrote Brooks. Rumor had it that he practiced his speeches in front of his bedroom mirror. Fastidious in his use of words, Sumner deplored Lincoln's homely language. When Lincoln said once that the rebels "turned tail and ran," or when he refused to give a preview of an important speech, saying he did not want to "have it all dribbled out of" him and have nothing to say tomorrow, Sumner thought the choice of words unworthy of a president. Throughout his presidency, Lincoln had to cope with this high-minded gadfly who sometimes supported him and sometimes fiercely opposed him. "The conscience of the Senate," he was called, but Sumner could also be an aggravation. As critical as he sometimes was, he never joined Greeley or the others in their opposition to the war or their willingness to compromise on slavery. "Lincoln's election would be a disaster," Sumner wrote in 1864, "but McClellan's [a] damnation." To the end, Lincoln and the Massachusetts senator shared much more in common than they had differences. Mrs. Lincoln agreed. Inordinately flattered when Sumner told her that for the first time in several administrations he actually enjoyed visiting the White House, she would sit for hours all dressed up, in the Blue Room, receiving his calls. "Mr. Sumner is a very high-toned gentleman," she once wrote, "and one of my best friends."

LINCOLN'S EXTENDED FAMILY: THE CABINET

WILLIAM HENRY SEWARD, SECRETARY OF STATE

Eight years Lincoln's senior, and for thirty years New York's leading politician, William Henry Seward had convinced himself that he would be the next president; when he ended up as Lincoln's secretary of state, at first he was incredulous, then grew to accept the lesser position gracefully. Kindly, optimistic, brilliant, Seward specialized in high finance, the ebb and flow of economic indicators, of trade, tariffs, transportation. His anti-slavery zeal was legendary, and his support of immigrants and Catholics marked him as far ahead of his time. In size Seward was a little man, only five feet four inches tall, which made his large ears seem bigger still, his chicken neck even thinner. His invalid wife stayed mostly up north in Auburn, New York, leaving Seward a bachelor in Washington, known for his sumptuous entertaining and for the perpetual cigar in his mouth or hand, the smell of tobacco permeating his out-of-style suits. Although Mary Lincoln despised Seward, calling him a "hypocrite" and a "sneak," the President slowly came to appreciate his secretary of state. Seward helped him in so many ways: made appointments for him with foreign diplomats, taught him proper governmental protocol, advised him on key political questions, helped him with his important written papers. By the fall of his first year in office, Lincoln, fonder of this man than of anyone else in his Cabinet, was regularly dropping in at Seward's home in the evenings. As the other secretaries became increasingly jealous, Seward's enemies came to believe that the secretary of state had gotten Lincoln under his control. "They will eat you up," Lincoln had been warned of his "compound Cabinet." Seward himself had tried to do just that, to seize power in the early days of the war. Thwarted, he came to love Lincoln, respect him, advise him, guard him. Together, they shared a love of animals, off-color jokes, and raucous laughter. With his own clean-living Baptist roots, Lincoln was continually amazed and amused by Seward's irreverent, worldly behavior. "You must be an Episcopalian," the President said to a mule driver one day, "because you swear just like Governor Seward, who is a churchwarden."

SALMON PORTLAND CHASE, SECRETARY OF THE TREASURY

New Hampshire-born Salmon Portland Chase had credentials similar to Seward's, for he had both governed Ohio and represented it in the Senate. He, too, had expected the presidential nomination at the convention in 1860 — or possibly the vice presidential. When Lincoln talked to him about heading the Treasury Department, Chase was hesitant; secretary of state would be a more likely path to the elusive presidency. But he took what Lincoln offered, and concentrated on running his department with skill, including overseeing the financing of the war. Despite similarities in background, it would have been hard to find two more opposite personalities than Chase and Seward. Next to the conservative, cigar-chomping New Yorker, Chase appeared puritanical, intensely religious, and politically radical, maintaining, along with his nickname of "Salmon the Solemn," an aura of considerable dignity. Unlike the short, rumpled Seward, Chase was tall, square-jawed, and handsome in an old-fashioned, classic way. Chase had suffered family tragedy: three wives and four children had died over the years. On abolitionist podiums he had been hit by rotten eggs, even a brick. He had defended so many blacks free of charge that he had acquired the name "attorney general for runaway slaves." Kate Chase Sprague, his beautiful, statuesque daughter, projected an air of refinement and delicacy, but she was also an insistent and persuasive campaign manager and booster for her father. For four years Chase second-guessed the President, was a cause of Cabinet infighting, and spread the story that Lincoln was inadequate, naive, and unqualified. As the new election year approached, Chase hungered for the presidency. Many Republican senators were fed up with Lincoln by now, and wondered who should replace him. Kate put her father's name forward at every opportunity. And behind Lincoln's back, Chase gingerly promoted his own candidacy. "I really feel as if, with God's blessing I *could* administer the Government of this country," he wrote. Although Lincoln at first dismissed the Chase threat as "a horsefly on the neck of a plough-horse" keeping him "lively about his work," Chase's politicking ended up costing him his Cabinet position.

GIDEON WELLES, SECRETARY OF THE NAVY

Lincoln recognized the devotion and ability of his secretary of the navy, but he also liked to make gentle jokes about the former Connecticut newspaperman with the huge wig that did not match his beard, jokes which Lincoln hoped no one would repeat to his old-fashioned, over-talkative "Father Neptune." A shy, dignified man but a humorless, suspicious, and acid-penned diarist, Welles had strong dislikes, including William Seward, Edwin Stanton, and Charles Sumner. General McClellan once wrote his wife that Welles was "the most garrulous old woman you were ever annoyed by"; Senator John Conness of California claimed that Welles "did not have tangible shape and one's arm could sweep through his form." Nevertheless, under his administration the navy grew from twelve available ships at the war's start to a creditable fleet of more than five hundred vessels and fifty thousand men.

MONTGOMERY BLAIR, POSTMASTER GENERAL

The easiest Cabinet job was postmaster general, and Lincoln used his choice not only to keep the mails running but, more important, to strengthen his position in the border states. In getting the six-feet-tall, straight-backed, blue-eyed Monty (nicknamed "the judge"), Lincoln got the whole powerful Blair family. They moved as one, the father in the lead. Francis Preston Blair had been the acknowledged brains behind Andrew Jackson and his principal speechwriter; sons Montgomery and Frank Jr. were powerhouses in their own right. Among the three, their influence spread from Virginia to Maryland to Kentucky to Missouri and was vital for the Union's cause. Though he was the only Cabinet member who advocated reinforcing Fort Sumter, Blair believed separation of the races had to follow emancipation, and spoke out sharply against abolitionists who supported the full equality of blacks and whites.

EDWARD BATES, ATTORNEY GENERAL

Along with Seward and Chase, Attorney General Edward Bates was yet another rival for the 1860 Republican presidential nomination whom Lincoln had defeated and then invited to serve in his Cabinet. In fact, Bates had been the first appointee Lincoln approached. He had known Bates since the River and Harbor Convention in Chicago in 1847, which Bates had chaired, and recognized him even then as the outstanding politician in the West. Born in Virginia in 1793, upon coming of age Bates moved to Missouri and launched into a long life of conservative politics. The "Old Fogey Whig," as Bates liked to call himself, served Lincoln without brilliance but with outspoken honesty before he stepped aside because of health at the end of 1864, allowing Lincoln to appoint James Speed from Kentucky, the brother of his best friend, in his place.

Brady   *New York*

CALEB BLOOD SMITH, SECRETARY OF THE INTERIOR

No president before had ever selected a man from Indiana for his Cabinet. Lincoln had two possible Hoosier candidates, and perhaps because of a deal between Indiana politicians and Lincoln's managers in return for votes, he seemed to feel pressured to choose one of them. The more qualified of the two was Schuyler Colfax, but ex-Congressman Smith, who had seconded Lincoln's nomination in Chicago, got the nod instead, because, as Lincoln wrote, Colfax "is sure of a bright future" but for the older Smith it "is now or never." Lincoln was right. The secretary of the interior served less than two years before he resigned, and in 1864 he died. He was succeeded in the then relatively less demanding job by John Palmer Usher, another Hoosier, and he by James Harlan of Iowa, who would become Robert Lincoln's father-in-law.

EDWIN McMASTERS STANTON, SECRETARY OF WAR

For most of Lincoln's presidency, Edwin McMasters Stanton was secretary of war, replacing Pennsylvania's Simon Cameron after eleven troubled months. The brilliant land and patent lawyer, who perfumed his beard, had been attorney general under President Buchanan. Now he went about making sense of the disorganized, scandal-ridden War Department with the intensity of a snake tamer, which he'd been in his youth. A series of tragedies had hardened and imbalanced this irascible, asthmatic, eccentric man: the death of a daughter, whose body Stanton had buried, then exhumed after a year and cremated, and whose ashes were kept in his room; the death of his wife, whom he personally dressed in her wedding gown for burial; the throat-slashing suicide of his brother. Stanton was incorruptibly loyal, but he put people off with his shouted orders, pounding of desks, and curious, arrogant procedures.

Lincoln's belief that adversaries served him better than friends was put to the test with Stanton, who had slighted Lincoln cruelly back in the 1850s when the two had locked horns in a Chicago law case. Even in the early 1860s Stanton was heard calling Lincoln "the original gorilla" and had commented that "Du Chaillu was a fool to wander all the way to Africa in search of what he could have so easily found in Springfield, Illinois." As usual, however, Lincoln held no grudges and always looked for the good in people. When he needed a replacement for Cameron, the President found Stanton's rudeness, temper, and impulsive nature outweighed by an enormous capacity for work, attention to detail, complete honesty, ability to make decisions, and anti-slavery sentiments. Sometimes Lincoln would drop by the War Department to watch "Old Mars," as he called him, "quell disturbances" while holding forth in his morning ritual of standing on a platform in his reception room and hearing anyone with an official problem. More often, the President was there to read the latest military telegrams from the front and discuss with Stanton the replies to the field. And if the secretary of war overstepped his bounds and called Lincoln "a fool" behind his back, Lincoln would smile when it was repeated to him, and say, "If Mr. Stanton said the President is a fool, it must be so, for the Secretary is generally right."

Lincoln and Salmon P. Chase. After a victory in the political arena, the President often liked to reward the vanquished. After removing Chase from the Cabinet, Lincoln appointed him to head the Supreme Court.

LINCOLN'S SUPREME COURT

Lincoln did not get a Supreme Court he could call his own until after his election to a second term. Then with his surprising appointment of Salmon P. Chase as chief justice, he put the final pin in place to ensure a Court that would stand behind the full ramifications of emancipation.

During his fifty months in office Lincoln made five appointments to the Court. When this picture was taken by Alexander Gardner, the men he selected had joined five already seated associate justices. The incumbents were: James Moore Wayne of Georgia *(sixth from right)*, chosen in 1835 by Andrew Jackson; John Catron of Tennessee *(missing)*, named in 1837 by Martin Van Buren; Samuel Nelson of New York *(fourth from right)*, nominated in 1845 by John Tyler; Robert Cooper Grier of Pennsylvania *(seventh from right)*, selected in 1846 by James Polk; and Nathan Clifford of Maine *(third from right)*, picked by James Buchanan in 1858. Two deaths, two resignations, and an additional seat on the bench voted by Congress eventually gave Lincoln five seats to fill. "I have been unwilling to throw all the appointments northward," Lincoln said at first, "thus disabling myself from doing justice to the south on the return of the peace..." But as the war continued, Lincoln put forward his candidates — all Unionists and all liberals. In January 1862 he appointed anti-slavery Noah Haynes Swayne of Ohio *(eighth from right)*. Six months later he selected Iowa Republican Samuel Freeman Miller *(second from right)*; in October of the same year he tapped his old Illinois friend Judge David Davis *(ninth from right)*; when a tenth seat was voted by Congress in 1863, Lincoln picked Unionist Stephen Johnson Field of California *(far right)*. Finally, when Chief Justice Taney died in 1864, in selecting Chase *(fifth from right)* to succeed him, Lincoln ensured an anti-slavery Court. In the process, he not only broke with a cadre of anti-Chase advisers, but at the same time bestowed on his troublesome, ambitious former Cabinet member, if not exactly what he craved, an important and dignified position nevertheless. "I shall never forget this," wrote Chase in response. "Be assured that I prize your confidence and good will more than nomination or office."

Along with the clerk of the Supreme Court who is standing, nine out of the ten justices in January 1865 sit for an Alexander Gardner portrait. (From 1863 to 1866 the Supreme Court had ten justices.)

WITH MANY, LINCOLN IS ANYTHING BUT POPULAR

During his presidency, Lincoln's popularity rode a seesaw of highs and lows. For many, he was an outright buffoon who endangered the nation by his presence. He offended conservatives and radicals alike, so the charges went—not only Southerners, Northern Democrats, and conservative Whigs but anti-slavery forces as well, drawing criticism from all sides: He moved too slowly. His patience was aggravating. He paid too much attention to border-state opinion. At first he was all for preserving slavery. Then, when he did issue his Emancipation Proclamation, it was too little, too late. He botched the war, firing the wrong generals and planning the wrong strategies. He antagonized Congress. He ran a government of misfits and thieves. He stifled civil rights. He pardoned the guilty. Instead of paying attention to business, he was always telling jokes and stories. He was called a "Simple Susan," an "Illinois beast," a "wet rag," a "Kentucky mule," a "political coward," a "butcher," an "imbecile," a "gorilla," a "tyrant." He was "weak," "timid," "foul-tongued," "pitiable," had "no education," was "shallow, dazed and utterly foolish."

Lincoln was denounced in private letters; many newspapers deplored him; his generals and his own Cabinet members publicly criticized him; and the radicals of his own party tried to grind him to shreds. In his first year and a half in office, there was much for his opponents to pick on. Indeed, Lincoln seemed entirely willing to preserve slavery if he could save the Union by force alone. He blocked the actions of Union commanders who took it upon themselves to emancipate slaves in rebel territory without the proper authorization. And when he did adopt emancipation in January 1863, it did not apply to Union slave states or Union-occupied rebel territory. In the election year of 1864 there were strong efforts to dump Lincoln for another candidate. Wearied by the vindictive critics in his own party, he had earlier said to his friend Orville Browning, "They wish to get rid of me, and I am sometimes half disposed to gratify them." Now even Browning was losing faith. "I am personally attached to the President," he wrote to a fellow politician, "and have...tried to...make him respectable; tho' I have never been able to persuade myself he was big enough for his position. Still, I thought he might get through, as many a boy has got through college, without disgrace, and without knowledge; but I fear he is a failure." As the election approached, though, events swung in Lincoln's favor. He was triumphantly reelected, his policies were supported, the war drove to its conclusion, and at the time of his second inauguration, he was at the height of his popularity. Even though his face was lined with sudden age, still it glowed. He had been able to withstand unscrupulous abuse and, in his own farsighted way, save the democratic principle for humankind.

Taken on the White House balcony by Henry F. Warren on March 6, 1865, this may be the last photograph of Lincoln alive.

LINCOLN STICKS CLOSE TO THE WHITE HOUSE, BUT ONE TRIP IN 1863 WILL GO DOWN IN HISTORY

Many thought Lincoln had hardly ever been out of the backwoods settlements of Kentucky, Indiana, and Illinois before he came to Washington. Actually, of the thirty-four states in the Union at the time of his nomination, he had visited twenty-three and had spoken in seventeen. There were only nine cities in the country with populations of 100,000 or more (New York, Philadelphia, Brooklyn, Baltimore, Boston, St. Louis, New Orleans, Cincinnati, and Chicago) and Lincoln had been in all of them. In fact, except for San Francisco, he had visited every city with a population of 50,000 or more. He had also crossed into Canada. Although his travels were limited while in office—he was away from Washington less than fifty nights—there were plenty of opportunities to photograph him on the road, inspecting forts, reviewing troops, conferring with generals, seeing battle areas firsthand, on a hurried trip to West Point, to Philadelphia to speak, to Richmond during the last days of fighting. Even so, President Lincoln was definitively captured by camera outside of Washington on only two occasions. The first was on October 4, 1862, near Harpers Ferry, on his trip to the Antietam battlefields (two photographs of which appear on the following pages). But by far Lincoln's most famous excursion while president was in November 1863 to speak at the little Pennsylvania town of Gettysburg, and here, too, he was photographed, albeit almost lost in a crowd.

Up until then, except for his inaugural address and a number of impromptu remarks, the great orator of the debates with Stephen A. Douglas had done no public speaking as president. His open letter to Springfield that summer, which literally changed the nation's view about its black soldiers, had been read aloud by a stand-in, James Conkling; his messages to Congress were sent over in printed form, to be read by clerks in a monotone. Now Lincoln wanted to say something clear and important in his own voice. It made little difference to him that he was to be the secondary speaker at Gettysburg, his job simply to add "a few appropriate remarks" to the main ones by the great Edward Everett. Lincoln planned to be "short, short, short," but he also hoped to say something true and lasting about the war, about dying for freedom. All his life he had ruminated about time. Stretching off before him in one direction was the great past of the founding fathers, whose vision had defined the kind of nation America was to be. In the other direction lay the vast, hopeful field of the future—where prosperity and peace, Lincoln believed, might one day extend to all people. In between was the chaos of the present where passions ruled and nothing was certain. In an early speech, Lincoln had compared this chaos to a mighty wind, a hurricane, that leveled all trees and wiped away every generation. And yet, each generation possessed its own special hour, its own set of opportunities and mandates and tasks. Time was a beckoner and an ally, as well as a destroyer.

As he said it would be, Lincoln's address on November 19, 1863, was "short"—only 270 or so simple words. But through them his deepest concerns came together in near perfection: how a war over slavery was, in fact, a test of the viability of the nation's destiny; how, in the midst of sacrifice and storm, there was a mandate to redeem the time, to give meaning to the struggle; how a great and important future still lay ahead for this country and for the world—"a new birth of freedom."

For trips, the one essential for Lincoln was his high hat. "His beaver hat was frequently reblocked; always looked fresh," the Reverend Dr. Gurley observed. Herndon disagreed, thinking it looked as if "a calf had just licked it." But, nevertheless, Herndon regarded his partner's hat as "an extraordinary receptacle. It was his desk and his memorandum book. Whenever... he wished to preserve an idea, he jotted it down on an envelope or stray piece of paper and placed it inside the lining. Afterwards when the memorandum was needed there was only one place to look for it." *Below:* Lincoln's hatbox for travel

Eleven days before delivering the Gettysburg Address, Lincoln posed for Alexander Gardner. From Boston, Edward Everett had kindly sent along his own speech. Already set in type, Everett's words may be in the envelope on the table next to Lincoln's right hand.

The only known occasion Lincoln was photographed on a war-related trip was when he visited Harpers Ferry and the Antietam battlefield in early October 1862. To the left is intelligence chief Allan Pinkerton, to the right Major General John A. McClernand. In both pictures Lincoln is slightly blurred from swaying.

THE SPEECH

Over the heads of spectators, a camera could see the parade approaching down Baltimore Street. The military units came first, the President and invited dignitaries just behind. Every minute along the way a cannon was fired. In a few moments the marchers would arrive at the new cemetery on the outskirts of the little town of Gettysburg, where today the eyes of the nation were focused. Not all the work was done; piles of coffins waited to be buried and skeletons of horses still lay about — gruesome evidence of the three-day battle in July. A speakers' platform had been erected, and a little tent had been set up close by for the convenience of Edward Everett, the nervous, elderly chief speaker who had a serious urinary ailment. An enormous crowd spread over the hillside. The marshals, wearing yellow sashes, kept order on horseback. Soldiers shoulder to shoulder, with guns in position, ringed the stand for security. The ceremony began. Prayers were said. "Old Hundred" was played. The chief speaker was introduced by Benjamin B. French, a Washington official. "Mr. Everett then arose," French wrote in his diary, "and without notes of any kind, pronounced an oration... two full hours in the delivery." The next speaker was Lincoln, the man the committee had thought was unable to give a dignified, heartfelt dedication address without politics or humor. A boy of fifteen named Gitt, "intent on being as close to Lincoln as was physically possible," had hidden himself early that morning beneath the raised platform that served as a stage. "Through a crack between the planks I could look directly into Lincoln's face," wrote Gitt. "Its deep lines, the wrinkled brow, the deep-set brooding eyes burned indelible images into my memory." Then Lincoln began to speak. A mere ten sentences, mostly made up of little words, common words. Together, they were destined never to be forgotten. Even though he didn't know it at the time, it was Lincoln's finest hour.

Late in the morning of November 19, 1863, a parade down Gettysburg's main thoroughfare preceded Lincoln's address.

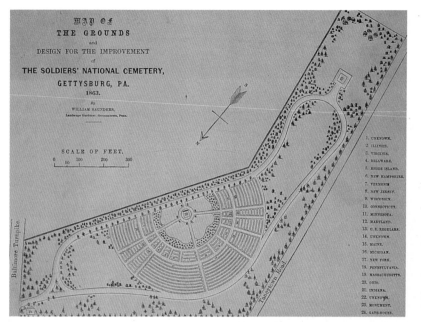

The graves fanned out in a semicircle in the middle of the boot-shaped piece of land. Soldiers from eighteen states had died at Gettysburg, and each state's contingent was buried in its own section, along with sections for U.S. Regulars and Unknown.

The regular village cemetery had been the site of plenty of action during the July battle. This is its gatehouse archway, through which spectators streamed to reach the new cemetery abutting the old.

Taken from the edge of the crowd, this picture shows the special flagpole erected for the day and the gatehouse archway. To the right are the jam-packed speakers' stand and Everett's special tent.

Mathew Brady was on the scene and Alexander Gardner was possibly there as well, along with other photographers — the Weaver brothers and probably the Tyson brothers — and all presumably were taking pictures. No one knows exactly who took what, for pictures were often bought or traded between photographers, and copying other men's work was standard procedure. But for the one picture in which Lincoln can be identified, the evidence points to Mathew Brady or one of his operators. In 1952, the photograph below was discovered among the collection of Brady negatives in the National Archives in Washington, D.C. Lincoln appears in the middle of the crowd, just to the right of center. Others who have been identified include John Hay, John Nicolay, Ward Hill Lamon, Benjamin B. French, John P. Usher, Governor Andrew Curtin and his son, and David Wills, Lincoln's overnight host and the Gettysburg attorney in charge of the cemetery's creation. The man with the blurred face three or four people to the right of Lincoln may be Edward Everett on his way to take his place beside Lincoln before the ceremony gets under way.

As the months wore on, Lincoln laughed less, slept
less, and took on more and more responsibilities.

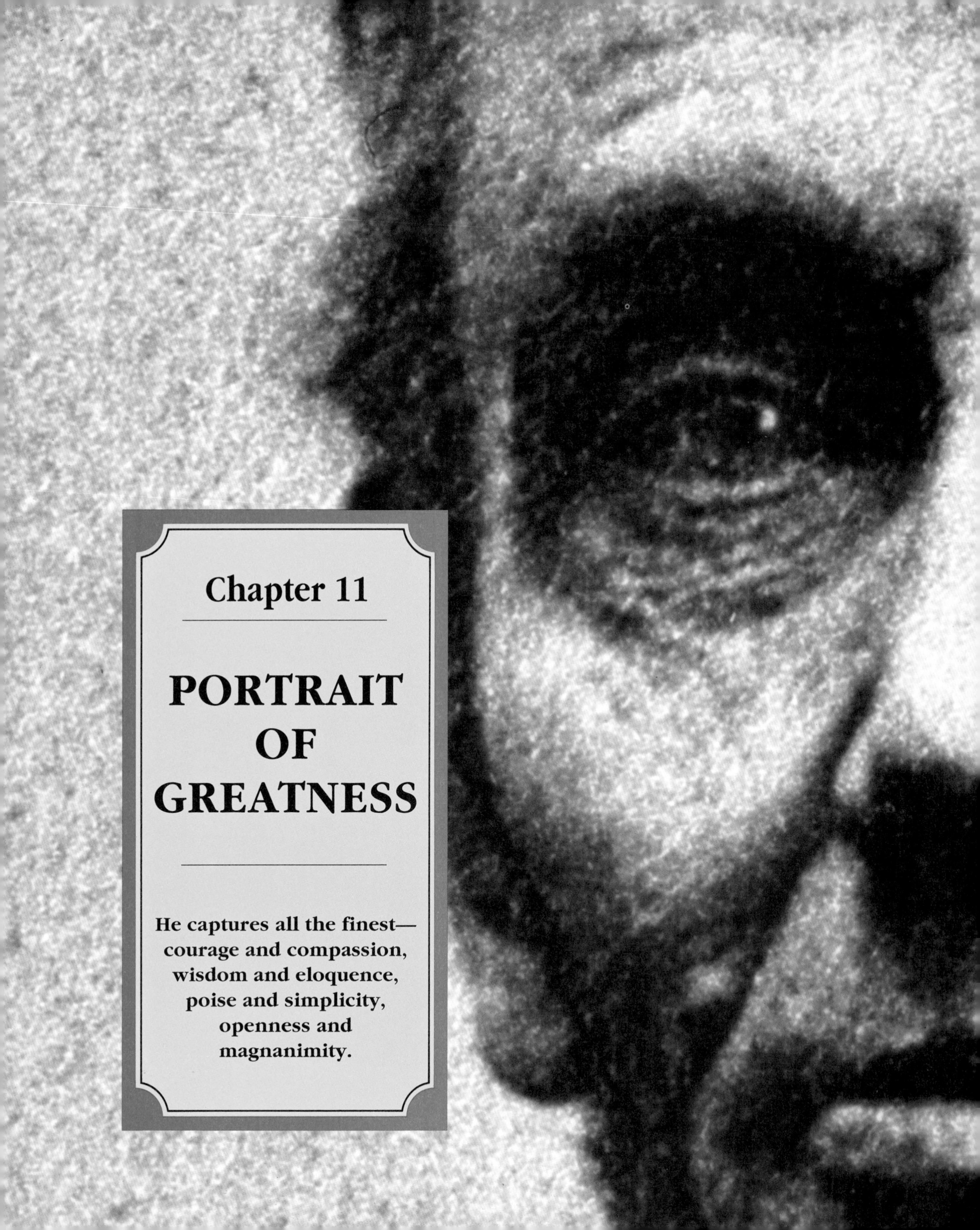

Chapter 11

PORTRAIT OF GREATNESS

He captures all the finest—
courage and compassion,
wisdom and eloquence,
poise and simplicity,
openness and
magnanimity.

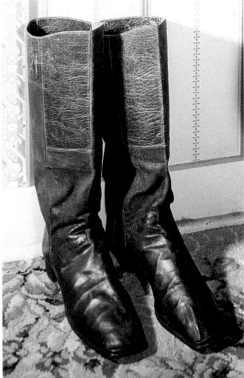

Lincoln's best boots had been made to measure by a master shoemaker. He had Lincoln stand on a piece of paper and then outlined his feet with a pencil *(above)* so that the uneven measurements could be reflected in two different boots *(below)*, each containing some felt between the layers of the sole, to keep them from squeaking.

PERSONAL TRAITS—ALONG WITH A FEW MARKS AND BRANDS

At the beginning of 1865, it had been only five years since Lincoln, unknown to the country, had described himself as "lean in flesh, weighing, on an average, one hundred and eighty pounds; dark complexion, with coarse black hair, and grey eyes—no other marks or brands recollected." Those years had marked him like no others, branded him in so many ways, that a new Lincoln had emerged, a Washington Lincoln as opposed to the Illinois prairie man who had been elected.

Sometimes, this new Lincoln had trouble sleeping, especially in winter, and lay in bed well past dawn, wrapped in his long yellow nightshirt, lost in thought. When he finally rose, he seemed to be "drawing out like a telescope." One observer thought he resembled an ostrich, another a "skeleton" occupying a suit. In former days he had fairly jumped into his clothes. Now he moved more slowly. He would often wear his soft, low slippers instead of his boots, not only during breakfast but while he worked as well—those backless slippers that made flip-flop sounds on the White House floors when he walked, a visiting relative reported. There were times when he wore these slippers even when greeting guests, who were sometimes shocked, thinking that was too informal dress for a president. One Southern governor claimed Lincoln had received him in bare feet, which wasn't beyond the realm of possibility. Actually, Lincoln occasionally went without socks, so that when he shucked off his boots—like the time he went wading in a brook on the Antietam battlefield—suddenly his huge naked feet were revealed. Lincoln's feet had given him some trouble; a chiropodist had been called in to treat his aching corns and bunions. They were size 14, as feet are measured today. They came down flat when walking and lifted up all at once, with no spring at all to their step. Lincoln was not only flat-footed, but also slightly pigeon-toed.

Lincoln's hands were a good indication of how far this man had traveled. All their coarseness, all the muscle flesh from his young years had vanished, and the very shape of his hands had changed. Now with the pen as their weapon, Lincoln's hands had actually turned graceful. But they were still strong, which was evident from his iron handshake or the firm double-handed greeting he favored so much.

With his nightshirt off, black hair was revealed on his arms, back, narrow shoulders, chest, and legs. His upper body still showed the remarkable muscle formation that Leonard Volk had commented on in 1860 when, making his life mask and taking Lincoln's other measurements for the bust he envisioned, the sculptor had asked him to remove his shirt. Over this frame, Lincoln usually pulled on an undershirt with long sleeves. There were 180 pounds of him when he came to Washington in 1861, but the years were shearing Lincoln down, and by 1865 he weighed but 160. His left shoulder was higher than his right and his walk was undulating and slightly off balance, making him resemble, someone said, "a mariner who had found his sea legs but had to admit there was a rough sea running." The Reverend Dr. Phineas D. Gurley, his pastor, said when Lincoln walked, he looked as if "he was about to plunge forward, from his right shoulder, for he always walked, when he had anything in his hand, as if he was pushing something in front of him." He was 6 feet 3¾ inches in his stocking feet, but he could go over 6 feet 4 if he drew himself up, which he loved to do when challenging another tall man to a measure.

Standing back to back with him, Lincoln would hold a book across their heads to see which way it slanted. He rarely missed guessing the height of other men, even Tom Thumb, who came just about to Lincoln's knee level.

Leaning over a recently installed sink in his room, Lincoln washed in Potomac River water piped straight into the White House. To clean his remarkably white and even teeth, Lincoln used a bone-handled toothbrush. He'd had a couple of teeth extracted, but all in all, having never chewed or smoked tobacco, Lincoln had teeth that were in excellent shape. His former black servant Solomon Johnson, who held a minor job in the Treasury Department, still came in to do Lincoln's beard and hair, tying a napkin around the President's neck and sometimes shaking the clippings out the White House window. It was coarse hair, not a fleck of white in it yet, but wiry, and better kept short, for it resisted taming and often didn't behave. Once he joked about it when asking Mrs. Lincoln's seamstress, Elizabeth Keckley, to brush it for him. "Well, Madame Elizabeth," he wanted to know, "will you brush my bristles down tonight?" While visiting at Fortress Monroe, before dinner Lincoln had asked a general if he might borrow a comb and was handed a delicate one made of shell. "Why, I can't do anything with such a thing as that," the President was remembered saying. "If you have anything you comb your horse's mane with, that might do."

Finally Lincoln climbed into his long-coated black suit, which hung on him two sizes too big. In his vest pocket he inserted his big, heavy watch, which not only told him the time but the date as well. Breakfast consisted of a boiled egg, toast, and coffee. Lunch could be as little as crackers and cheese, or a biscuit and milk, or grapes, or his favorite, a pear. Sometimes, when work piled up, leaving no time for lunch, Lincoln would eat an apple on his way over to the War Department and a second one on his way back. Dinner, taken between five and six o'clock, usually consisted of two courses; but ask Lincoln afterward what they had been and he'd be at a loss—he ate what was put before him without thinking, without savoring. His drink was water—Adam's ale he called it. When he was entertaining and wine was served, he would lift his glass and merely touch it to his lips, not because of pledges from his early temperance days; he just didn't like the stuff or how it made him feel. Early in his White House days, Lincoln had taken "blue mass" pills for chronic constipation but later gave the laxative up because he said it made him "peevish."

Lincoln liked to get to bed by ten or eleven, but he was often up until one or two, having left the White House through the cellar and passed through the gate leading to the War Department close by. There he would monitor the telegraph messages from the battlefronts and confer with his secretary of war. Before bed he might even wander alone and unrecognized through the streets of Washington, something he liked to do especially during storms.

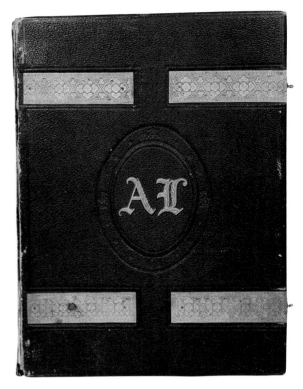

The Lincoln family photo album.

The Lincoln's family photo album during the White House years was this green leather book with brass clasps that had been made in France and carried the President's initials in gold. Like most American families, the Lincolns devoted the first pages to the famous—Cabinet ministers, generals, actors. Then followed their children and relatives. Four *cartes de visite* could be inserted into little windows on each of the twenty-four heavy pages, front and back. Evidence shows that the Lincolns added to the album with enthusiasm in the beginning but lost interest after the death of Willie.

LINCOLN HUMOR SAMPLER

On one occasion when Lincoln replaced a member of his Cabinet, some senators demanded that the President fire the lot. This reminded Lincoln of the farmer who had seven skunks to deal with. "I took aim," said the farmer, "blazed away, killed one, and he raised such a fearful smell that I concluded it was best to let the other six go."

•

Since an Indian named Laughing Water had been introduced to Lincoln as Minihaha, when he met Crying Water he said, "I suppose your name is Miniboohoo?"

•

When General Grant was criticized for drinking, Lincoln said he wished he knew Grant's brand so he could send it to his other generals.

•

Lincoln suggested that Douglas was using the horse-chestnut style of argument—"a specious and fantastic arrangement of words, by which a man can prove a horse-chestnut to be a chestnut horse."

•

A frontiersman lost his way in an uninhabited region on a dark and tempestuous night. The rain fell in torrents, accompanied by terrible thunder and more terrific lightning. His trouble increased when his horse halted, being exhausted with fatigue and fright. Presently a bolt of lightning struck a neighboring tree, and the crash brought the man to his knees. He was not an expert in prayer, but his appeal was short and to the point: "O Lord, if it is all the same to you, give us a little more light, and a little less noise!"

•

Lincoln was asked how he liked being president, and he answered with the story of the tarred and feathered man whose neighbors were riding him out of town on a rail. When they inquired how he liked it, the man replied: "If it wasn't for the honor of the thing, I would much rather walk."

Cartoonists ridiculed Lincoln's joke-telling whenever they could think of a new way to do it. Here he is portrayed as "The National Joker, Salary 25,000 dollars Per Annum."

Another artist, this one working for *Harper's Weekly,* puts Lincoln's jokester reputation to work in a political cartoon. "They say I tell many stories," Lincoln once remarked. "I reckon I do, but I have learned from long experience that plain people...are more easily influenced through the medium of the broad and humorous illustration than in any other way; and what the hypercritical few may think, I don't care."

THE RING OF HIS LAUGHTER

Lincoln loved to laugh. Out of this brooding man came great bellows of laughter, and, for a while, anyway, it made him forget life's deadly seriousness. The problems of his presidency drained him, made him ill with gloom, but laughter was his medicine, and it entered into his very system, coursing through him, tickling his innards, purging him of despair, giving him release. It was not just moodiness or the blues that needed fixing; it was his own peculiar sad framing of the world, focused on humanity's grave failings and the terrible need for right in a universe of wrong. It could be said, too, that Lincoln merely had a love of nonsense and the ridiculous, and told his stories for the sheer joy of laughter. Lincoln's humor was original only in the manner in which he dished it up. More often than not, he was retelling stories and anecdotes that he remembered from childhood, many from his father, or that he heard during his years on the circuit, from farmers and plainsmen and boat people, some even from joke books. Many he embellished and changed for his own purposes. When he told them, his face lit up with expectation as he closed in on the climax or punch line. His listeners found his stories sidesplittingly funny, and he was usually the first to start laughing, so hard sometimes that he could only sputter out the end of the story through high, convulsive gasps. Then he would lift his knees to his chest and wrap his great arms around them as he rocked back and forth in his chair, wheezing with mirth. For the most part, it was gentle, grocery-store humor. He loved especially his "little stories" about farmers back in the West: the farmer with the piece of stony, barren land who assured a passerby, "I'm not as poor as you think I am; I don't own this land"; or the farmer who insisted he wasn't greedy—"I just want the land that jines mine!" He caught people's foibles and gave them a twist. He said the reason his attorney general's beard was white, while his hair was not, was because Bates used his jaws more than his brain. The humor seldom got flat-footed and obvious. Once, after signing his name, he was asked to add "President of the United States" and he put down his pen and said, "Well, I don't think I'll say 'This is a horse.'" He never told a dirty joke, as such, even though many of his tales were risqué, so peppered with barnyard language they couldn't be repeated in the parlor. Absurdities were his stock-in-trade, pointed up by exaggeration and understatement. Once, to illustrate the illogic of a project, he told about a fellow who remarked on his new boots, "I shall never get 'em on, 'til I wear 'em a day or two, and stretch 'em a little." Lincoln's humor was often self-deprecating and filled with puns. Maybe its most distinctive quality, though, was his strange, offbeat, funny way of using language, some of the best examples of which can be found in his military correspondence: the U.S. Navy became "Uncle Sam's web-feet." Swiftness in the field became "a question of legs." And he told his generals to "hive" the enemy, to "fret him and fret him," and to "chew and choke."

HIS LOVE OF INVENTION AND THE POWER OF HIS THOUGHT

When, more than a decade ago, Lincoln had chosen not to visit his dying father, Thomas, in Goosenest Prairie, he showed how far he had distanced himself not only from his father but from everything he symbolized — the harshness and impoverishment of the frontier, the grueling grind of a life of manual labor, the absence of all intellectual horizons. When Lincoln looked back to his childhood and ignored his poetic instinct to romanticize the good old days, more often than not those days evoked images of death for him, of antiquated ways and backbreaking labor. He preferred things new and up-to-date, and had become an early and outspoken proponent of the railroad, urban development, and a centralized bank. With a keen interest in technology and labor-saving devices, Lincoln wholeheartedly supported all efforts at transforming primitive, backwoods America into a modern land of plenty.

It was not long after taking office in Washington that Lincoln got a chance to deal with the kind of mind that was helping transform the country. Thaddeus Sobieski Coulincourt Lowe had been trying to get the backing of the Smithsonian Institution for an Atlantic Ocean balloon crossing. Professor Joseph Henry, secretary of the institution and the greatest American scientist of his time, had told the inventor that he considered such a trip entirely possible, given his knowledge of wind currents; but he found the attempt much too dangerous for the Smithsonian to sponsor and recommended shorter trials in the interior of the country first. When Lincoln took office, Lowe was trying to interest the government in his ''aeronautic machinery'' for military observation purposes. With Lincoln's backing, Lowe performed an aerial ascent over Washington in his *Balloon Enterprise* in June 1861, taking up with him an operator and a telegraph apparatus that was attached to a wire connecting it to the White House. From his perch high over the city, Lowe sent a telegram to Lincoln: ''This point of observation commands an area nearly 50 miles in diameter. The city, with its girdle of encampments, presents a superb scene. I have pleasure in sending you the first dispatch ever telegraphed from an aerial station and in acknowledging indebtedness to your encouragement for the opportunity of demonstrating the availability of the science of aeronautics in the military service of the country. T.S.C. Lowe.''

Recognizing genius and encouraging it among the military took not only a very special kind of mind but courage of conviction and forcefulness as well, for Washington's military leaders were for the most part arch-conservatives, opposed philosophically to experimentation and change. Lincoln simply brushed aside static thinking. He paid little heed to criticism, obeyed his instincts, and when a new weapon or military device interested him, his own inventive, questioning, practical mind analyzed it and its possible uses. He had his own way of weeding out the unworkable schemes. Body armor got serious attention at the beginning of the war, and many steel-vest inventors tried to make their way to Lincoln. Supposedly, he fended them off with a standing offer of an official military test of their invention — with the inventor wearing it. Even though there were plenty of impractical, even ridiculous weapons presented, and, even for those presenting good ideas, much red tape to wade through, 16,000 new patents were issued by the Union during the war. In contrast, only 266 new patents were issued by the Confederate government.

Lincoln loved models, devices, engines, tools, big machinery. The Navy Yard

Dr. Joseph Henry

Some people made him nervous because they knew so much, but Lincoln enjoyed being in the company of brilliant men like Professor Joseph Henry, head of the Smithsonian Institution and the most distinguished American scientist since Benjamin Franklin. Saying that the first quality of a statesman should be ''pre-science,'' Henry once remarked that ''the most far-seeing head in this land is on the shoulders of that awkward rail-splitter from Illinois.''

Many who knew Lincoln recognized his remarkable mind. One such admirer was his erudite minister to Austria, John Lothrop Motley, writing in 1865.

On the very first interview that I had with him in the summer of 1861, he impressed me as a man of the most extraordinary conscientiousness. He seemed to have a window in his breast. There was something almost childlike in his absence of guile and affectation of any kind.... [It is] impossible for me to pretend to form an estimate as to his intellectual power, but I was struck by his simple wisdom, his straightforward, unsophisticated common sense. What our Republic, what the whole world has to be grateful for, is that God has endowed our chief magistrate at such a momentous period of history with so lofty a moral nature and with so loving and forgiving a disposition.

His mental abilities...and his faculty of divining the right amid a conflict of dogmas, theories, and of weighing other men's opinions while retaining his own judgement, almost...[amount] to political genius...

In a midterm assessment of Lincoln's leadership, author Harriet Beecher Stowe, like Professor Joseph Henry, focuses on Lincoln's clarity of vision.

There have been times...of impetuous impatience, when our national ship seemed to lie water-logged and we have called aloud for a deliverer of another fashion,—a brilliant general, a dashing, fearless statesman, a man who could dare and do, who would stake all on a die, and win or lose by a brilliant *coup de main*. It may comfort our minds that since He who ruleth in the armies of nations set no such man to this work, that perhaps He saw in the man whom He did send some peculiar fitness and aptitudes therefor.

Slow and careful in coming to resolutions, willing to talk with every person who has anything to show on any side of a disputed subject, long in weighing and pondering, attached to constitutional limits and time-honored landmarks, Lincoln certainly was the *safest* leader a nation could have at a time when the *habeas corpus* must be suspended, and all the constitutional and minor rights of citizens thrown into the hands of their military leader. A reckless, bold, theorizing, dashing man of genius might have wrecked our Constitution and ended us in a splendid military despotism.

Among the many accusations which in hours of ill-luck have been thrown out upon Lincoln, it is remarkable that he has never been called self-seeking, or selfish. When we were troubled and sat in darkness, and looked doubtfully towards the presidential chair, it was never that we doubted the good-will of our pilot—only the clearness of his eyesight. But Almighty God has granted to him that clearness of vision which he gives to the true-hearted...

was exciting to visit, with its steam hammers, blast furnace, rolling mill, explosives lab, chain cable shop, many foundries, and round-the-clock production. He loved to contemplate how things worked, to use his knack for math, his surveying knowledge, and what he had learned as a patent lawyer, and apply it all to the explosion of knowledge and know-how that was already producing, in the military, everything from submarines to poison gas. More important, exploring minds like Lincoln's were already envisioning the vast scientific leaps the world might take in the name of peace and progress. In a lecture he had written (and given twice) back in Springfield and planned to expand, Lincoln previewed the future—foreseeing the harnessing of the wind, the taming of tides, the further uses of captured steam, and the mastery of the sun's explosive heat and firepower.

"It requires close, severe analysis," wrote Lincoln's law partner William Herndon, "to understand the man who was a riddle and a puzzle to his neighbors among whom he lived." But above all, he was "a close, cautious, persistent, profound terrible *thinker*." By all accounts, Lincoln's thought processes were slow but penetrating. "His mind was like polished steel," wrote his friend Joshua Speed, "a mark once made upon it was never erased." He continually astounded people with his memory of names, dates, and facts, and with his ability to quote long passages of poetry after a single reading. In one of his earliest speeches, he called education "the most important subject which we as a people can be engaged in," enabling every person to "read the histories of his own and other countries...to say nothing of the...scriptures and other works...." The written word, he thought, was humankind's greatest invention, "enabling us to converse with the dead, the absent, and the yet unborn." It was his most special love, his most especial gift. And yet, Lincoln's mind was not bookish. His appetite for books in his youth had stemmed from a hunger to better himself in a world that could be revealed in no other way. But books were never an end in themselves for him. After the self-tutoring of his early years, his law studies, his later mastery of Euclid, and later still his self-education in the texts of military science, Lincoln never immersed himself in book learning again. In most instances, he substituted foresight and common sense for the study of documents. He was a worshiper of Reason and a ponderer of life and death. "Whenever he had an important case on hand," wrote law colleague John H. Littlefield of his late days in Springfield, "he would withdraw himself more or less from society...[s]ometimes...[with] his young son Tad and...go out on the prairie.... By the time he returned to the house he would have a clear conception of the case and have the knotty points unravelled." It was often said of Lincoln that he could think harder than any other man. Lost in thought, he seemed to be not of this world. But when his decision was made or his problem solved, he laughed, pursed his lips, and often played with a kitten or puppy to help bring himself back to reality. Then he would toss the animal aside, his law partner Herndon claimed, adding "he did the same with people." "Mr. Lincoln had a kind of poetry in his nature," said Mary, but "[n]one of us—no man nor woman—*could* rule him after he had made up his mind." It was this capacity for powerful, direct thought and hard decision, even at the expense of people's feelings, that made Lincoln so effective.

For Lincoln, testing out a new gun was just as much a part of the war as planning strategy. This is his own breach-loading Spencer carbine — a gift.

To float a vessel that had run aground, Lincoln invented a boat with "buoyant chambers" and "sliding spars." In 1849 he took this model of his device that worked on air pressure to Washington and applied for a patent. Although never put to use, it received Patent No. 6469. Following is Lincoln's description of his invention.

What I claim as my invention and desire to secure by letters patent, is the combination of expansible buoyant chambers, placed at the sides of a vessel, with the main shaft or shafts C, by means of the sliding spars or shafts D, which pass down through the buoyant chambers, and are made fast to their bottoms and the series of ropes and pulleys, or their equivalents, in such a manner that by turning the main shaft or shafts in one direction, the buoyant chambers will be forced downwards into the water, and at the same time expanded and filled with air for buoying up the vessel by the displacement of water, and by turning the shaft in an opposite direction, the buoyant chambers will be contracted into a small space, and secured against injury.

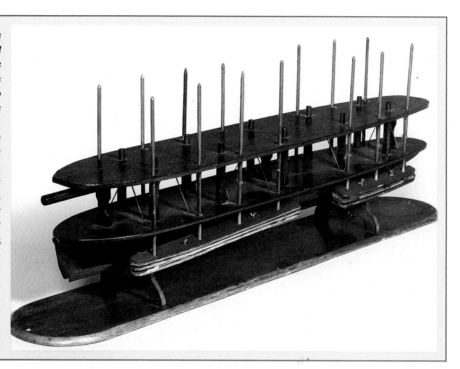

Lincoln could hold his own with the best military minds in the country. Here he confers with *(left to right)* Generals Sherman and Grant and Admiral David Porter.

One of the successful naval ideas that Lincoln backed early in the war was the use of mortar boats for river fighting.

HIS HEART GOES OUT TO THOSE IN DISTRESS

Washington had become a city of hospitals; twenty-one of them cared for up to 14,000 wounded and dying, with thousands more in convalescence homes. In addition, public halls, schools, even private homes were commandeered when emergencies arose. By order, church bells were muffled so as not to disturb the wounded. Lincoln was a constant visitor among the casualties, moving from bed to bed, shaking whatever hands could shake his, often working into his warm banter some humorous reference to his and their respective heights. "Hello, comrade," he greeted a Pennsylvania soldier much taller than even he. "Do you know when your feet get cold?" At the entrance to a ward, a nurse cautioned: "You don't want to go in there; they're only rebels." "You mean Confederates," Lincoln gently corrected her and entered.

Lincoln could almost feel the pain and suffering of others; it filled him with a very real agony. After shooting a wild turkey when he was seven, he felt such remorse that he never killed game again. He returned birds to their nests, pulled a pig from the mud, risked his life for a dog. And how much more important to him than animals were people. Soldiers had to die in war, but Lincoln was determined to save as many as he could from disciplinary execution. His evenings were filled with cases to study and pardons to be issued. He was especially adamant that sleeping on guard duty did not deserve the death penalty. "I don't think shooting will do him any good," Lincoln observed wryly. "I say let him go!" As Friday approached, "Black Friday" he called it—"the day they execute farmers' boys for falling asleep at their posts down on the Potomac"—he often bluntly dismissed his friends in order to attend to such matters. "Get out of the way, Swett, tomorrow is butcher day and I must go through these papers and see if I cannot find some excuse to let these poor men off," Lincoln's friend Leonard Swett remembered being told. Forfeiture of pay, hard labor, and dishonorable discharge were some of the alternate punishments Lincoln ordered to save the lives of stragglers and deserters. In one stroke of the pen in 1864 he commuted sixty-two death sentences. Only when it came to cases involving some heinous offense—such as rape or slave-trading—did the President refuse to commute. "He strove at all times," wrote Secretary of the Interior John P. Usher, "to relieve the citizens on both sides of the inconveniences and hardships resulting from war." Seldom was noble purpose and sympathy for others blended so eloquently as in a letter that Lincoln wrote to Mrs. Bixby, a mother bereaved by the loss, it was reported to him, of five sons in the war.

Lincoln's letter to Mrs. Bixby (at the bottom of the page) and Thomas Nast's woodcut of "Lincoln and the Little Orphan Boy" (right) both came, in the eyes of the nation, to symbolize Lincoln's kind heart. The following article by F. B. Carpenter is from Harper's Weekly.

Among the large number of persons waiting to speak with Mr. Lincoln...was a small, pale, delicate looking boy.... The President saw him standing, looking feeble and faint, and said, "Come here, my boy, and tell me what you want." The boy...said, "Mr. President, I have been a drummer in a regiment for two years, and my colonel got angry with me and turned me off; I was taken sick, and have been a long time in a hospital. This is the first time I have been out, and I came to see if you could not do something for me."

The President looked at him kindly and tenderly, and asked him where he lived. "I have no home," answered the boy. "Where is your father?" "He died in the army," was the reply. "Where is your mother?" continued the President. "My mother is dead also. I have no mother, no father, no brothers, no sisters, and," bursting into tears, "no friends—nobody cares for me."

Mr. Lincoln's eyes filled with tears, and he said to him, "Can't you sell newspapers?" "No," said the boy, "I am too weak, and the surgeon of the hospital told me I must leave, and I have no place to go." The scene was wonderfully affecting. The President drew forth a card, and addressing on it certain officials to whom his request was law, gave special directions to "care for this poor boy."

The wan face of the little drummer lit up with a happy smile as he received the paper, and he went away convinced that he had one good and true friend, at least, in the person of the President.

Executive Mansion,
Washington, Nov. 21, 1864

Dear Madam,—

I have been shown in the files of the War Department a statement of the Adjutant General of Massachusetts, that you are the mother of five sons who have died gloriously on the field of battle.

I feel how weak and fruitless must be any words of mine which should attempt to beguile you from the grief of a loss so overwhelming. But I cannot refrain from tendering to you the consolation that may be found in the thanks of the Republic they died to save.

I pray that our Heavenly Father may assuage the anguish of your bereavement, and leave you only the cherished memory of the loved and lost, and the solemn pride that must be yours, to have laid so costly a sacrifice upon the altar of Freedom.

Yours, very sincerely and respectfully,
A. LINCOLN

Thomas Nast's woodcut of "Lincoln and the Little Orphan Boy."

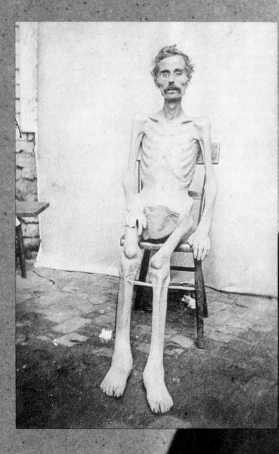

Left: A barely living testament to the war's brutality. In May 1864, Lincoln sent Lucius E. Chittenden to Annapolis to inspect the condition of four hundred Union men just released from rebel prisons. What he saw there horrified him. "They were men no longer—they were skeletons." Chittenden reported back. "Their minds had gone with their strength.... Many had only stumps where their fingers and toes had been...." "Can such things be possible?" Lincoln exclaimed upon reading Chittenden's full report. "There must be some explanation for it. The Richmond people are Americans—of the same race as ourselves. It is incredible!"

THE MUSIC AND RHYME HE LOVED IS USUALLY ROUSING —

"I never sung in my life and never was able to," Lincoln told a troupe of singers in an Illinois hotel who were trying to get him to join in. "But I'll tell you what I'll do for you…I'll repeat to you my favorite poem." Half closing his eyes, he began: "Oh! why should the spirit of mortal be proud?/Like a swift-fleeting meteor, a fast-flying cloud,/A flash of the lightning, a break of the wave,/He passeth from life to his rest in the grave." It was the first of many melancholy stanzas on the frailty of life by William Knox, and Lincoln quoted it so frequently he became known for it. Also among his favorites were the rhymes and sentiments of another Scot, Robert Burns, whose poems seemed to capture a young man's love of nature, and which reminded Lincoln of the tender songs of his youth—such cradle ballads, sentimental hymns, and dancing jigs as "Annie Laurie," "Rock of Ages," and "Skip-to-my-Lou." As an older man, Lincoln was drawn to the more complex and sophisticated soliloquies of Shakespeare and to opera arias. The President went to the theater so often in Washington that he was accused of trivializing wartime. But without this favorite form of relaxation, Lincoln said he "couldn't go on." It was not only theatrical music and poetry that engaged President Lincoln. Anything true and moving touched him, from blackface minstrel jingles and the dusty beat of hoofers to plaintive slave songs and the sighing cries for freedom. When there was no other music close at hand, he asked his friend Ward Hill Lamon to play banjo and sing songs like "The Blue-tailed Fly," or anything by Stephen Foster. In summertime, he attended the twice-weekly concerts of the Marine Band. But he also brought the first guest artists ever to appear at the White House, who together formed an odd conglomeration of musical talent: the young and beautiful opera star Meda Blanchard; an American Indian singer named Larooqua, known as the "aboriginal Jenny Lind"; a midget strutter from Barnum's who gave a spirited rendition of "Columbia, the Gem of the Ocean"; Teresa Carreño, the temperamental nine-year-old Venezuelan piano prodigy; the Hutchinson Family, who had practically sung Lincoln into office campaigning throughout the West. The skies resounded with "Yes, we'll rally round the flag, boys, we'll rally round again," "Yankee Doodle," and "The Battle Hymn of the Republic," and "Dixie," which Lincoln called for after Richmond fell, saying the Union had captured it back. And how could he escape from "Hail to the Chief," the royal strains of which he heard on the Capitol steps in 1861 at his oath of office and then, finally, after a thousand renditions in between, one last time, as he made his entrance to Ford's Theatre to a standing ovation.

In January 1862 the famous Hutchinson Family *(left)* sang for Lincoln at the White House, John Hutchinson, the father and leader of the group, presiding. Another performer who charmed the Lincolns was the temperamental nine-year-old concert pianist from Venezuela, Teresa Carreño *(right)*. In sharp contrast to these decorous White House musicians was the group of contrabands *(below)* which Lincoln came upon as he was riding through the city to the Soldiers' Home one summer evening in 1864. Legend has it that he took off his hat, and with tears in his eyes sang spirituals with them for over an hour.

B-5240

"YOU ARE IN CONSTANT DANGER"

How the President had avoided being assassinated during his first term was a mystery—the capital was rife with Lincoln-haters, war had stimulated an atmosphere of violence, threats came in each mail, and little protection was provided the Chief Executive. Security at the White House, especially, was almost nonexistent. Although there was supposed to be a front doorman, normally Edward Moran, and an usher on the second floor, they were often lax, and any assassin or maniac could easily get to the President.

As his second term approached, Lincoln may have recalled the ominous incident on election night of 1860 in Springfield, when, after collapsing exhausted into a sofa, he had suddenly seen a strange double image of himself in the mirror—one face robust, the other ghostly pale. According to the story, Mary Lincoln's instant response was that the double image anticipated a two-term presidency, but that the ghostly second image predicted death before the end of the second term. Now, four years later, following another election victory, Washington's marshal, Ward Hill Lamon, who bore the responsibility for Lincoln's safety, was getting increasingly concerned. In the early years he had encouraged the President to take horseback rides alone out in the countryside, advising him that "no one needs such exercise more than you do (and you ought to have it every day)." But by Lincoln's second term, Lamon felt differently. "*You are in danger*. Tonight, as you have done on several previous occasions, you went unattended to the theater.... You ought to know, that your life is sought after, and will be taken unless you and your friends are cautious." But Lincoln was unheeding. He liked breaking free of the crowds, eluding guards, and walking alone outside, especially at night. "It was impossible to induce him to forgo those lonely and dangerous journeys," complained Lamon. He eluded his special guard, Company K of the 150th Pennsylvania Volunteers; and even the Union Light Guard, assigned to Lincoln after the summer of 1863, failed to keep up with him. Once, outside the Soldiers' Home, an assassin's bullet just missed him, passing right through his high hat. To those who warned him of danger, Lincoln retorted: "So you think the Richmond people would like to have Hannibal Hamlin here any better than myself? In that one alternative, I have an insurance on my life worth half the prairie-land of Illinois. And besides, if there were such a plot, and they wanted to get at me, no vigilance could keep them out." Stanton and Lamon, among others, disagreed with him, and by late 1864 they had detailed four special plainclothes policemen to take turns guarding the President. Lincoln disliked this encumbrance, but agreed to abide by it. Privately, he was worried; he carefully saved death threat letters in a special envelope inside his office desk drawer.

Even more disturbing was a dream that Lincoln had, which he described to Lamon: "There seemed to be a death-like stillness about me. Then I heard subdued sobs, as if a number of people were weeping. I thought I left my bed and wandered downstairs.... It was light in all the rooms; every object was familiar to me... I kept on until I arrived at the East Room, which I entered. There I met with a sickening surprise. Before me was a catafalque, on which rested a corpse wrapped in funeral vestments.... 'Who is dead in the White House?' I demanded of one of the soldiers. 'The President,' was the answer, 'he was killed by an assassin!' Then came a loud burst of grief from the crowd, which awoke me from my dream. I slept no more that night..."

To the end of his life Lincoln remained fascinated by dreams, which had the power both to frighten him and to fill him with joy. Ward Hill Lamon remembered Lincoln's words on the subject one day in 1865.
It seems strange to me how much there is in the Bible about dreams. There are, I think, some sixteen chapters in the Old Testament and four or five in the New in which dreams are mentioned; and there are many other passages scattered throughout the book which refer to visions.... Nowadays dreams are regarded as very foolish, and are seldom told, except by old women and by young men and maidens in love.... I had one the other night which has haunted me ever since.

Lincoln then narrated his dream of seeing himself dead in a coffin in the White House. Lamon remembered Lincoln later trying to downplay the fears it had engendered.
Hill, your apprehension of harm to me from some hidden enemy is downright foolishness. For a long time you have been trying to keep somebody—the Lord knows who—from killing me. Don't you see how it will turn out? In this dream it was not me, but some other fellow, that was killed. It seems that this ghostly assassin tried his hand on some one else.

Ward Hill Lamon, who had sworn to protect Lincoln, made the President promise he wouldn't go to the theater when Lamon was out of town—which he was on the night of April 14, 1865.

Even with a guard posted at the door, the summer White House — a cottage on the grounds of the Soldiers' Home, outside Washington — was an easy target. Only a last-minute change in his plans prevented Lincoln from being kidnapped here on the night of March 17, 1865.

LINCOLN AND GOD

While Lincoln was "a religious man always," according to Mary his first deep thinking about God was not until 1862, "when Willie died—never before." Mary was wrong; even she did not know everything about the inner life of her intensely private husband.

As a boy, preachers had put Lincoln off. They seemed predictable, crude, easy to mimic, and their frontier religion contained too many objectionable features. Later, in Springfield, Lincoln not only didn't join the First Presbyterian Church—or any other parish, ever—but preferred to spend his Sundays horsing around with his boys or simply staying away from home all weekend on the circuit.

In the 1840s, Lincoln's political opponent Peter Cartwright was calling him a blasphemous "infidel," a scoffer at religion. Lincoln readily admitted that he was not a member of any Christian church, but he disclaimed ever being disrespectful of organized religion. Lincoln did not deny that his own beliefs inclined toward fatalism, "that the human mind is impelled to action…by some power, over which the mind…has no control." Predestination was part of it. Men were instruments in some foreordained plan. But Lincoln's beliefs went far beyond simple fatalism.

"He had his own religion," decided his old law partner William Herndon, a religion based on "exalted notions of right….He had no prejudice against any class…tolerating—as I never could—even the Irish." It was a religion of broad sympathies and high moral passion. Inspired by the Bible, it dealt with the immense mystery of time and death and creation. The more he pondered, the more he came to believe that God had created all human beings fundamentally equal. His anti-slavery efforts in the late 1850s became fueled with religious passion.

Although Mary was wrong that Lincoln thought little about God before Willie's death, she was right that, after it, his concern for the spiritual was intense and expanding. "It is my earnest desire to know the will of Providence," he declared just prior to issuing the Emancipation Proclamation *"And if I can learn what it is I will do it!"* Now he saw himself more and more as an especially appointed agent of the Almighty, chosen to preside over the worst crisis in American history, and coming to see that the immense loss of life in the war could be justified by one thing alone—complete and permanent freedom for the slaves.

Skeptical of dogma, refusing to believe in eternal punishment, comparing himself to a doubting Thomas, guided by the nobility of the Bible, directed by dreams and signs, "feeling and reasoning" his way through "a twilight," coming to think of himself as a homely prophet to an America he described as "God's almost chosen people," Lincoln revealed, late in his presidency, why he had "never united [himself] to any church." To Congressman Henry C. Deming of Connecticut he explained, "I have found difficulty in giving my assent…to the long, complicated statements of Christian doctrine….Where any church will inscribe over its altar, as its sole qualification for membership, the Savior's condensed statement of both Law and Gospel, 'Thou shalt love the Lord thy God with all thy heart, and with all thy soul, and with all thy mind, and thy neighbor as thyself,' that church will I join with all my heart and all my soul."

AN ANSWERED PRAYER

Major General Daniel E. Sickles lost a leg at the Battle of Gettysburg and was brought soon after to lodgings in Washington to recuperate. There he was visited by President Lincoln and afterward wrote out this memorandum of their conversation.
"Mr. Lincoln, we heard at Gettysburg that here at the capital you were all so anxious about the result of the battle that the government officials packed up and got ready to leave at short notice with the official archives."

"Yes," he said, "some precautions were prudently taken, but for my part, I was sure of our success at Gettysburg."

"Why were you so confident?" I asked.

There was a brief pause. The President seemed to be in deep meditation.…Turning to me he said: "…I felt that the great crisis had come.…I went to my room and got down on my knees in prayer.

"Never before had I prayed with so much earnestness. I wish I could repeat my prayer. I felt I must put all my trust in Almighty God. He gave our people the best country ever given to man. He alone could save it from destruction. I had tried my best to do my duty and found myself unequal to the task. The burden was more than I could bear.…I asked him to help us and give us victory now. I was sure my prayer was answered. I had no misgivings about the result at Gettysburg."

Rising to go, Mr. Lincoln took my hand in his and said with tenderness: "Sickles, I have been told, as you have been told perhaps, your condition is serious. I am in a prophetic mood today. You will get well."

General Daniel E. Sickles did recover. Here he poses with members of his staff.

The twenty or so months between these portraits, both taken at the Brady gallery, brought great change to the President's face.

Chapter 12

THE TRAGIC CONCLUSION

First a night of horror, then a stricken people say goodbye in a twenty-day funeral pageant.

When this photograph was taken, Lincoln's body had just been removed from this humble, blood-soaked bed where he died.

AN ASSASSIN'S BULLET RINGS DOWN THE CURTAIN

Junius Brutus Booth, the greatest Shakespearean actor of his day, left a legacy of family acting talent. The photograph at right, taken shortly before his death, shows him with his eldest son, Edwin. Twelve years later, on November 25, 1864, three of his actor sons appeared together in a benefit performance of *Julius Caesar* at New York's Winter Garden. Below, posing for that celebrated performance, is John Wilkes Booth *(left)*, who played Marc Antony in the production. Edwin, the most famous of the three, holds the shoulder of Junius, Jr.

STRANGE TRAITS IN A BRILLIANT FAMILY

John Wilkes Booth's father was so eccentric that he was often called insane. Junius Brutus Booth died in 1852 when John Wilkes was fourteen, and although America considered him her greatest actor, he frequently appeared on stage barely able to stand after drinking a bottle of brandy. At times, he had been known to be so filled with rage as to have almost killed other actors. He liked to play practical jokes. Once, on a river steamboat, he put his money in the pockets of a sleeping clergyman, then sounded the alarm that he had been robbed. Another time, he asked someone to attend a funeral with him, and when the coffin was opened it was found to be filled with dead pigeons, over which the senior Booth mourned as if they were human.

John Wilkes had more than a touch of his father's strangeness. In 1864 his older brother Edwin wrote: "Dear mother is happy with her children about her, Thank God! but she still has an absent one, the youngest boy, strange, wild and ever-moving; he causes us all some degree of anxiety." A fierce supporter of the South, John Wilkes would have caused his family even more anxiety had they known of his growing obsession—to gather around him a band of followers and do away with Lincoln.

On several occasions, John Wilkes Booth had already touched the Lincolns. Tad had seen him act and said "he makes me thrill," and the actor had presented the President's son with a rose. But when Lincoln invited Booth to visit him between acts of a play, which he occasionally did with stars he admired, the request was ignored. Another time Lincoln was at the theater with some of Mary's relatives when the actor stepped near the President's box and shook his finger in his direction. Mrs. Helm, Mary's half-sister, said, "Mr. Lincoln, he looks as if he meant that for you." And Lincoln replied, "Well, he does look pretty sharp at me, doesn't he?" And just this month, three days before Good Friday, Booth and his co-conspirator Lewis Paine had listened to Lincoln's last public speech, delivered from a second-story window of the White House. Booth did not try to hide his hatred, as he openly urged Paine to take out his revolver and shoot Lincoln right there in the window.

Mary Surratt, a handsome widow of forty-five and a Southern sympathizer, was the mother of twenty-year-old John Surratt, a courier for the Confederacy, whom Booth charmed into becoming one of his partners in crime.

Mrs. Surratt ran a tavern in Maryland. At the end of 1864, thirteen miles north of her establishment, she opened this Washington boardinghouse as well, and it was here that Booth and his group of conspirators often met.

John Surratt had two years earlier left a Catholic seminary where he was studying to become a priest.

"I never saw Mr. Lincoln so cheerful and happy," remarked Hugh McCulloch, the new secretary of the treasury, on that beautiful, bright morning of April 14. No one could miss noticing the difference in him. For months the President had looked pale and haggard and old, and unbearably sad, as if his life were being "eaten out from the inside," he himself recognized. Under the frightful ordeal of war, "the boisterous laughter became less frequent year by year," remembered John Hay, and "he aged with great rapidity." Today, however, Lincoln felt light and buoyant, stood erect, and even told people how happy he was, which scared Mary, who felt that saying it right out like that was bad luck. The President paid her no heed. The terrible long war was over and it was finally sinking in. Even his dreams the night before had been good. After a long stretch of nightmares and even a vision of his own death, Lincoln had had his good dream again—the dream of the mysterious ship sailing toward an unknown shore, a dream, he insisted, that always arrived just prior to receiving excellent news. When he came downstairs for breakfast, "his face was more cheerful than I had seen it for a long time," noted Lizzie Keckley. Even his hair, which was normally unattended to, and which sometimes stood out "in every direction like that of an electric experiment doll," was today "neatly combed." He just looked good. It didn't feel like Good Friday at all—the day of the Crucifixion—but more like Easter. And on this excellent spring morning, said White House guard Smith Stimmel, "all nature seemed to bask in the warm sunshine of assured peace."

Normally Lincoln ate his solitary egg alone, but today was to begin with the rare treat of a family breakfast. Twenty-one-year-old Robert was home and everyone was beaming with pride at his having been, for the last two months, a member of General Grant's own staff. He had even been present at Lee's surrender at Appomattox, waiting on a porch outside the courthouse. "Captain Robert came into the room with a portrait of General Lee in his hand," remembered Lizzie Keckley. Lincoln placed the picture on the table in front of him and studied it "thoughtfully." Then, unexpectedly, he said, "It is a good face; it is the face of a noble, noble, brave man. I am glad that the war is over at last."

For months the Maryland-born actor John Wilkes Booth had been finding it difficult to pay attention to his career. He had never been as good an actor as his brother Edwin or his famous father, Junius. John's theatrical success depended largely on his dashing good looks, on tricks like his dazzling swordsmanship, and on his ability to portray frighteningly realistic outbursts of anger while on stage. "He...generally slept smothered in steak or oysters to cure his own bruises," wrote actress Kate Reignolds, who herself had often been roughed up by Booth during plays. And "in his blind passion he constantly cut himself."

The last big show of Booth's career had been a family affair at New York's Winter Garden Theatre, with all three Booth brothers collaborating, for the first time ever, in a production of *Julius Caesar*. Playing to a packed house, in a once-only performance on November 25, it had been proclaimed the greatest theatrical event in New York history. But by then the youngest Booth had already begun to come unhinged.

An ardent white supremacist who believed slavery to be "one of the greatest

(continued on page 346)

Above is a detail from a photograph showing the overall scene at Lincoln's second inauguration on March 4, 1865. It may show just how close John Wilkes Booth was to the little speaker's table during Lincoln's address. The young man in the high hat on the balustrade has been identified as Booth *(see arrow)* and the man just below him as John Ford, Booth's good friend and the owner of Ford's Theatre. *Left:* A telling portrait of the dapper actor, playing himself.

Booth's hatred of Lincoln and the North had by late 1864 grown so intense he could no longer contain it. "This country was formed for the *white* man not for the black," he seethed as a plot spawned in his mind to kidnap the President. For this he would need helpers; he turned first to two old school chums from Maryland—Sam Arnold and Michael O'Laughlin, both of whom had served time in the Confederate Army and were looking for excitement. Then, in December, Booth picked up a third man, a Confederate spy named John Surratt, son of a woman who was now keeping a conveniently hospitable Washington boardinghouse.

Through Surratt, Booth gained access to two other willing souls, little David Herold, a dim-witted nineteen-year-old former pharmacist's clerk who was deeply drawn by Booth's magnetism, and George Atzerodt, a German-born wagon painter who made money on the side as a Potomac ferryman for Confederate spies needing to cross the river.

The last to join Booth's team, and the most dangerous and brutal of all, was Lewis Thornton Powell, alias Paine, alias Mosby, a Florida clergyman's son gone bad—a giant thug of a man with inhuman willpower who had once nearly beaten a Negro maid to death.

By March 1865, Booth was supplying several of these men in Washington with room and board and liberal quantities of drink. As of yet there was talk only of kidnapping. But following an abortive March 17 attempt to capture Lincoln outside the Soldiers' Home, Booth began to hint at the possibility of a murder. Almost immediately, Arnold, O'Laughlin, and Surratt shook free from the conspiracy. Furious, and drinking more brandy than ever, Booth consoled himself that at least he still had his three main men—Paine, Atzerodt, and Herold. In addition to these were a few more or less willing dupes: Mary Surratt, who agreed to run errands and messages for Booth; John Lloyd, who hid rifles for him in Maryland; Edman Spangler, a scene-shifter at Ford's Theatre who often held Booth's horse for him; and Dr. Samuel Mudd, who may or may not have recognized the crazed and charismatic actor when he turned up on the doctor's porch looking for help.

Lewis Paine, who had deserted the Confederate Army after Gettysburg, was the team's "young giant," muscular, iron-willed, and brutal.

Wiry, beady-eyed George A. Atzerodt, a ferryman for Confederate spies, was considered by some "a notorious coward," especially when drinking.

An old friend of the Booth family, stagehand Edman Spangler, who slept nightly at Ford's Theatre, often obliged Booth by taking care of his horse while the actor visited with friends inside.

Stoop-shouldered, "baboon"-browed David E. Herold, everyone said, was a "pretty little man" with the mind of an eleven-year-old.

blessings that God ever bestowed upon a favored nation,'' and who considered himself ''soul, life and possessions...for the south,'' Booth had early in his life betrayed a sadistic streak, once exterminating all the cats on his father's farm. Over the course of the winter of 1864–65, this streak had begun to assert itself again; his own sister Asia noticed in him a slow, steady ''turn towards...evil.''

By late in the year Booth had taken to living at Washington's National Hotel, keeping horses at a stable off F Street, behind Ford's Theatre, and buying drinks for an assortment of strange characters. Through his friendship with Edman Spangler, a theatrical set man, he had gained access to Ford's Theatre night and day, by any of its many entrances.

By early 1865 Booth had begun to hatch a plot that involved kidnapping President Lincoln—and thus derailing the Union war effort. Booth's hope was to capture and then smuggle Lincoln across the Potomac River into Confederate hands, where presumably he would be used to blackmail the North into coming to terms.

By March, he had enlisted help, including that of Lewis Thornton Powell, alias Lewis Paine, a Florida ne'er-do-well with muscles like iron. In all, five members of Booth's kidnapping team were probably present at Lincoln's second inauguration, with Booth so close, he said, that if he wanted to he could have done the President in ''that very day.'' But after a fruitless attempt at a kidnapping on March 17, when Lincoln failed to show up, as expected, at the Soldiers' Home, Booth's team had suddenly disbanded, leaving their leader more restless than ever and increasingly dependent upon alcohol.

The war's end, which produced the sudden new specter of what Booth called ''nigger citizenship,'' threw him into a literal frenzy. By this time, he was downing a quart of brandy a day just to keep his nerves under control.

On April 14, Booth's morning began at the stroke of midnight, when, lying wide awake in his room at the National Hotel, he wrote his mother telling her that even though he was ''in haste,'' all was well. To his diary, Booth admitted that the time had come for him to do something ''decisive.'' When later that morning Booth learned of Lincoln's plans to attend Ford's Theatre in the evening, that decisive ''something'' began to take shape, progressing far beyond his earlier ideas of a kidnapping. The only hope now was to throw the nation into an open revolution—and that called for murder.

After a day of official duties, including a full Cabinet meeting with General Grant to discuss the future of the Southern states, Lincoln took time in the late afternoon for a leisurely carriage ride with Mary. He was still in radiant good humor. ''I never saw him so supremely cheerful,'' said Mary of that last ride together. ''His manner was even playful....I asked him if anyone should accompany us. He immediately replied, 'No, I prefer to ride by ourselves today!' During the drive he was so gay, that I said to him laughingly, 'Dear Husband, you almost startle me, by your great cheerfulness;' he replied, 'And well may I feel so, Mary, I consider this day the war has come to a close.' And then added, 'we must *both* be more cheerful in the future—between the war and the loss of our darling Willie—we have both, been very miserable.'''

Lincoln's mind was on the future. That very morning he had told Schuyler Colfax that he believed the possibilities for America's future were almost limitless.

LINCOLN'S LAST DAY

At a midday meeting on April 14, Lincoln surprised his Cabinet members and General Grant by mentioning a dream he had. Gideon Welles recorded that it came in answer to the question of whether news from General Sherman would soon be coming.

The President remarked it would, he had no doubt, come soon, and come favorable, for he had last night the usual dream which he had preceding nearly every great and important event of the War.... I inquired what this remarkable dream could be. He said it related to...water; that he seemed to be in some singular, indescribable vessel, and that he was moving with great rapidity.... [T]hat he had this dream preceding Sumter, Bull Run, Antietam, Gettysburg, Stone River, Vicksburg, Wilmington, etc....

"I had," the President remarked, "this strange dream again last night, and we shall, judging from the past, have great news very soon. I think it must be from Sherman."

William Henry Crook, one of four plain-clothesmen assigned to guard the President in 1865, had a last conversation with Lincoln on the night of April 14.

Mr. Lincoln had told me that afternoon of a dream he had had for three successive nights, concerning his impending assassination. Of course, the constant dread of such a calamity made me somewhat nervous, and I almost begged him to remain in the Executive Mansion that night, and not to go to the theater. But he would not disappoint Mrs. Lincoln and others who were to be present. Then I urged that he allow me to stay on duty and accompany him; but he would not hear of this, either.

"No, Crook," he said, kindly but firmly, "you have had a long, hard day's work already, and must go home to sleep and rest. I cannot afford to have you get tired out and exhausted."

It was then that he neglected, for the first and only time, to say good-night to me. Instead, he turned, with his kind, grave face, and said: "Good-bye, Crook," and went into his room.

ALL DAY LONG LINCOLN TRIES TO ASSEMBLE GUESTS FOR THE THEATER THAT NIGHT

For some, Mary Lincoln's undignified, even unbalanced behavior of late rendered an evening at the theater with her unthinkable. Just two weeks ago at City Point, she had blurted out at her traveling companion Julia Grant, as the refined woman took a seat on a ship's coil of ropes, "How dare you sit in the presence of the wife of the President?" On April 14, even though the theater party had been based around the Grants, at the last minute they withdrew and headed north on the pretext of visiting their children at school in New Jersey. The Stantons had been asked too. But Ellen Stanton and Julia Grant had vowed that neither one of them would give Mary Lincoln the satisfaction, and she and her husband also sent their regrets. On impulse, Lincoln had turned to War Department telegraph officer Thomas Eckert and asked him to join them; but Eckert's boss, Secretary of War Stanton, disapproved of Lincoln's theater-going, considering it dangerous, and said he needed the powerful Eckert to stay at work.

So it went throughout the day. Speaker of the House Schuyler Colfax turned Lincoln down because he was leaving on a trip for the Pacific coast the next morning. George Ashmun of Massachusetts, who had presided over the 1860 Republican Convention and banged the gavel that saw Lincoln nominated, had a previous engagement. Lincoln's good friends from Illinois, Governor Richard J. Oglesby and ex-Governor Richard Yates, laughed a lot with Lincoln during the early evening but then excused themselves to meet other friends, as did another Illinois invitee, Isham N. Haynie. Ex-Congressman William A. Howard of Detroit had already made arrangements to leave Washington that day. Governor of the Idaho Territory William H. Wallace and Mrs. Wallace pleaded weariness. Noah Brooks had a cold. Robert Lincoln, just back from the field, told his father he wanted nothing more than to go to sleep. The refusals had kept pouring in all day long. At about 7:45 p.m., Lincoln and his wife boarded their carriage, rode over to the residence of New York Senator Ira T. Harris at Fifteenth and H streets, and picked up the only two people who had said yes.

Above are fourteen people Lincoln invited to the theater on April 14 who turned him down. At the top are General Grant and his wife, Julia. Next are Edwin M. Stanton and his wife, Ellen, and below them, Robert Lincoln and Thomas T. Eckert. In the bottom two rows, left to right, are Schuyler Colfax, Noah Brooks, Richard J. Oglesby, and Richard Yates, then George Ashmun, William A. Howard, William H. Wallace, and Isham N. Haynie.

He predicted that immigration would "land upon our shores hundreds of thousands...from over-crowded Europe," that America was destined to become "the treasury of the world." Now with his Mary, he wanted to dream about their own personal future.

"He was like a boy out of school," wrote Isaac Arnold, who interviewed Mary soon afterward. "He spoke of his old Springfield home,...the law office, the court room, the green bag for his briefs and law papers, his adventures when riding the circuit....'We have laid by,' said he to his wife, 'some money....We will go back to Illinois, and I will open a law-office at Springfield or Chicago.'...In imagination he was again in his prairie home, among his...books, and...with his old friends."

The day that had begun so well still had a grand finale ahead. If Lincoln could get through a few dozen more visits and presidential duties between this carriage ride and a late dinner, there was an evening at the theater to look forward to. Throughout the war, theater had been his chief diversion, his method of escape from the constant stream of visitors, his time to rest and daydream and disappear into the darkness. Despite repeated warnings from Stanton and others—and a promise made to Ward Hill Lamon that he would not go out to the theater while Lamon was away on business—Lincoln was glad that he would be attending Ford's Theatre that evening, even though the play, *Our American Cousin,* was known to be a lightweight and rather mediocre farce.

During the afternoon, Wilkes Booth, as many called him, paid a strange visit of his own to Ford's Theatre. Climbing up to the President's box, he bored a chunk out of its door to make a peephole and then fashioned a simple wooden doorjamb which could effectively lock the box's outer entrance from the inside.

Earlier that morning Booth had purchased a new getaway horse, and after finishing his preparations at the theater, at about 4:00 p.m., he showed up at Pumphrey's stable to pick up the mare. After returning to the theater to make arrangements with his friend Edman Spangler to hold his horse that evening, and then buying a round of drinks for his friends at Taltavull's bar next door to the theater, Booth went home to his hotel to think. He had called a meeting of his fellow conspirators for 8:00 p.m. in Paine's room at Herndon House, on Ninth and F streets—just a short walk from Ford's Theatre.

In the original conspiracy plot, there had been a careful orchestration of roles. Sam Arnold, Booth's school chum from Maryland, was given the job of actually seizing the President in his box seat. George Atzerodt, alias "Port Tobacco," was to apply handcuffs to Lincoln and then help Booth lower him onto the stage where Lewis Paine, code name "Mosby," was to catch Lincoln and hold on to him until the others got down. John Surratt, the Confederate spy, was to facilitate their escape over the Eastern Branch bridge.

But if kidnapping was unduly complicated, causing dissension among the conspirators, murder was much simpler to accomplish and required fewer participants. At 8:00 p.m., just two hours prior to the deed, Booth handed out the new assignments. Simultaneously, Atzerodt would assassinate Vice President Andrew Johnson, and Lewis Paine would kill Secretary of State William Seward. Little Davie Herold, son of a government clerk and described as "doltish" and

(continued on page 352)

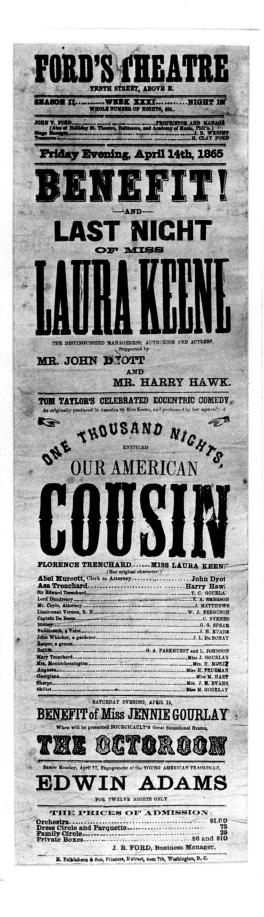

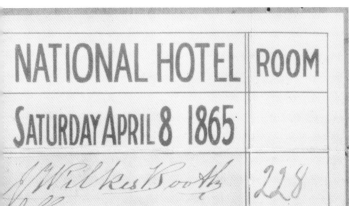

NATIONAL HOTEL | ROOM

SATURDAY APRIL 8 1865

J. Wilkes Booth | 228

Unmarried and footloose, John Wilkes Booth moved around a lot; his last room was at the National Hotel in Washington. The register entry *(left)* shows that he took Room 228 six days before his final, brutal act at Ford's Theatre *(below)*. From 1833 this was the site of the First Baptist Church of Washington. In 1859, John Thomson Ford, a successful manager of theaters in Richmond and Baltimore, bought the building and transformed it into a lavish, modern theater. On December 30, 1862, it burned to the ground, but Ford built it up again, more elegant than ever. *Far left:* The flier for Good Friday's performance

Access to the lobby of Ford's Theatre was provided by any of five archway entrances that led in from Tenth Street. The building to the right was Taltavull's Star Saloon, which could be entered from the street or from a side entrance that opened into the theater itself. Eventually the government bought the theater from Ford for $100,000, and, trying to obliterate the blemish from its streets, tore out its insides, making it into a storehouse for army records and a medical museum. Today the theater is restored—stage, President's box, and all—to its exact state on April 14, 1865 *(left)*.

This photograph, taken the day after the shooting, shows how the proscenium box on the right of the stage was decorated for the President's party. Taken from far back and high up in the family circle (the top tier of benches), it also shows the dress circle (the tier of seats just below), on the same level as the President's box, from which Lincoln's guard for the night watched the play. Usually a partition separated the box into two small rooms, but one of Booth's accomplices, the scenery man and carpenter Edman Spangler, had removed it that afternoon. A newspaper described the double box *(right)* as "fitted with elegance and taste, the curtains the finest lace and buff satin, the exterior ornamentations are lit up with a chaste chandelier, suspended from the outside." In his leap over the box rail, Booth knocked the framed engraving of George Washington askew with his boot, and in doing so, his spur caught in the draped flag, tearing off some blue material as he dropped off-balance toward the stage below.

In a closer view of the Lincolns' side of the box, the door through which Booth entered is clearly visible behind the rocking chair in which the President sat. Above is a close-up of the door paneling, with the freshly cut peephole Booth is thought to have bored and then enlarged with his pen-knife. The following day, a large gimlet with an iron handle was found in Booth's trunk in his room at the National Hotel.

"irresolute," was instructed to help Paine escape from Washington. Booth himself would kill the President.

Our American Cousin had already been playing for some time to the packed house when the Lincoln carriage finally arrived, on a night that had turned foggy and cold. With the Lincolns was Major Henry R. Rathbone and Clara Harris, the lovely daughter of a senator. Accompanying them was a White House plainclothesman, John F. Parker, and an attendant—probably White House footman Charley Forbes. As the executive party entered the second-floor double box, where a large cushioned rocking chair awaited the President, the play was suddenly halted, the orchestra struck up "Hail to the Chief," and the entire audience rose and cheered for their beloved President. Then all settled back into the darkness for the resumption of the drama. Unbeknownst to Lincoln, the newly hired Parker now abandoned his post. "He left it almost immediately," said Parker's colleague William Crook. "He confessed to me the next day that he went to a seat at the front of the first gallery, so that he could see the play." Forbes, too, at some point during the play left his vestibule chair just outside the box, taking an empty seat in Section A. Booth could not have asked for anything better.

At one point during the course of the play, Lincoln was observed shivering in the drafty box. The outside temperature had plummeted twenty degrees, and he got up and pulled on his overcoat. At another point, the stage manager's wife noticed him "leaning forward, with his arm on the cushioned edge of the box, his chin resting in his hand...looking deep into space as if in deep thought." Just a little before 10:00 p.m., Mary put her arms around her husband and they had the last conversation of their life. "What will Miss Harris think of my hanging on to you so?" Mary whispered. "She won't think anything about it," Lincoln answered her tenderly.

Booth had been in and out of the theater throughout the evening; John Buckingham, the ticket-taker, had seen him come into the lobby at least five different times. Booth was a close acquaintance of the theater's owner, John Ford, who allowed the actor to receive his mail there, and, having performed in the theater himself, Booth could wander the side aisles and even backstage at will, without causing suspicion. Planned for that evening was a special patriotic song written by the orchestra leader, William Withers, Jr., which was to be sung by the cast. Laura Keene, the owner of the performing company and its star, was hoping that the President and his party would linger for a few moments after the final curtain to hear it, and she sent a message, she said later, up to Lincoln's box with her request. No messenger was seen delivering this message. But at thirteen minutes after ten, Booth, who had taken a last long drink of whiskey at Taltavull's, showed Lincoln's attendant a card that gained him admission to the President's box. Once inside the outer door, he jammed it with the bar he had fashioned, peeked through the hole in the inner door, and, finding things to his liking, pushed the door open and silently stepped in.

During the evening the Lincolns had been discussing the Holy Lands, and now, Mary remembered later, her husband had suddenly said, "How I should like to visit Jerusalem sometime!" The sentiment was out of keeping with the play onstage, a pun-filled, slapstick comedy of an American backwoodsman

Henry R. Rathbone   Clara Harris

After so many people had turned down their invitation to accompany them to the theater that night, the Lincolns finally settled for a young couple they both admired. Clara Harris was the daughter of Senator Ira T. Harris of New York, who had once asked Mary Lincoln, "Why isn't Robert in the army?" The question had made Mary blanch, but she chose to forget the senator's lapse and still considered him a dear friend and his daughter "a very superior woman." She also liked Henry R. Rathbone, destined to be the senator's stepson, and so, obviously, did Clara, for even though they were about to become stepbrother and stepsister, the two were engaged to be married. Just a month before, the President had appointed the twenty-eight-year-old Rathbone as assistant adjutant general of volunteers, with the rank of major. Unable to prevent the tragedy at Ford's Theatre that night, Rathbone never forgave himself for not protecting Lincoln better. Even though the couple married and moved with their children to Germany, where he was made American consul stationed in Hanover, Rathbone still brooded and finally became deranged. One evening, around Christmas time, using the excuse that his wife paid too much attention to the children, he killed her. He spent the rest of his life in the Hildescheim Asylum for the Criminally Insane.

Actress Laura Keene

Stage manager and actor Harry Hawk

A married Englishwoman in her forties with two children, Laura Keene had made a business out of presenting and playing the lead in *Our American Cousin*. Tossing her auburn curls and batting her beady brown eyes, she had played the young girl Florence Trenchard more than a thousand times, still able to create an appealing ambience of youth with plenty of greasepaint and a charming, natural style of acting. Harry Hawk's main job was tour manager for Keene's company, and he only doubled as comedian when called upon. Though not as good an actor as Joseph Jefferson, who usually played Asa Trenchard, the backwoods American, his performance in the role was more than adequate.

visiting his refined English cousins. Now Lincoln spied General Burnside in the audience below and was leaning forward to get a better look at him. Onstage, Harry Hawk, the company stage manager who was doubling as the male comic lead, was raucously reciting the last words Lincoln would ever hear. A scheming mother had just discovered the American Cousin to be poor and mannerless. "Don't know the manners of good society, eh?" Hawk intoned. "Well, I guess I know enough to turn you inside out, old gal—you sockdologizing old mantrap."

At this precise moment Clara Harris turned around. "Major Rathbone arose and asked the intruder his business. He rushed past the major without making a reply." Then, placing a small derringer-style pistol "close to the President's head—actually into contact with it—[Booth] fired."

Everything in the box suddenly became a whirl of smoke and confusion. Rathbone sprang forward to seize Booth but was sliced in the upper arm by the assassin's large knife. Lincoln was propelled forward, his forehead striking the rail. Mrs. Lincoln's very first reaction was that he was pitching headfirst over the railing. She grabbed at him and held him up, and Lincoln's head slumped to the right, his chin resting on his chest as if he were dozing. Booth leapt from the balcony, catching the spur of his boot in the Treasury flag draped over the box. From the stage, Harry Hawk saw the bad landing that snapped the bone in Booth's leg. At first, everybody in the audience was stunned; could all this be a surprise addition to the play? Brandishing his huge knife that a witness said "glinted like a diamond," Booth shouted "Sic semper tyrannis" ("Thus it shall ever be for tyrants"). And then he was gone into the wings, slashing at the orchestra leader behind the sets, hopping through the door at the back of the theater, knocking over the boy who held his waiting horse, and clattering down the alley into the night. Someone finally screamed out the single word "Booth!" and the whole audience began to cry out the name, louder and louder. "Booth!" "Booth!" "Booth!" In the box, the vacuum of silence following the pistol report was over. Mary Lincoln, clutching at her husband, shrieked "Help!" three times before her voice turned to gibberish. "Stop that man!" screamed Clara Harris. "Won't somebody stop that man!" The audience now was screaming "Hang him!"

"There will never be anything like it on earth," wrote Helen Truman, who was present in that crazed and terrified crowd. "The shouts, groans, curses, smashing of seats, screams of women, shuffling of feet and cries of terror created a pandemonium that . . . through all the ages will stand out in my memory as the hell of hells."

EVIDENCE OF A MURDER

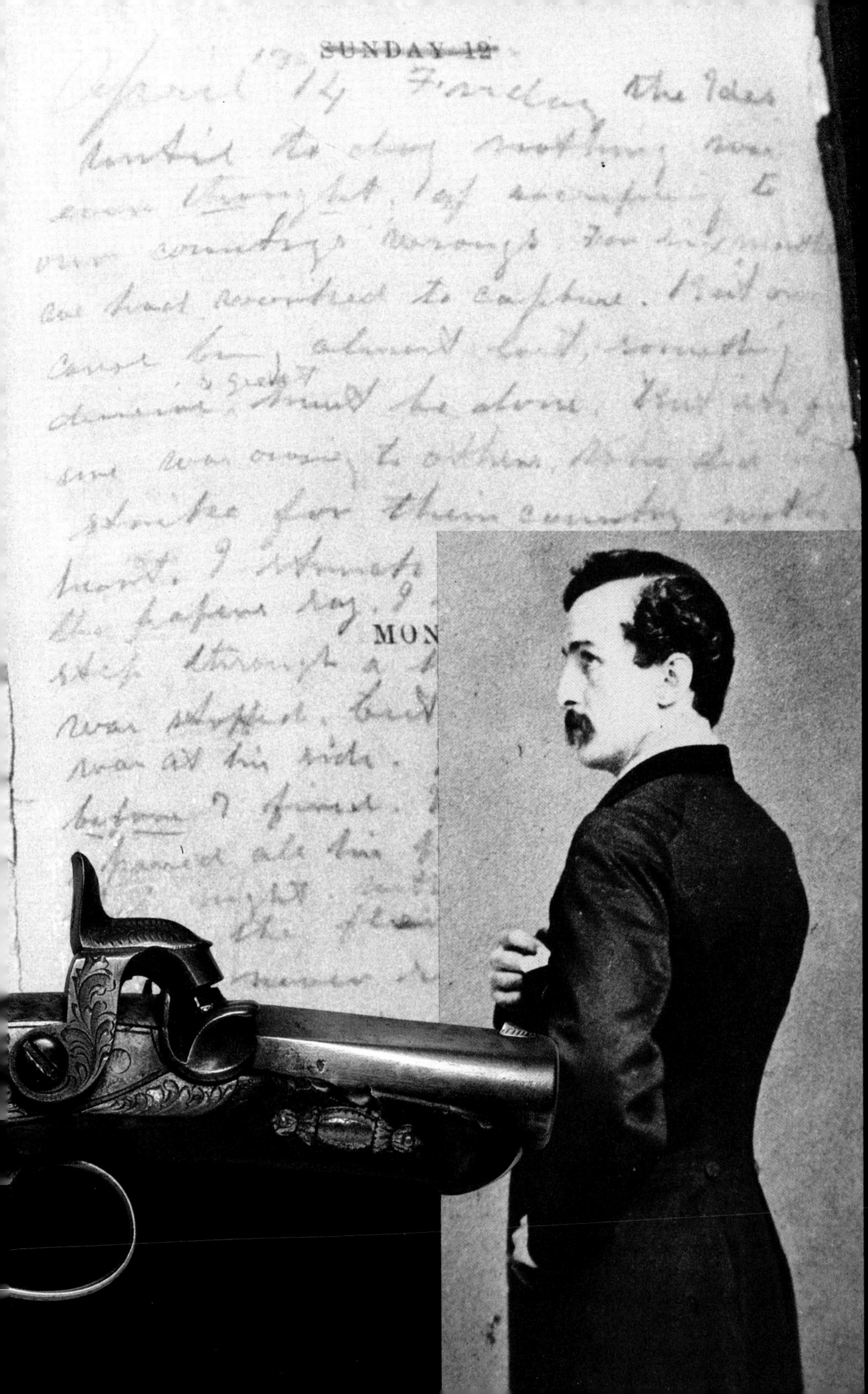

[handwritten diary text, partially legible]

April 14 Friday the Ides

Until to day nothing was ever thought of sacrificing to our country's wrongs...

MON

As Booth approached Lincoln from behind the President sat forward in the rocker *(below)*. The tiny, muzzle-loading derringer *(bottom left, actual size)* was a type of pistol much used in the South. Only six inches long, it could easily be hidden in a hand or a pocket. The one bullet it fired, made of a mixture of antimony, tin, copper, and soft lead, was almost half an inch in diameter and exceedingly hard. As Booth *(below left)* and his weapon approached the President's chair, Lincoln spotted General Burnside in the audience below and leaned farther forward for a better look. Then he may have caught a glimpse of what was behind him, for all of a sudden his head turned sharply to the left. At this moment the shot was fired, the bullet hitting Lincoln behind his left ear and tunneling directly into his brain. Not long after, Booth wrote despondently in his diary *(top left)*: "Until today, nothing was ever thought of sacrificing to our country's wrongs. For six months we had worked to capture.... I can never repent it, though we hated to kill. Our country owed all her troubles to him, and God simply made me the instrument of His Punishment."

NIGHT OF BLOOD, NIGHT OF DYING

In the Ford Theatre's orchestra, not forty feet away, sat twenty-three-year-old Dr. Charles Leale, transfixed by the horror of the moment. "I saw someone open the door of the box, and heard him call for a Surgeon and help," Leale wrote two years later. When he got to Lincoln, Leale found the President almost dead. He was paralyzed, had no pulse at all in his wrist, and breathed only in occasional, snorting gasps.

First Leale stretched Lincoln out on the floor, and, remembering the knife that the assassin had brandished onstage, he searched for a stab wound, calling for the collar and coat to be cut away. Finding blood on Lincoln's left shoulder but no source, Leale now felt through the President's hair and "soon discovered a large firm clot of blood" behind the left ear. The clot, "which was firmly matted with the hair, I removed, and passed the little finger of my left hand directly through the perfectly smooth opening made by the ball.... When I removed my finger which I used as a probe, an oozing of blood followed and he soon commenced to show signs of improvement."

A second doctor, Charles Sabin Taft, also twenty-three, now arrived, half climbing, half pushed, over the box railing. Taft helped by pumping Lincoln's arms while Leale pressed down the back of the President's tongue, which was acting as a stopper to the windpipe, frantically massaged the chest over the heart, and applied mouth-to-mouth resuscitation. All at once, Lincoln's heart fluttered and his breathing began again on its own. Even so, Leale announced, there was no hope. "It is impossible for him to recover."

Dr. Leale had first put his own white handkerchief on the floor under Lincoln's head, but then, when Laura Keene was admitted to the box, he rather grudgingly gave her permission to hold the head in her lap. As smudged, melting greasepaint transformed her face from the young girl she had been playing to the middle-aged woman she was, the actress dabbed water onto the President's forehead while blood slowly spread over her yellow satin skirt. A spoonful of diluted brandy was pressed between Lincoln's lips, and he swallowed it. Word was sent to countermand the carriage called to take the President back to the White House; the closest bed would be found. A third doctor, Charles A. Gatch, had made his way into the box, and now the growing cluster of physicians was joined by a fourth, Dr. Africanus F. A. King. At a signal from Leale, King took the President's left shoulder, Taft the right, Leale the head, with Dr. Gatch and several other men from the audience bearing the rest of the body, and they all lifted in unison. Soldiers cleared a passageway through the crowd as the awkward little group inched its way out into the street.

The unconscious President could not see or hear the nightmare of despair and screaming and panic outside. Through the uproar, made madder still by the sickly glow of gaslights, a young man named Henry Safford beckoned the doctors across the street to the Petersen home, and in a few moments, Lincoln's great, slack form had been carried up the front steps of a narrow, three-story house and into a small, shabby bedroom at the back of the hallway. The room was awash with the heavy, sweet smell of blooming lilacs from outside the open windows. A single gas jet hissed out its dim, greenish light. The walnut cottage bed was too short. Leale at first tried to break off the foot rail. Failing, he arranged Lincoln diagonally, his head next to the door and his feet sticking out the opposite side.

Charles Augustus Leale was the first doctor to reach Lincoln. Only two months out of medical school, he had specialized in the heart, the lungs, and gunshot wounds, and was a chief surgeon in an army hospital. Leale directed that Lincoln be carried from the theater and across Tenth Street to the house *(below)* of a German tailor named Petersen.

At about 10 o'clock, while sitting in the front parlor reading, I heard a commotion in front of the house. Going to the window I saw the provost guard running up and down the street as though looking for someone, and the audience rushing out of the building. Everybody seemed panic stricken, and I raised the window and sang out, asking of those below what was the matter, and they replied that the President had been shot.

I was soon down at the door and across the street and edging my way through the crowd half way into the theater, and finding it impossible to go further, as everyone acted crazy or mad, I retreated to the steps of the house, and some five minutes later when the bearers of the body had brought him nearly across the street one of the leaders asked: "Where can we take him?" As there was no response from any other house I cried out: "Bring him in here." On either side of the house the residents, I had understood, were secessionists or not very loyal.... The family with whom I lived was named Peterson [sic]. They were worthy Germans, who were away at the time.... It was a three-story brick house, with two parlors on one side of the hall and a stairway on the other. The two parlor doors were locked, and without hesitation Lincoln was taken up the steps and carried through the hall to a light, airy bedroom at the rear.... There was an actor named Mathews who a few months before the assassination had occupied the same bedroom into which Lincoln was taken, and in this room Booth, the assassin, had visited him, and it is thought he had endeavored to prevail on Mathews to take part in the murderous plot he was arranging.

Lincoln was carried from Ford's Theatre onto Tenth Street. The artist who painted this scene had been sketching on his balcony across the street when the dramatic sight presented itself.

No one was monitoring who could enter the house, or even the room, and at first it was crowded with people. Finally, soldiers cleared everybody out but the doctors. Mary Lincoln made her arrival, crying, "Where is my husband? Where is he?" and then throwing herself upon him. She was asked to leave as well. A locked parlor door in the front of the house was broken down; it would become Mrs. Lincoln's sanctuary during the night ahead. From a second adjoining parlor, Secretary Stanton set up a communications post from which to run the now presidentless country, interview eyewitnesses, and dispatch soldiers in a web around Washington to try to trap the assassins. Havoc still reigned. Major Rathbone lay in the hallway, unconscious from loss of blood. Clara Harris tried to tend the wailing, frantic Mary Lincoln and save the life of her fiancé at the same time. Official Washington had begun to appear, all wanting access to the tiny room—Cabinet members, department heads, senators, army officers, friends, close associates, Lincoln's son Robert.

Staying in command until the arrival of Surgeon General Joseph K. Barnes and the Lincoln family physician, Dr. Robert King Stone, Dr. Leale had time to undress his patient, examine him thoroughly, order bottles of hot water prepared and mustard plasters made. Leale was annoyed when Dr. Taft tried brandy again. He didn't stop him, but as he said he knew would happen, the President almost strangled. Dr. Stone called for the same remedy later, with the same result.

There would be other doctors during the night, ten of them—Doctors Abbott, Crane, Curtis, Ford, Hall, Notson, Lieberman, May, Todd, and Woodward. Sixteen men of medicine in all would tend Lincoln during his hours of dying, would take his pulse and inspect his bulging eye, listen to his hoarse breathing, shake their heads and check their watches, and touch the President wherever they could, make contact in some way. Dr. Barnes probed the wound. Dr. King took notes. Dr. Abbott kept a medical chart, recording pulse and breathing rate and other vital signs. Thirty-three entries in all were made as Lincoln slowly slipped away.

"About once an hour," Gideon Welles noted, "Mrs. Lincoln would repair to the bedside of her dying husband and with lamentation and tears remain until overcome by emotion." At one point during the long night, when Lincoln's breathing had developed a frightening rattle, she let out a "piercing cry," wrote Leale, "and fell fainting to the floor. Secretary Stanton, hearing her cry, came in and called out loudly 'Take that woman out and do not let her in again.'" Managing to remain in the room throughout the night was Senator Charles Sumner, who had earlier forced his way in despite Surgeon General Barnes's insistence that he was not needed. All night long this great "conscience of the Senate," who had grown so close to Lincoln that they played like boys together, sat by the blood-stained bed holding Lincoln's hand and weeping. The President's breathing sounded to him "almost like a melody."

No testimony had yet been given on the second attack of the evening. For, almost at the very same instant that Booth's bullet penetrated President Lincoln's brain, another assassin was slashing away with a knife at the neck of Secretary of State Seward.

Over a week earlier, Seward had been badly hurt in a carriage accident, his arm broken, his jaw fractured on both sides, and his head suffering a bad concussion. Returning from Richmond on April 9, Lincoln had rushed to the secretary's side, stretched himself out on Seward's bed with his face right next to his closest friend in government, and given Seward a blow-by-blow account of events on the front. "Seward [was] listening with interest," wrote his son Frederick, "but [was] unable to utter a word without pain." On the night of Lincoln's attack, Seward lay half asleep in a third-floor bedroom in his home near the White House, his cracked jaw and broken arm being tended by his young daughter Fanny and George T. Robinson, a soldier recuperating from an injury, who had been temporarily assigned to nursing duty. At 10:10 p.m. Booth's most trusted follower, the former army nurse Lewis Paine, appeared at Seward's front door and thrust himself past William Bell, a black servant, saying he had medicine to deliver in person to the secretary of state. Frederick, who was the assistant secretary of state, was awakened and sleepily met the strapping Paine on the staircase, blocking his way. Suddenly, Paine pulled a gun, and when it wouldn't fire he smashed young Seward with its butt, cracking his skull in two places and exposing the brain. Reaching the secretary of state's room, Paine knifed Robinson in the forehead, dashed him to the floor, punched Fanny out of the way and set upon the elder Seward, slicing each side of his neck and opening up his cheek so deeply that his tongue showed through. Only the strange metal jaw-brace Seward was wearing prevented

Above: The Sewards, father and son, secretary of state and assistant secretary of state, respectively, were both attacked and almost killed by Lewis Paine *(below).* Frederick Seward's sister, Fanny *(right),* was tending her father when Paine entered the bedroom and knocked her to the floor.

It was the ninth day since the carriage accident in which my father had been injured, and he still lay helpless and suffering.... The family took turns in watching at his bedside, and two invalid soldiers were sent to assist in his care....

Night came, and about ten o'clock...the gaslights were turned low, and all was quiet....

There seemed nothing unusual...when a tall, well dressed, but unknown man presented himself below and, informing the servant he had brought a message from the doctor, was allowed to come up the stairs.

Hearing the noise of footsteps in the hall, I came out and met him....

Suddenly turning...he sprang up and forward, having drawn a Navy revolver, which he levelled, with a muttered oath, at my head, and pulled the trigger.

And now, in swift succession, like the scenes of some hideous dream, came the bloody incidents of the night, — of the pistol missing fire, of the struggle in the dimly lighted hall, between the armed man and the unarmed one, — of the blows which broke the pistol of the one, and fractured the skull of the other, — of the bursting in of the door, — of the mad rush of the assassin to the bedside, and his savage slashing, with a bowie knife, at the face and throat of the helpless Secretary, instantly reddening the white bandages with streams of blood, — of the screams of the daughter for help, — of the attempt of the invalid soldier nurse to drag the assailant from his victim, receiving sharp wounds himself in return, — of the noise made by the awaking household, inspiring the assassin with hasty impulse to escape, leaving his work done or undone, of his frantic rush down the stairs, cutting and slashing at all whom he found in his way, wounding one in the face, and stabbing another in the back, — of his escape through the open doorway, — and his flight on horseback down the avenue.

Five minutes later, the aroused household were gazing horrified at the bleeding faces and figures in their midst, were lifting the insensible form of the Secretary from a pool of blood, — and sending for surgical help.

---

the attack from being fatal. The sharp blade of Paine's knife was cold as it slid through his face, Seward recalled later, and the torrents of blood washing down him freely felt like rain. There were more struggles, more stabbings, but in a moment Paine was gone, down the stairs again, slashing at whoever got in his way, calling out, "I am mad! I am mad!" and disappearing into the night. For a while Seward lay still, eyes closed. Those attending him listened for a heartbeat. All at once Seward opened his eyes and said, "I am not dead, send for a surgeon, send for the police, close the house!"

Seward would live. But as morning approached at the Petersen house, with a cold rain beginning to fall and huge crowds gathering outside along Pennsylvania Avenue, for Lincoln the end was not far off. Gideon Welles, who had remained most of the night beside Lincoln's bed, described the approaching conclusion: "The giant sufferer lay extended diagonally across the bed. He had been stripped of his clothes. His large arms, which were occasionally exposed, were of a size which one would scarce have expected from his spare appearance. His slow, full respiration lifted the clothes with each breath that he took. His features were calm and striking. I had never seen them appear to better advantage than for the first hour, perhaps, that I was there. After that, his right eye began to swell and that part of his face became discolored."

Dr. King, the young English obstetrician who had helped in the theater box, made notes. "Jerking" he called Lincoln's breathing at 6:25 a.m. Fifteen minutes later "the expiration prolonged and groaning—a deep, softly sonorous cooing sound at the end of each expiration." And in five more minutes "respiration uneasy and grunting, lower jaw relaxed." Then "a minute without breath—face growing dark." At about 6:45 a.m., as death approached, cool, collected Robert Lincoln finally broke down—throwing himself against Charles Sumner's shoulder and sobbing openly.

James Tanner, who had lost both his legs at the Second Battle of Bull Run, was a boarder in the house next door. A stenographer, Tanner had been called upon to take down the testimony of eyewitnesses throughout the night. Now, as morning came, the peg-legged little man entered the death room and later described Lincoln's end. "His stertorous breathing subsided a couple of minutes after seven o'clock. From then til the end only the gentle rise and fall of his bosom gave indication that life remained. The Surgeon General was near the head of the bed. Sometimes sitting on the edge, his finger on the pulse of the dying man. Occasionally he put his ear down to catch the lessening beats of his heart....The first indication that the dreaded end had come was at twenty-two minutes past seven, when the Surgeon General gently crossed the pulseless hands of Lincoln across the motionless breast and rose to his feet. The Reverend Dr. Gurley stepped forward and lifting his hands began 'Our Father and our God.'...Mr. Stanton raised his head, the tears streaming down his face. A more agonized expression I never saw on a human countenance."

Then, as a look of "unspeakable peace" settled on Lincoln's countenance, the stern, efficient secretary of war, never known for his poetry, whispered, "Now he belongs to the ages."

DIFFERENT RECORDS OF THE NIGHT OF DYING

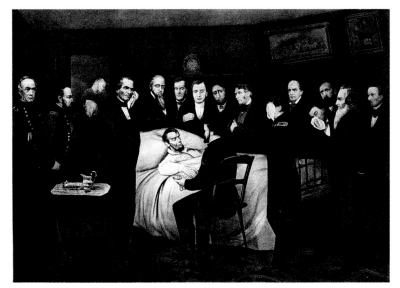

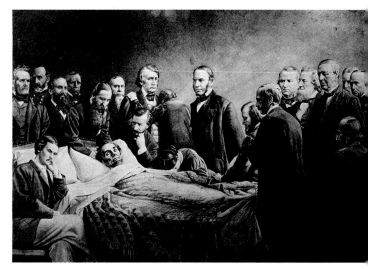

Published by Currier & Ives, this scene of the moment of death includes the new chief justice of the United States, Salmon P. Chase *(fifth from right)*, who never even showed up that night.

The photographer Alexander Gardner copyrighted this scene, which features the Reverend Phineas D. Gurley standing at the center. Twice during the night Gurley said prayers while everyone knelt.

In *The Death of Lincoln,* an oil painting by Alonzo Chappel, the nine-by-sixteen-foot room has grown and now holds forty-seven mourners, all of whom were actually there at one time or another during the night.

Secretaries Stanton and Welles look on at far left, while
Gurley prays and Andrew Johnson holds Lincoln's hand.
The absent Chase is shown here too *(second from right)*.

In another Currier & Ives print subtitled "The Nation's Martyr,"
Robert Lincoln weeps, Tad, actually not present, buries his face
in his mother's skirts, and Clara Harris mourns just behind.

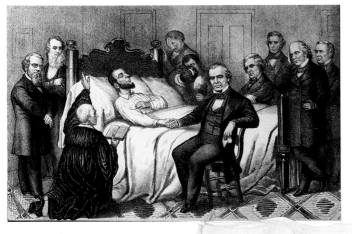

The final contents of Lincoln's pockets

For years afterward, the long night of dying was recorded over and over again. Artists crammed the room with three or four times as many doctors, family members, and dignitaries as could possibly have fitted into the small room at one time. A few of those depicted were never present at all that night. All five of the renditions of the deathbed scene presented here show Vice President Andrew Johnson keeping vigil. Actually, Johnson was in the room for only a few minutes and was quickly removed when Mrs. Lincoln, who hated him, made one of her frequent, emotional entrances. The print directly above shows Tad with his mother at bedside. Mary Lincoln cried out to her comatose husband, "Oh, that my Taddy might see his father before he dies!"; but the frantic Tad was back at the White House, finally put to bed by one of the doormen.

Mementos from that night were saved as important objects. Among these were the contents of Lincoln's pockets, including a pocketknife, a linen handkerchief, a sleeve button, a fancy watch fob, two pairs of spectacles, a tiny pencil, and a leather wallet *(left)*. The wallet contained a Confederate five-dollar bill and nine old newspaper clippings—two pieces of praise and five others dealing with some of the issues that were on Lincoln's mind during his final months. They were the clippings of a politician who was partial to humor and enthralled with power in its many guises.

VOICES FROM THE SAD MORNING

Many in the city of Washington awakening that Saturday morning were not aware of the barbarous acts committed in their midst during the night. Even though their streets had echoed with the din of disaster, some had slept right through it and peacefully stirred into the morning, expecting a normal spring day ahead. Noah Brooks, who was about to replace John Nicolay as Lincoln's chief secretary and had stayed home Friday night, sleeping off a "violent cold," had heard a commotion but had drifted quickly back to sleep. Upon getting the terrible news, Brooks dressed and went out and found "an extraordinary spectacle" in the drizzly streets.

They were suddenly crowded with people — men, women, and children thronging the pavements and darkening the thoroughfares. It seemed as if everybody was in tears.... Men and women who were strangers accosted one another.... The President still lived, but at half-past seven o'clock in the morning the tolling of the bells announced to the lamenting people that he had ceased to breathe.... Instantly flags were raised at half-mast all over the city.... Wandering aimlessly up F Street towards Ford's Theatre, we met a tragical procession. It was headed by a group of army officers walking bareheaded, and behind them, carried tenderly by a company of soldiers, was the bier of the dead President, covered with the flag of the Union, and accompanied by an escort of soldiers who had been on duty at the house where Lincoln died. As the little cortège passed down the street to the White House, every head was uncovered, and the profound silence which prevailed was broken only by sobs and by the sound of the measured tread of those who bore the martyred President back to the house which he had so lately quitted full of life, hope, and courage.

Benjamin B. French had been one of the many who had stood by the "bed of death." It took him a year to summon the will to write down all he had seen. Here French remembered

how my hand was rung by Mrs. Lincoln as she sat on a sofa in an adjoining room... how, at the request of the family, I got into the President's carriage and rode to Secy.

Welles's after Mrs. Welles — how I waited there until she could rise from her sickbed, dress, and take a little refreshment — how we rode to the White House, where I remained to take charge of it & see that it was placed in proper care, while the carriage bore Mrs. Welles to Mr. Peterson's [sic] in 10th St. where the President lay — how I returned to my home and breakfasted — how, just as I had finished, the bells commenced tolling — how I returned to the President's house in time to accompany the remains in & to the guestchamber where they were deposited — how I saw them taken from the box in which they were enclosed, all limp and warm, and laid upon the floor, and then stretched upon the cooling board.

Ten minutes after Lincoln's death, William M. Stewart, senator from Nevada, happened on Senator Solomon Foot, "the grand old gray-haired statesman from Vermont, who was chairman of the Republican caucus and master of ceremonies in the Senate." Foot was hailing a carriage in front of Willard's Hotel. In his reminiscences, Stewart told how Foot

put his hand on my shoulder as the news of the President's death reached us... and said "We must get the Chief Justice at once and swear in the Vice-President. It will not do in times like these to be without a President."... Mr. Chase was in his library, pacing back and forth, in deep thought. We explained our business, and he got into the vehicle with us, and went to the... Kirkwood House.... I sprang out, went to the desk, and asked the clerk what room the Vice-President occupied. "I will send up your card," he said. "No, you won't," I said. "I'll go up myself."... A Negro boy showed us the room, and I rapped on the door. There was no answer. I rapped again and again. Finally I kicked the door, and made a very loud noise. Then a voice growled: "Who's there?"... After some little delay Johnson opened the door and we entered. The Vice-President was in his bare feet and only partially dressed.... Chief Justice Chase said very solemnly: "The President has been assassinated. He died this morning. I have come to administer the oath of office to you." Johnson seemed dazed at first. Then he jumped up, thrust

The silver Nelaton probe used to explore Lincoln's wound during his night of dying never dislodged the flattened bullet, which finally fell from Lincoln's brain into a basin during the autopsy.

A typical badge of mourning. Like the tens of thousands of little personal statements of loss that appeared all through the North, this one was made from a tiny tintype copy of one of Brady's finest Lincoln portraits.

his right arm up as far as he could reach, and said in a thick, gruff, hoarse voice: "I'm ready." The Chief Justice administered the oath. Johnson—President Johnson—went back to his bedroom, and we retired.

Lincoln's intimate friend Orville Browning was at the White House that sad April morning and wrote down in his diary what he witnessed.

The corpse was laid in the room on the North side of the second story, opposite Mrs. Lincoln's room. His eyes were both very much protruded—the right one most—and very black and puffy underneath. No other disfiguration. The skull was opened under the supervision of Surgeon Genl Barnes and Dr Stone, and the ball removed. It was a Derringer [sic] ball, much flattened on both sides. It entered at the base of the brain an inch and a half or two inches back of the left ear, and ranging upward and transversely in the direction of the right eye, lodged in the brain about two thirds of the way from where it entered to the front. He never had a moment's consciousness after he was shot.

While tending Mary Lincoln, Mrs. Welles asked, "Is there no one, Mrs. Lincoln, that you desire to have with you in this terrible affliction?" and Mary answered, "Yes, send for Elizabeth Keckley." The black seamstress was not located until eleven o'clock on Saturday morning.

I was quickly shown to Mrs. Lincoln's room, and on entering, saw Mrs. L. tossing uneasily about upon a bed.... She was nearly exhausted with grief, and when she became a little quiet, I asked and received permission to go into the Guests' Room, where the body of the President lay in state.... Never did I enter the solemn chamber of death with such palpitating heart and trembling footsteps as I entered it that day. No common mortal had died. The Moses of my people had fallen in the hour of his triumph.... When I entered the room, the members of the Cabinet and many distinguished officers of the army... made room for me, and, approaching the body, I lifted the white cloth from the white face of the man that I had worshipped as an idol—looked upon as a

demi-god. Notwithstanding the violence of the death of the President, there was something beautiful as well as grandly solemn in the expression of the placid face. There lurked the sweetness and gentleness of childhood, and the stately grandeur of god-like intellect.... Returning to Mrs. Lincoln's room, I found her in a new paroxysm of grief.... [L]ittle Tad was crouched at the foot of the bed with a world of agony in his young face.... I bathed Mrs. Lincoln's head with cold water, and soothed the terrible tornado as best I could.

Six physicians tended Lincoln's body in the White House and assisted in the post-mortem. Edward Curtis, a young assistant surgeon in the medical corps, was one of them. Here, in a letter to his mother written a week later, Curtis describes the scene.

A week ago today Dr. Woodward and myself were ordered by the surgeon general to make a post-mortem examination, in his presence, on the body of the President. Accordingly, at 11 o'clock we assembled at the White House in the room where the body lay.... It contained but little furniture: a large, heavily-curtained bed, a sofa or two, bureau, wardrobe and chairs comprised all there was. Seated around the room were several general officers and some civilians, silent or conversing in whispers, and to one side, stretched upon a rough framework of boards and covered only with sheets and towels, lay, cold and immovable, what but a few hours before was the soul of a great nation.... The surgeon general was walking up and down the room when I arrived.... Dr. Woodward and I proceeded to open the head and remove the brain down to the track of the ball.... Not finding it readily, we proceeded to remove the entire brain, when, as I was lifting the latter from the cavity of the skull, suddenly the bullet dropped out through my fingers and fell, breaking the solemn silence of the room with its clatter, into an empty basin that was standing beneath. There it lay upon the white china, a little black mass no bigger than the end of my finger—dull, motionless and harmless, yet the cause of such mighty changes in the world's history as we may perhaps never realize.

‘‘NOW HE BELONGS TO THE AGES’’

Made two months before Lincoln's death by
sculptor Clark Mills, this mask, John Hay said,
showed "the peace that passeth understanding."

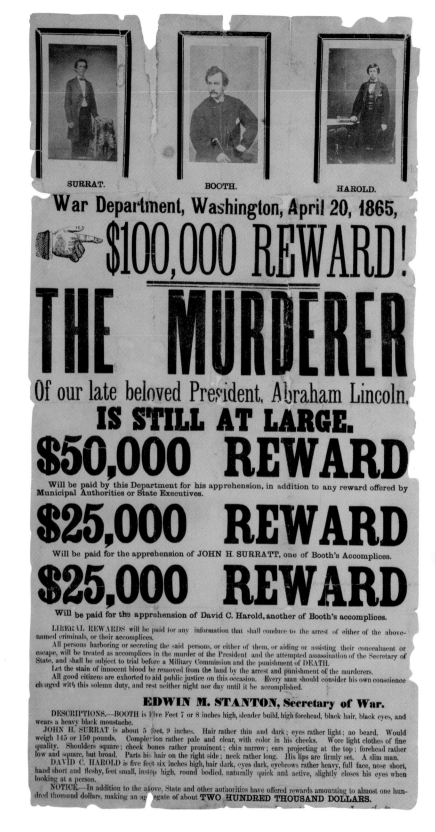

SURRAT.   BOOTH.   HAROLD.

War Department, Washington, April 20, 1865,

$100,000 REWARD!

THE MURDERER

Of our late beloved President, Abraham Lincoln,

IS STILL AT LARGE.

$50,000 REWARD

Will be paid by this Department for his apprehension, in addition to any reward offered by Municipal Authorities or State Executives.

$25,000 REWARD

Will be paid for the apprehension of JOHN H. SURRATT, one of Booth's Accomplices.

$25,000 REWARD

Will be paid for the apprehension of David C. Harold, another of Booth's accomplices.

LIBERAL REWARDS will be paid for any information that shall conduce to the arrest of either of the above-named criminals, or their accomplices.

All persons harboring or secreting the said persons, or either of them, or aiding or assisting their concealment or escape, will be treated as accomplices in the murder of the President and the attempted assassination of the Secretary of State, and shall be subject to trial before a Military Commission and the punishment of DEATH.

Let the stain of innocent blood be removed from the land by the arrest and punishment of the murderers.

All good citizens are exhorted to aid public justice on this occasion. Every man should consider his own conscience charged with this solemn duty, and rest neither night nor day until it be accomplished.

EDWIN M. STANTON, Secretary of War.

DESCRIPTIONS.—BOOTH is Five Feet 7 or 8 inches high, slender build, high forehead, black hair, black eyes, and wears a heavy black moustache.

JOHN H. SURRAT is about 5 feet, 9 inches. Hair rather thin and dark; eyes rather light; no beard. Would weigh 145 or 150 pounds. Complexion rather pale and clear, with color in his cheeks. Wore light clothes of fine quality. Shoulders square; cheek bones rather prominent; chin narrow; ears projecting at the top; forehead rather low and square, but broad. Parts his hair on the right side; neck rather long. A slim man.

DAVID C. HAROLD is five feet six inches high, hair dark, eyes dark, eyebrows rather heavy, full face, nose short, hand short and fleshy, feet small, instep high, round bodied, naturally quick and active, slightly closes his eyes when looking at a person.

NOTICE.—In addition to the above, State and other authorities have offered rewards amounting to almost one hundred thousand dollars, making an aggregate of about TWO HUNDRED THOUSAND DOLLARS.

A fortune in reward money was offered to whoever could catch the conspirators, leading thousands of soldiers and detectives and ordinary citizens to drop everything and join in the search.

Thomas A. Jones, a Confederate mail agent on the Maryland side of the Potomac who sheltered Booth and Herold for six days in a pine woods, later told his story.
I heard of the murder of President Lincoln on Saturday afternoon, April 15, 1865. Two federal officers brought me the news. The next day a young man came to me from Samuel Cox's house...and said...that Booth and his companion were secreted in a thicket of dense pines about a mile from the house. Cox said I must get Booth and his companion, whom I afterward learned was Herold, across the river. I consented, and after getting instructions from Cox how to approach the parties, which were to give two sharp whistles at intervals of some seconds as I entered the pines, I started out to find their hiding place.... Booth...was lying on the ground wrapt in a blanket. A crutch was lying by his side and his foot was bandaged. His face was pallid and drawn, as if he was worn with pain and anxiety. He was dressed, as well as I can now recollect, in dark clothes. He was abrupt in his questioning, and about the first sentence he uttered was to inquire what people had to say of his crime. He asked me to get him some newspapers, which I did. He frankly admitted that he was the murderer of the president and expressed no regret for the act. We then discussed ways and means of getting himself and Herold across the river, and where he could get necessary medical attention. As the country was overrun with federal soldiers, it was decided that Booth was to remain where he was until a more favorable opportunity for escape was presented. Had I desired it, I could have got $100,000 for betraying Booth, as that amount was offered in my presence by an officer of the federal government. I was then a ruined man financially, but the thought of betraying him never once entered my mind for a single instant.

Davie Herold was "more like a boy than a man," said his former employer Francis Walsh, "easily persuaded and led." Where his mentor John Wilkes Booth led him was to a burning barn and an early end. "This brave boy with me," Booth had said in his diary's last entry, "who often prays...with a true and sincere heart, was it a crime in him?" Once surrounded in the Garrett tobacco barn, Booth yelled out, "Cap there is a man in here who wants to surrender mighty bad." After urging Herold to give himself up, Booth shouted once again: "I declare before my Maker that this man here is innocent of any crime whatever."

Red-haired, prematurely bald Samuel Alexander Mudd claimed that he did not recognize Booth on the morning of April 15. He cut off Booth's left boot, set his broken leg, and sent him off with a hand-made pair of crutches.

Like everything else in Booth's life, his final acts were pure melodrama. "I passed all...pickets," he bragged to his diary after his deadly pistol shot and cry of triumph. "Rode sixty miles that night, with the bone of my leg tearing the flesh at every jump."

Arriving an hour ahead of the official blockade of the city, Booth had convinced Sergeant Silas T. Cobb to let him pass over the Navy Yard Bridge despite the 9:00 p.m. curfew. Just minutes behind him was the idiot accomplice Davie Herold, using the alias of Smith. United in Maryland, Booth and Herold made a midnight stop at Lloyd's Tavern, Surratsville, to pick up whiskey and a rifle. Mary Surratt had warned John Lloyd that very morning that these would be needed soon. Though Lloyd was dead drunk, he remembered that the men bragged about having killed Lincoln. The two headed off next, by moonlight, to get Booth medical attention. Dr. Samuel A. Mudd had met Booth before, but may have failed to recognize the now-bearded man introduced to him as Mr. "Tyson" or "Tyser." The doctor as of yet knew nothing of the assassination, and later testified that even when he saw "Tyson's" fake whiskers removed and watched a very real black mustache carefully shaved off with Mudd's own razor and soap, he still did not know it was Booth. Nor did he notice the words "J. Wilkes" written inside the high leather boot which he cut away from the man's left foot in order to treat the fractured leg.

Somehow, after leaving Mudd's place on Saturday afternoon, and after getting lost in the swamps and then paying a black man named Swann to rescue them, Booth and Herold found their fate in the hands of a crusty, pro-Southern mail-runner named Thomas A. Jones.

For six long rainy days and five nights, Booth and Herold hid out in the scrubland behind Jones's brother's farm, as soldiers and policemen, part of a massive manhunt, swarmed the area, eager for reward money, passing once within 200 yards of them. I have been "hunted like a dog through swamps and woods," wrote Booth in his diary late in the week. "[W]et, cold, and starving, with every man's hand against me, I am...in despair." At one point, lest their whinnying be heard, it was decided to shoot the two horses and sink them in the bog; when the horses' bodies failed to submerge, and great birds of carrion swarmed in over the carcasses, all three men feared imminent discovery and capture.

Each day, Jones brought the men food and newspapers. Booth devoured both—becoming alternately proud and furious at descriptions of his deeds. "I struck boldly, not as the papers say," he lashed back in his diary. "Our country owed all our troubles to [Lincoln], and God simply made me the instrument of his punishment." Booth was desperate to cross into Virginia, but there was the mounting question of whether his leg would hold out; it "had become terribly swollen and infected," noted Jones, all black and painful to the touch.

On Friday night, April 21, one week after the assassination, Jones quietly led the two men to a flat-bottomed fishing boat, sold it to them for eighteen dollars, and then explained how to make the crossing through the inky, cold darkness over a flood tide that had transformed the lazy river into something strangely fierce.

WASHINGTON BIDS FAREWELL

The men of Lincoln's government were determined that the farewell to their fallen chief would be an event never before equaled in the United States. Work to make it so started immediately. Benjamin B. French, the commissioner of public buildings, designed a magnificent, eleven-foot-high catafalque—the "Temple of Death," it was called—which was constructed in the East Room. To fit it in, one of the giant chandeliers had to be removed; the other two were shrouded in black bags. When Lincoln's body was brought downstairs Monday evening, the men who carried his coffin took off their shoes so that as they passed Mrs. Lincoln's bedroom door, there would be no hint of what was happening. On Tuesday morning Lincoln's body went

The "Temple of Death" sat on a higher platform than this artist depicted; and he included the widow, seated

Frank Leslie's Illustrated put an engraving of the murder on its front page.

Members of the Union Army's Invalid Corps wore pale blue uniforms and were assigned special duties for the funeral.

beneath the black-bagged chandelier, although she was actually never present.

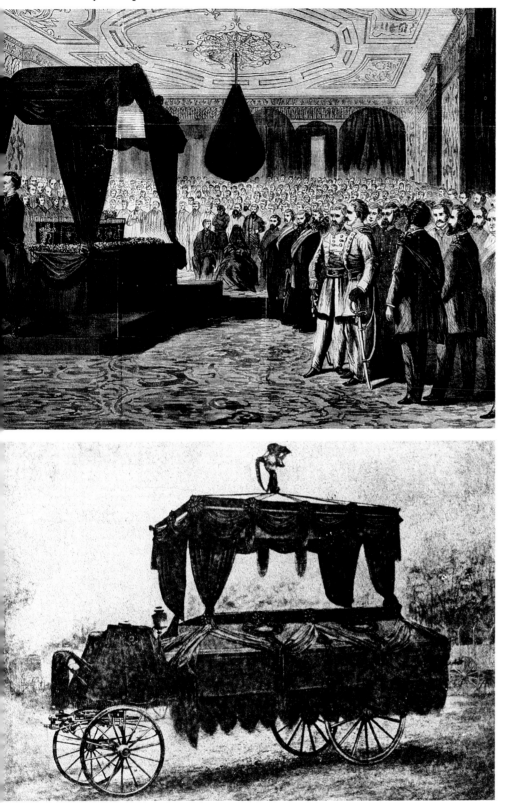

Although its canopy was topped by a gilt eagle in mourning, the Washington hearse looked very much like a decorated wagon.

Mary Lincoln's seamstress, Elizabeth Keckley, the best friend she had left in the world, was a witness to little Tad's devotion to his mother.

Tad's grief at his father's death was as great as the grief of his mother, but her terrible outbursts awed the boy into silence. Sometimes he would throw his arms around her neck, and exclaim, between his broken sobs, "Don't cry so, Mamma! don't cry, or you will make me cry, too! You will break my heart."

Mrs. Lincoln could not bear to hear Tad cry, and when he would plead to her not to break his heart, she would calm herself with a great effort, and clasp her child in her arms.

Every room in the White House was darkened, and every one spoke in subdued tones, and moved about with muffled tread. The very atmosphere breathed of the great sorrow which weighed so heavily upon each heart. Mrs. Lincoln never left her room, and while the body of her husband was being borne in solemn state from the Atlantic to the broad prairies of the West, she was weeping with her fatherless children in her private chamber. She denied admittance to almost every one, and I was her only companion, except her children, in the days of her great sorrow. . . .

Tad had been petted by his father, but petting could not spoil such a manly nature as his. He seemed to realize that he was the son of a President — to realize it in its loftiest and noblest sense. One morning, while being dressed, he looked up at his nurse, and said: "Pa is dead. I can hardly believe that I shall never see him again. I must learn to take care of myself now." He looked thoughtful a moment, then added, "Yes, Pa is dead, and I am only Tad Lincoln now, little Tad, like other little boys. I am not a President's son now. I won't have many presents any more. Well, I will try and be a good boy, and will hope to go some day to Pa and brother Willie, in heaven."

on view. Wednesday was the funeral day. A series of levels had been constructed in the East Room, making it into an amphitheater so that all who attended, even those far in the back, could see the proceedings. General Grant sat alone at the head of the coffin. Robert Lincoln sat at the foot, along with Springfield brothers-in-law Ninian Edwards and Clark M. Smith. President Johnson, ex–Vice President Hamlin, and the members of the Cabinet stood at the east side of the coffin. In the entire gathering of six hundred invited guests, only seven women were present—the wives of Stanton, Welles, Usher, and Dennison,

When the hearse reached the Capitol, the end of the funeral procession was just passing these spectators at the Treasury Building.

370

General Grant wore mourning black on his left arm.

two Chase daughters, and a nurse. Mrs. Lincoln stayed upstairs, unable to attend. Four ministers conducted the service, and at the very same time, all over the country, twenty-five million citizens were attending similar memorial services in their own churches. After the service, an enormous procession, arranged by Ward Hill Lamon, wound through Washington. Recuperating, William Seward watched from his house on Lafayette Square. At first no one had dared tell him that Lincoln was dead, but on Sunday he had spotted from his window flags at half mast, and knew what they meant. When the fourteen-foot-long hearse bearing Lincoln's body arrived at the Capitol, its six gray horses halted in front of the east portico and twelve Veteran Reserve Corps sergeants carefully lifted the coffin onto their shoulders and bore it up the great stairs and into the rotunda. These shoulders would be the only ones to carry Lincoln through the ten cities before Springfield where additional funerals had been planned. All day Thursday the public streamed past the open coffin. Noah Brooks climbed the winding stairs that led to the dome and later described what he had seen. "From that lofty point, the sight was weird and memorable. Directly beneath me lay the casket in which the dead President lay at full length, far, far below; and, like black atoms moving over a sheet of gray paper, the slow-moving mourners, seen from a perpendicular above them, crept silently in two dark lines across the pavement of the rotunda, forming an ellipse around the coffin and joining as they advanced toward the eastern portal and disappeared."

General Sherman's black crepe armband was more prominent.

Up Pennsylvania Avenue the procession went. Here it is just approaching the hill that stretches up to the Capitol.

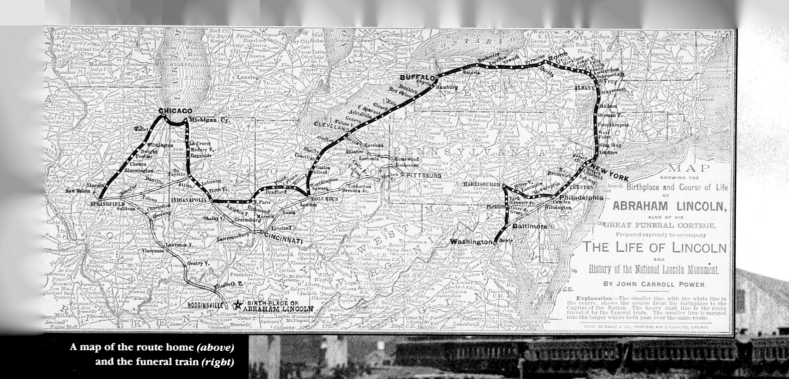

A map of the route home *(above)* and the funeral train *(right)*

At dawn on Friday, April 21—just a week after Lincoln's last awakening—his body left Washington in a nine-car funeral train with three hundred dignitaries and the casket of his son Willie aboard. Baltimore was the first stop on the 1,700-mile journey, which, except for the omission of Cincinnati, would duplicate in reverse Lincoln's trip east in 1861. Baltimore, the city where Lincoln might easily have been murdered four years earlier, where the first attack on Union troops had occurred, which had been home to John Wilkes Booth, now paid tribute to Lincoln. The city's newfangled hearse had French glass windows three-quarters of an inch thick and special cushion springs to ease the jolts. The three hundred honored travelers lunched in silence at the Eutaw House, and, though it rained hard, ten thousand people saw Lincoln before the schedule demanded the train move on. In Harrisburg, thunder and lightning filled the skies during the hectic nighttime viewing, and Lincoln's face had to be chalked and his body dusted the next morning. Reporter George Alfred Townsend described to his readers how the embalming had been done: "There is no blood in the body.... He lies in sleep, but it is the sleep of marble. All that made this flesh vital, sentient and affectionate is gone forever." In Philadelphia there were riots, dresses ripped off, spectators almost crushed or trampled to death, as unruly three-mile-long lines wound through the city and overzealous police tried to keep order. One visitor wrote home, "The beloved remains are knocking the machinery of social life here into a cocked hat." Except for the hearse and its escort, new railroad cars were provided for the trip from Philadelphia to New York. The people of Trenton, New Jersey—hurt because theirs was the only state capital on the route where a funeral procession and a viewing had not been scheduled—watched, but were a bit sullen, as the train made a short stop at its station. Their hats stayed on. In Newark, though, along the path to the Hudson ferry, all hats came off out of respect, even women's bonnets.

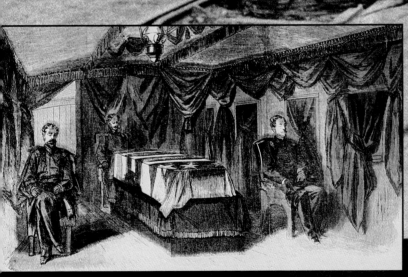

When the casket was on the train, it was draped with a large American Flag and surrounded by an honor guard.

Philadelphia's hearse moved slowly through the crowds on Broad Street. At Independence Hall, 300,000 people viewed the body.

IN NEW YORK CITY LINCOLN IS PHOTOGRAPHED IN DEATH

After the coffin had been arranged on a dais and before the crowds on the steps of City Hall were let in, New York photographer Jeremiah Gurney, Jr., took a number of photographs of Lincoln's body lying in state. An outraged Stanton ordered the plates broken and prints destroyed. And they were—all except one small print which was sent to Stanton, who, fearful of Mary Lincoln, secretly kept it among his papers. His son, Lewis, found the print twenty-two years later and mailed it to John Nicolay, thinking he and Hay might use it in their ten-volume life of Lincoln. They didn't, and the print did not surface again until 1953, when a fifteen-year-old boy found it secreted in the Nicolay papers at the Illinois State Historical Library. Below and at far right are a series of telegrams between Washington & New York that supposedly led to the destruction of the death pictures.

TELEGRAMS KILL A PICTURE

Washington City,
April 25, 1865 — 11:40 p.m.

Brigadier-General Townsend,
Adjutant-General, New York:

I see by the New York papers this evening that a photograph of the corpse...was allowed to be taken yesterday in New York. I cannot sufficiently express my surprise and disapproval of such an act while the body was in your charge. You will report what officers of the funeral escort were or ought to have been on duty at the time this was done, and immediately relieve them.... You will also direct the provost-marshall to go to the photographer, seize and destroy the plates and any pictures or engravings that may have been made, and consider yourself responsible if the offense is repeated.

Edwin M. Stanton,
Secretary of War.

In New York City, crowds gather on the steps of City Hall, awaiting the arrival of the body.

Inside City Hall, before the viewing begins, the open coffin was photographed. Rear Admiral Charles H. Davis stands at the head of the coffin, Brigadier-General E. D. Townsend guards the foot. This is the only picture of Lincoln in death that was preserved.

Albany, N.Y.,
April 26, 1865
(Received 10:40 a.m.)

Hon. E. M. Stanton,
Secretary of War:

Your dispatch of this date is received. The photograph was taken when I was present.... I have telegraphed General Dix your orders about seizing the plates. To whom shall I turn over the special charge given me in order to execute your instructions to relieve the officer responsible...?

E. D. Townsend,
Assistant Adjutant-General.

Washington City,
April 26, 1865 — 12:30 p.m.

Brig. Gen. E. D. Townsend,

...You being in charge, and present at the time, the sole responsibility rests upon you; but having no other officer...that can relieve you and take your place you will continue in charge of the remains under your instructions until they are finally interred....

Edwin M. Stanton,
Secretary of War.

Albany, N.Y.,
April 26, 1865

Hon E. M. Stanton:

General Dix, who is here, suggests that I should explain to you how the photograph was taken. The remains had just been arranged in state in the City Hall, at the head of the stairway, where the people would ascend on one side and descend on the other.... The photographer was in a gallery twenty feet higher than the body, and at least forty distant from it. Admiral Davis stood at the head and I at the foot of the coffin. No-one else was in view. The effect of the picture would be general, taking in the whole scene, but not giving the features of the corpse.

E. D. Townsend.

120,000 PEOPLE MARCH IN THE COUNTRY'S LARGEST CITY

IMPORTED SADDLERY

From City Hall, the procession headed up Broadway to Fourteenth Street, then over to Fifth Avenue, up Fifth to Thirty-fourth Street, and then across to Ninth Avenue and the depot. Windows along the route rented for up to $100 a person. At first, it was decided, Negroes would not be allowed to march, but an order from Washington countermanded that. A black contingent brought up the rear, but by the time its members started out in the almost four-hour-long procession, the funeral train had already departed the city. According to accounts by reporters, Lincoln's lips looked glued together, his jaw had fallen, and his face had turned black. The reporters were sure that New York would be the last of the open-coffin funerals; after this, the coffin lid would just have to be kept screwed down.

IN THE MIDDLE OF THE FUNERAL TRIP, THE ASSASSIN IS CORNERED AND KILLED

John Wilkes Booth had become the century's most heinous criminal. "Do recognize him somewhere and kill him," wrote one outraged American on the back of a *carte-de-visite* portrait *(above)*. Finally, the assassin was cornered and shot in a burning tobacco barn *(below)*.

From the time of their river departure on the night of Friday, April 21, Booth and Herold had had nothing but trouble. Their boat had been swept off course and it had taken them another full day to get across into Virginia; they had been forced to sleep in a black family's barn and to hire a man named Rollins to take them across the Rappahannock; they had been seen by too many witnesses, and all the while Booth's foot was becoming increasingly swollen and painful. Finally, on Tuesday night they ended up in a tobacco barn in Caroline County pawning themselves off as the Boyd brothers.

Three officers each claimed credit for the capture that followed: Lt. Edward P. Doherty of the army, and Lts. Everton J. Conger and Luther Baker of the Secret Service. Early in the morning of Wednesday, April 26, they and their men surrounded their captives' hiding place, shouted out to Booth to give up, received Davie Herold with his arms raised, and then set fire to the barn to try to smoke out Booth himself. Then one of Doherty's men, a religious fanatic named Boston Corbett, heard the voice of "Providence" tell him to shoot Lincoln's murderer; he took aim and fired through a chink in the barn wall, sending a bullet through Booth's neck. As the barn fire roared higher and higher, Doherty, Conger, and Baker pulled the fatally wounded man free. "Tell mother I die for my country," Booth whispered in Conger's ear. Then they carried him up to the porch of Garrett's house, still alive but paralyzed, his hands "useless" now, he said, "useless." They gave him water to drink, turned him on his side three times, emptied out the contents of his pockets, and listened to him beg to be killed mercifully.

Two and a half hours after Corbett's shot was fired, not much earlier in the day than Lincoln himself had died, Booth the unhappy actor made his final exit.

Pulled out of the burning barn and dragged up to a porch of a Virginia farm-house *(above)*, Booth whispered, ''I did what I thought was best,'' and then died.

THE CROSS-COUNTRY FUNERAL CONTINUES

BUFFALO

Buffalo had performed a mock funeral soon after Lincoln's death, so it was a second time around for the catafalque as it edged its way through this city's crowds toward a viewing that was well planned and without incident.

CLEVELAND

The open coffin was on display again, beneath this hurriedly constructed pagoda in Cleveland's Monument Square; it was the only city along the route that offered outdoor viewing. Without steps, doors, halls, or rooms to slow them, more than ten thousand citizens an hour were accommodated.

COLUMBUS

The procession in Columbus moved slowly toward the State House. The eighth funeral, two weeks after Lincoln's death, featured a seventeen-foot-long hearse drawn by six white horses and the fire department's hook-and-ladder bearing forty-two young lady singers.

INDIANAPOLIS

It rained so hard in the capital of the state of Lincoln's boyhood that the grand procession was canceled and photographs were impossible. A procession had to be set up the next day after the funeral train's departure, using left over crowds and a fake coffin.

REMAINS OF
ABRAHAM LINCOLN
THE GREATEST MAN OF OUR CENTURY
assassinated April 14ᵗʰ 1865.

Indianapolis legend has it that during this stop there were attempts to photograph the corpse and to make a death mask. Neither result has ever turned up, but this lithograph by Indiana artist George Koch may have been made from a photograph of the dead Lincoln adorned with an Indiana laurel wreath.

CHICAGO — "HUSHED BE THE CITY.... LET THE LAKE REST."

During the Chicago visit, the funeral train rested upon a trestle that stretched out over Lake Michigan.

"He who writes this is weeping," one Illinois newspaper spoke. "He who reads it is weeping.... Hushed be the city. Hung be the heavens in black. Let the tumult of traffic cease. Let the streets be still. Let the lake rest. Let the winds be lulled, and the sun be covered up. The bells—toll them. The guns—let their melancholy boom roll out."

Thirty-six maidens in white accompanied the coffin as it passed under an arch that, along with decorations, cost $15,000.

People marched down Michigan Avenue, Lake Street, and Clark Street to Court House Square, in a procession that rivaled New York's.

Chicago citizens streamed out of the Court House after viewing Lincoln. By the time Lincoln's body reached Chicago, blackness had spread over the entire face, but constant powderings kept it presentable.

Suddenly, everything in Springfield seemed sacred. There was hardly a building there that Lincoln hadn't been in, nor a street he hadn't walked. He had touched so many people over the years. He had ridden so many miles over the very same prairie that now saw the approach of "the black train," as it parted the wildflowers, following by ten minutes a pilot engine that had preceded it all the way from Washington, to check the safety of the stretch ahead. It had been raining the night before but now the sun shone purely, lighting the ribbons of people on every road leading to Springfield, lighting the signs along the track. "Home," they said; "bear him tenderly home."

Robert would be there. Just as he had not missed the first, he would not miss the last of his father's dozen funerals. But gently he would have to leave his mother in little Tad's hands for a few days — Mary, who had not yet risen from her bed of agony, who was trying to make contact with her dead husband through bedside séances conducted by message-bearing spiritualists, who had missed the country's pageant farewell completely. Her house in Springfield, their house, was the focus of attention now. Everyone went there, drawn as if Lincoln were still alive, wanting to stand on the floor he had stood on, touch the same walls, have a picture taken out in front beside the tree he had planted a decade ago, be somehow comforted by the one house he had ever called his own.

The back parlor of the Lincoln home was draped in black for the occasion. In little more than four years, sixty-five thousand curious people had paid the house a visit, giving the long-suffering tenants a busy time.

Members of the official Congressional Committee, who had been on the train all the way from Washington, posed for a photographer in front of the Lincoln house.

Lincoln's horse, Old Bob, was brought out of pasture retirement for the day, dressed in a mourning blanket, held quiet for a photograph, and given the choice position immediately following the hearse in the last procession.

THE LARGEST PROCESSION THE WEST HAS EVER SEEN

On May 4, at 10 a.m., the last viewer was ushered out of the Hall of Representatives in the Statehouse and embalmer Charles Brown went to work, making his charge look presentable one last time, even though no more public viewings were scheduled. Time and time again during the journey, Brown had dressed Lincoln's body in a clean collar and shirt and underclothes. Those along the route who bent their heads quickly enough to peek under the closed part of the coffin observed that Lincoln was wearing "clean white gloves," the *New York Times* had said. He would have hated them. Once, after finishing a Washington receiving line in his white dress gloves, the President quoted a friend as thinking Lincoln's hands in that condition resembled "canvassed hams." Nor would he have liked the hearse chosen for his final ride; it was too elegant. As the procession

formed, though, Lincoln would have liked the fact that his old horse followed directly behind him. And he would have liked it that Robert was riding in a buggy with Lizzie Grimsley, the member of the Todd family closest to Mary, who had visited them in the White House and become such a favorite of the boys. He would have been sad that, other than Robert, his only blood relative present was John Hanks, who represented not only himself and all the Hanks family but Sarah Bush Lincoln as well, too weak to come the long distance from her Goosenest Prairie cabin. On hearing of her stepson's murder, she had sighed, "I know'd they'd kill him," and someone close to her said, "She never had no heart after that to be chirp and peart like she used to be." Lincoln would have liked the fact that Thomas Pendel, his doorman back at the White House, was in the crowd,

representing all the servants in the President's house; he had been on the train from the beginning. And Lincoln would have liked the fact that Billy the Barber was marching, but he wouldn't have liked the place in the procession assigned to him. As usual, Negroes brought up the rear. No procession in the West had ever been so large. Beneath the scorching heat of the day, it wound through Springfield and onto the country road that led to the cemetery. Music blared, singers sang, muffled drums beat out the step. There was a festive air, but mostly there was a deep, underlying sadness that pervaded everything to do with this day. There was an overpowering feeling of loss, and people had to keep a grip on themselves when the realization came over them, through the dust and music, that they would never see Abraham Lincoln again.

The mayor of St. Louis lent Springfield his city's gold-silver-and-crystal hearse, made in Philadelphia at a cost of $6,000.

Right: Springfield citizens line up in front of the Statehouse to pay their last respects to their slain neighbor inside.

THE "BLACK PAGEANT" IS FINALLY DONE

Lincoln's body was brought to a limestone receiving tomb at Oak Ridge Cemetery, a little room carved into the steep hillside on top of which a majestic monument to this man would rise. His large coffin and Willie's small one were gently placed side by side just inside the heavy iron gates and strewn with spring flowers from the gardens of his Springfield neighbors. A million Americans in eleven great cities had looked upon his face, and thirty times that many had prayed or sung for him or watched the marvelously orchestrated progress of the black pageant. Arches across the tracks, mottoes, and tableaux had greeted his engine as it huffed at twenty miles an hour across the country. Ministers with their parishioners, kneeling and singing hymns, had said goodbye all along the tracks. Over and over, hats were raised, hands held over hearts. Old men in chairs were carried close. Young girls wearing white dresses with black sashes kissed the coffin. Guns fired. Bands played. Hilltops were black with people. At night torches, bonfires, and candles lit the way west. Roses were tossed in carpets beneath the hearse's wheels. Farmers stopped in their fields and knelt as the train crossed the plains. At bridges, soldiers stood at attention, frozen in their salutes. The trees along the way were filled with people. Butchers, bricklayers, carpenters, and tailors came dressed to show who they were. Everywhere flags flew, or were draped, or occasionally were worn. Muffled drumbeats and pictures of Lincoln merged together with soft singing and tears and black cloth. How else could this life have ended? people were already beginning to ask. How else?

The last day was a hot day; umbrellas were raised all through the crowd for shade from the sun as masses of Illinois mourners gathered before the receiving tomb at Oak Ridge Cemetery and on the hillside behind.

THE AFTERMATH

Still to come:
a multiple hanging,
another son's demise,
a widow's madness,
a body that won't
stay buried, a legend
that won't stop growing.
It is over, and yet
"the great American story"
will never truly
be over.

To remember him by — on parlor tables, in the windows of homes, in shopfronts, wherever people gathered, tributes to Lincoln appeared, like this one, constructed of a black cross, a picture, and a forest of skeleton leaves arranged inside a glass dome.

TWELVE WEEKS AFTER THE ASSASSINATION, FOUR PAY THE PRICE OF INVOLVEMENT

With the death of John Wilkes Booth, the nation lost the chief object of its fury; in his place, seven men and one woman became the means of expiation. These eight had been captured in a furious dragnet ordered by Edwin Stanton, in which civil liberties were ignored and dozens falsely arrested. The accused had been fitted with arm and leg manacles, kept in tiny, dirty cells, and, except for Mary Surratt, forced to wear padded canvas head bags that lacked openings save for a small eating hole. For days they lived under these conditions, swollen and disoriented and afraid, Paine alone displaying massive self-control.

In a military trial, in which no clear distinction was made between the earlier kidnapping conspiracy and the later murder plot, the court found one after another of Booth's friends guilty as charged. Herold, Paine, and Atzerodt, the most active accomplices, were sentenced to death by hanging. O'Laughlin and Arnold, unjustly accused of helping plan the murder, got life sentences at hard labor, as did Dr. Mudd, who was probably even less guilty than they. Edman Spangler, no more than an innocent dupe, got six years. And then there was Mary Surratt, portrayed as the incubator of the entire plot, and as guilty as Booth himself, although it is almost certain she knew nothing beyond the kidnapping scheme. But John Lloyd testified that she had delivered field glasses to Lloyd's Tavern on the morning of the assassination, along with a message to have Booth's rifle waiting for him that night, and so she too was sentenced to death. On July 7, having failed to gain President Johnson's intervention, Mary Surratt was led onto a high scaffold with the other three to be hanged, tied up like an umbrella to prevent flailing, and fitted with hood and noose. At a signal, soldiers below knocked away the posts that held up the front half of the gallows floor. Paine alone, whose neck refused to break, lived on for five long minutes. Again and again he had sworn that Mrs. Surratt was innocent. The "commission was without authority and its proceedings void," commented Orville Browning in his daily diary. "The execution of those persons [was]...murder."

From left: **Mary Surratt, Lewis Paine, David Herold, George Atzerodt**

THE SAD TALE OF LINCOLN'S HAUNTED, "UNHINGED" WIDOW

It was Mary Lincoln's curse to live on for seventeen years after her husband's murder. For months after April 14 she could think or talk of nothing else, repeating her description of the attack to anyone who would listen, "as if she had lost all power of choice in the topics of her conversation," said Isaac Arnold. Every sudden noise reminded her of the dreaded pistol blast. She accused the guard John Parker, who had abandoned his post at Ford's Theatre on the night of the murder, of complicity in the assassination. "I shall always believe you guilty," she told him bitterly. And when President Andrew Johnson failed to pay her the expected condolence visit, or even send her a note, she decided he too must have taken part in the conspiracy. For forty days she lay in bed in the White House, as looters and souvenir hunters ransacked the mansion, stealing the costly treasures she had spent so much of her time accruing. When she was finally eased out of the residence and shipped off to Chicago so that President Johnson could move in, rumors flew about that it was she who had stripped the house of its movable belongings—its "beds and bedding and table linen and...housekeeping utensils" of which "there was absolutely nothing left," testified Commissioner Benjamin French. What else could have been inside those massive trunks and approximately seventy-five to one hundred boxes she took with her? But over the next seventeen excruciating years it was Mary herself who was stripped, slowly but surely, until she had lost everything she cared about. "Why, why was not I taken when my darling husband was called from my side?" became her constant refrain.

Over the course of the years, Mary's peculiarities became more and more noticeable. For one, her fetish for finery took on new dimensions. Although she never again wore anything but the deepest widow's black, she continued to buy new clothes with a passion and stored them away in her precious trunks. Her proclivity to spiritualism, held somewhat in check during her years alongside the skeptical Lincoln, now bloomed, convincing many that she had become "unhinged." Her obsession with money became a daily trauma; terrified of poverty and burdened by store debts, she begged friends to help. Unlike the widows of generals, governors, and Cabinet members, for whom money was easily raised, Mary's allies found it

"Only my darling Taddie prevents my taking my life," wrote a haunted Mary Lincoln in 1867. It was a difficult position for a teenager to be put in, especially for a young man so twisted by tragedy he no longer resembled his father's beloved "Tadpole" *(above)*. Although he remained his mother's constant companion for four more years, on July 15, 1871, eighteen-year-old Thomas Lincoln succumbed to tuberculosis, and joined his two brothers and his father in the grave.

"[From the moment] her husband was shot down by her side . . . to the day of her death, Mrs. Lincoln never saw a well day nor a happy hour," attested her close friend Noyes Miner. "[H]er mind was unhinged by the shock."

The only Lincoln offspring to live beyond adolescence, Robert *(above)* became a smooth, successful lawyer and politician. At the time of his mother's death in 1882 he was James A. Garfield's secretary of war; later, he witnessed Garfield's assassination and slow demise. Twice named as a contender for the presidency, and serving for four years as Benjamin Harrison's minister to England, Robert Todd Lincoln lived on until 1926, the wealthy president of the Pullman Car Company, the official guardian of his father's papers, and a happy resident in his Vermont mansion, with a passion for golf.

Wearing widow's attire the rest of her life, Mary sometimes could not even turn her neck, so rigid was the mourning bonnet and collar *(left).*

almost impossible to raise funds in her name—she was just too unpopular. When she read in the papers that the friends of former Governor Andrew of Massachusetts had contributed $100,000 for his widow, she railed, "What did *he* do compared to President Lincoln?" Attempting to raise money herself by a special New York sale of her elaborate wardrobe, and using the false name of "Mrs. Clarke" to avoid publicity, Mary became the object of even more ridicule and humiliation when no one wanted the old clothes. All across America she was despised; one newspaper called her a "mercenary prostitute." Mary claimed that all she wanted was to be clear of her debts and to own her own quiet home, "where I can freely indulge my sorrows." Thwarting her in this simple wish were two men: Supreme Court Justice David Davis, who withheld her inheritance in a fashion almost criminal; and in the shadows behind him, unbeknownst to Mary as of yet, her own son Robert. When Mary impulsively bought a house without being able to afford it, and then, almost as quickly, had to give it up, Robert declared, "I am done wasting time in urging you to beware [my] advice."

At least Mary had the past to dream of. But had she? Her husband's law partner William Herndon now came up with a story Mary could not abide—that the love of Lincoln's life had been Ann Rutledge, the New Salem maiden who had died so young. From Herndon's lectures and writings the country became convinced that the President had gone to his grave pining for Ann and that he had never loved his wife. Mary retaliated with thinly veiled threats at Herndon, and insisted to all who would listen that Lincoln's heart had not been "in any unfortunate woman's grave—but in the proper place with his loved wife and children."

Then, when her "best and kindest friend," Lizzie Keckley, in the absence of Mary's long-promised financial help, brought out a ghostwritten reminiscence of the White House years, as accurate and interesting as it was, Mary felt that she had been cast in a bad light. Determined it was a deadly betrayal, Mary severed all ties with the woman who had been her deepest emotional support ever since Willie's death.

By 1868 she had had enough. Taking Tad along with her, she abandoned the country which she felt had abandoned her and went into hiding in Germany. Clinging to her youngest son, calling the two of them "wanderers in a strange land," she made valiant attempts to find happiness abroad.

Three years later, with Tad now sounding more like a German than an American, she agreed to come home. A new government pension awaited her, which, combined with her inheritance, would finally make her a rich woman. The cold ocean crossing, however, proved too much for Tad, and within months he had developed tuberculosis. For six weeks he lingered on, growing thinner and thinner. His lungs finally filled with liquid which made the terrified boy gasp for his life. Finally, unable to breathe, he expired. It was more than Mary could stand. "Ill-luck presided my birth and has been a faithful attendant ever since," she cursed.

With only her cold, indifferent son Robert left, Mary's main refuge now was spiritualism. Moving into a spiritualist commune, she developed the "gifts" of how to see spirit faces, sometimes many at a time, and how to communicate "across the veil" with her dead husband. At least he would watch over his once "petted and idolized wife."

In the spring of 1875, Robert decided to have Mary institutionalized. Motivated at least in part by his desire to protect her estate and thus his inheritance, Robert figured that, living on her own, she drained away $5,000 per year, whereas at Bellevue Hospital in Illinois, he could have her managed for one-fifth this amount. He hired spies to gather information about her and her growing drug use—chloral hydrate, laudanum, and opium were now taken to excess—and paid doctors to swear in court to her insanity. In her own vivid manner, she had once described her migraine headaches as feeling as if an Indian were removing the bones of her face and pulling wires out of her eyes. Using such talk as positive proof of lunacy, with the help of Judge David Davis and Leonard Swett, Robert attempted to have her put away for life.

When Mary finally broke free from the mental wards and was declared "sane" by an independent court, she severed all ties with her only remaining offspring, calling him a "wicked monster." "You have tried your game of robbery long enough," she hissed.

Seeking peace in exile again, for the next three long, sad years Mary lived alone in a dingy hotel in southern France, refusing to travel as she had before, her hatred of Robert festering, her eyes weakening, her body

---

A great niece of Mary Lincoln's, Mary Edwards Brown, was sixteen when, in 1882, she helped care for Lincoln's widow in her last days. More than seventy years later she was interviewed by Dorothy Kunhardt. I was a girl of sixteen when Aunt Mary was ill in Grandmother Edwards' house, the winter before she died. A few years before that her son Robert had to have her committed to a sanitarium because she did queer things like getting into the elevator in a hotel when she was undressed; she

Young Mary Edwards

thought it was the lavatory. Mother went to call on her at the sanitarium and Aunt Mary said, "Tell Elizabeth"—that was Grandmother, Mrs. Ninian Edwards—"to come and get me and I won't be any trouble." But she was, a lot of trouble.

She kept writing letters all the time to rich men in the country saying how poor she was and living in despicable circumstances and the nation should be ashamed. She often told my mother, "Robert says I'm crazy, but he is crazy too. He was bit by a mad dog when he was a boy." It was very hard on Cousin Robert. He suffered a lot and his mother wouldn't speak to him and said he was a robber, that he had stolen her silver and her jewelry. But Mother always told us that we mustn't say anything unkind about Aunt Mary in her last years because she wasn't herself.

She had a lot of money that she kept in a money belt, even under her nightdress, but sometimes she hid it other places. One day she said Grandmother had stolen her money. Mother was there (she always got along with Aunt Mary because she never argued with her like Grandmother did). Well, Aunt Mary had a commode with a piece of Oriental carpet on top—she kept it beside her bed. Mother and Grandmother got her up on that and Grandmother dived her hand in under the mattress and there was a big roll of bills.

In the room next to her, Aunt Mary had 64 trunks. Grandmother's maid left because she was afraid to sleep under that room, with all that weight. The trunks were filled with bolts of curtain materials and dress goods. Aunt Mary had a lot of clothes in her trunks made out of elegant foreign material she bought abroad, and she had basted it together to look like dresses—to escape the customs duty. She wouldn't stop buying. Once she bought 300 pairs of gloves at one time and two dozen watches. She had about a hundred shawls. Every day she got up and went through those trunks for hours. Grand-

racked with arthritis. Finally, after a series of bad falls made it almost impossible for her to walk, Mary agreed to come home to Springfield. Her sister Elizabeth would take her into the house where Mary and her husband had been married so many years earlier.

Nervous, wearing a money belt now to prevent the theft of her savings bonds, accusing Robert of madness and swearing that even his father had always disliked him, Mary lived out the last years of her life alone, all the shades in her bedroom drawn, drinking bottles of paregoric, packing and repacking her sixty-four trunks of clothing by candlelight. On July 15, 1882, on the eleventh anniversary of Tad's death, Mary descended into a coma. The next day she got her greatest wish—to join the rest of the family in death.

mother said it was funny, if Aunt Mary was so sick, that she was able to be up all day bending over her trunks.

She had terrible headaches. And she was puffed up. She took a lot of bottles of "restorative," it was called, and it had paregoric in it, same as opium, but you could get those things without a prescription then. She didn't know much about diseases, but what she thought she had was a condition where her blood was turning to water, and when too much water hit her heart she would die. Her fingers swelled up so she had to take off her wedding ring—it was a wide ring and worn very thin. After Aunt Mary died, Mother hunted it up and got it back again on her finger. Mother laid Aunt Mary out, too. The newspapers wrote about the ring when she was lying in her coffin in Grandmother's parlor with the wedding lamps lighted, how the ring was Etruscan gold and was shining on her finger and there was a smile on her face.

At a séance in Boston, using the name of Mrs. Tundall to avoid recognition, Mary Lincoln believed that she had made contact with her dead husband, sensing him laying his hands on her shoulders. Later, working out of Brady's studio, the spirit photographer William Mumler — who was once indicted for fraud — captured an "authentic" spirit image of the same event.

THIRTY-SIX YEARS LATER, LINCOLN GETS HIS ''QUIET PLACE''

On the broiling hot afternoon of May 4, 1865, in the new iron lock of a limestone vault at Oak Ridge Cemetery in Springfield, Illinois, a large key was turned, then handed ceremoniously to John Stuart, Lincoln's first law partner. It was the end of one story and the beginning of another.

Lincoln was not to lie in the peace he deserved quite yet. For the next thirty-six years, in fact, his body was moved time and again, almost kidnapped by a band of ransom-hungry grave robbers, hidden under a dirt floor, the coffin cut open and the body inspected to make sure the right remains were inside. For Lincoln, not until the second year of the twentieth century did he attain final rest, in a place where only a bomb could reach.

Springfield had fought hard for the honor of being the site of Lincoln's official burial ground. At first, Mary Lincoln had objected, saying that the ''quiet place'' her husband recently had spoken of to lie in after death was certainly not in downtown Springfield, where the town fathers wanted to bury him alone, without his family members. Warning them that it was a widow's prerogative to decide where her husband was to be buried, she suggested that she might easily choose Chicago, beside the lapping waters of Lake Michigan, or even the crypt beneath the rotunda of the Capitol which had been built for George Washington but never used. Mary finally accepted a compromise in Springfield—a spacious memorial on eight acres of a country graveyard, with a fitting tomb to be erected and paid for by the State of Illinois at a cost of $180,000. Six years later, with the work partially completed, Lincoln's body, along with those of his three sons, was deposited in the new crypts as work on the obelisk continued. The ''quiet place'' seemed closer. But in the autumn of 1876, eleven years after Lincoln's death, a counterfeiting ring hatched a plan to break into the tomb at night, grab Lincoln's body, drive it by wagon to the hills of northern Indiana, bury it in sand, and wait for the ransom terms to be met—$200,000, plus the release of the counterfeiters' star engraver from Joliet State Prison. It almost worked. Lincoln's coffin was half out the door when lawmen swooped down.

Thirty-six years after his death, a group gathers at the Lincoln tomb to witness Lincoln's final burial.

Fearful of another attempt, Lincoln's old friends now hid the coffin in the labyrinth of passageways beneath the obelisk and finally secretly buried it there. For the next ten years, the public unknowingly paid homage to an empty sarcophagus. After Mrs. Lincoln's death, her body, too, was switched in the dead of night from her public crypt to her husband's makeshift grave. Over the next two decades, Lincoln and family were exhumed, buried again, and exhumed once more during a restoration of the faulty building. But in 1901, under Robert Lincoln's instructions, the macabre charade ended. A hole thirteen feet deep was dug below the main cata-comb floor. A four-foot base of cement was laid and an iron cage sunk into it. The coffin would be lowered into the cage and cement poured, creating a block eight feet long by eight feet deep. At the final burial ceremony, a plumber cut a little window in the lead of the coffin just over Lincoln's face. A pungent odor arose. There was the face, still white from the chalk applied by the undertaker on the funeral trip west back in 1865. There were the nose and chin, as prominent as in life. There were the little black bow tie in place, and the suit of black cloth Lincoln had worn at his second inauguration, now whitened with mildew. There was the head, fallen to one side on the sunken pillow.

Seventeen honored Springfield citizens were asked to peer inside the coffin on this final day, and as each one confirmed the identity of the coffin's occupant, their thoughts could not have been far different from those of the young doctor Edward Curtis, who had held Lincoln's brain in his hand thirty-six years before: "As I looked, I felt more profoundly impressed than ever with the mystery of that unknown something which may be named 'vital spark'... whose absence or presence makes all the immeasurable difference, between an inert mass of matter...and...a living brain, by whose silent and subtle machinery, a world may be ruled.''

HOW THE ABRAHAM LINCOLN WE KNOW TODAY BEGAN TO TAKE SHAPE

For Lincoln, the trip to sainthood was speedy. The apotheosis began on the day after his death in thousands of pulpits across the nation. Ministers and their congregations chose to forget the real man and to replace him with a sanitized version, pure and great, up there in the heavens beside George Washington, awash in martyrdom and divinity. The first biographies written after his death followed suit. They were stories of a Christ-like log cabin boy who grew up to become president and free the slaves, no flesh and blood, no human frailty along the way.

There was something in Lincoln that made him seem different from ordinary men. Visible during his own lifetime, it was even more apparent after his death. "The news of his going," wrote William Herndon, "struck me dumb...the deed...so huge in consequences, that it...[did] not appear like a worldly reality." "No common mortal had died," declared White House seamstress Lizzie Keckley. "The Moses of my people had fallen in the hour of triumph."

His death inspired an enormous outpouring of words about this remarkable human being, who had freed the slaves and preserved the Union, and then himself been slain on Good Friday, as if for the sins of the nation. In the year of his death alone, more than 450 pamphlets, speeches, and sermons about him erupted into print, many of them comparing Lincoln to Christ. The son of a "saintly" mother and an illiterate carpenter, Lincoln had been sent by God to save his people, they said.

Back in 1860, Lincoln himself had composed a brief autobiographical statement, which became the starting point for all subsequent treatments of his life. A year after his death, the first real Lincoln biography appeared, written by a New York editor who had never met his subject—Josiah G. Holland. It was eulogy writ large, a long, sanitized hymn of praise in which Lincoln continued his ascent into sainthood. Isaac N. Arnold's substantial biography of the same year, written by a man who had known Lincoln well, was filled with fascinating first-hand remembrance, but it too was strangely oversimplified, with Lincoln not as saint, but as "Great Emancipator." John G. Nicolay's personal notes from the 1860s and John M. Hay's diary of the White House years, perhaps because they were never meant to be biographies, contained vivid and contemporaneous depictions of Lincoln, key to all later research; as did the diaries of other important insiders such as Gideon Welles, Edward Bates, Salmon P. Chase, and Orville Browning. But years later, when the massive ten-volume official biography by Nicolay and Hay became the most comprehensive history ever written of Lincoln's presidency, and a gold mine of important detail, its final form, censored by Robert Lincoln, had a strangely partisan and impersonal quality to it, and did not succeed in capturing Lincoln the man.

Isaac Newton Arnold

John George Nicolay and John Milton Hay

The three Lincoln intimates above were the most important early biographers. Their work conveyed valuable factual records of Lincoln's life without any of the warts, a job left for Lamon and Herndon *(right)*, whose earthy biographies helped reveal "the real Lincoln" but were considered improper when they were published. Although the most valuable source of all, Herndon's work included mistakes and exaggerations that are still part of the Lincoln myth today.

Ward Hill Lamon

William Henry Herndon

Lincoln's body first resided in Oak Ridge Cemetery's public receiving vault *(shown in the lower right-hand corner of this picture).* Inside a year, it was moved to a temporary vault higher up the hill to the left. In 1871 the almost completed Lincoln Tomb at the top of the hill received the bodies of the recently deceased Tad, then Eddie, Willie and Abraham. Mary joined them in 1882.

Partly in reaction to what they perceived as blatant falsification, William H. Herndon, Lincoln's last law partner, and Ward Hill Lamon, Lincoln's friend and self-appointed body guard, each commenced his own biography, to be based upon first-hand knowledge, and promising to show him flaws and all. Herndon's goal, with the help of fellow writer Jesse Weik, was to reveal the "true Lincoln," "just as he lived, breathed—ate and laughed." To this purpose he dedicated the rest of his life, collecting information and testimony from hundreds of eyewitnesses, as well as recording his own clearest memories. He was interested in Lincoln's humor, his sadness, his friendships, his failings, his early loves, his secrets, his marital troubles, his ugly face—matters totally overlooked by the eulogists. And Lamon, supplementing his own research with Herndon's material, did the same. "If you and I had not told the exact truth about Lincoln," Herndon wrote to Lamon in later days, "he would have been a myth [with]in a hundred years..." Theirs, too, was in part a mythic Lincoln. And yet, nowhere does the actual man live on more vividly than in the pages of Herndon's biography.

In our own century, we have at once carried forward the Lincoln legend and uncovered ever more of the Lincoln of history. We have done intensive study and writing on Lincoln's own words, on the accounts of his contemporaries, and on the key sources of his era. And we have taken advantage of the chief ingredient that the early writers lacked: chronological distance. Strangely, while there is now good access to the corpus of Lincoln's own writings, the all-important letters and messages sent to him, long kept under lock and key by order of Robert Lincoln, remain largely unpublished.

From the rhapsodic power of Carl Sandburg, to the comprehensive accuracy of James G. Randall, a few great twentieth-century biographies have emerged, and continue to emerge. Despite all that is known, despite the maelstrom of Lincoln literature over the past century and a quarter, we still yearn to know and to ponder Lincoln's story anew—to understand and to see and to wonder at the extraordinary human being who gave rise to the myths even within his own lifetime.

1846

1865

ACKNOWLEDGMENTS

This book began with an idea for a television program, and we are indebted to Capital Cities/ABC for commissioning the film. John Sias, Robert Iger, and Ted Harbert had the bold vision and commitment that permitted such a large-scale documentary to be made for network television. We thank them. We also thank Esther Newberg at ICM for all her help in bringing us together with Knopf. Esther realized the importance of this book when the idea for it was only barely shaped. And we thank Ashbel Green. As our editor, Ash not only has huge personal interest in this period of history but his help and support made it possible for us to deliver this book under enormous time constraint. With Nancy Clements supervising the copy editing and Ellen McNeilly in charge of the printing of the book, we were in most capable hands.

In addition to our principal consultant, David Herbert Donald, we thank three others who carefully read the manuscript for accuracy: Richard Current, Harold Holzer, and Brian Pohanka each offered important criticism and suggestions, both in regard to text as well as photographs. (Thoughtfully, Holzer and co-author Mark E. Neely, Jr., made available important pictures from their book, *The Lincoln Family Album*.) In addition, Ralph Graves did skillful early editing and offered invaluable layout advice. The generous input of these men has helped sharpen both the content and the shape of this book.

Many institutions provided us with photographic images, but leaders of two of them must be singled out. Mark Neely is director of The Lincoln Museum and has not only furnished us with valuable pictures but with helpful suggestions as well. And Thomas Schwartz, curator of the Illinois State Historical Library, has been an enormous help. He has opened that vast collection and offered many creative recommendations.

We thank James Mellon for allowing us to copy his exquisite collection of Lincoln portraits; Lloyd Ostendorf, friend and colleague of Frederick Hill Meserve, who has been very generous with his time and his collection of photographs; Jack Smith for trustingly supplying us with his collection of original lithographs; Tom Truscott of the Lincoln Bookshop in Chicago for his help locating research material. We salute Gabor Boritt, Mark Katz, and Richard E. Sloan for their support and for the materials they have provided.

We thank the National Portrait Gallery, the owner for the last decade of more than 5,400 Mathew Brady original glass negatives formerly in the Meserve Collection. We express gratitude to the National Archives and the Library of Congress for photographs, and to Diane Hamilton, who did photo research with Anne-Marie Cunniffe at these institutions. Thanks also to Joan Chaconas for her guidance and help. We are grateful to the Chicago Historical Society and to Ford's Theatre National Historic Site for their assistance. We also thank Dorance Smith for the help and access he provided at the White House. We thank Dan Brambilla of Proskauer Rose Goetz and Mendelsohn for his good legal work with both the book and the documentary. And we are indebted to Edwin London and his fine team at Gelfand, Rennert & Feldman for steering us through business complexities on both projects.

No book of photographs could be completed without expert help in the darkroom. We thank Hanns Kohl, chief of the Time-Life lab, for his meticulous work and for luring former lab chief Peter Christopoulos out of retirement to oversee a difficult and painstaking printing job. And we especially thank Diego Padro of The Original Image and his partner, Alice Vera. Their darkroom, across the street from our office in Mount Kisco, New York, and their skillful printing and copy photography are most appreciated. Another fine photo copyist to whom we owe thanks is Tony Holmes.

We express gratitude to Gedeon de Margitay for the careful corrections he made on the text and for overseeing the picture credits and producing the index for this book.

For the typesetting of this book we are indebted to Robert H. Strampfer, Creative Service Director of Time Inc. Magazines, as well as to his colleague, Ellen Nitschmann, the company's typesetting supervisor. Ellen was personally responsible for setting all the type, and her patience and thoroughness were remarkable. We also thank Carol Stanford, who typed the manuscript for the entire book as well as the script for the television documentary in its many versions. She was throughout a pleasure to work with.

We also wish to thank all the many staff members of Kunhardt Productions. In particular, Nancy Malin, Jody Abramson, Mia Freund, James Edgar, Edmond Garesche, and Christopher Edgar were asked to juggle both television research and book research, completing both on schedule. Without their help along with the help of two interns, Alexandra Zabriskie and Monica Darer, this book could not have been completed so quickly.

We are especially appreciative of art director and production manager Gene Light. While nearly all books today are laid out on computer screens, Gene decided that for this complex and evolving work he would do it the old-fashioned way: by hand. After 6 gallons of rubber cement, 2,000 razor blades, and dozens of garbage bags filled with his paper scraps, he has designed and pulled together a most complicated book. His fast, creative work has been central to this entire project.

In addition to paying tribute to Frederick Hill Meserve and Dorothy Meserve Kunhardt, we thank the late Josephine Cobb. Once the famed iconographic expert of the National Archives, in her lifetime she helped three generations of this family in their Lincoln projects. Today Miss Cobb is helping still another generation, her collection of pictures, manuscripts, and research files having been left to our family.

Finally, we thank the three Kunhardt wives—Katharine, Margie, and Suzy—not only for their loving support throughout this project but for raising children and dogs without much help from their husbands. The older generation of children—Jean, Sandra, Sarah, and Michael—some of whom have children of their own, have been patient and enthusiastically supportive. It has been harder on the next generation—Jessie, Philip, Harry, Peter, Abby, Teddy, and George have not seen much of their fathers for the past year. We thank them all.

BIBLIOGRAPHY

I. SELECTED REFERENCES

Basler, Roy P. et al. (eds.), *The Collected Works of Abraham Lincoln* (Springfield, Ill.: Abraham Lincoln Association, 1953), 8 vols.

Dictionary of American Biography (New York: Scribners, 1943), 20 vols.

Hamilton, Charles, and Lloyd Ostendorf, *Lincoln in Photographs, An Album of Every Known Pose* (Norman: University of Oklahoma Press, 1963).

Johnson, Robert Underwood, and Clarence Cough Buel (eds.). *Battles and Leaders of the Civil War* (New York: The Century Company. 1884-1888), 4 vols.

Meserve, Frederick Hill, *Historical Portraits and Lincolniana* (New York: Privately Printed, 1915), 28 vols.

Meserve, Frederick Hill, and Carl Sandburg, *The Photographs of Abraham Lincoln* (New York: Harcourt, Brace & Co., Inc., 1944).

Miers, Earl Schenck, Editor-in-Chief, *Lincoln Day by Day* (Washington: Lincoln Sesquicentennial Commission, 1960), 3 vols.

Neely, Mark E., Jr., *The Abraham Lincoln Encyclopedia* (New York: McGraw-Hill, Inc., 1982).

Segal, Charles M. (ed.), *Conversations with Lincoln* (New York: G. P. Putnam's Sons, 1961).

II. SELECTED PRIMARY SOURCES

An Eyewitness, Recollections of Lincoln and Douglas (New York: Privately Printed, 1899).

Angle, Paul M. (ed.), *Created Equal? The Complete Lincoln-Douglas Debates of 1858* (Chicago: The University of Chicago Press, 1958).

Angle, Paul M. (ed.), *Herndon's Life of Lincoln* (Cleveland and New York: The World Publishing Co., 1949).

Barnes, John S., "With Lincoln from Washington to Richmond in 1865" in *Appleton's Magazine*, vol. II (May, June 1907), pp. 515-524, 742-751.

Bates, David Homer, *Lincoln in the Telegraph Office* (New York: The Century Co., 1907).

Beale, Howard K. (ed.), *The Diary of Edward Bates* (Washington, D.C.: Annual Report of the American Historical Association for 1930, vol. IV, 1933).

Beale, Howard K. (ed.), *The Diary of Gideon Welles* (New York: W. W. Norton & Co., 1960), 3 vols.

Brooks, Noah, "Personal Recollections of Abraham Lincoln," in *Harper's Monthly* (July 1865), pp. 222-230.

Brooks, Noah, *Washington in Lincoln's Time* (New York: The Century Co., 1896).

Browning, Orville H., *The Diary of Orville Hickman Browning*, edited by Theodore C. Pease and James G. Randall (Springfield, Ill.: Illinois State Historical Library, 1925-1933), 2 vols.

Carpenter, Francis B., *Six Months at the White House with Abraham Lincoln* (New York: Hurd and Houghton, 1866).

Chambrun, Charles A. P., Marquis de, *Impressions of Lincoln and the Civil War, a Foreigner's Account* (New York: Random House, 1952).

Chase, Salmon, *Inside Lincoln's Cabinet: The Civil War Diaries of Salmon P. Chase*, edited by David Donald (New York: Longmans, Green & Co., 1954)

Chittenden, Lucius E., *Recollections of President Lincoln and His Administration* (New York: Harper & Brothers, 1891).

Crook, William H., "Lincoln as I Knew him. Compiled and written down by Margarita S. Gerry," in *Harper's Monthly*, vol. 114, pt. 1 (Dec. 1906), pp. 107-114; vol. 115, pt. 1 (June 1907), pp. 41-48.

Crook, William H., "Lincoln's Last Day; new fact now told for the first time. Compiled and written down by Margarita S. Gerry," in *Harper's Monthly*, vol. 115, pt. 1 (Sept. 1907), pp. 519-530.

Crook, William H., *Memories of the White House: The Home Life of Our Presidents from Lincoln to Roosevelt* (Boston: Little, Brown and Co., 1911).

Crook, William H., *Through Five Administrations* (New York: Harper & Brothers, 1907).

Curtis, George William (ed.), *The Correspondence of John Lothrop Motley* (New York: Harper & Brothers, 1889), 2 vols.

Cuthbert, Norma B. (ed.), *Lincoln and the Baltimore Plot, 1861: From Pinkerton Records and Related Papers* (San Marino, Calif.: Henry E. Huntington Library, 1949).

Dana, Charles A., *Recollections of the Civil War: With the Leaders at Washington and in the Field in the Sixties* (New York: D. Appleton & Co., 1898).

Douglass, Frederick, *The Life and Times of Frederick Douglass, Written by Himself* (Hartford, Conn.: Park Publishing Co., 1882).

Everett, Edward, *Orations and Speeches* (Boston: Charles C. Little & James Brown, 1850).

Fessenden, Francis, *Life and Public Services of William Pitt Fessenden* (Boston: Houghton, Mifflin and Co. 1907), 2 vols.

Forney, John W., *Anecdotes of Public Men* (New York: Harper & Brothers, 1873-1881), 2 vols.

French, Benjamin Brown, ed. Donald B, Cole and John J. McDonough, *Witness to the Young Republic, A Yankee's Journal, 1828-1870* (Hanover, N.H.: U. Press of New England, 1989).

Gilmore, James R., *Personal Recollections of Abraham Lincoln and The Civil War* (London: John Macqueen, 1899).

Grant, Ulysses S., *Personal Memoirs of U.S. Grant* (New York: Charles L. Webster & Co., 1885), 2 vols.

Grimsley, Elizabeth Todd, "Six Months in the White House," in *Journal of the Illinois State Historical Society* (Oct. 1926), 43-73.

Hay, John, "Life in the White House in the Time of Lincoln," in *Century Magazine*, No. 19 (Nov. 1890), pp. 33-37.

Hay, John, *Lincoln and the Civil War in the Diaries and Letters of John Hay* selected by Tyler Dennett (New York: Dodd, Mead and Co., 1939).

Herndon, William H., "Mrs. Lincoln's Denial, and What She Says." (Broadside, Jan. 12, 1874. Mass. Hist. Soc.).

Hertz, Emanuel, *The Hidden Lincoln* (New York: The Viking Press, 1938).

Howells, W. D., *Life of Abraham Lincoln* (1860; reproduced by Indiana University Press, 1960).

Keckley, Elizabeth, *Behind the Scenes: Thirty Years a Slave, and Four Years in the White House* (New York: G. W. Carleton, 1868).

Koerner, Gustave, *Memoirs of Gustave Koerner, 1809–1896*, edited by Thomas J. McCormack (Cedar Rapids, Iowa: The Torch Press, 1909), 2 vols.

Lamon, Ward H., *Recollections of Abraham Lincoln, 1847–1865*, edited by Dorothy Lamon Teillard (Chicago: A. C. McClurg & Co., 1895).

Littell, E., *Littell's Living Age; April, May, June 1865* (Boston: Littell, Son & Co., 1865).

McClellan, George B., *McClellan's Own Story* (New York: Charles L. Webster & Co., 1892).

McClure, Alexander K., *Lincoln and Men of War-Times* (Philadelphia: Times Publishing Co., 1892).

McCulloch, Hugh, *Men and Measures of Half a Century* (New York: Charles Scribner's Sons, 1889).

Mearns, David C. (ed.), *The Lincoln Papers* (Garden City, N.Y.: Doubleday & Co., 1948), 2 vols.

Meigs, Montgomery C., "General M. C. Meigs on the Conduct of the Civil War," in *American Historical Review* (Jan. 1921), pp. 285–303.

Miner, The Rev. N.W., "Mrs. Abraham Lincoln, A Vindication," (MS., Illinois State Historical Library).

Mitgang, Herbert (ed.), *Lincoln as They Saw Him* (New York: Rinehart and Co., 1956).

Nicolay, Helen, *Lincoln's Secretary: A Biography of John G. Nicolay* (New York: Longmans, Green & Co., 1949).

Official Records of the Union and Confederate Armies, The War of Rebellion (Washington: Government Printing Office, 1880–1901, 4 series, 70 vols. in 128).

Poore, Ben: Perley, *Reminiscences of Sixty Years in the National Metropolis* (Philadelphia: Hubbard Brothers, 1886), 2 vols.

Pratt, Harry E. (ed.), *Concerning Mr. Lincoln, in Which Abraham Lincoln Is Pictured as He Appeared to Letter Writers of His Time* (Springfield, Ill.: Abraham Lincoln Association, 1944).

Rankin, Henry B., *Intimate Character Sketches of Abraham Lincoln* (Philadelphia: Lippincott, 1924).

Rankin, Henry B., *Personal Recollections of Abraham Lincoln* (New York: Putnam, 1916).

Report of the Commissioner of Patents for the Year 1849 (Washington: Office of the Printers to the Senate, 1850).

Rice, Allen Thorndike (ed.), *Reminiscences of Abraham Lincoln by Distinguished Men of His Time* (New York: North American Review Publishing Co., 1886).

Russell, William H., *My Diary North and South* (Boston: T. O. H. P. Burnham, 1863).

Schuckers, Jacob W., *The Life and Public Services of Salmon Portland Chase* (New York: Appleton, 1874).

Scott, Winfield, *Memoirs of Lieutenant-General Scott, LL.D.* (New York: Sheldon, 1864), 2 vols.

Scripps, John Locke, *Life of Abraham Lincoln*, edited by Roy P. Basler and Lloyd A. Dunlap (Bloomington, Ind.: Indiana University Press, 1961).

Seward, Frederick W., *Reminiscences of a War-Time Statesman and Diplomat, 1830–1915* (New York: G. P. Putnam's Sons, 1916).

Sherman, William T., *Personal Memoirs of General W. T. Sherman* (New York: D. Appleton & Co., 1875), 2 vols.

Speed, Joshua F., *Reminiscences of Abraham Lincoln and Notes of a Visit to California. Two Lectures* (Louisville, Ky.: J. P. Morton, 1884).

Stimmel, Smith, *Personal Reminiscences of Abraham Lincoln* (Minneapolis: William H. M. Adams, 1928).

Stoddard, William O., *Inside the White House in War Times* (New York: Charles L. Webster & Co., 1892).

Stoddard, William O., *Lincoln's Third Secretary; the Memoirs of William O. Stoddard*. Edited with an introduction by William O. Stoddard, Jr. (New York: Exposition Press, 1955).

Villard, Henry, *Lincoln on the Eve of '61: A Journalist's Story*, edited by Harold G. and Oswald G. Villard (New York: Alfred A. Knopf, 1941).

Villard, Henry, *Memoirs of Henry Villard* (Boston and New York: Houghton, Mifflin and Co., 1904), 2 vols.

Weed, Thurlow, *Autobiography of Thurlow Weed* (Boston: Houghton, Mifflin and Co., 1883).

Welles, Gideon, *Diary of Gideon Welles*, edited by John T. Morse, Jr. (Boston: Houghton Mifflin Co., 1911), 3 vols..

Whipple, Wayne, *The Story-Life of Lincoln* (Philadelphia: John C. Winston Co., 1908).

Whitney, Henry C., *Life on the Circuit with Lincoln* (Boston: Estes & Lauriat, 1892).

Wilson, Rufus R. (ed.), *Intimate Memories of Lincoln, Assembled and Annotated by Rufus Rockwell Wilson* (Elmira, N.Y.: Primavera Press, 1945).

Wilson, Rufus R. (ed.), *Lincoln Among his Friends: A Sheaf of Intimate Memories, Assembled and Annotated by Rufus Rockwell Wilson* (Caldwell, Id.: Caxton Printers, 1942).

III. SELECTED LINCOLN LITERATURE

Abdill, *Civil War Railroads* (Seattle: Superior Publishing Company, 1961).

Abraham Lincoln: Tributes From His Associates (intro. by William Hayes Ward) (New York: Thomas Y. Crowell & Company, 1895).

Addresses and Funeral Solemnities on the Death of John Quincy Adams (Washington: J. & G. S. Gideon, 1848).

Ames, Mary Clemmer, *Ten Years in Washington—Life and Scenes in the National Capital—As a Woman Sees Them* (Hartford, Conn.: A. D. Worthington & Co., 1874).

Angle, Paul M., *A Portrait of Abraham Lincoln in Letters by His Oldest Son* (Chicago: The Chicago Historical Society, 1968).

Angle, Paul M., *A Shelf of Lincoln Books, A Critical Selective Bibliography of Lincolniana* (New Brunswick, N.J.: Rutgers University Press, 1946).

Angle, Paul M., *Here I Have Lived, A History of Lincoln's Springfield, 1821–1865* (Springfield, Ill.: Abraham Lincoln Association, 1935).

Angle, Paul M. (ed.), *The Lincoln Reader* (New Brunswick, N.J.: Rutgers University Press, 1947).

Angle, Paul M., and Miers, Earl Schenck, *The Living Lincoln* (New Brunswick, N.J.: Rutgers University Press, 1955).

Angle, Paul M., and Miers, Earl Schenck, *The Tragic Years* (New York: Simon & Schuster, 1960), 2 vols.

Arnold, Isaac N., *The History of Abraham Lincoln and the Overthrow of Slavery* (Chicago: Clarke, 1866).

Arnold, Isaac N., *The Life of Abraham Lincoln* (Chicago: Jansen, McClurg & Co., 1885).

Baker, Jean H., *Mary Todd Lincoln, A Biography* (New York and London: W. W. Norton & Co., 1987).

Ballard, Colin R., *The Military Genius of Abraham Lincoln* (London: Oxford University Press, 1926).

Bancroft, George, *Memorial Address* (Washington: Government Printing Office, 1866).

Baringer, William E., *A House Dividing: Lincoln as President-Elect* (Springfield, Ill.: Abraham Lincoln Association, 1945).

Baringer, William E., *Lincoln's Rise to Power* (Boston: Little, Brown and Co., 1937).

Baringer, William E., *Lincoln's Vandalia, A Pioneer Portrait* (New Brunswick, N.J.: Rutgers University Press, 1949).

Barnes, Thurlow Weed, *Memoir of Thurlow Weed* (Boston: Houghton, Mifflin and Co., 1884).

Barrett, Joseph H., *Abraham Lincoln and His Presidency* (Cincinnati: The Robert Clark Company, 1904), 2 vols.

Bartlett, D. W., *The Life and Public Services of Hon. Abraham Lincoln* (New York: Derby & Jackson, 1860).

Barton, William E., *Abraham Lincoln and His Books* (Chicago: Marshall Field & Co., 1920).

Barton, William E., *The Lineage of Lincoln* (Indianapolis: The Bobbs-Merrill Co., 1929).

Barton, William E., *The Paternity of Abraham Lincoln . . .* (New York: George H. Doran Company, 1920).

Barton, William E., *The Women Lincoln Loved* (Indianapolis, The Bobbs-Merrill Co., 1927).

Barzun, Jacques, *Lincoln The Literary Genius* (Evanston, Ill.: The Schiori Private Press, 1960).

Basler, Roy P., *The Lincoln Legend* (Boston and New York: Houghton Mifflin Co., 1935).

Basler, Roy P. (ed.), *Walt Whitman's Memoranda During the War [&] Death of Abraham Lincoln* (Bloomington: Indiana University Press, 1962).

Bayne, Julia Taft, *Tad Lincoln's Father* (Boston: Little, Brown and Co., 1931).

Beveridge, Albert J., *Abraham Lincoln, 1809–1858* (Boston and New York: Houghton Mifflin Co., 1928), 4 vols.

Boritt, Gabor S., *Lincoln and the Economics of the American Dream* (Memphis: Memphis State University Press, 1978).

Bradford, Gamaliel, *Wives* (New York: Harper & Brothers, 1925).

Brooks, Noah, *Abraham Lincoln* (New York: G. P. Putnam's Sons, 1888).

Brooks, Noah, *Abraham Lincoln and the Downfall of American Slavery* (New York: G. P. Putnam's Sons, 1902).

Browne, Francis Fischer, *The Everyday Life of Abraham Lincoln* (New York: Thompson, 1886).

Browne, Francis Fischer, *The Everyday Life of Abraham Lincoln* [expanded second edition] (Chicago: Browne & Howell Co., 1913), 2 vols.

Browne, Robert H., *Abraham Lincoln and the Men of His Time* (Chicago: The Blakely-Oswald Printing Company, 1907, original copyright 1900), 2 vols.

Bruce, Robert V., *Lincoln and the Tools of War* (Urbana and Chicago: University of Illinois Press, 1989 edition, previously published by Bobbs-Merrill Co., 1956).

Bryan, George S., *Great American Myth* (New York: Carrick and Evans, 1940).

Bullard, F. Lauriston, *Abraham Lincoln and the Widow Bixby* (New Brunswick, N.J.: Rutgers University Press, 1946).

Bullard, F. Lauriston, *Tad and His Father* (Boston: Little, Brown and Co., 1925).

Carr, Clark E., *Lincoln at Gettysburg* (Chicago: A. C. McClurg & Co., 1906).

Carruthers, Olive, and R. Gerald McMurtry, *Lincoln's Other Mary* (Chicago and New York: Ziff-Davis Publishing Company, 1946).

Charnwood, Lord, *Abraham Lincoln* (New York: Henry Holt & Co., 1917).

Clark, Allen C., *Abraham Lincoln in the National Capital* (Washington, D.C.: W.F. Roberts Co., 1925).

Clark, Champ, and the Editors of Time-Life Books, *The Assassination* (Alexandria, Va.: Time-Life Books, 1987).

Coleman, Charles H., *Abraham Lincoln and Coles County, Illinois* (New Brunswick, N.J.: Scarecrow Press, 1955).

Coleman, Charles H., ed. David Donald, *Divided We Fought, A Pictorial History of the War, 1861–1865* (New York: Macmillan, 1961).

Colver, Anne, *Mr. Lincoln's Wife* (New York: Farrar & Rinehart, Inc., 1943).

Conwell, Russell H., *Why Lincoln Laughed* (New York: Harper and Brothers Publishers, 1922).

Cramer, John Henry, *Lincoln Under Enemy Fire* (Louisiana: State University Press, 1948).

Croy, Homer, *The Trial of Mrs. Abraham Lincoln* (New York: Duell, Sloan & Pearce, 1962).

Current, Richard N., *The Lincoln Nobody Knows* (New York: McGraw-Hill Book Co., 1958).

Current, Richard N., and James G. Randall, *Lincoln, the President: Last Full Measure* (New York: Dodd, Mead & Co., 1955).

Curtis, William Eleroy, *The True Abraham Lincoln* (Philadelphia: J. B. Lippincott Co., 1903).

Davis, John P. (ed.), *The American Negro Reference Book* (Englewood Cliffs, N.J.: Prentice-Hall, Inc., 1966).

Dodge, Daniel Kilham, *Abraham Lincoln, Master of Words* (New York and London: D. Appleton & Company, 1924).

Donald, David Herbert, *Charles Sumner and the Rights of Man* (New York: Alfred A. Knopf, 1970).

Donald, David Herbert, *Lincoln's Herndon* (New York: Alfred A. Knopf, 1948).

Donald, David Herbert, *Lincoln Reconsidered: Essays on the Civil War Era* (New York: Alfred A. Knopf, 1956).

Evans, W. A., *Mrs. Abraham Lincoln* (New York: Alfred A. Knopf, 1932).

Fehrenbacher, Don E., *Lincoln in Text and Context, Collected Essays* (Stanford, Calif.: Stanford University Press, 1987).

Fehrenbacher, Don E., *Prelude to Greatness: Lincoln in the 1850s* (Stanford, Calif.: Stanford Univ. Press, 1962).

Ferguson, W. J., *I Saw Booth Shoot Lincoln* (Boston: Houghton Mifflin Co., 1944).

Foster, Genevieve, *Abraham Lincoln's World* (New York: Charles Scribner's Sons, 1944).

Franklin, John Hope, and Alfred A. Moss, Jr., *From Slavery to Freedom* (New York: Alfred A. Knopf, 1988).

Frassanito, William A., *Antietam, The Photographic Legacy of America's Bloodiest Day* (New York: Charles Scribner's Sons, 1978).

Freedman, Russell, *Lincoln, A Photobiography* (New York: Ticknor & Fields, 1987).

Gray, Wm. C., *Life of Abraham Lincoln* (Cincinnati: Western Tract & Book Society, 1867).

Grierson, Francis, *Abraham Lincoln, The Presidential Mystic* (New York: John Lane Company, 1917).

Gross, Anthony, *Lincoln's Own Stories* (New York: Harper & Brothers, 1912).

Hamlin, Charles Eugene, *The Life and Times of Hannibal Hamlin* (Cambridge: Riverside Press, 1899).

Hapgood, Norman, *Abraham Lincoln, The Man of the People* (New York: The Macmillan Co., 1899).

Harkness, David J., and R. Gerald McMurtry, *Lincoln's Favorite Poets* (Knoxville: The University of Tennessee Press, 1959).

Helm, Katherine, *The True Story of Mary, Wife of Lincoln* (New York: Harper & Brothers, 1928).

Hendrick, Burton J., *Lincoln's War Cabinet* (Boston: Little, Brown and Co., 1946).

Herndon, William H., and Jesse William Weik, *Herndon's Lincoln* (Springfield, Ill.: The Herndon's Lincoln Publishing Co., 1888).

Hertz, Emanuel, *Lincoln Talks, A Biography in Anecdote* (New York: The Viking Press, 1939).

Hesseltine, William B., *Lincoln and the War Governors* (New York: Alfred A. Knopf, 1948).

Hill, John Wesley, *Abraham Lincoln—Man of God* (New York: G.P. Putnam's Sons, 1920).

Holland, J. G., *The Life of Abraham Lincoln* (Springfield, Mass.: Gurdon Bill, 1866).

Holloway, Laura C., *The Ladies of the White House* (Philadelphia: Bradkey & Company, 1883).

Holzer, Harold, Gabor S. Boritt, and Mark E. Neely, Jr., *The Lincoln Image, Abraham Lincoln and the Popular Print* (New York: Charles Scribner's Sons, 1984).

Houser, A. M., *Lincoln's Education* (New York: Bookman Associates, 1957).

Illustrated Life, Services, Martyrdom and Funeral of Abraham Lincoln and the Hon. George Bancroft's Oration (Philadelphia: F. B. Peterson & Brothers, 1865).

Katz, Mark D., *Witness to an Era, The Life and Photographs of Alexander Gardner* (New York: Viking, 1991).

Kennedy, Frances H., *The Civil War Battlefield Guide* (Boston: Houghton Mifflin Co., 1990).

Kimmel, Stanley, *The Mad Booths of Maryland* (New York: Dover, 1969).

Kimmel, Stanley, *Mr. Lincoln's Washington* (New York: Coward-McCann, Inc., 1957).

Kincaid, Robert L., *Joshua Fry Speed: Lincoln's Most Intimate Friend* (Harrogate, Tenn.: The Filson Club, 1943).

Kunhardt, Dorothy M., and Philip B. Jr., *Twenty Days* (New York: Harper and Row, 1965).

Kunhardt, Dorothy M., and Philip B. Kunhardt, Jr., *Mathew Brady and His World* (Alexandria, Va.: Time-Life Books, 1977).

Kunhardt, Philip B., Jr., *A New Birth of Freedom: Lincoln at Gettysburg* (Boston: Little, Brown and Co., 1983).

Lair, John, *Songs Lincoln Loved* (New York: Duell, Sloan & Pearce, 1954).

Lamon, Ward Hill, *The Life of Abraham Lincoln, From His Birth to His Inauguration as President* (Boston: James R. Osgood & Co., 1872).

Lee, R.E., *Recollections and Letters of General Robert E. Lee by his son Captain Robert E. Lee* (New York: Doubleday, Page and Company, 1904).

Leech, Margaret, *Reveille in Washington* 1860–1865 (New York: Harper & Row, 1941).

Lester, Julius, *To Be A Slave* (New York: Scholastic, 1968).

Lewis, Lloyd, *Sherman: Fighting Prophet* (New York: Harcourt, Brace & Co., 1932).

Lewis, Lloyd, *Myths After Lincoln* (New York: Harcourt, Brace & Co., 1929).

Lewis, Montgomery S., *Legends that Libel Lincoln* (New York: Rinehart & Company, Inc., 1946).

The Life and Public Services of Hon. Abraham Lincoln of Illinois and Hon. Hannibal Hamlin of Maine (Boston: Thayer & Eldridge, 1860).

Livermore, Thomas L., *Numbers & Losses in the Civil War* (Bloomington: Indiana University Press, 1957).

Lorant, Stefan, *Lincoln—A Picture Story of His Life* (New York: Harper & Brothers, 1952).

Ludwig, Emil, *Lincoln* (Boston: Little, Brown and Co., 1930).

Luthin, Reinhard H., *The Real Abraham Lincoln* (Englewood Cliffs, N.J.: Prentice-Hall Inc., 1960).

Maltby, Charles, *The Life and Public Services of Abraham Lincoln* (Stockton, Calif.: Daily Independent Steam Power Print, 1884).

Martin, Edward Winslow, *Behind the Scenes in Washington* (The Continental Publishing Co. & National Publishing Co., 1873).

Marx, Rudolph, M.D., *The Health of the Presidents* (New York: G. P. Putnam's Sons, 1960).

Maynard, Nettie Colburn, *Was Abraham Lincoln a Spiritualist?* (Philadelphia: Rufus C. Hartranft, 1891).

McClure, Alexander K., *"Abe" Lincoln's Yarns and Stories* (New York: Western W. Wilson, 1901).

McClure, J. B. (ed.), *Anecdotes of Abraham Lincoln, and Lincoln's Stories* (Chicago: Rhodes & McClure Publishing Co., 1889).

McFeely, William S., *Frederick Douglass* (New York: W. W. Norton, 1991).

McPherson, James M., *Abraham Lincoln and the Second American Revolution* (New York: Oxford, 1990).

McPherson, James M., *The Negro's Civil War* (New York: Pantheon, 1965).

Mellon, James (ed.), *The Face of Lincoln* (New York: Bonanza Books, 1979).

Meredith, Roy, *Mathew Brady's Portrait of an Era* (New York and London: W. W. Norton & Co., 1982).

Meredith, Roy, *Mr. Lincoln's Camera Man Mathew Brady* (New York: Charles Scribner's Sons, 1946).

Meserve, Frederick H., *The Photographs of Abraham*

Lincoln (New York: Privately Printed, 1911).

Miller, Francis Trevelyan, *Portrait Life of Lincoln* (Springfield, Mass.: The Patriot Publishing Co., 1910).

Monaghan, Jay, *Diplomat in Carpet Slippers: Abraham Lincoln Deals with Foreign Affairs* (Indianapolis: Bobbs-Merrill, 1945).

Morris, B. F., compiler, *Memorial Record of the Nation's Tribute to Abraham Lincoln* (Washington, D.C.: W. H. & O. H. Morrison, 1865).

Morse, John T., *Abraham Lincoln* (Boston: Houghton, Mifflin and Co., 1893), 2 vols.

Mudge, Z. A., *The Forest Boy, a Sketch of the Life of Abraham Lincoln* (New York: Carlton & Porter, 1867).

National Historical Society, *The End of an Era, The Image of War, 1861–1865* (Garden City, N.Y.: Doubleday, 1984).

Neely, Mark E., Jr., and Harold Holzer, *The Lincoln Family Album* (New York: Doubleday, 1990).

Nevins, Allan, *The Emergence of Lincoln* (New York: Charles Scribner's Sons, 1950), 2 vols.

Nevins, Allan (ed.), *Lincoln and the Gettysburg Address* (Urbana: University of Illinois Press, 1954).

Nevins, Allan, *The War for the Union* (New York: Charles Scribner's Sons, 1959).

Nevins, Allan, and Irving Stone (eds.), *Lincoln: A Contemporary Portrait* (Garden City, N.Y.: Doubleday, 1962).

Newhall, Beaumont, *The Daguerreotype in America* (New York: Duell, Sloan and Pearce, 1961).

Newman, Ralph G. (ed.), *Lincoln for the Ages* (Garden City, N.Y.: Doubleday, 1960).

Newton, Joseph Fort, *Lincoln and Herndon* (Cedar Rapids, Iowa: The Torch Press, 1910).

Nicolay, Helen, *Personal Traits of Abraham Lincoln* (New York: The Century Co., 1913).

Nicolay, John G., *A Short Life of Abraham Lincoln* (New York: The Century Co., 1904).

Nicolay, John G., *The Outbreak of Rebellion* (New York: Charles Scribner's Sons, 1881).

Nicolay, John G., and John Hay, *Abraham Lincoln: A History* (New York: The Century Co., 1890), 10 vols.

Oakleaf, Joseph Benjamin, *Lincoln Bibliography* (Cedar Rapids, Iowa: The Torch Press, 1925).

Oates, Stephen B., *Abraham Lincoln, The Man Behind the Myths* (New York: Harper & Row, 1984).

Oates, Stephen B., *Our Fiery Trial* (Amherst: U. of Mass. Press, 1979).

Oates, Stephen B., *With Malice Toward None* (New York: Harper & Row, 1977).

The Old Salem Lincoln League, *Lincoln and New Salem* (Petersburg, Ill.: The Old Salem Lincoln League, 1820), bound pamphlet.

Oldroyd, Osborn H., *The Assassination of Abraham Lincoln* (Washington, D.C.: O. H. Oldroyd, 1901).

Oldroyd, Osborn H., *The Lincoln Memorial* (Chicago: Gem Publishing House, 1882).

Page, Elwin L., *Abraham Lincoln in New Hampshire* (Boston and New York: Houghton Mifflin Co., 1929).

Power, J. C., *Abraham Lincoln—His Great Funeral Cortege from Washington City to Springfield, Illinois—With a History and Description of the National Lincoln Monument* (Springfield, Ill.: J. C. Power, 1872).

Power, J. C., *Abraham Lincoln, His Life, Public Services, Death and Great Funeral Cortege* (Chicago and Springfield, Ill.: H. W. Rokker, 1889).

Pratt, Harry E., *The Personal Finances of Abraham Lincoln* (Springfield, Ill.: The Abraham Lincoln Association, 1943).

Quarles, Benjamin, *The Negro in the Civil War* (Boston: Little, Brown and Co., 1953).

Randall: James G., *Lincoln the Liberal Statesman* (New York: Dodd, Mead & Co., 1947).

Randall, James G., *Lincoln the President: Midstream* (New York: Dodd, Mead & Co., 1952).

Randall, James G., *Lincoln the President: Springfield to Gettysburg* (New York: Dodd, Mead & Co., 1946), 2 vols.

Randall, James G., *Lincoln and the South* (Baton Rouge: Louisiana State Univ. Press, 1946).

Randall, Ruth Painter, *Mary Lincoln, Biography of a Marriage* (Boston: Little, Brown and Co., 1953).

Raymond, Henry J., *History of the Administration of Abraham Lincoln* (New York: J. C. Derby & N. C. Miller, 1864).

Rhodes, James A., and Dean Jauchins, *The Trial of Mary Todd Lincoln* (Indianapolis and New York: The Bobbs-Merrill Co., 1959).

Riddle, Donald W., *Congressman Abraham Lincoln* (Urbana, Ill.: University of Illinois Press, 1957).

Ross, Harvey Lee, *Lincoln's First Years in Illinois* (Elmira, N.Y.: Primavera Press, 1946).

Rothschild, Alonzo, *Lincoln—Master of Men: A Study in Character* (Boston: Houghton, Mifflin and Co., 1906).

Russell, William H., *The Civil War in America* (Boston: Gardner A. Fuller, 1861).

Sandburg, Carl, *Abraham Lincoln: The Prairie Years* (New York: Harcourt, Brace & Co., 1926), 2 vols.

Sandburg, Carl, *Abraham Lincoln: The War Years* (New York: Harcourt, Brace & Co., 1939), 4 vols.

Sandburg, Carl, and Paul M. Angle, *Mary Lincoln—Wife and Widow* (New York: Harcourt, Brace & Co., 1932).

Schurz, Carl, *Abraham Lincoln, A Biographical Essay by, with an Essay on the Portraits of Lincoln by Truman H. Bartlett* (Boston and New York: Houghton, Mifflin and Co., 1907).

Schurz, Carl, *The Reminiscences of Carl Schurz* (New York: McClure Co., 1908), 3 vols.

Seale, William, *The President's House, A History* (Washington, D.C.: White House Historical Association, 1986), 2 vols.

Sermons Preached in Boston on the Death of Abraham Lincoln, Together with the Funeral Services in the East Room of the Executive Mansion at Washington (Boston: J.E. Tilton and Co., 1865).

Seward, Frederick W., *William H. Seward* (New York: Derby & Miller, 1891), 3 vols.

Shaw, Albert, *Abraham Lincoln, The Year of His Election—A Cartoon History* (New York: The Review of Reviews Corporation, 1929).

Shutes, Milton H., M.D., *Lincoln and the Doctors* (New York: The Pioneer Press, 1933).

Sparks, Edwin Erle (ed.), *The Lincoln-Douglas Debates* (Springfield, Ill.: Illinois State Historical Library, 1908).

Stampp, Kenneth M., *And the War Came: The North and the Secession Crisis, 1860–1861* (Baton Rouge, La.: Louisiana State University Press, 1950).

Starr, John W., Jr., *Lincoln and the Railroads* (New York: Dodd, Mead & Co., 1927).

Stephenson, Nathaniel Wright, *Lincoln* (Indianapolis: The Bobbs-Merrill Company, 1922).

Stimmel, Smith, intro. by William Hayes Ward, *Abraham Lincoln: Tributes From His Associates* (New York: Thomas Y. Crowell, 1895).

Stoddard, William O., *Abraham Lincoln: The True Story of a Great Life* (New York: Fords, Howard & Hulbert, 1884).

Strozier, Charles B., *Lincoln's Quest For Union: Public and Private Meanings* (Urbana: Ill.: University of Illinois Press, 1987).

Strunsky, Rose, *Abraham Lincoln* (New York: The MacMillan Co., 1914).

Swinton, William, *History of the Seventh Regiment, National Guard* (New York and Boston: Fields, Osgood and Co., 1870).

Tarbell, Ida M., *Father Abraham* (New York: Moffat, Yard & Co., 1909).

Tarbell, Ida M., *In the Footsteps of Lincoln* (New York: Harcourt, Brace & Co., 1929).

Tarbell, Ida M., *The Life of Abraham Lincoln* (New York: Lincoln History Society, 1924), 4 vols.

Taylor, John M., *William Henry Seward: Lincoln's Right Hand* (New York: Harper Collins, 1991).

Temple, Wayne C., *Lincoln the Railsplitter* (La Grosse, Wis.: The Willow Press, 1961).

Thayer, William M., *From Pioneer Home to the White House* (Boston: James H. Earle, 1888).

Thayer, William M., *The Pioneer Boy and How He Became President* (Boston: Walker, Wise and Co., 1863).

Thayer, William Roscoe, *The Life and Letters of John Hay* (Boston and New York: Houghton, Mifflin and Co., 1908).

Thomas, Benjamin P., *Abraham Lincoln: A Biography* (New York: Alfred A. Knopf, 1952).

Thomas, Benjamin P., *Lincoln's New Salem* (Springfield, Ill.: The Abraham Lincoln Association, 1934).

Thomas, Benjamin P., *Portrait for Posterity* (New Brunswick, N.J.: Rutgers University Press, 1947).

Thomas, Benjamin P., and Harold M. Hyman, *Stanton: The Life and Times of Lincoln's Secretary of War* (New York: Alfred A. Knopf, 1962).

Townsend, William H., *Lincoln and the Bluegrass* (Lexington, Kentucky: University of Kentucky Press, 1955).

Townsend, William H., *Lincoln and Liquor* (New York: The Press of the Pioneers, Inc., 1934).

Trollope, Anthony, *North America* (New York: Harper & Brothers, 1862).

Truesdell, Winfred Porter, *Col. Elmer E. Ellsworth* (Champlain, N.Y.: The Print Connoisseur, 1927).

Turner, Justin G., and Linda Levitt Turner, *Mary Todd Lincoln, Her Life and Letters* (New York: Alfred A. Knopf, 1972).

Tyler, Samuel, *Memoir of Roger Brooke Taney, LL.D.* (Baltimore: John Murphy & Co., 1872).

Van Deusen, Glyndon G., *William Henry Seward* (New York: Oxford University Press, 1967).

Warren, Louis A., *Lincoln Lore, Bulletin of the Lincoln National Life Foundation* (Fort Wayne, Indiana, starting with No. 1, dated April 15, 1929).

Warren, Louis A., *Lincoln's Parentage and Childhood* (New York and London: The Century Co., 1926).

Warren, Louis A., *Lincoln's Youth* (New York: Appleton, Century, Crofts, Inc., 1959).

Washington, John E., *They Knew Lincoln* (New York: E. P. Dutton & Co., 1942).

Weaver, John D., *Tad Lincoln: Mischief Maker in the White House* (New York: Dodd, Mead & Co., 1963).

Wecter, Dixon, *The Hero in America* (New York: Charles Scribner's Sons, 1941).

Weichmann, Louis J., *A True History of the Assassination of Abraham Lincoln and of the Conspiracy of 1865* (New York: Alfred A. Knopf, 1975).

Weik, Jesse W., *The Real Lincoln: A Portrait* (Boston: Houghton Mifflin Co., 1922).

Welles, Gideon, *Lincoln and Seward* (New York: Sheldon & Co., 1874).

West, Richard S., Jr., *Mr. Lincoln's Navy* (New York: Longman's, Green & Co., 1957).

Whipple, Wayne, *The Story of Young Abraham Lincoln* (Chicago: Goldsmith Co., 1934).

White, Charles T., *Lincoln and Prohibition* (New York and Cincinnati: The Abingdon Press, 1921).

Williams, Kenneth P., *Lincoln Finds a General* (New York: The MacMillan Company, 1949).

Williams, T. Harry, *Lincoln and His Generals* (New York: Alfred A. Knopf, 1952).

Williams, Wayne C., *A Railsplitter For President* (Denver, Colorado: University of Denver Press, 1951).

Wilson, Francis, *John Wilkes Booth* (Boston and New York: Houghton Mifflin Co., 1929).

Wilson, Rufus R., and introduction by R. Gerald McMurtry, *Lincoln in Caricature* (New York: Horizon Press, 1953).

Woldman, Albert A., *Lawyer Lincoln* (Boston: Houghton Mifflin Co., 1936).

Wolf, William J., *The Religion of Abraham Lincoln* (New York: Seabury, 1963).

THE EYEWITNESSES

Included in this book are over 100 extended quotations from Lincoln and from people who lived through events alongside Lincoln. These words of "the eyewitnesses" have been taken from the following primary sources, identified more fully in the bibliography.

Page 6 Quoted in *Frank Leslie's Illustrated Newspaper,* March 2, 1861, p. 234

Page 13 *Collected Works,* IV, 130

Page 15 Ibid., 241

Page 16 David C. Mearns, *The Lincoln Papers,* vol. II, pp. 442–443

Page 17 Allen T. Rice, *Reminiscences of Abraham Lincoln,* pp. 37 f.

Page 35 Wayne Whipple, *The Story of Young Abraham Lincoln,* p. 31; *The Hidden Lincoln,* ed. Hertz, p. 278

Page 36 *The Hidden Lincoln,* pp. 281, 282; *The Story of Young Abraham Lincoln,* p. 54

Page 37 Ida Tarbell, *The Life of Abraham Lincoln,* vol. 1, pp. 43–44, 17

Page 38 *The Hidden Lincoln,* pp. 279, 280–281

Page 39 Ibid., pp. 346–347

Page 42 Ibid., pp. 350–352

Page 43 F. B. Carpenter, *Six Months at the White House,* pp. 96–98

Page 45 *Collected Works,* I, 5–9

Page 46 John Locke Scripps, *Life of Abraham Lincoln,* pp. 71–72

Page 48 *Collected Works,* I, 48–49

Page 52 Joshua F. Speed, *Reminiscences of Abraham Lincoln,* pp. 21–22

Page 58 Sandburg and Angle, *Mary Lincoln—Wife and Widow,* pp. 179, 180–181

Page 59 Turner and Turner, *Mary Todd Lincoln, Her Life and Letters,* p. 27

Page 61 *Collected Works,* I, 260–261

Page 64 Ruth Painter Randall, *Mary Lincoln, Biography of a Marriage,* pp. 73–74

Page 75 *Collected Works,* I, 465–466, 477–478; Turner and Turner, *Mary Todd Lincoln,* pp. 36–38

Page 77 *Collected Works,* II, 81–82

Pages 80–81 Henry C. Whitney, *Life on the Circuit with Lincoln,* pp. 55, 64, 69

Pages 84–85 *Herndon's Life of Lincoln,* ed. P. Angle, pp. 268–276, 280

Page 96 *The Hidden Lincoln,* p. 382

Page 97 From a photostat of a typed, unpublished manuscript, corrected in the author's hand, "My Early Recollections of Abraham Lincoln, Our Greatest American With a Few Incidents Gathered Elsewhere," by Elizabeth A. Capps

Page 99 *Collected Works,* II, 15–16

Page 108 *Memoirs of Henry Villard,* vol. 1, pp. 92 ff.

Page 116 Noah Brooks, *Abraham Lincoln,* pp. 186–187

Page 119 "Making the Life Mask of Lincoln," in *The Magazine of History,* vol. 21, #1, Extra Number 81, p. 24

Page 122 Addison G. Proctor, "The Nomination of Lincoln," in *Lincoln Centennial Association Addresses,* pp. 80 ff.

Page 123 *The Lincoln Papers,* pp. 234–237

Page 148 W. H. Russell, *My Diary North and South,* pp. 58–59

Page 149 *Collected Works,* IV, 341–342

Page 154 Charles M. Segal, *Conversations with Lincoln,* pp. 124–125

Page 157 James M. McPherson, *The Negro's Civil War,* p. 162

Pages 158–159 *The Reminiscences of Carl Schurz,* vol. II, pp. 284–286

Page 159 *McClellan's Own Story,* vol. II, pp. 90–91

Page 162 *Official Records of the Union and Confederate Armies* (O. R.), Series III, vol. 1, p. 661

Page 163 Tyler Dennett, *Lincoln and the Civil War in the Diaries and Letters of John Hay,* pp. 34–35

Page 164 *The Diary of Edward Bates,* ed. Howard K. Beale, pp. 212–213

Page 165 Ibid., p. 220

Pages 168–169 *Collected Works,* IV, 421–441

Page 172 Segal, *Conversations with Lincoln,* pp. 153–154

Page 173 Ibid., pp. 154–155

Page 188 *Inside Lincoln's Cabinet, The Civil War Diaries of Salmon P. Chase,* pp. 149–150

Page 191 Segal, *Conversations with Lincoln,* p. 210

Page 193 *Collected Works,* V, 509–510

Page 195 Dennett, *Lincoln and The Civil War in the Diaries of John Hay,* pp. 111–112

Page 198 *Collected Works,* V, 342–343

Page 199 Ibid., 518–537

Page 205 Grace Greenwood, "Reminiscences of Abraham Lincoln," in *Abraham Lincoln: Tributes From His Associates,* pp. 108–112

Page 209 Quoted in Segal, *Conversation with Lincoln,* pp. 258–259

Pages 224–225 Quoted in Katherine Helm, *Mary, Wife of Lincoln,* pp. 221–233

Page 228 *Collected Works,* VI, 406–410

Page 229 *Collected Works,* VIII, 36–53

Page 235 Quoted in Herbert Mitgang, *Lincoln as They Saw Him,* pp. 377–378

Page 235 Smith Stimmel, *Personal Reminiscences of Abraham Lincoln,* pp. 38–40

Page 237 F. B. Carpenter, *Six Months At The White House,* pp. 58–59

Page 239 *Collected Works,* VII, 281–282

Page 240 Isaac Arnold, *The Life of Abraham Lincoln,* p. 375

Page 243 *Collected Works,* VII, 419; *Inside Lincoln's Cabinet,* p. 223

Page 245 N. Brooks, *Washington in Lincoln's Time,* pp. 174–175

Page 245 Dennett, *Lincoln and the Civil War,* p. 209

Page 246 *Collected Works,* VII, 512

Page 253 *Collected Works,* VIII, 100–101

Pages 258–259 Ibid., 136–152

Page 265 Ibid., 303

Page 267 Ibid., 332–333

Page 269 William H. Crook, "Lincoln's Last Day," in *Harper's Monthly,* vol. 115, pt. 1 (Sept. 1907)

Page 269 *Collected Works,* VIII, 413

Pages 272–273 Ibid., 309–405

Page 283 F. B. Carpenter, *Six Months At The White House,* pp. 91–92

Page 321 W. H. Russell, *My Diary North and South,* pp. 37–38

Page 326 *The Correspondence of John Lothrop Motley,* ed. George W. Curtis, vol. II, pp. 202–203

Page 327 Quoted in Mitgang, *Lincoln as They Saw Him,* p. 378

Page 329 *Report of the Commissioner of Patents for 1849,* Part I, p. 262

Page 330 *Collected Works,* VIII, 116–117

Page 330 *Harper's Weekly,* Vol. X, No. 539 (April 27, 1867), p. 257

Page 334 Ward H. Lamon, *Recollections of Abraham Lincoln,* pp. 113 ff.

Page 336 Quoted in R. R. Wilson, *Intimate Memories of Lincoln,* pp. 573–574

Page 346 *Diary of Gideon Welles,* vol. 2, pp. 282–283

Page 346 Crook, *Memories of the White House,* pp. 39 ff.

Page 357 Henry S. Safford, in Boston *Globe,* February 12, 1909; as quoted in "The Lincolnian," by the Lincoln Group of the District of Columbia, vol. VIII, No. 5, Dec. 1962

Page 359 F. W. Seward, *Reminiscence of a War-Time Statesman and Diplomat,* pp. 258–260

Page 362 N. Brooks, *Washington in Lincoln's Time,* p. 231

Page 362 B. French, *Witness to the Young Republic,* p. 507

Pages 362–363 *Reminiscences of William M. Stewart,* pp. 193 ff.

Page 363 *The Diary of Orville Hickman Browning,* vol. II, p. 20

Page 363 E. Keckley, *Behind the Scenes,* pp. 185–190

Page 363 Edward Curtis, unidentified newspaper clipping, quoting April 22, 1865 letter to his mother

Page 366 cf. Oldroyd, *The Assassination of Abraham Lincoln,* pp. 101–110

Page 369 E. Keckley, *Behind the Scenes,* pp. 190 ff.

Pages 374–375 O. R., Series I, vol. XLVI, Part III, pp. 952–965

Pages 396–397 *Life Magazine,* Feb. 9, 1959, pp. 57–60

INDEX

PICTURE CREDITS

All photographs of Abraham Lincoln in this book have been reproduced from prints in the Meserve-Kunhardt Collection or the Mellon Collection. All other pictures that were obtained from outside sources specifically for this book are credited in the listings that follow. Whenever there is no credit given the picture is from the Meserve-Kunhardt Collection. As well as giving the sources for the almost 800 pictures in the book, a second type of information is conveyed here. For each photograph of Abraham Lincoln himself, the photographer is named, plus the location and date, whenever they are known.

2: By Christopher S. German, Springfield, Ill., Feb. 9, 1861. **4:** By Christopher S. German, Springfield, Ill., Feb. 9, 1861 (top); Illinois State Historical Library (bottom). **5:** By F. DeB. Richards, Philadelphia, Pa., Feb. 22, 1861. **8:** Probably by Preston Butler, Springfield, Ill., May 20, 1860. **9:** By Preston Butler, Springfield, Ill., Aug. 13, 1860 (top); Chicago Historical Society (bottom right). **10-11:** By Alexander Hesler, Springfield, Ill., June 3, 1860. **12:** By Samuel G. Alschuler, Chicago, Ill., Nov. 25, 1860 (left); by Mathew Brady, New York, N.Y., Feb. 27, 1860, beard added later by artist (bottom right). **13:** Manuscript from The Lincoln Museum. **18:** *Harper's Weekly* (bottom left). **19:** Manuscript from The Chicago Historical Society. **23:** *Harper's Weekly.* **24:** Alexander Gardner, Mathew Brady Gallery, Washington, D.C., Feb. 23 or 24, 1861 (left); Detail from another photograph taken by Gardner the same day (top right). **26:** Library of Congress (top). **27:** *Leslie's Illustrated Newspaper* (top). **28-29:** By an unknown photographer, Washington, D.C., March 4, 1861. **30:** By Christopher S. German, Springfield, Ill., Feb. 9, 1861. **32-33:** Illinois State Historical Society; Manuscript from the Illinois State Historical Library. **34:** Manuscript from the Illinois State Historical Library (top left). **36:** The Lincoln Museum (left). **37:** The Lincoln Museum (top). **38:** Illinois State Historical Library (top); The Lincoln Museum (bottom). **39:** Lloyd Ostendorf (top); Illinois State Historical Library (bottom). **41:** Columbia University Library (top left); Chicago Historical Society (top right); Library of Congress (center); Brown University Library (bottom). **44:** Lloyd Ostendorf (top); Chicago Historical Society (bottom). **45:** Library of Congress (bottom). **46:** Illinois State Historical Library (both top, center left); Illinois State Historical Society (bottom right); Lloyd Ostendorf (center right). **47:** Illinois State Historical Society (bottom left); Illinois State Historical Library (top and bottom right). **49:** Illinois State Historical Library (top); Chicago Historical Society (bottom). **50:** Probably by N. H. Shepherd, Springfield, Ill., 1846 (top left); Illinois State Historical Library (top right). **53:** Illinois State Historical Library. **54-55:** Illinois State Historical Library. **57:** Illinois State Historical Library (2nd from top left); Library of Congress (top center); Illinois State Historical Library (two on top right and 2nd row left); The Lincoln Library (2nd row right); Probably by N. H. Shepherd, Springfield, Ill., 1846 (3rd row left); Illinois State Historical Library (two in bottom row). **61:** Lloyd Ostendorf (right). **62:** Lincoln Memorial University (top). **65:** Illinois State Historical Library (top center and bottom left). **67:** Probably by N. H. Shepherd, Springfield, Ill., 1846. **68-69:** By J. A. Whipple, Springfield, Ill., summer 1860. **70:** Illinois State Historical Library (top); *Leslie's Illustrated Newspaper* (bottom two). **71:** McLean County Historical Society (left); Chicago Historical Society (right). **72:** Library of Congress (bottom). **74:** Library of Congress (top and bottom left). **77:** Springfield Historical Preservation. **78:** By Amon J. T. Joslin, Danville, Ill., spring 1857 or 1858. **79:** By an unknown photographer, probably Illinois, about 1858. **81:** Springfield Historical Preservation (bottom). **82-83:** Illinois State Historical Library. **84:** By Samuel G. Alschuler, Urbana, Ill., Apr. 25, 1858. **86:** By Calvin Jackson, Pittsfield, Ill., Oct. 1, 1858. **87:** By Abraham M. Byers, Beardstown, Ill., May 7, 1858. **89:** Library of Congress. **90:** The Lincoln Museum (left). **91:** The Lincoln Museum (all). **94:** Probably by Preston Butler, Springfield, Ill., summer 1858 (top left); By an unknown photographer, probably in Illinois in 1858 (top right); By Samuel M. Fassett, Chicago, Ill., Oct. 4, 1859 (bottom left); Probably by Preston Butler, Springfield, Ill., May 20, 1860 (bottom right). **95:** Probably by Roderick M. Cole, in Peoria, Ill., about 1858 (top left); Unknown photographer, probably 1859 (top right); Probably by William Shaw, Chicago or Springfield, Ill., spring or summer 1860 (bottom left); Unknown photographer, probably Springfield, Ill., spring or summer 1860. **96:** By an unknown photographer, Springfield, Ill., May or June, 1860. **100:** Alexander Hesler, Chicago, Ill., Feb. 28, 1857. **101:** By Edward A. Barnwell, Decatur, Ill., May 9, 1860. **103:** Probably by Preston Butler, Springfield, Ill., May 20, 1860. **104:** By Johan Carl Frederic Polycarpus Von Schneidan, Chicago, Ill., 1854. **107:** New Salem Museum. **109:** By William Judkins Thomson, Monmouth, Ill., Oct. 11, 1858 (top); Illinois State Historical Library (bottom). **110:** By an unknown photographer, probably Springfield, Ill., spring or summer 1860. **111:** National Archives (bottom right). **113:** By T. P. Pearson, Macomb, Ill., Aug. 26, 1858. **114:** *Harper's Weekly* (bottom). **115:** By Mathew Brady, New York, N.Y., Feb. 27, 1860. **116:** Henry Groskinsky. **121:** *Harper's Weekly* (top, all). **124:** By an unknown photographer, 1860. **125:** By Preston Butler, Springfield, Ill., Aug. 13, 1860. **126-127:** By an unknown photographer, Springfield, Ill., summer 1860. **128:** By an unknown photographer, Springfield, Ill., summer 1860. **129:** By J. A. Whipple, Springfield, Ill., summer 1860. **131:** The Collection of Mr. & Mrs. Jack L. Smith. **132-133:** Lloyd Ostendorf (top); Illinois State Historical Library (bottom left); Springfield Historic Preservation (bottom right). **136:** Alexander Hesler, Springfield, Ill., June 3, 1860. **140:** Probably by Christopher S. German, Springfield, Ill., Sept. 1858. **141:** By Christopher S. German, Springfield, Ill., Jan. 13, 1861. **144-145:** By Alexander Gardner, Mathew Brady Gallery, Washington, D.C., Feb. 23 or 24, 1861. **146:** *Harper's Weekly* (bottom). **147:** *Leslie's Illustrated Newspaper* (top right and center left); *The New York Illustrated News* (bottom left). **148:** *Leslie's Illustrated Newspaper* (bottom). **149:** *Harper's Weekly* (top inset). **151:** By an unknown photographer, Washington, D.C., possibly May 19, 1861 (top right); *Harper's Weekly* (bottom left). **152:** National Archives (bottom). **159:** *Harper's Weekly* (bottom). **160:** By an unknown photographer, Washington, D.C., 1861 (top right); *Leslie's Illustrated Newspaper* (bottom). **164:** Library of Congress (top). **167:** National Archives. **170-171:** Alexander Gardner for Mathew Brady, near Harpers Ferry, Md., Oct. 3, 1860. **174-175:** *Leslie's Illustrated Newspaper* (top center). **176:** By an unknown photographer at Mathew Brady Gallery, Washington, D.C., 1862 (top). **177:** Union League of Philadelphia (top). **178:** Chicago Historical Society (bottom left). **185:** U.S.Am.I.H. (top right); New York Public Library (bottom left); Lloyd Ostendorf (bottom inset). **186:** National Archives (top); Minnesota Historical Society (bottom). **187:** Lloyd Ostendorf (top right). **190:** Alexander Gardner for Mathew Brady, near Harpers Ferry, Md., Oct. 4, 1862. **194:** Minnesota Historical Society (top). **195:** Manuscript from The Minnesota Historical Society (top left). **196:** Architect of the Capitol. **197:** By an unknown photographer at Mathew Brady Gallery, Washington, D.C., 1862; Library of Congress (manuscript inset). **200-201:** By an unknown photographer, possibly Mathew Brady, Gettysburg, Pa., Nov. 19, 1863. **202:** Fort Monroe Casemate Museum (bottom). **209:** Probably by Thomas Le Mere, Mathew Brady Gallery, Washington, D.C., Apr. 17, 1863 (left). **214:** Old Courthouse Museum, Vicksburg, Miss. (top). **216:** By Alexander Gardner, Washington, D.C., Aug. 9, 1863 (left); National Portrait Gallery, Smithsonian Institution (bottom right). **218:** *Leslie's Illustrated Newspaper* (top left); Lloyd Ostendorf (top right). **220:** The Collection of Mr. and Mrs. Jack L. Smith (top). **222-223:** By Alexander Gardner, Washington, D.C., Nov. 8, 1863; Library of Congress (manuscript insets). **230-231:** By Anthony Berger, Mathew Brady's Gallery, Washington, D.C., Feb. 9, 1864. **232:** By Mathew Brady, Washington, D.C., Jan. 8, 1864 (top left). **233:** Western Reserve Historical Society (bottom left). **234:** By Anthony Berger, Mathew Brady Gallery, Washington, D.C., Feb. 9, 1864 (both). **237:** White House Historical Society (top). **240:** *Harper's Weekly* (top left). **243:** The Collection of Mr. and Mrs. Jack L. Smith (left, except insets). **244:** Library of Congress (top right and center); University Library, Dundee (bottom). **249:** Utah State Historical Society (top left). **251:** Library of Congress (bottom right). **252:** The Lincoln Museum (top left); *Harper's Weekly* (right). **253:** By Alexander Gardner, Washington, D.C., 1865. **255:** *Harper's Weekly* (top). **256:** By Lewis E. Walker, Washington, D.C., about 1864. **257:** Library of Congress. **260-261:** By Alexander Gardner, Washington, D.C., Mar. 4, 1865. **264:** National Archives (top right). **265:** By Lewis E. Walker, Washington, D.C., about 1864 (bottom right). **266-267:** By Alexander Gardner, Washington, D.C., Mar. 4, 1865. **269:** Chicago Historical Society (center); Department of the Navy (bottom). **270:** By Lewis E. Walker, Washington, D.C., 1863-64. **274-275:** By Anthony Berger, Mathew Brady Gallery, Washington, D.C., April 20, 1864. **276:** By Anthony Berger, Mathew Brady Gallery, Washington, D.C., Feb. 9, 1864 (left). **277:** White House Historical Association (center right). **278:** Western Reserve Historical Society (top); *Leslie's Illustrated Newspaper* (center); By an unknown photographer, Mathew Brady Gallery, Washington, D.C., 1862 (bottom left). **279:** By Alexander Gardner, Washington, D.C., Nov. 8, 1863. **280-281:** By Anthony Berger, Mathew Brady Gallery, taken at the White House, Apr. 26, 1864. **282:** By Anthony Berger, Mathew Brady Gallery, Washington, D.C., Feb. 9, 1864 (left); The New York Historical Society (center). **284:** Smithsonian Institution (bottom). **288:** By Mathew Brady, Washington, D.C., Jan. 8, 1864 (bottom). **292:** By Alexander Gardner, Washington, D.C., 1865. **294:** By an unknown photographer, Mathew Brady Gallery, Washington, D.C., 1862. **295:** By Alexander Gardner, Washington, D.C., Aug. 9, 1863. **302:** By Mathew Brady, Washington, D.C., Jan. 8, 1864. **306:** By Henry F. Warren, taken at the White House, March 6, 1865. **309:** By Alexander Gardner, Washington, D.C., Nov. 8, 1863. **310-311:** By Alexander Gardner for Mathew Brady, near Harpers Ferry, Md, Oct. 4, 1862. **314-315:** By an unknown photographer, possibly Mathew Brady, Gettysburg, Pa., Nov. 19, 1863. **316-317:** By Anthony Berger, Mathew Brady Gallery, Washington, D.C., Feb. 9, 1864. **318-319:** By Alexander Gardner, Washington, D.C., 1865. **320:** By Anthony Berger, Mathew Brady Gallery, Washington, D.C., Feb. 9, 1864 (left); Courtesy of Gabor S. Boritt (top right). **322:** The Lincoln Museum. **323:** By Alexander Gardner, Washington, D.C., Nov. 8, 1863. **324:** By Alexander Gardner, Washington, D.C., Aug. 9, 1863. **325:** *Harper's Weekly* (bottom). **327:** By an unknown photographer, Mathew Brady Gallery, Washington, D.C., 1862. **328:** By Anthony Berger, Mathew Brady Gallery, Washington, D.C., Feb. 9, 1864. **329:** Smithsonian Institution (top and center); White House Historical Association (bottom left); *Harper's Weekly* (bottom right). **331:** By Mathew Brady, Washington, D.C., Jan. 8, 1864. **332:** By an unknown photographer, probably Washington, D.C., about 1864. **333:** Library of Congress (bottom). **335:** By Alexander Gardner, Washington, D.C., Aug. 9, 1863. **337:** By Lewis E. Walker, Washington, D.C., about 1864. **338:** By an unknown photographer, Mathew Brady Gallery, Washington, D.C., 1862. **339:** By Mathew Brady, Washington, D.C., Jan. 8, 1864. **342:** Harvard Theater Collection (bottom). **344:** By Alexander Gardner, Washington, D.C., March 4, 1865 (right). **347:** By Alexander Gardner, Washington, D.C., 1865 (top left); The Bostonian Society (bottom, left); Library of Congress (bottom right). **354:** By Alexander Gardner, Washington, D.C., Nov. 8, 1863. **355:** Edward Owen, Ford's Theatre, NHS (pistol); Henry Ford Museum and Greenfield Village (right). **356:** *Leslie's Illustrated Newspaper* (bottom). **357:** Edward Owen, Ford's Theatre, NHS (right). **358:** The Seward House (top). **360:** Chicago Historical Society (bottom). **361:** Michael Latil, Smithsonian Institution (bottom). **366:** McClellan-Lincoln Collection, Brown University (left). **368-369:** *Leslie's Illustrated Newspaper* (top center). **373:** *Leslie's Illustrated Newspaper* (bottom left). **375:** By Jeremiah Gurney, Jr., New York, N.Y., Apr. 24, 1865. **378:** Collection of Mr. and Mrs. Jack L. Smith (bottom). **394:** The Lincoln Museum. **402:** Probably by N. H. Shepherd, Springfield, Ill., 1846. **403:** By Alexander Gardner, Washington, D.C., 1865.

FILM CREDITS

LINCOLN

Produced and Directed by
Peter W. Kunhardt

Produced and Written by
Philip B. Kunhardt, III
Philip B. Kunhardt, Jr.

Edited by
John Martin
Kris Liem
Elizabeth Ackerman

Music by
Alan Menken

Narrated by
James Earl Jones

Voices
Jason Robards, *Abraham Lincoln*
Glenn Close, *Mary Todd Lincoln*
Oprah Winfrey, *Elizabeth Keckley*
Frank Langella, *John Wilkes Booth*
Cliff Robertson, *Noah Brooks*
E. G. Marshall, *Gideon Welles*
Dabney Coleman, *Stephen A. Douglas*
Eli Wallach, *William Crook*
Olympia Dukakis, *Elizabeth Grimsley*
Arnold Schwarzenegger, *John G. Nicolay*
Richard Thomas, *John Hay*
Robby Benson, *William O. Stoddard*
Ossie Davis, *Frederick Douglass*
Jill Clayburgh, *Emilie Helm*
Fred Gwynne, *Edwin M. Stanton*
Rod Steiger, *Ulysses S. Grant*
John Shea, *John S. Barnes*
Jim Dale, *William H. Russell*
Philip Bosco, *Frederick Seward*
Keith Carradine, *William H. Herndon*
Robert Vaughn, *Isaac Arnold*
F. Murray Abraham, *Salmon P. Chase*
Burgess Meredith, *Winfield Scott*
Barnard Hughes, *Horace Greeley*
Richard Widmark, *Ward Hill Lamon*
Rex Everhart, *Joshua Speed*
Laurence Luckinbill, *Charles A. Leale*
Blythe Danner, *Elizabeth Todd Edwards*
Gordon Parks, *Henry Highland Garnett*
Henry Morgan, *Benjamin B. French*
Stacy Keach, *George B. McClellan*
Stockard Channing, *Clara Harris*
Maureen Stapleton, *Sarah Bush Lincoln*
Ned Beatty, *Dennis Hanks*

Additional Voices
Adam LeFevre, Wyman Pendleton, Gordon
Connell, Peter Coffeen, Chris Sena, Brian
Mancinelli, Steven Hall, Robert Katims,
Ed Lyndeck, Gordon Rigsby, Curt Chaplin,
Jay Gregory, Albert Verdesca, Joseph Cannito,
Arthur Goodman and James Smith

Coordinating Director
James A. Edgar, III

Coordinating Producer
Jody Abramson

Director of Photography
Allan Palmer

Additional Music
Walter Levinsky
Richard Lieb

Orchestration
Michael Starobin

Sound Effects Editor
Susan Wagner

Assistant Editors
Janet Cristenfeld
Michael J. Balabuch
Marygrace O'Shea
Darrell Hanzalik

Senior Production Assistant
Mia Freund

Production Assistants
Christopher Edgar
Edmond Garesche
Peter Mottur
Carol Stanford
Elizabeth Darst
Anne-Marie Cunniffe

Business Administration
Nancy Malin

Legal
Dan Brambilla

Interns
Monica Darer
Alexandra Zabriske
David Kolenda

Additional Photography
Dan White
Foster Wiley
Erich Roland
Laurie Hoen
Jeffrey Stonehouse
Allen Moore

Consultants
David Herbert Donald
Harold Holzer
Brian Pohanka
Esther Newberg
Richard Plepler

A NOTE ON THE TYPE

The text of this book was set in an adaptation of Garamond designed by Tony Stan in 1977 for the International Typeface Corporation.
The original, designed by Claude Garamond (1480-1561), first appeared in books printed in Paris around 1532. There have been many subsequent versions designed for both European and American type founders in the twentieth century, many of which were based on the Jean Jannon cut of the mid-seventeenth century.
ITC Garamond is distinguished by a greater x-height than most versions; the ascenders and descenders are proportionately shorter. The curved letters are very round.

Composed by Ellen Nitschmann of Time Inc. Magazines, New York, New York.
Film preparation by Capper, Inc., Knoxville, Tennessee. Printed and bound by R.R. Donnelley & Sons, Willard, Ohio. Designed by Gene Light.
Production directed by Ellen McNeilly.